ISBN 978-1-331-92732-7
PIBN 10255440

English
Français
Deutsche
Italiano
Español
Português

www.forgottenbooks.com

Mythology Photography **Fiction**
Fishing Christianity **Art** Cooking
Essays Buddhism Freemasonry
Medicine **Biology** Music **Ancient**
Egypt Evolution Carpentry Physics
Dance Geology **Mathematics** Fitness
Shakespeare **Folklore** Yoga Marketing
Confidence Immortality Biographies
Poetry **Psychology** Witchcraft
Electronics Chemistry History **Law**
Accounting **Philosophy** Anthropology
Alchemy Drama Quantum Mechanics
Atheism Sexual Health **Ancient History**
Entrepreneurship Languages Sport
Paleontology Needlework Islam
Metaphysics Investment Archaeology
Parenting Statistics Criminology
Motivational

TRANSACTIONS

OF THE

AMERICAN PHILOLOGICAL ASSOCIATION.

1884.

VOLUME XV.

Published by the Association.

CAMBRIDGE:

JOHN WILSON AND SON.

University Press.

1885.

352

CONTENTS OF VOL. XV.

TRANSACTIONS

OF THE

AMERICAN PHILOLOGICAL ASSOCIATION,

1884.

I. — *The Genitive Case in Sophokles.*

By THOMAS D. GOODELL, Ph. D.,

PUBLIC HIGH SCHOOL, HARTFORD, CONN.

I.

On pedagogical as well as on other grounds the uses of the Greek genitive need to be more thoroughly understood, and more clearly presented in the elementary grammars; for no department of Greek syntax is more productive of confusion of thought in young pupils. The grammars most in use differ greatly in their classification and in the statement of principles. Here, as elsewhere, categories based originally on mistaken notions are still retained, for the supposed comfort of the learner, after their reason for existence has long been recognized as illusory. Careful statement, with accompanying statistics, of the actual usage of the case, from Homer down, is urgently needed. It is the aim of this paper to give such a statement with reference to Sophokles. The classification employed will be different in some respects from others which have been widely adopted; and will be more or less superior to them, it is hoped, because according more closely with the historical development of the case. And, in particular, the ablatival uses of the genitive will be shown to be more numerous, and in some directions more clearly defined, in Sophokles at least, than the grammars would lead one to suppose.

Before proceeding farther, a word may be said in regard to certain restrictions adhered to in this paper, and in regard to the method of recording the facts observed. In the first place, the fragments are not included in this survey, except incidentally. And this for two reasons : chiefly because they offer nothing which would materially affect the conclusions derived from the rest of Sophokles, but also because to include them would require an entirely disproportionate amount of textual discussion. What we are seeking now is primarily the general proportions of Sophoklean usage. The entire plays give these sufficiently, even if the text of the fragments did not present special difficulties. But the ratio of doubtful or corrupt lines to sound ones in the fragments is of course much the greater ; and it would not be worth while to make elaborate studies of the text of the worst lines in an author— especially when the investigator's decisions would carry with them no weight unless accompanied by a full account of his reasoning — merely in order to determine whether a given construction, common everywhere, occurs, say, three hundred or three hundred and one times. A few points of special interest in the fragments will be mentioned in their natural connection. In the entire plays, also, variations in text are not touched upon, except where the usage is peculiar, or where a single example would affect statistics considerably. The text followed is that of Schneidewin as revised by Nauck, and references are made to the following editions of the separate plays: Ai., 7th cd., 1877; O. T., 7th ed., 1876; O. K., 7th ed., 1878 ; Ant., 8th ed., 1880; El., 5th ed., 1877; Tr., 5th ed., 1880; Phil., 7th ed., 1876. Lyric references — that is, to all lines not in trimeter or tetrameter dialogue — are distinguished by heavy-faced numerals. Further, the genitives themselves are counted, not the governing words ; a word attracted into the genitive is counted and assigned to the governing word on which the attracting genitive depends ; but appositives are not counted.

In any study of the Greek genitive we must constantly recognize the fact that a part of the Indo-European ablative has become identical with it in form. So far as can be done with certainty, or with a high degree of probability, these cases should be separated, and treated as two. It is true, before the language reached that stage which appears in Homer the union had become, in some common constructions, so complete that the line of demarcation is obliterated. Or, more fully, we may say that, even in Homer, there occur side by side, contemporaneously, survivals from all along the line of development from Indo-European separateness in form and usage to complete coalescence in form and confusion of usage. But an accidental identity in form should not lead us to confound constructions totally different in origin and nature. Accordingly, the genitives in Sophokles will be here divided into three classes, to be taken up in their order : first, true genitives; secondly, ablatival genitives; thirdly, genitives whose origin and development cannot at present be traced with certainty, or a high degree of probability. However, it is not to be overlooked that the first two classes run into the third perplexingly,—indeed, the third is in part a sort of catch-all for the remnants, — and that any two observers may differ here and there as to which way the fluctuating line of probability inclines. Furthermore, the prepositions, which occur with each class of genitives, will most conveniently be treated last.

II.

The true genitive is originally adnominal; that is, its primary function is to limit the meaning of a substantive. Its other functions have grown out of this by one extension after another, sometimes traceable, sometimes not. The case-ending may be said to denote merely that some relation exists between the genitive and its noun ; the nature of that relation is in no sense expressed by the case-ending, but is determined wholly by the context and by the nature of the two things named. All this merely paraphrases the statement of Whitney (Sanskrit Gr., § 294): " The proper value of the genitive is adjectival; it belongs to and qualifies a noun, designating something belonging to the latter in a manner which the nature of the case, or the connection, defines more nearly."

In Sophokles, as elsewhere, this original adnominal genitive constitutes a very large and a fairly distinct class. When, however, we attempt to subdivide this class into genitives subjective, objective, partitive, genitives of possession, material, specification, etc., we at once stumble upon perplexities. Let any one take a hundred consecutive examples from any writer and try to put each one in its appropriate pigeonhole. The partitions have to come out immediately. Many examples belong in two or three at once; more still will not fit any. The simple experiment proves the impossibility of making such subdivisions. The reason is that the relations actually subsisting between things connected in the genitive construction include about all the relations which ever subsist between separate entities. At any rate, those relations are so "flexible, changeable, vague, and multiform and doubtful," — to make a special application of Clough's words, — that any complete subdivision of the adnominal genitive on this basis is impracticable. All the varieties to which the grammars give separate names appear frequently in Sophokles, but statistics cannot be given. Nor, if possible, would such subdivision be of much profit. It would add nothing to our understanding of the nature of the case, little to our knowledge of the history of the case, nothing to our understanding of the thought of a Greek author. As to the last assertion let us examine illustrations in our own language. For nearly all the categories of the adnominal genitive laid down in the grammars may be perfectly illustrated by Shakespearian and other good English usage. Very brief search and consideration furnish the following examples.

Subjective genitive: "*Night's* predominance"; "*ruin's* wasteful entrance"; "without *my* stir"; "*his* present death"; "the *sun's* return." Objective genitive: "Fought against *my* captivity"; "every one did bear *thy* praises in his *kingdom's* great defence"; "labored in his *country's* wreck"; "in our *country's* purge"; "thy personal venture in the *rebels'* fight." Genitive of measure or value: "Grief of an *hour's* age"; "an *hour's* delay"; "a *fortnight's* space"; "a *moment's* hesitation"; "a *year's* time." Genitive of the whole: "The *house's* top"; "a tale *whose* lightest word"; "my *heart's* core." Genitive of specification: "*Sinai's* mount"; "*Nebo's* lonely mountain." Genitive of connection, in family, state, etc.: "The *Norways'* king"; "*Bellona's* bride-groom"; "*John's* father, son," etc.

These and similar lists might be almost indefinitely extended, and the genitive of possession is too common to need mention. There are also an endless number of genitives which elude classification as absolutely as many in Greek. Note, for example, the following: "A *summer's* cloud"; "*heaven's* breath"; "this *night's* great business"; "each *day's* life"; "*life's* feast"; "my *sceptre's* awe." True, some of these and others like them may be forced into various categories; but such forcing is not classification. Surely, so far as pupils are concerned, no practical and sufficient end would be served by requiring them to attempt or think of any such dissection of the adnominal genitive in Shakespeare.[1] Then why in Sophokles? At most the terms "subjective," etc. can be useful only occasionally, in case of real ambiguity, as a convenient mode of indicating the actual meaning of the passage.

Under this simplest type of genitive, depending on a noun or pronoun, are included 46.3+ per cent of all the genitives in Sophokles, and 86.3+ per cent of the true genitives. The extensions and offshoots of this type, familiar as most of them are, common in all writers, and in great part pro-ethnic in origin, are thus seen to be comparatively infrequent.

We should expect in poetry some combinations of nouns in the genitive construction which would be strange in prose. The poet's preference for a concise mode of expression may lead him to select a genitive instead of a prepositional phrase or a clause. And in particular Sophokles's fondness for a somewhat artificial style, for a new and artistic rather than a familiar turn of words, tends to variations from prose usage. Hence we find examples like these: κλέπτης αὐτοῦ ψηφοποιός, Ai. 1135; τόλμης πρόσωπον, O. T. 533; σχολῇ κακοῦ, O. T. 1286; λυγρῶν πόνων ἱκετῆρες, O. T. 185; ἄρρητ᾽

---

[1] Of course, in giving English genitives, *of* has not been regarded as a genitive sign, any more than ἀπό or any other preposition would be so regarded in Greek.

ἀρρήτων, O. T. **465**; δόκησις λόγων, O. T. **681**; μῆνιν πράγματος, O. T. **699**; θανάτων πύργος, O. T. **1199**; ἔδρας γῆς; O. K. **45**; ὁ Θήβας ἐλελίχθων, Ant. **153** (in which example the peculiarity lies merely in the fact that the participle is made a substantive); νόσων φυγάς, Ant. **364**; μῦθος φίλων ('talk about friends'), Ant. **11**; θρήνων ᾠδάς, El. **88**; στέρνων πληγάς, El. **90**; φάσμα νυκτός, El. **501**; τἀκείνου σωτήρια ('means of safety proceeding from him'), El. **924**; ὠδῖνας αὐτοῦ ('about him'), Tr. **42**; εὐμάρεια πόρου, Phil. **704.**

Sometimes the noun with which the genitive is connected is omitted, or is continued from a preceding phrase, to which the genitive is joined by some conjunction, most often ὡς: e. g. φρενός, Ai. **482**; θεοῦ, Ai. **998**; κώδωνος, Ai. **17**; φεύγοντος, Ant. **256**. (It may be said here that this use of ὡς, ὥσπερ, εἴπερ appears several times in Sophokles connecting similar constructions under other classes of genitives.)

Sometimes, as in prose, the genitive is put alongside of a possessive adjective, as if agreeing with a genitive implied in that possessive: as, θανόντος, Ai. **1016**; μόνης, Tr. **775**.

Then there are many occurrences of the genitive dependent on a pronoun, as τίς, τὶς, οὐδείς, μηδείς, ὅστις, some form of the article followed by μέν or δέ, or even on the article alone in some survivals of its earlier pronominal use, or even, finally, on a pronoun understood. Most of these are simple enough, and common in prose and poetry of all periods. Examples are: ἐν τῷ πράγματος, Ai. **314**; ἐν τῷ συμφορᾶς, Ant. **1229**; ὅστις ὑμῶν, O. T. **224**; θεῶν του, O. T. **42**; ἐς τοσοῦτον ἐλπίδων, O. T. **771**; τοὐκεῖθεν ἄλσους, O. K. **505**.

A noun or pronoun, with a genitive dependent on it, may have an adjective in the superlative degree connected with it, either directly, as an attributive, or through a verb, as a predicate adjective, to denote that one individual or certain individuals of a class possess a quality in a higher degree than any others of the class. We may call this the genitive with superlatives; but it evidently belongs primarily with the noun or pronoun; and this even when the superlative itself, by omission of its noun, becomes a substantive. Examples of this sort, then, are to be classed as adnominal; and the case is the same with genitives accompanying a superlative adverb, the genitive depending on a noun or pronoun, expressed or understood, and the adverb belonging to a verb, adjective, or other adverb. The reason for here separating these examples from those just considered is that the grammars so separate them; and in fact the presence of the superlative marks the examples distinctly enough to justify the practice. In its nature prosaic, this construction appears but eighty-three times in the seven plays (2.0+ per cent of all, 3.8— per cent of true genitives), and lyric lines furnish less than their quota. Indeed, the genitive with a superlative adverb nowhere occurs in lyric metre. A few examples are cited: στρατοῦ, Ai. 502; πημονῶν, O. T. 1230; τῶνδε, Tr. 312. In two instances the genitive with superlatives is probably to be regarded as ablatival, of the same nature as the genitive with comparatives, and is counted under that head. The examples are τῶν προτέρων, Ant. **100** ff.; τῶν ἐντόπων, Phil. **1171**.

A number of common adverbs retain enough of their earlier force as nouns to admit, in dependence on them, a genitive of the whole. There occur in Sophokles thirty-four adnominal genitives of this description (0.8+ per cent of all, 1.6— per cent of true genitives) with the adverbs ἄλλη, ἔνθα, ἐνθάδε, ἵνα, μηδαμοῦ (?), οἷ, οἷπερ, ὅποι, ποῖ, ποῦ, πού, ὡς. E. g., with ἄλλη, Tr. 906; with ἔνθα, Ai. 659; with ἐνθάδε, Phil. 899; with ἵνα, O. T. 367 and 413; with μηδαμοῦ, [Phil. 256]; with οἷ, El. 1035; with οἷπερ, El. 404; with ὅποι, El. 922; with ποῖ, O. T. **1309**; with ποῦ, Ai. 102; with πού, Phil. **1124**; with ὡς, O. T. 345.

The adnominal genitive is used by Sophokles in the predicate with the verbs εἰμί, γίγνομαι, νομίζομαι, ὀνομάζομαι, ἐπονομάζομαι, φαίνομαι, γράφομαι, καλοῦμαι, ἐπακούω, ποιοῦμαι, κυρῶ, ὄπωπα, εἶπον, ὑπάρχει (?), αὐδῶμαι. Of these εἰμί, as everywhere, is the most common. The following are the examples with the other verbs: ὁ νοῦς ὅταν | αὐτοῦ γένηται, O. K. 660; πατρὸς | ἄλλου γενοῦ του, Tr. 1205. In Phil. 305 f., πολλὰ γὰρ τάδε | ἐν τῷ μακρῷ γένοιτ᾽ ἂν ἀνθρώπων χρόνῳ, ἀνθρώπων is commonly taken with χρόνῳ. But the objection of Blaydes, quoted with approval by Nauck, that with ἀνθρώπων we should expect βίῳ rather than χρόνῳ is well founded ; and in reading ἀνθρώπῳ Blaydes at least gives the meaning of the passage, which is, 'Many events of this sort might in the long stretch of time fall to the lot of men.' But why not retain ἀνθρώπων as a predicate genitive after γένοιτο, which stands close beside it? Although the idea is ordinarily expressed by γίγνομαι with the dative, yet the predicate genitive is not unnatural in itself, and is no more unparalleled than ὅταν αὐτοῦ γένηται, O. K. 660, in the sense of 'become master of itself,' or 'come to itself.' It is certainly less hard to explain thus than to put ἀνθρώπων with χρόνῳ. τοῦ θεῶν νομίζεται, O. K. 38 ; οὐ τοῦ κρατοῦντος ἡ πόλις νομίζεται, Ant. 738 ; ὁ τῆς ἀρίστης μητρὸς ὠνομασμένος, Tr. 1105 ; πατρὸς | τὴν δυστάλαιναν δαῖτ᾿ ἐπωνομασμένην, El. 283 ; ὡς οὐκέτ᾿ ὄντος γὰρ συμβόλαιά σου | ἐφαίνετο, Phil. 884 ; τὸν ἐκ θεῶν | φανέντ᾿ ἄναγνον καὶ γένους [τοῦ Λαΐου], O. T. 1383. This example is not included in the count, for the text cannot possibly be right, whatever be the true correction. οὐ Κρέοντος προστάτου γεγράψομαι, O. T. 411 ; Παλλάδος καλούμεναι | Ἀθῆναι, O. K. 107 ; καλοῦ τῆς μητρός, El. 367 ; οἷον ἐγὼ γᾶς Ἀσίας οὐκ ἐπακούω, O. K. 695 ; ποιοῦ σεαυτῆς, Ant. 547 ; ἀδελφῆς . . . | κυρεῖ, Ant. 486 ; ὁποῖον οὐ | τῶν σῶν τε κἀμῶν οὐκ ὄπωπ᾿ ἐγὼ κακῶν, Ant. 6 ; ποίας ὑμᾶς πατρίδος ἢ γένους εἰπών, Phil. 222 ; σχῆμα Ἑλλάδος | [στολῆς ὑπάρχει], Phil. 223 ; οἶσθα γὰρ ὧν αὐδῶμαι, Phil. 852.

There are in addition nine passages, furnishing fourteen genitives, which require fuller consideration. The genitives are certainly adnominal in origin, and may best be treated in connection with the predicate genitive. The passages are as follows: ποίου κέκραγας ἀνδρὸς ὧδ᾿ ὑπέρφρονα; | ποῦ βάντος ἢ ποῦ στάντος οὖπερ οὐκ ἐγώ; Ai. 1236 f. ; ποίου γὰρ ἀνδρὸς τήνδε μηνύει τύχην; O. T. 102 ; μαντεῖα | ἃ τοῦδ᾿ ἐχρήσθη σώματος, O. K. 355 ; κεἰ δεῖν᾿ ἐπερρώσθη λέγειν | τῆς σῆς ἀρωγῆς, O. K. 662 ; τοῦ κασιγνήτου τί φῄς, | ἥξοντος ἢ μέλλοντος; El. 317 ; τοῦ με τήνδ᾿ ἐφίστασαι βάσιν; Tr. 339 ; τῷ παιδὶ φράζω τῆς τεχνωμένης τάδε, Tr. 928 ;

τῆς μητρὸς ἥκω τῆς ἐμῆς· φράσων ἐν οἷς | νῦν ἔστιν, Tr.
1122; Φ. ἀναξίου μὲν φωτὸς ἐξερήσομαι, | γλώσσῃ δὲ δεινοῦ
καὶ σοφοῦ, τί νῦν κυρεῖ. Ν. ποίου δὲ τούτου πλήν γ᾽ Ὀδυσ-
σέως ἐρεῖς; Phil. 439 ff.

In all these except Tr. 339 the meaning is just about what
would be expressed were περί used;· but no one would now
explain them by saying λείπει περί, or, in Tr. 339, λείπει
ἕνεκα. Nor is it quite satisfactory to say that ποίου ἀνδρός,
for instance, depends directly on ὑπέρφρονα, still less on
κέκραγας. Is not a clue to the right explanation to be
found in such varieties of the predicate genitive as πατρί-
δος, Phil. 222; κακῶν, Ant. 6; γᾶς, O. K. 695, quoted above?
Then compare with these such expressions as τί τόδε λέγεις;
or οἷόν τι ποτὸν τόδε νηῦς ἐκεκεύθει, Hom. ι 348, showing
a not infrequent predicate accusative. In the nine passages
above quoted, the genitive is to be regarded as a development of the predicate genitive; and the force of Ai. 1236
may be roughly given thus : 'What sort of a man is he with
whose name you clamorously connect such haughty words?'
So O. T. 102 might be rendered, 'Whose does he, by his
announcement, declare this fate to be?' So O. K. 355,
'Prophecies which were, by utterance of the oracle, declared
as mine,' i.e. 'as having reference to me.' In like manner the
other passages might be rendered. In each instance, except
Tr. 339, we have a verb of declaring, a direct object (or with
the passive a subject), and a genitive, which in several instances does not stand very near the object. In O. K. 355,
and in some others, the genitive might perhaps be regarded
as connected directly with the noun or pronoun ; but in Ai.
1236 and O. T. 102 the genitive cannot be so construed ; and
the examples all seem to belong together. The most doubtful ones are Tr. 1122 and Phil. 439, where it is difficult to say
with certainty that the genitive does not depend directly on
the indirect question. Then in Tr. 339 it is difficult to say
whether a still further extension of the idiom has taken place,
in that the verb of declaring is only implied, or the genitive
should be taken to modify the rest of the sentence as a
whole. This genitive seems to be a good deal like the geni-

tive of price, which also is probably a development of the predicate genitive. And besides, in most of the passages under consideration the genitive has come to have the aspect of an adverbial modifier of the predicate, and from being so regarded may well have been used in connections which completely obscured the origin of the locution. In other words, we may have here instances of the beginnings of a distinct function of the genitive.

With these apparently belong seven examples of the genitive with verbs of hearing and learning (i. e. having something told one), where the genitive is to be translated *about.* They are : τούτων ἀκοῦσαι, O. K. 485 ; κλύων σοῦ, O. K. 307 ; κλύουσαν | ὀνειράτων, El. **481** ; κλύουσα παιδός, Ant. 1182; ἔραμαι πυθέσθαι . . . τᾶς δειλαίας . . . | ἀλγηδόνος, O. K. **514** ; ὧν πεύσει, El. 35 ; σὲ πατρὸς οὕτω δαρὸν ἐξενωμένον | τὸ μὴ πυθέσθαι ποῦ ἔστιν αἰσχύνην φέρειν, Tr. 65. This genitive is certainly more nearly akin to those discussed immediately above, than it is to the common genitive of the thing heard with these and like verbs.

Another special development of the predicate adnominal genitive is the genitive denoting the place or time within the limits of which an action takes place. These idioms evidently belong together, and are to be compared with Homeric ἑσπέριοι ἀφίκοντο, εὗδον παννύχιοι, παλίνορσος ἀπέστη, ἄψορροι ἀπονέοντο, etc. The type is marked by Delbrück[1] as proethnic, and it throws light on the idioms discussed immediately above. The Sophoklean examples are : νυκτός, Ai. 21, **141**, 285, El. 780, Phil. 606 ; χρόνου, O. K. 397, 821, El. **477**, 817, Tr. 173 ; ἡμέρας, El. 698 ; θέρους, Phil. 1340 ; χειμῶνος, Ai. 1143; πεδίων, O. K. **689**; τοῦ προσωτάτω, Ai. 731 ; ἑρκέων, Ai. 1274 ; πυρᾶς, El. 901. Among these seventeen examples, then, appear five expressions of time and four of place, although νυκτός and χρόνου are most frequent. In El. 901 πυρᾶς illustrates very clearly the predicative origin of the construction. No account has been taken of the common adverbs in -ου, which undoubtedly belong in the same category, case-forms petrified into adverbs.

---

[1] Syntakt. Forschungen, iv. p. 45.

. The genitive absolute has advanced a step farther along the line of these predicate genitives; or rather, in most instances of the genitive absolute this farther step has been taken. For we may distinguish three stages: First, the genitive is so closely and directly connected with a noun that one might hesitate whether to call it adnominal or to call it absolute. For example, οὗ δῆτα ποικίλως αὐδωμένου | δέχου τὰ συμφέροντα τῶν ἀεὶ λόγων, Phil. 130 f. Secondly, it has the aspect of a predicate genitive similar to those of time and

TRUE GENITIVE.

		Ai.	O.T.	O.K.	Ant.	El.	Tr.	Phil.	Total.	Total.
With substantives and pronouns,	Dial.	158	220	280	167	211	203	186	1,425	1,895
	Lyr.	69	49	67	103	55	60	67	470	
With superlative adjectives,	Dial.	10	9	9	4	12	6	12	62	75
	Lyr.	1	2	3	4	1	2	0	13	
With superlative adverbs,	Dial.	2	2	1	0	2	1	0	8	8
	Lyr.	0	0	0	0	0	0	0	0	
With adverbs of time, etc.,	Dial.	4	5	1	1	9	6	2	28	34
	Lyr.	0	1	1	0	0	1	3	6	
In predicate,	Dial.	1	9	8	8	11	8	8	53	60
	Lyr.	0	0	3	0	0	0	4	7	
Predicate Genitive translated 'about' or 'because of,'	Dial.	3	1	4	1	4	3	2	18	20
	Lyr.	0	0	1	0	1	0	0	2	
Genitive of place and time,	Dial.	5	0	2	0	4	1	2	14	17
	Lyr.	1	0	1	0	1	0	0	3	
Genitive Absolute,	Dial.	11	16	11	6	10	14	6	74	84
	Lyr.	3	1	0	2	2	1	1	10	
Total,	Dial.	194	262	316	187	263	242	218	1,682	2,193
	Lyr.	74	53	76	109	60	64	75	511	
Total,		268	315	392	296	323	306	293	2,193	

23.3+ per cent are lyric.

place, as in El. 101 f., οὐδεὶς τούτων οἶκτος φέρεται | σοῦ, πάτερ, οὕτως | ... θανόντος. Thirdly, this predicate genitive appears to modify the action as a whole, or the verb itself, giving vaguely a cause, condition, etc. of the main action. This last stage is that of most genitives absolute, and may be compared with Tr. 339, τοῦ με τήνδ᾽ ἐφίστασαι βάσιν; The usage of Sophokles presents little that is peculiar or especially noteworthy. A few examples occur of a participle standing alone in the absolute construction; as, τελουμένων, El. 1344; κατθανόντος, Ant. 909.

The synopsis on the preceding page indicates the numbers and distribution of the classes of genitives thus far discussed.

III.

The Homeric uses of the ablatival genitive are nearly all retained by Sophokles, and still others are added. How far his peculiarities in this respect are due to his own invention, extending deliberately the range of certain types, and how far to fastidious choice of phrases from predecessors, cannot now be determined. Nor can we decide, without the statistics for other writers and periods, just how the usage of Sophokles compares with that of his contemporaries and predecessors. But certain it is that we find the ablatival genitive surprisingly well defined and numerously illustrated in his surviving plays. This genitive occurs mostly with verbs, to a considerable extent with verbs compounded with prepositions; but the preposition is seldom the essential governing element. The most convenient classification of the examples for our purpose will be, first, the genitive of separation; second, of source; third, of agent; fourth, of cause; fifth, of comparison; sixth, with compounds of πρό. As grammatical categories go, these are tolerably distinct, although connected as closely as the various meanings of the English *from*. Taking them up in order, the genitive of separation (including under that term departure, deprivation, failure, and the like) occurs with the following words and in the places noted. A few variations from the strict alphabetical order, with compounds under their simple verbs when these latter occur, have been allowed for etymological reasons.

ἄγω, Phil. 613, 630; ἀείρω, Ant. 417; ἀλύσκω, Ant. 489, El. 626; ἁμαρτάνω, El. 1320, Phil. 231 (two; here the meaning is, virtually, 'to fail to receive from'); ἀμπλακεῖν, Ant. 554, 910, 1234; ἀμύνω, O. T. 894; ἀνακουφίζω, O. T. 24; ἀναπνέω, Ai. 274 (cf. ἐκπνέω, and also Frag. 147 Dind., οὐ μύρου πνέον); ἀνατίθημι, Ai. 476 (articular inf.); ἀνίημι (cf. ἀφίημι, μεθίημι, παρίημι), O. T. 264, 265; ἀπαΐσσω, Ai. 448; ἀπαλλάσσω (cf. ἐναλλάσσω, καταλλάσσω), O. K. 786, Ant. 400, 769, El. 783, 1335, 1336; ἀπαράσσω, Tr. 1016; ἀπατάω, Ai. 807; ἀπαυδάω, O. T. 236; ἄπειμι (εἰμί), Ant. 1170, Tr. 165; ἄπειμι (εἶμι, cf. also ἔξειμι, βαίνω, μολεῖν, etc.), O. T. 229, 431 (where ἀποστραφείς is added); ἀπορέω, Phil. 898; ἀποσκεδάννυμι, O. T. 138; ἀποβλάπτω, Ai. 941; ἀποσπάω, Ai. 1025, 1176, O. T. 1432, O. K. 895, El. 809; ἀποστάζω, Ant. 959 (cf. Frag. 342 Dind., κεραυνίου | νώτου καταστάζοντα φάρος, 'letting slip down, droop, from'); ἀποστατέω, O. T. 743, Ant. 993; ἀποστέλλω, El. 71; ἀποσυλάω, see ἐξωθέω; ἀπωθέω (cf. ἐξωθέω), Ai. 446, O. T. 233, 234, 641, 670, El. 1325; ἀφίημι (cf. ἀνίημι, etc.), O. T. 1521, Ant. 1085 (the last passage is variously construed, some editors, with the Scholiast, explaining καρδίας as = κατὰ καρδίας, others putting καρδίας with τοξεύματα; Nauck makes it ablatival); ἐξαφίημι, Tr. 72; ἀφορμάομαι, O. K. 1401; ἀτιμάζω, O. K. 50, Ant. 21 (cf. ἄτιμος, O. T. 789).

βαίνω (cf. μολεῖν and ἔρχομαι), O. T. 152, O. K. 226 (with ἔξω πόρσω added); ἀποβαίνω, O. K. 167; ἐκβαίνω, Ai. 892; ἐπιβαίνω, Phil. 194; βάλλω, O. T. 622 (with ἔξω added). In regard to this and similar examples, where ἔξω is added, it is not easy to say whether the genitive is "governed" by the verb or by ἔξω. In their origin, of course, the prototypes of such phrases contained an ablative modifying the verb; the question now is, with which the poet, in thought, would have connected the genitive. From the freedom with which Sophokles uses the ablatival genitive with simple verbs of motion, it appears on the whole more probable that ἔξω was secondary in his mind. ἐκβάλλω, Ai. 808, O. K. 1307, El. 648.

δεῖ, O. T. 394, 406, Ant. 1098, El. 612, 1494, Phil. 647, 1049, 1060; δεῖται, O. T. 1148, 1292 (two), O. K. 1170 (two); δέχομαι, O. T. 1163, 1164.

ἐκβιάζω, Phil. 1129; ἔκκειμαι, Ant. 1011; ἐκκυλίνδω, O. T. 812; ἐκπλέω, Phil. 1375; ἐκπνέω (cf. ἀναπνέω), Ai. 1148; ἐκραίνω (?), Tr. 781; ἐκρίπτω, O. T. 1410 (?) (with ἔξω added, cf. what is said under βάλλω, above), El. 510; ἔκτοπος (cf. compounds of *alpha privative*), O. K. 232; ἐκτρέπομαι, O. T. 851; ἐξαιτέω, Tr. 10; ἔξειμι (εἶμι, cf. ἄπειμι), O. K. 909; ἐξοδοιπορέω, El. 20; ἐξωθέω (cf. ἀπωθέω), O. K. 428, 1296, 1330 (κἀπεσύλησεν is added); εἴργω, O. K. 836, Ant. 48; ἀπείργω, Ai. 51; ἐλαύνω, O. T. 97; ἀπελαύνω, O. K. 599; ἐξελαύνω, O. K. 356, 376, 823; ἐλεῖν (cf. λαμβάνω), O. T. 1522; ἀνελεῖν, O. T. 1035, El. 1139; ἐξελεῖν, O. K. 541; ἐναλλάσσω (cf. ἀπαλλάσσω and καταλλάσσω), Ai. 208; ἔρημος, O. T. 57, 1509, O. K. 1719, El. 1405; ἐρύκω, Tr. 131; ἐρυστός, Ai. 730; (ἔρχομαι, Frag. 675 Dind., μικροῦ δ᾽ ἀγῶνος οὐ μέγ᾽ ἔρχεται κλέος; cf. O. K. 572, γῆς ὁποίας ἦλθον, which is not counted because of the proximity of ἀπό in the previous line, although perhaps it should have been;) ἀπέρχομαι, O. K. 1165; ἐξέρχομαι, O. K. 45, El. 777; ἔχω, El. 375 (O. K. 1618, an example which, like that in O. K. 572, is not counted, because of ἐξ in the previous line); ἀνέχω, O. T. 174.

ἵστημι, O. T. 142; ἀφίστημι, El. 776 (two), 912, Phil. 865; ἐξανίστημι, Ant. 297; ἐξίστημι, Ant. 1105; μεθίστημι, Phil. 463.

καταλλάσσω (cf. ἀπαλλάσσω and ἐναλλάσσω), Ai. 744; κενός, O. K. 931, Ant. 756, El. 403; κηκίω, Phil. 696 (cf. 784 f. ἐκ βυθοῦ | κηκῖον); κομίζω, O. T. 580, O. K. 1412; κρεμαστὸς (αὐχένος), Ant. 1221; κτάομαι, Phil. 1371; κυρέω, O. K. 1290 (two; ἀπό, line 1289, would be still in the listener's mind); κύρω, O. K. 1082 (?).

λαμβάνω, O. T. 1004, 1012, 1349; λείπω, Ai. 543, Ant. 548, El. 474, Tr. 266, 936; ἀπολείπω, El. 1169; λοιπός, El. 1127; λήγω, (Ai. 274, counted under ἀναπνέω,) O. K. 346, 1722, El. 104 (two), 353, 379, Tr. 911, Phil. 1395; λύω, Tr. 181; ἐκλύω, O. T. 1002; λωφάω, Ai. 61.

μαλάσσω, Phil. 1334; μεθίημι (cf. ἀνίημι, etc.), Ai. 372,

O. K. 838 ; μεταγιγνώσκω, Ai. **717** (two) ; μολεῖν, El. 908 ; μόνος, Ai. 511, μοῦνος, O. K. 1250.

νοσφίζω, Phil. 1427; ἀπονοσφίζω, Phil. 979.

ὁρίζω, Phil. 636 ; ὀρφανός, Ant. 425 ; ὀρφανίζω, Tr. 942.

παρίημι (cf. ἀνίημι, etc.), O. K. **1212** ; παύω, Ai. 788, El. 798, Phil. 1379, 1424 ; ἀναπαύω, O. K. 1114 ; ἀποπαύω, Ai. **1205** ; πέμπω, O. T. 1518 (ἄποικον perhaps has some influence) ; ἐκπέμπω, O. T. 309, 951, El. 1130 (?) ; πίπτω, Phil. 1002 (Schol. ἄνωθεν πεσὼν ἀπὸ πέτρας ; Wecklein-Wunder also connect πέτρας directly with πεσών) ; ἐκπίπτω, Ai. 1177, O. K. 766, El. 750 ; περάω, O. T. 674. (πνέω, Frag. 147 Dind., οὐ μύρου πνέον.)

ῥιζόω, O. K. 1591 (with γῆθεν).

(σπένδω, Frag. 49 Dind., ἔσπεισα βαιᾶς κύλικος) ; στείχω, Ant. 10. After observing the use of the ablatival genitive with μολεῖν, ἔρχομαι, ἐλθεῖν, βαίνω, there seems no just ground for objecting to the same syntax with στείχω. στερέω, Ai. 511, O. K. 857, 1443, Ant. 13, 574, 890, El. 1210, Tr. 177 ; ἀποστερέω, O. T. 1379, El. 813, 814 ; ἀποστερίσκω, O. K. 375 ; σφάλλω, Tr. 1113 ; σῴζω, Ant. 1162, Phil. 919; ἀνασῴζω, El. 1133 ; ἀποσῴζω, Phil. 1379.

τήκομαι, Ant. 1008; τητάομαι, O. K. 1200, 1618, El. 1326, Phil. 228, 383 ; τυγχάνω, O. K. 1168, Phil. 1315.

(ὑφαιρέω, Frag. 34 Dind., ὑφῃρέθη σοῦ κάλαμος ὡσπερεὶ λύρας.)

φέρω, El. 324 ; φεύγω, O. K. 1024, Phil. 1044 ; φυλάσσω, O. K. **161**.

ψεύδω, Ai. 1382, Tr. 713.

Here belong also a number of genitives with adjectives having *alpha privative* as their first and most important element. In these cases the compound is a more picturesque or more suggestive substitute for an adjective of want, and is construed accordingly. As the second element is more or less prominent the construction shades off into the ablatival genitive of agent, or into the "objective" genitive with adjectives containing more or less of verbal force. Of the following, which are here classed under this head of separation, a few might perhaps be put under the genitive of agent. It is not

important to fix the exact dividing line between two classes
which shade into each other so naturally. In none of this list
does it seem necessary to consider the genitive "objective."

ἄγευστος κακῶν, Ant. **582**; ἀκραιφνεῖς τῶν κατηπειλημένων,
O. K. 1147; ἀλαμπὲς ἡλίου, Tr. 691; ἄλυπος ἄτης, El. 1002,
γήρως, O. K. 1519; ἄμμορος πάντων, Phil. **182**; ἄμοιρος τα-
φῆς, Ai. 1326, τῶν θεῶν, Ant. 1070; ἄνατος κακῶν, O. K.
786; ἀνήλιον | ἀνήμερόν τε | χειμώνων, O. K. **678**; ἀπάτωρ
ἐμοῦ, O. K. 1383 (cf. ἄπαις ἔρσενος γόνου, Hdt., etc.); ἄπειρος κακῶν, Ant. 1191, γνώμης, Ant. 1250, τῶνδε, Tr. 309;
(in O. T. **1094** f. the infinitives αὔξειν and χορεύεσθαι depend on ἄπειρος in **1088**, but are not counted here, because
without the article ;) ἄποπτος ἄστεως, O. T. 762, ἡμῶν, El.
1489; ἄπυρον ἀκτῖνός τ' ἀεὶ | θερμῆς ἄθικτον, Tr. 685; γόων
οὐκ ἀσήμονες φθόγγοι, O. K. 1668; ἄσκευον ἀσπίδων τε καὶ
στρατοῦ, El. 36; ἄτιμος τοῦ τεθνηκότος, El. 1214, οὐδενός,
El. 1215, ὧν μὲν ἱκόμην | ἄτιμον, O. T. 788; ἄχαλκος ἀσπί-
δων, O. T. **190**; ἀψόφητος κωκυμάτων, Ai. 321.

We must add to these the following examples, wherein one
cannot say to which of two words the genitive belongs; it
rather belongs to both, or to the phrase as a whole. κυνῆς
ἅλμα κουφιεῖν, Ai. 1287; ἀπωστὸς γῆς ἀπορριφθήσομαι, Ai.
1019; ἄφορμος ἐμᾶς χθονὸς ἔκθορε, O. K. **233**; δράμημα
νωτίσαι πάτρας | ἄπουρον, O. T. **192**; ἔλαμψε γὰρ τοῦ νιφό-
εντος ἀρτίως φανεῖσα | φάμα Παρνασοῦ, O. T. **475**; ὅπως |
σοῦ πρὸς δόμους ἐλθόντος εὖ πράξαιμί τι, O. T. 1006. This
is said by the ἄγγελος with evident reference to the words
of Oedipus two lines above, χάριν λάβοις ἐμοῦ; hence σοῦ is
to be taken as ablatival, with the idea of receiving a present
in the euphemism εὖ πράξαιμί τι. So Wecklein-Wunder also,
as appears from the comment, "Bene Ed. Oxon. 'ut a te bene-
ficii aliquid consequerer.'" For a somewhat similar turn of
words see Tr. 191, πρὸς σοῦ τι κερδάναιμι.

Several interesting facts are brought out by these lists of
examples. In general, the freedom with which this genitive
of separation is used with all sorts of words and expressions
denoting removal, issue, deprivation, distinction, separation,
receiving, is surprising. No one word occurs many times with

it; the number is not swelled by a few frequent phrases. Apparently Sophokles felt free to indicate these relations by the genitive with almost any word; so that, although many compounds of ἀπό and ἐξ appear in the lists, especially with verbs of motion, yet enough simple verbs of motion are so construed to show that the poet scarcely felt it necessary to help out such phrases with ἀπό or ἐξ, or any other preposition. Metre or euphony often seems to determine whether simple or compound shall be used. See e. g. under λείπω. Accordingly, where the only objection to a MS. reading is the presence of an ablatival genitive of separation, that reading should without hesitation be retained. Passages to be considered with this principle in view are ἕλῃ μου, O. T. 1522, and ἀνδρῶν μοῦνος, O. K. 1250, where the genitive offers no difficulty.

Obviously some of the examples enumerated above — namely, those with verbs of receiving — might with some propriety be classed under the head of source; but without strongly objecting to such disposal of them, it seems better for our purpose to reserve the term "genitive of source" to include the genitive with two classes of verbs: first, those of hearing and learning; secondly, verbs denoting birth. These verbs, with references, are the following : —

(a.) ἀκούω, O. T. 42, 547, 729, 841, O. K. 33, 452, 551, 1171, 1352, El. 926, 927, Tr. 431 ; εἰσακούω, Ai. 318, Tr. 424.

κλύω, Ai. 1072, O. T. 235, 305, O. K. 412, 413, 792, 1117, 1350, **1766** (possibly adnominal; here classed as ablatival, first, because so far from ταῦτα, secondly, because with these verbs the genitive usually denotes source when referring to persons, if the accusative of the thing accompanies it), El. 293, 424, 877, Tr. 189, Phil. 1273.

μανθάνω, Ai. 800, 801, O. T. 546, 574, 575, O. K. 593, Ant. 723, 725, 1032, El. 565, 889, Tr. 187, 408 ; ἐκμανθάνω, O. T. 1438 (not governed by ἐκ, cf. 1443), O. K. 114.

εἰδέναι, El. 668. Possibly this genitive goes with χρῄζω ; but, first, the order indicates otherwise ; secondly, compare O. K. 1149, ἃ γ᾽ εἴσει καὐτὸς ἐκ ταύταιν ; finally, when this verb means 'to learn,' as here and in El. 40, and else-

where not infrequently, why should it not be construed like
μανθάνω?

πυνθάνομαι, O. T. 333, Tr. 387.

(*b.*) γίγνομαι, O. T. 1168, El. 775, Phil. **181**, 1284.

φύω, O. T. 1015, 1082, O. K. 1378, Ant. 38, **144, 145, 866**,
El. 1171 (also Frag. 470 Dind., θνητῆς φύς); ἐκφύω, Ai. 487,
488, 1295, O. T. 1499.

φυτεύω, O. K. 1324.

βλαστάνω, Tr. 403 (also Frag. 518 Dind.); ἀποβλαστάνω,
O. K. **534**.

O. T. 1063 may be added, οὐδ᾽ ἐὰν τρίτης ἐγὼ | μητρὸς
φανῶ τρίδουλος, where the case seems to hover between the
adnominal and ablatival genitive, with the idea of source the
more prominent.

Under this head belong also a few examples in which the
genitive of source, without a preposition, is employed to denote the agent. The following appear in Sophokles: ἄφαρ-
κτος φίλων, Ai. **910**; τῶν φίλων νικώμενος, Ai. 1353; ἄθικτος
ἡγητῆρος, O. K. 1521; κακῶν | δυσάλωτος, O. K. **1722**; φίλων
ἄκλαυτος, Ant. **848**; μαντικῆς ἄπρακτος, Ant. 1034; κείνης
διδακτά, El. 344; ἐκδιδαχθεὶς τῶν κατ᾽ οἶκον [Tr. 934]; κρα-
τίστου πατρὸς τραφείς, Phil. 3 (cf. οἷος ἐξ οἵου ἐτράφης, Ai.
557; also τραφεὶς μητρὸς εὐγενοῦς ἄπο, Ai. 1229, and μητέ-
ρων τεθραμμένοι, Aesch. Sept. 792); ἐλπίδων | ἄπιστον, Phil.
867; φωνῆς | προσφθεγκτός, Phil. 1066.

As already remarked, some few of those placed under the
genitive of separation with compounds of *alpha privative* may
perhaps belong here instead. Thus Wunder, for example,
agreés with Brunck in so disposing of γήρως, O. K. 1519.

The genitive is used to denote cause in exclamations in the
following passages: with οἴμοι, Ai. **367, 900, 908**, 980, O. K. **202**,
982, 1399 (two), 1400, Ant. 82, **1265**, El. 1143 (with τάλαινα),
1179, 1209 (with τάλαινα), Tr. **971, 972**; with ἐή, O. K. **149**;
with φεῦ, El. 920, 1183.

With other words the genitive of cause is difficult to separate from genitives wholly doubtful in character. The following, however, seem to belong here: (βαρυνθήσεσθε, Frag. 627
Dind.); ἐντρέπομαι, Ai. 90, O. T. 724, 1226, El. 520; κήδο-

could have explained it away. Moreover, I believe that the former idea is earlier in time, in spite of its appearing later in Greek literature. It is wholly unsafe to assume without question, as is so often done, that beliefs and customs which meet us first in post-Homeric authors are of post-Homeric origin. Such an assumption must be tested by a wide survey of the development of human thought and institutions. Now the fancy expressed in Hom. Ψ, regarded as the initial form of the exclusion-idea, finds no very plausible explanation in primitive ways of thinking; whereas it is easy to see how it might have been developed as an offshoot from the simple natural notion that the unburied walk the earth, coupled with the belief in Hades as the proper home of the dead. Be that as it may, it is noteworthy that the idea of Hom. Ψ does not reappear in classical Greek literature, unless it be in Hom. λ. Here, after telling how Odysseus, having reached the appointed spot on the edge of Hades, dug a trench, and filled it with the blood which was to reanimate for a time the νεκύων ἀμενηνὰ κάρηνα, the poem proceeds (51 ff.):

πρώτη δὲ ψυχὴ Ἐλπήνορος ἦλθεν ἑταίρου·
οὐ γάρ πω ἐτέθαπτο ὑπὸ χθονὸς εὐρυοδείης·
σῶμα γὰρ ἐν Κίρκης μεγάρῳ κατελείπομεν ἡμεῖς
ἄκλαυτον καὶ ἄθαπτον, ἐπεὶ πόνος ἄλλος ἔπειγεν.

The commentators, ancient and modern,[1] say in substance: "Elpenor appeared first, because, his corpse having remained unburied, he could not go down δόμον Ἀΐδος εἴσω." (Merry.) But, in spite of this unanimity, I venture to doubt whether the poet had any such thought in mind. If one reads the whole episode through without prejudice, he will be struck by the absence of any explicit reference to Elpenor's being excluded from the society of the other shades. Even the suppliant himself, in his entreaty to Odysseus for burial, hints at nothing of the sort. And if his being the first to have speech with Odysseus must be accounted for, his own

---

[1] Faesi is apparently an exception. See his note on Ψ 72 (edition of 1865). Ameis and Koch, in their notes on ω 187, virtually unsay what they have said on λ 51.

eagerness to be heard would furnish a plausible enough reason.
True, this ghost, unlike the rest, seems able to hold converse
without drinking of the dark blood ; and for this there is the
old explanation that, not being yet admitted to the interior of
Hades, he has not yet tasted of the water of Lethe.   But, not
to dwell on the fact that Homer appears to know nothing
of Lethe, this explanation seems to me a case of treating
" literature" like " dogma," — an unwarrantable attempt to
make a poetical picture square with a supposed doctrinal
formula.   The inconsistency is best left as the poem leaves
it, unexplained ; especially as the whole passage (lines 51–83)
is open to strong suspicion of being interpolated.   The idea,
then, embodied in Hom. Ψ, that the soul of an unburied corpse ·
is doomed to wander on the hither margin of the underworld,
seems more like the fancy of an individual poet than an
article of popular faith.   The popularity of the Homeric
·poems must of course have made this fancy familiar to the
Greek world, and Vergil elaborates it in the sixth book of the
Aeneid ; but if we may judge by the silence of post-Homeric
Greek authors, it struck no deep root in the Greek mind,
while at the most it was crowded and overshadowed by other
conflicting ideas.

For it is now time to point out that entrance into Hades
was commonly thought of as taking place at the moment of
death, and that whether burial was to follow or not.   The
wide-spread belief in a subterranean realm of shades probably
grows out of the custom of burial.   " Hell," as M. Guyau puts
it, " is nothing but an extended tomb."   (Morale d'Épicure,
p. 106.)   But the Greeks, at the stage where we first meet
them, were no longer distinctly conscious of this.   Hades·had
come to be the proper home of all disembodied spirits: to it
the spirit took its flight when life expired.   Thus, to take a
typical instance, we read (Λ 262 f.) :

ἔνθ' 'Αντήνορος υἷες ὑπ' 'Ατρείδῃ βασιλῆι
πότμον ἀναπλήσαντες ἔδυν δόμον "Αϊδος εἴσω.

More striking are the cases where the descent to Hades is
mentioned in immediate connection with the fact of non-
burial.   Thus Achilles (X 344 ff.) refuses to the dying

Hector the rites of burial; but immediately after we read (361 f.) :

> ὧς ἄρα μιν εἰπόντα τέλος θανάτοιο κάλυψεν,
> ψυχὴ δ' ἐκ ῥεθέων πταμένη Ἀϊδόσδε βεβήκει.

See also H 327 ff., and the familiar lines which begin the Iliad. But passages like these, though inconsistent with the notion of the soul's lingering in or near the unburied body, are reconcilable, it may be urged, with the language of Patroklos in Ψ. It is admitted that, standing by themselves, they would not prove much. But then they do not stand by themselves. The twenty-fourth book of the Odyssey is more circumstantial, and treats the presence of unburied men in Hades as a matter of course. Here the shades of the suitors are conducted by Hermes to the lower world. Their destination is left in no manner of doubt (11 ff.) :

> πὰρ δ' ἴσαν Ὠκεανοῦ τε ῥοὰς καὶ Λευκάδα πέτρην,
> ἠδὲ παρ' Ἠελίοιο πύλας καὶ δῆμον Ὀνείρων
> ἤϊσαν· αἶψα δ' ἵκοντο κατ' ἀσφοδελὸν λειμῶνα,
> ἔνθα τε ναίουσι ψυχαὶ, εἴδωλα καμόντων.
> εὗρον δὲ ψυχὴν Πηληιάδεω Ἀχιλῆος
> καὶ Πατροκλῆος, κ. τ. λ.

And when one of their number has told to Agamemnon the story of their slaughter, he ends by saying (186 ff.) :

> ὧς ἡμεῖς, Ἀγάμεμνον, ἀπωλόμεθ', ὧν ἔτι καὶ νῦν
> σώματ' ἀκηδέα κεῖται ἐνὶ μεγάροις Ὀδυσῆος·
> οὐ γάρ πω ἴσασι φίλοι κατὰ δώμαθ' ἑκάστου,
> οἵ κ' ἀπονίψαντες μέλανα βρότον ἐξ ὠτειλέων
> κατθέμενοι γοάοιεν· ὃ γὰρ γέρας ἐστὶ θανόντων.

Post-Homeric literature supplies illustrations of the same way of thinking.

> κεῖται δὲ νεκρὸς περὶ νεκρῷ, τὰ νυμφικὰ
> τέλη λαχὼν δείλαιος ἔν γ' Ἀΐδου δόμοις,

says the messenger in the Antigone (1240 f.), while the bodies of Haemon and Antigone still lie where they had just fallen. Alkestis, in Euripides's drama, when about to die, sees Charon and Pluto waiting impatient (252 ff.) :

> ὁρῶ δίκωπον ὁρῶ σκάφος,
> νεκύων δὲ πορθμεὺς

ἔχων χέρ' ἐπὶ κοντῷ Χάρων μ' ἤδη καλεῖ· τί μέλλεις;
ἐπείγου· σὺ κατείργεις.
.   .   .   .   .   .
ἄγει μ' ἄγει μέ τις, οὐχ ὁρᾷς;
νεκύων ἐς αὐλὰν
ὑπ' ὀφρύσι κυαναυγέσι βλέπων πτερωτὸς Ἅιδας.

Later, after her death, but before her burial, the chorus sing
(435 ff.) :

ὦ Πελίου θύγατερ,
χαίρουσά μοι εἰν Ἀίδα δόμοισιν
τὸν ἀνάλιον οἶκον οἰκετεύοις.
ἴστω δ' Ἀίδας ὁ μελαγχαίτας θεὸς ὅς τ' ἐπὶ κώπᾳ
πηδαλίῳ τε γέρων
νεκροπομπὸς ἵζει,
πολὺ δὴ πολὺ δὴ γυναῖκ' ἀρίσταν
λίμναν Ἀχεροντίαν πορεύ-
σας ἐλάτᾳ δικώπῳ,

where the second sentence seems most naturally to imply
that the passage in Charon's ferry-boat has already taken
place. Again, Lucian suggests (De Luctu, 16) that, while
a father is engaged in frantic funeral laments over the body
of his son, the son might get leave of Aeakos and Pluto
to slip out from his nether prison and remonstrate against
this ill-judged grief. The soul, then, according to this, is
already established in Hades before the funeral rites are performed. Still more to the present purpose is the story told
in a scholium on Pindar, Ol. i. 97. According to this authority, Sisyphus, being near death, gave orders to his wife to
leave him unburied. She obeyed ; but he, descending to
Pluto, accused his wife of neglect, and obtained permission to
revisit the earth and punish her.

The evidence quoted in the two foregoing pages shows, not
only that the Greeks were in the habit of speaking conventionally and thoughtlessly of the soul as departing to Hades
immediately after death, but that this idea might be dwelt
upon and developed into a picture or story, which, for the
time being at least, seemed real. There is surely just as
much reason, and just as little, for extracting from the twenty-
fourth book of the Odyssey as from the twenty-third book of
the Iliad a dogma, and representing it as *the* belief of the

outside the regular legion formation of about the size of a maniple (*circiter* cxx), and is probably so used here. That this *centuria* contained no more than one hundred and twenty men cannot be positively decided from the language of Caesar (*voluntarii eiusdem centuriae*). Bearing in mind, however, the shortness of Caesar's military career (p. 52), and also the fact that his legionaries numbered hardly half those of Pompey, viz. twenty-two thousand to forty-five thousand (cc. 88, 89), one hundred and twenty need not seem altogether improbable as representing the whole number of Caesar's *evocati* (*voluntarii*), even over against Pompey's two thousand. Besides, we have the repeated testimony of Plutarch that Crastinus commanded one hundred and twenty men (p. 47). But it does not necessarily follow that Caesar massed all his *evocati* (*voluntarii*) under Crastinus. Such an inference from his so prominently mentioning the fact that Pompey scattered his own *evocati* all along his line of battle (c. 88. 5) is at best uncertain.

The bearing of this view of the commission of Crastinus on the question what the *antesignani* were, is negative, but important. Caesar does not call the troop which Crastinus commanded *antesignani*, but *voluntarii*. So the author of the Bellum Africanum, in a passage cited[1] to uphold the old view that the *antesignani* were a special detached corps in each legion,[2] speaks not of *antesignani*, but of *expediti*, a word of as general meaning as *electi*. The new view that the *antesignani* were the four front cohorts in the legion's usual line of battle is so well upheld by Göler,[3] that it is strange to find him, in his impossible interpretation of the Crastinus episode, neglecting to compare it with the exploit of the *antesignani* at Ilerda (B. C. i. 43).

3. What was the exploit of Crastinus?

It was to set an inspiring example to Caesar's whole line of battle, and especially to the tenth legion, on whose suc-

---

[1] Jähns, in Bursian's Jahresbericht, 1881, ii. p. 208. See also, ibid., the summary of Planer's "Caesars Antesignanen."

[2] Marquardt, *op. cit.*, ii. p. 343.

[3] *Op. cit.*, ii. p. 37, note 4.

cess the fate of the day had been made to depend, by leading
a large body of re-enlisted veterans in such a fierce charge
upon the enemy's extreme left that it was thrown into some
confusion, and would have been easily driven back when the
shock of the onset of the regular line came, had not Crastinus fallen. Caesar had planned the movement as one of
three precautionary measures which should frustrate Pompey's known design of turning his right wing. These measures would probably all have proved in vain, had it not been
for a fourth precaution, which seems to have flashed into
Caesar's mind at the last moment. Pompey concentrated
even more strength upon his left wing than Caesar had antici-
pated (c. 88, *fin.*). Fearing then the certain defeat of his own
cavalry in spite of the fact that they had been strengthened
by infantrymen, in which case everything would have de-
pended upon the success of Crastinus and the tenth legion,
Caesar formed the famous *quarta acies*, which, in concert
with his cavalry, crushed so utterly the hopes of Pompey
(c. 89. 4 ; 93. 5–8). But even when this *quarta acies*, after
routing the cavalry of Pompey, had fallen in one and the
same charge (*eodem impetu*) upon the rear of his infantry
left, this was still holding its ground bravely against the tenth
legion (*pugnantibus etiam tum ac resistentibus*). Crastinus
had fallen. Pompey's left had fought better than Caesar had
thought they could against his favorite tenth legion, even
after a path had been opened up for it into the enemy's ranks
by the *voluntarii;* but when the cavalry of Pompey scurried
off to the hills, and Caesar's *quarta acies* fell upon the rear
of Pompey's left wing, the death of Crastinus and the failure
of his exploit to accomplish all that had been intended by it
were more than made good. Pompey's left wing broke and
fled ; and now Caesar ordered up his reserves, the *tertia acies*,
when Pompey's whole line followed the shattered left wing.
Caesar had not merely foiled the tactics of his enemy, but
turned them back upon him with complete success. As Florus
so well puts it (ii. 13 [= iv. 2], 47) : " Sed nec minus admira-
bilior illius exitus belli. Quippe cum Pompeius adeo equi-
tum copia abundaret, ut facile circumventurus sibi Caesarem
videretur, circumventus ipse est."

Very discriminating is Caesar's estimate of his obligations for this victory; first and foremost, the *quarta acies:* "Neque vero Caesarem fefellit quin ab iis cohortibus quae contra equitatum in quarta acie collocatae essent initium victoriae oriretur" (c. 94. 3). But to Crastinus, even though only partially successful, he gives that praise for which the veteran was willing to die: "Sic enim Caesar existimabat, eo proelio excellentissimam virtutem Crastini fuisse, optimeque eum de se meritum iudicabat."

IV. — *Alliteration in Latin.*[1]

By TRACY PECK,

PROFESSOR IN YALE COLLEGE.

THE Latin language shares with other languages a disposition to emphasize an idea by some form of repetition, as by the reduplication of the root, the iteration of the same word or words, anaphora, the *figura etymologica*, assonances in any part of a word, puns, and rhyme : but in the manifold uses of *alliteration* the Latin probably goes far beyond any other cultivated speech. Alliteration is here used in its narrowest sense, the recurrence, namely, of the same initial letter (or its phonetic equivalent) in two or more contiguous words. There are abundant indications of its existence in the popular language, and in religious and legal phraseology, even before the rise of any regular literature. It is especially prominent in the earlier writers of the Republic : it obtrudes itself with over-frequency in Ennius and Plautus, — the former often playing with it as with a newly acquired toy, the latter employing it for merely comical effects ; in Terence it so far fades away as to escape observation unless it is sought for ; in Lucilius, who protested against the devices and mannerisms of rhetoricians and grammarians, it is comparatively though not altogether ignored ; in the fragments of Pacuvius, and, still more, of Accius, it again becomes very conspicuous ; in every book of Lucretius there are hundreds of palpable instances ; it again declines in the poets of the Augustan age, except in Vergil, whose verse is full of illustrations, though here as elsewhere the imperial laureate shows his exquisite taste by treating alliteration strictly as a means to higher ends. Though there

---

[1] Free use has been made of these works : — Naeke, *De Allitteratione Sermonis Latini*, Rhein. Mus., 1829; Maehly, *Ueber Allitteration*, Neues Schweiz. Mus., 1864; Jordan, *Beiträge zur Geschichte der latein. Sprache*, Berlin, 1879; Kvičala, *Beiträge zur Erklärung der Aeneis*, Prag, 1881; and, especially, Wölfflin, *Die Allitterierenden Verbindungen der latein. Sprache*, München, 1881.

are many cases of conscious alliteration in all the great prose
writers of Rome, it can hardly be called a peculiarity of any
but Cicero and Sallust, and perhaps Tacitus, and then, through
a kind of renaissance, of Fronto and Apuleius.   In all these
writers, and in its sporadic appearance elsewhere, alliteration
is found much more frequently with consonants than with
vowels, and in poetry its favorite place is at the end of the
verse.   Thus Lucretius and Vergil are very fond of throwing
the fifth and sixth feet of the hexameter into detached and
alliterative words.   Kvíčala counts 277 instances of this movement in the Aeneid ; in the fifth book of Lucretius it certainly
occurs more than fifty times.

It might fairly be asked if the decline of alliteration, and its
displacement in verse by rhyme, — like the displacement of
quantity by accent, — have not been a loss to literature.   Less
obtrusive and less inevitable than rhyme, less amenable to
laws of position and recurrence, very often much less mechan-
ical, it seems to me to contribute an æsthetic enjoyment of a
higher and more delicate order.

Though the word *alliteration* seems to have been invented by
Pontanus in the fifteenth century, the Romans were certainly
aware that the device was in use among themselves.   Thus
the author of the Rhetorica ad Herennium (iv. 12) calls it
" eiusdem litterae nimia assiduitas."   Donatus remarks on the
solus Sannio servat of Terence (Eun. 780), " Haec figura παρό-
μοιον dicitur."   In connection with Vergil's *casus Cassandra
canebat* (A. iii. 183) Servius says : " Haec compositio iam viti-
osa est, quae maioribus placuit, ut *Anchisen agnoscit amicum*
(A. iii. 82), et *sale saxa sonabant* (A. v. 866)."   Significant,
too, is the dictum of Martianus Capella (De Arte Rhet. 33) :
" Compositionis vitium maximum est non vitare cuiuslibet litterae assiduitatem in odium repetitam."   Spartianus, in his Life
of the Emperor Geta (5), says : " Habebat etiam istam consue-
tudinem ut convivia et maxime prandia per singulas litteras
iuberet scientibus servis, velut in quo erat *anser, apruna, anas,*
item *pullus, perdix, pavus, porcellus, piscis, perna*; et quae in
eam litteram genera edulium caderent; et item *fasianus, far-
rata, ficus,* et talia."

Those who to-day doubt, as Lachmann doubted,[1] the presence of alliteration as a characteristic in Latin diction, should in this particular compare such contemporary and fairly comparable writers as Lucretius and Catullus, Cicero and Caesar, Vergil and Horace. And it is difficult to see how any one can deny this large presence who comes upon such passages as these from representative writers: —

"O Tite tute Tati tibi tanta tyranne tulisti." Enn. Ann.

"Africa terribili tremit horrida terra tumultu." Ibid.

"At tuba terribili sonitu taratantara dixit." Ibid.

"Maior mihi moles, maius miscendumst malum." Accius, Atr.

"Non potuit paucis plura plane proloqui." Plaut. Men. 252.

"Quanta pernis pestis veniet, quanta labes larido,
    quanta sumini absumedo, quanta callo calamitas,
    quanta laniis lassitudo." Id. Capt. 900.

"Viva videns vivo sepeliri viscera busto." Lucr. v. 993.

"Neu patriae validas in viscera vertite vires." Verg. A. vi. 833.

"Ita sensim sine sensu aetas senescit." Cic. de Sen. xi.

The grammarian Diomedes gives this line, which is probably a cento from the second Aeneid: —

"Machina multa minax minitatur maxima muris."

Less on the surface than in the above extracts, but very effective and artistically very beautiful, is the alliteration in this descriptive passage from Ennius: —

"Incedunt arbusta per alta, securibus caedunt,
    percellunt magnas quercus, exciditur ilex,
    fraxinus frangitur atque abies consternitur alta,
    pinus proceras pervertunt: omne sonabat
    arbustum fremitu silvai frondosai."

Vergil's (A. vi. 179–182) imitation of the last passage well illustrates the different management of the same peculiarity by the two poets.

Of course a distinction must be made between accidental alliteration and that which is clearly premeditated, and statistics and theories are worthless which are based upon the natural and almost unavoidable juxtaposition of alliterative

---

[1] *Allitteration*, in Ersch und Gruber's Encyclopädie.

words. It should be said, too, that to quite an exceptional extent the Latin contains words of the same initial letter which naturally often appear together. Among such common phrases are *virtutes vitia, longus latus, publicus privatus, maximus minimus, plebs populusque, populus et patres, doceo disco, toga tunica, victus vestisque, flumina fontes, prope procul, ager aedes, aequo animo, aurum argentum, fundo fugo, aes alienum, septem sapientes.* Caesar's "*Veni vidi vici*" (Suet. J. C. 37) seems as natural in form as it is comprehensive in content, though Plutarch (Caes. 50) appears to have noticed only its rhyme, not its alliteration. Nor does one see how Christ's description of himself (John xiv. 6) was to go into Latin except with alliteration : " Ego sum *via* et *veritas* et *vita.*"

The common impression that alliteration in Latin originated in poetry seems clearly a mistake. It is hardly to be found in the extant fragments of the oldest verse, as in the hymns of the Arval brethren and of the Salii ; but it is found in many very ancient phrases and formulae of a popular and priestly and juridical character. These are some of the alliterative proverbial expressions, many of which demonstrably antedate the appearance of formal Latin poetry : — *Vivus vidensque* (Ter. Eun., Lucr. iii., Cic. Sest.), *oleum et operam perdere* (Plaut. Poen., Cic. passim), *nec vola nec vestigium* (Varro), *sex septem, acus aciaeque* (Titinius, Petron. 76), *inter os et offam* (Cato), *inter manum et mentum* (Id.), *inter sacrum saxumque* (Plaut. Capt., Apul.), *vitio vertere, semel saepius, cave canem, ad carceres a calce* (Varro, Sat., Cic. de Sen., Id. de Am.), *sine fuco ac fallaciis* (Cic. Att. i. 1), *cras credo* (Varro), *est modus matulae* (Id.), *mutuum muli scabunt* (Id.), *fortes fortuna* (Ter., Cic., et al.), *sucus et sanguis* (Cic. Br. Att. iv. 16), *sudor et sanguis* (Enn., Cic., Plin. Ep., Tac. G.), *ad restim res redit* (Caecil., Ter. Ph.), *satis superque, viva vox, a vestigio ad verticem* (Plin. N. H. vii. 77), *albus an ater, nec vas nec vestimentum* (Ter. Heaut., Cato, Sall. C.). In Aulus Gellius (xiv. 2) *vox viva* is set proverbially against *muti magistri* (books), while Cicero (de Leg. iii. 1) defines *magistratus* as *lex loquens*, and *lex* as *mutus magistratus.*

Here are some alliterative religious and legal expressions of great antiquity : — *Di duint, felix faustum fortunatumque, sit salvus sator salva sint sata* (Cato), *ius iudiciumque, manus et mancipium, tabulae testesque, sane sarteque, purus putus* (Aul. Gell. vii. 5), *arae et altaria, tecta templa, templa tesca, per lancem liciumque, pater patratus, sacro-sanctus.* The directors of the mint were called *triumviri auro argento aeri flando feriundo* (Orelli, Insc. 569) ; sellers of swine guaranteed that their wares were free *a febri et a foria* (Varro, R. R. ii. 4); the praetor solemnly uttered his *do dico addico ;* of the Senate it was reported *censuit consensit conscivit* (Liv. i. 32). Rome's faithful allies were called *fortes fideles* (Liv. passim), her enemies were often described as *fusi fugati,* and to her foreign envoys and public guests were assigned *loca lautia.* The traditional epithets of several divinities attest the great antiquity of alliteration ; as, *Dea dia, mater matuta, bona* (once *duona*) *Dea, Venus victrix, Iuno iuga, Fors Fortuna.* Observe, also, *Venus volgivaga* (Lucr. iv.), and such combinations of gods and heroes as *Iuppiter Iuno, Vulcanus Vesta, Romulus Remus, Titus Tatius, Semo Sancus, Picumnus Pilumnus.* Among the marriage divinities was a *Deus domiducus* (August. C. D. vi. 9).

Noteworthy in the cases of alliteration, amounting almost to a law in the earliest instances, is the frequency of asyndeton.

But the object of this paper is rather to present some philological aspects of alliteration than to treat it on its rhetorical or historical sides.

The argument in regard to the guttural sound of *c* before all vowels is amply confirmed by alliteration ; indeed, were we without other guides as to the ancient pronunciation of this letter, this guide alone would be almost conclusive. Of abundant examples in all periods and styles, these may suffice : — *quae cava corpore caeruleo cortina receptat* (Enn.), *cava caerula candent* (Id.), *claudus caecus mutus mancus* (Plaut. Merc.), *cito cursim* (Id. Poen.), *cedo calidum consilium cito* (Id. Mil.), *crispus crassus caesius* (Ter. Hec.), *carmina cantu concelebrare* (Lucr. v.), *cymbala circum concava* (Id. ii.), *caeca caligo* (Lucr., Verg.), *cum caedes cum civium cruor cum cinis* (Cic. pro Sulla), *caedes incendia* (Cic., Tac., passim), *certus clarus* (Ter., Cic., Hor., Liv.), *comitia consulum cum candidatis civiliter celebrans* (Tac. H. ii. 91).

Even among progressive Latinists there is some tendency to approximate the sound of *o*, in many positions, to that of *a*. The tendency seems to me to be a vicious one from every point of view, and to be against the teaching of such evidently alliterative and frequently occurring combinations as *oro obsecroque, ora oculique, oleum et operam perdere, opera aut otium, ope atque opera*. Equally valuable is the negative evidence from the apparent absence of examples of *o* and *a* in alliteration. Had the two vowels sometimes been uttered alike, we should expect to find them brought together. Thus, we do find *au* combined with *o* in the plebeian or colloquial speech; as, from Plautus, *aurum orichalcum, ope auxiliumque, aurata ornata, omen auspicium*. More frequently, however, *au* is found in conjunction with its first element; as, *agenda audendaque, alit auget, aluit auxit armavit* (Cic. Att. viii. 3), *auctor actor, adiuvant augent amant* (Plaut. Men.), *altas aëris auras* (Lucr. iii.), *attentas aures animumque* (Id. vi.), *animus atque aures avent avide* (Enn. Trag.).

The seemingly studied juxtaposition of initial *ae* and *a*, and the apparent lack of examples of *ae* and *e*, are of some weight against the theory that *ae* was pronounced like *e*, or approximately like it. Thus, *anni aetas vox vires* (Cato contra Galb.), *agere aetatem, agere aevum, aequo animo, aes alienum, ager aedes, aeris acervus et auri* (Hor. Ep. i. 1), *animo aegra amore saevo saucia* (Enn. Trag.). This does not affect the evidence that early among the peasants, and much later quite generally, *ae* and *e* were practically identified.

It is well known that a Latin *l* is sometimes the representative of *d*, and that *du* sometimes sank to a *b*. Having the testimony of Roman grammarians that *lacrima* was once *dacrima*, as well as the forms of the word in cognate languages, we do not hesitate to read *dacrima* in Ennius's Epitaph, which is otherwise rich in alliteration: —

> "Nemo me dacrimis decoret nec funera fletu
> faxit: cur? volito vivus per ora virum."

The combinations *domi bellique* and *bona Dea* in all probability had their origin in a fondness for alliteration in the days when *belli* and *bona* were *duelli* and *duona*.

The alliterative union of vocalic and consonantal *u* has been denied, as by Wölfflin [1]: but there is certainly some support for a different view, and *pro tanto* an argument for the proper pronunciation of consonantal *u*, in such expressions as *transversum unguem, ab unguibus usque ad verticem* (Cic. Rosc. Com.), *qui vobis universis et populo placent* (Ter. Ad. prol.), *utilius veṛu in sulco quam gravis galea in proelio* (Syrus); Horace's *quid valeant umeri* (A. P. 40) is certainly in an alliterative neighborhood, and Lucretius appears to have wished to fill with the *u* sound this line, — *ventorum validis fervescunt viribus undae* (iii. 493). It should here be borne in mind that vowels were employed alliteratively much less often than consonants.

In the sequence of alliterative words, if but one contains the vowel *a*, it usually follows, — certainly in the classical period. This principle naturally holds in prose more than in poetry, and it has been already said that in the dactylic hexameter there is a fondness for throwing the alliterative words into the last two feet of the verse. In illustration of this general rule, I give *ferro flammaque, longe lateque, colles campique, silvae saltusque* (Lucr., Verg., Tac.), *multi et magni, potus atque pastus* (Cic. Div. i. 60), *plebs patresque, mitis et mansues* (Aul. Gell. v. 14), *membra manusque, mundus magnus* (Lucr. passim), *moles magna* (Acc., Verg.), *lepidus et lautus* (Plaut., Ter.), *gloria et gratia, fundere fugare, fides fama, crispus crassus caesius* (Ter. Hec.), *video et valeo, certus clarusque, nec cor nec caput, vince et vale.*

If the words in alliteration are unequal in length, the shorter one usually precedes. Thus, *aurum argentum, acer acutus, bonus benignus, cursus certamenque* (Plin. Ep. viii. 20), *cura custodiaque* (Ibid. vii. 19, Cic. Fam. xv. 2), *gerrae germanae, ferus ferreus, fortis fidelis, vinctus verberatus, verba verbera, cor corpusque, fama fortuna, pudor pudicitia, damnum dedecus, fons fundamentum, dat dicat dedicat, nec vas nec vestimentum, vietus vetus veternosus* (Ter. E. 688), *porro penitus-penetrata* (Lucr. i.), *male monita memoria* (Caecil.), *magistratus lex est loquens, lex autem mutus magistratus* (Cic. de Leg. iii. 1).

---

[1] *Ueber d. allit. Verbindungen der lat. Sprache,* p. 4.

In textual criticism and in exegesis some help has been derived from alliteration, and this legitimate source is likely to be more and more resorted to.   In Cicero's quotation[1] (T. D. i. 16) from some ancient poet the manuscripts differ between *falso sanguine* and *salso sanguine*.   As sense and tradition hesitate between the readings, alliteration may well decide in favor of *salso*.   Kvíčala[2] avails himself of this aid in trying to settle the text and meaning of more than three hundred places in the Aeneid, though probably very few will assent to all his conclusions.   From his examples I select a few.   In iv. 460, *voces* rather than *gemitus* is almost required by the alliterative context:

> "Hinc exaudiri voces et verba vocantis
>   visa viri."

If nothing else can decide between *ciet manes* and *movet manes* (iv. 490), alliteration may pronounce for the latter. The very effective and varied repetition of sounds in vi. 683,

> " Fataque fortunasque virum moresque manusque,"

seems conclusive against Peerlkamp's change of *manus* to *animos*.   It has been a question from the early Roman commentators to the latest American editors[3] whether, at vi. 806, Vergil wrote *virtutem extendere factis*, or, as is favored by the resulting alliteration, *virtute extendere vires*.   And perhaps by Vergil's undeniable fondness for alliteration we may best explain his use of *mores* in *mores et moenia* (i. 264), where we might look for *leges* or *iura*, and his odd phrase *pubes tuorum* in *puppesque tuae pubesque tuorum* (i. 399),[4] and his bold expression *auri aura* (vi. 204), and his puzzling employment of *secat* in *quam quisque secat spem* (x. 107).

---

[1] See J. Maehly, Neues Schweiz. Mus., 1864, p. 229.
[2] *Neue Beiträge zur Erklär. der Aeneis*, pp. 387–415.
[3] Greenough (1881) *v. e. v*; Frieze (1883) *v. e. f.*
[4] Quint. ix. 3. 75 : " Verbum verbo non dissimile valde quaeritur."

V. — *On the Relation of the Anglo-Norman Vowel System to the Norman Words in English.*

By HANS C. G. VON JAGEMANN,

PROFESSOR IN EARLHAM COLLEGE, RICHMOND, IND.

THE introduction of Latin elements into the English language is due to four principal causes : the occupation of Britain by the Romans, the conversion of the Britons to the Christian Church, the conquest of England by the Normans, and the revival of classical learning in the sixteenth century. We are therefore accustomed to speak of these elements respectively as Latin of the first, second, third, and fourth period.

This division is not altogether satisfactory. It accounts, for instance, for *leal* and *loyal* on the one hand, and *legal* on the other, the first two being Latin of the third period, the third Latin of the fourth period ; but it fails to explain the doublet *leal* and *loyal.* A similar group is *peer, pair,* and *par,* and others will be mentioned in the course of this investigation. Again, there is a class of words, a fair specimen of which is *require,* which is decidedly classical Latin in form, and which we should therefore suppose to belong to the Latin of the fourth period ; yet it is found in Chaucer. Subdivisions of the above classes are therefore needed, if we wish to account for the various forms in which Latin words appear in English.

The words belonging to the first two classes are so well known and so few in number that we need not dwell upon them. The third class, however, is the most important one, the words belonging to it being very numerous, and next to the Anglo-Saxon constituting the most important element in the English language.

At the time of the Norman conquest there was no French language in the modern sense of this word, but instead of it we have a number of dialects, the principal ones being the Wallonian, the Norman, the Picard, the Burgundian, and that of the Île-de-France. The last-named dialect, of which the Modern French is the direct descendant, possessed during the eleventh century no pre-eminence whatever over the other dialects, but, considering both its literary productions and its territorial extent, it was perhaps the least important of them all. These four dialects must be regarded as independent developments of the Low Latin, and not as having grown out of a common French type.

The French words which were introduced into English during the first centuries following the Norman conquest came of course directly from the Norman dialect, or rather from that particular species of it known as the Anglo-Norman, which was the original Franco-Norman transplanted on English soil and left there to independent development. In consideration now of the great differences which existed between the phonetic system of the Anglo-Norman dialect and that of the Old French proper, it would certainly be a great mistake to look in the Old French for the original types of this class of Romance words in English. We have to go to the Anglo-Norman dialect. This seems so perfectly plain and self-evident that it is strange it should ever have been overlooked. Nevertheless, works on English etymology pay, as a rule, no attention to it. Mr. Skeat in his Dictionary constantly derives English words from their Old French (Île-de-France) cognates, without troubling himself to account for the strange changes which their pronunciation and orthography must have undergone were they to be derived in that fashion, — changes which cannot be explained by phonetic laws known to have worked on English soil, and which Mr. Skeat occasionally disposes of by using the very convenient, but rather unscientific, term "corruption." (Compare the article on *mister.*) A knowledge of the peculiar forms which these words had in Anglo-Norman will at once reveal the fact, not only that no corruption has taken place, but that the original Anglo-Norman forms have in many cases been remarkably well preserved, making allowance, of course, for the changes which the English phonetic system in general has undergone since the Norman conquest, particularly by the mutation of vowel sounds.

This may be illustrated by the following example. The earliest and most common Middle-English form of *hour* is *ure*, Ancren Riwle, pp. 6, 8, 20, etc. Mr. Skeat refers us to OF. *hore, heure;* he pays no attention to the ME. *ure*, but gives us only the later Chaucerian *houre*. The matter is very simple : the Norman dialect has a preference for *u*, and substitutes it, as a rule, for Latin *ō* where we have *ou* or *eu* in the French proper. Hence we get from Latin *hōra* the Anglo-Norman *ure*, Set Dormanz, l. 767, Petit Plet, ll. 168, 548, etc. This gives us the ME. *ure* mentioned above, which then passes into the MOD.E. *hour*, just as most other ME. *ū*'s pass into MOD.E. *ou ;* viz. ME. *hûs* $>$ MOD.E. *house*, ME. *ût* $>$ MOD.E. *out*, etc. Were we now to derive our word, as Mr. Skeat does, from the OF. *hore*, we should have *hor(e)* in ME. and *hoor(e)* in MOD.E. ; for as a rule ME. *ô* passes into MOD.E. *oo ;* for instance, ME. *bone* $>$ MOD.E. *boon*, ME. *lome* $>$ MOD.E. *loom*, ME. *mone* $>$ MOD.E. *moon*, etc. Here is, then, a clear case of Modern English pronunciation and spelling being directly traceable to the Anglo-Norman vowel system.

In the following pages I propose to show how far the influence of the Anglo-Norman vowel system extends ; but before doing so it would be well to state that we cannot expect to find perfect regularity, and give the reason why.

In the first place, there existed dialectic differences within the Anglo-Norman itself, which future investigations may classify according to time and locality. Then again, while it is right to assume that every Englishman acquiring the use of a new Norman word endeavored to pronounce it to the best of his sense of hearing and his capacity of reproducing, it is equally natural to suppose that his attempts to pronounce the new sounds exactly as the Normans pronounced them were as a rule unsuccessful. As far as the English side is concerned, it would thus be useless to go into the niceties of Anglo-Norman phonetics. It is impossible to suppose that the English distinguished in hearing and in pronunciation the five or six *e* sounds which Chardry never mixes in his rhymes. (Vid. Koch, Einleitung, pp. 25, 26.) Again, the preference of any given English dialect for its own peculiar sounds must in each case have influenced the pronunciation of Norman words, and it is hence perfectly natural that the same word was pronounced and spelt in different fashions by English writers living in different localities. A thorough treatment of this subject should therefore be based on a complete glossary of all Norman words occurring in Middle-English classified according to time and locality. Unfortunately, such a glossary does not exist. Attempts toward such a collection have indeed been made, but what has been produced is untrustworthy.[1] Mr. Skeat's work is an invaluable help, to be sure, since the Middle English references are numerous and generally exact ; but of course not all the Middle English forms are given, and the author, misled by Modern English spelling, which is largely influenced by Modern French, is apt to give us exceptional forms rather than the more regular ones.[2]

This brings up another point, which will go far toward

---

1 I refer particularly to the collection given in Morris's "Outlines of English Accidence." By a comparison with my own glossary, I find, for instance, that out of a total of 92 Romance words occurring in "King Horn" Mr. Morris has omitted 20, or about 22 per cent ; viz. *arme* (840), *cheres* (403, 1063), *age* (1324), *wicket* (1074), *still* (and horn let the tires *stille*, 676), *sire* (805, etc.), *seint* (665), *rivere* (230), *rive* (132), *pris* (898), *preie* (763), *lay* (1477), *joye* (1346), *ile* (1318), *heirs* (897), *geaunt* (802), *fine* (262), *feste* (477), *faille* (638), *dute* (344). The compiler evidently did not go through the text, but simply glanced through Lumby's very incomplete glossary, as will be seen from the fact that *denie* is mentioned as a French word, being evidently taken for the ME. *deny*, while the passage where it occurs reads, " al þe curt gan *denie*," meaning, of course, "the whole court resounded," *denie* being the AS. *dynnan*, MOD.E. to *din*. By a similar mistake, *pure* is counted as a Norman word, but the passage where it occurs reads, " Aþulf was in the ture — abute for to *pure*," meaning, in order to "peer" about ; *peer* is a good Anglo-Saxon word.

2 Mr. Skeat depends for his Old French forms largely on Burguy's Glossary in the "Grammaire de la Langue d'Oil," and from among the abundance of Old French dialectic forms that are given there he does not always select those peculiar to the Norman, which are most likely to explain English pronunciation, English orthography being largely under the influence of the French proper. Often he gives us a whole set of Old French forms which are in no way important for English. Comp. the article on *juggler.*

explaining many irregularities, namely, the influence which spelling and pronunciation of one set of Romance words in English have exercised upon spelling and pronunciation of another. If the English were ever conscious of the Anglo-Norman as a dialect distinct from, but equally legitimate with, the French proper, it seems that they had lost this consciousness very soon ; for while in the earliest Middle-English Norman words are found in precisely the same form which they have in the dialect, later writers are found to be more and more under French influence. Thus only the most striking characteristics of the Anglo-Norman were preserved in English ; minor peculiarities were lost. Many words which in the earliest Middle-English appear in a pure Anglo-Norman garb, are later refashioned after a French model. Sometimes, however, the Anglo-Norman word had gotten a hold on the popular language, and in that case it was preserved by the side of its French cognate. Still later, both forms were subject to being remodelled after a Latin fashion to suit the etymologizing tendency of the period of the Renaissance ; sometimes the older forms would stand, and a third or Latin form would be added to form a triplet.

More correct, then, than the division cited above would be the following classification of Latin elements introduced into English later than the Norman conquest : —

1. Norman words : *leal,* ME. *real, feeble, peer, mister, leisure, defeat, grief, dainty, frail, conquer,* ME. *acqueren,* etc.

2. French words : *loyal, royal, foible, pair, master, poise, coy,* etc.

3. Latin words : *legal, regal, par, magister, defect, grave, dignity, fragile, acquire, quiet.*

A word may therefore belong either to one of these classes, like *leisure, poise,* or to two, like *defeat* and *defect, coy* and *quiet,* or to all three, like *leal, loyal,* and *legal.* On the other hand, it may belong to one class at a certain period, and to another class at another period, like ME. *acqueren* and MOD.E. *acquire.* In the following pages I propose to show the relation of the first class to the other two, as far as the vowel system is concerned.

I. THE VOWELS e AND i.

A. *ê and ĭ.*

The vowels *ĕ* and *ĭ* of the Classical Latin passed in Low Latin into one sound, which was undoubtedly that of an *é fermé*. (Comp. Romania, x. p. 36.) This sound passed in the common Old French into *ei*, and later, probably through the influence of the Eastern dialects, into *oi*. In Norman it was preserved as *ei*, but especially in the later Anglo-Norman it is subject to contraction. Thus we have: —

> Lat. *rĕgem* > AN. *rei*, SD. 223, F. *roi*.
> " *lĕgem* > " *lei*, SD. 224, F. *loi*.
> " *fĭdem* > " *fei*, Jos. 73, F. *foi*.
> " *quĭd* > " *quei*, Jos. 40, F. *quoi*, etc.

In English words of Norman origin this peculiarity of the Anglo-Norman dialect is very well preserved; for although in Modern English the original *ei* is graphically represented in many different ways, yet it has regularly an *e* or *i* sound; the French *oi* is found only exceptionally.

a. LATIN TONIC *ĕ* AND *ĭ* IN OPEN SYLLABLES (*ĕ* and *ĭ* "libre").

feeble. Lat. *flêbilis* > AN. *feble*, SD. 155, Jos. 1115 > ME. *feble*, AR. pp. 54, 56, 136, etc. > MOD.E. *feeble.* — The OF. form *foible* (MF. *faible*) gives us the doublet *foible*.

faith. Lat. *fĭdem* > AN. *fei*, SD. 234 > ME. *fey*, Havelock 255, later with E. suffix > *feith, feyth, faith.* OF. *foi, foit.*

veil. Lat. *vēlum* > AN. *veil* > ME. *veil*, AR. p. 420. F. *voile*.

parish. Lat. *parēcia* (*paroecia*) > ME. *parische*, Chaucer. F. *paroisse.* Derivative: *parēcianum* > ME. *parishen* > MOD.E. *parishion-er*.

heir. Lat. *hēres* > A.N. *heir*, PP. 1101 > ME. *eir, eyre, heire, heyre*, Chaucer, William of Pal. F. *hoir*.

beverage. **bĭb(ĕ)rat(i)cum* > *beverage*, Shak. W. T. i. 2. 346. According to its vocalism, the word must have been used before Shakespeare's time. OF. *boivre*, hence *boivrage, bovrage.* MF. *breuvage*.

ME. **curteys.** Lat. *cortēsis* (for *cortensis*) > AN. *curteis*, PP. 1215 > ME. *corteys, curteys*, William of Pal.; corrupted > MOD.E. *courteous.* Derivative: AN. *curteisie*, PP. 281, *curtesie*, SD. 1223, PP. 1012 > ME. *kurteisie, kurtesie*, AR. pp. 70, 416. F. *courtois, courtoisie*.

eyre. Lat. *ĭter* > N. *eire:* "le *eire* des feluns perirat," Bartsch, Chrestomathie Franç. 53. 20, in a Norman translation of the Psalms. The OF. form is *oire* or *err.*

prey. Lat. *prēda* > N. *preie,* Bartsch, Quatre Livres des Rois 59. 2 > ME. *preie, preye,* Rob. of Gl. F. *proie.*

trey. Lat. *trēs* > N. *treis,* Chanson de Roland 275, 995 > ME. *trey,* Chaucer. F. *trois.*

money. Lat. *monēta* > AN. *munee,* SD. 532 > ME. *muneie, moneie,* Chaucer. OF. *monoie,* MF. *monnaie.*

lamprey. Low Lat. *lamprēta* > ME. *laumprei, laumpree,* Havelock. F. *lamproie.*

array. Low Lat. *arrēdium* > N. *arreie* > ME. *arraie, arraien.* OF. *arrôi, arroier.*

fair. Lat. *fēriae* > N. *feire* > ME. *feyre, feire.* F. *foire.*

ME. secree. Lat. *secrētum* > AN. *secrei, segrei,* Jos. 826 > ME. *secre, secree,* Chaucer, Piers Plowm. OF. *secroi,* but under Lat. influence both MOD.E. and MF. *secret.* The correct Middle English form is preserved in *de-cree,* ME. *decre, decree,* Robert of Brunne, Chaucer, while we have a combination of the two in *discreet,* ME. *discret,* Piers Plowm.

receive. Lat. *recĭpere* > AN. *receivre, recevre,* Jos. 817 > ME. *receiven, receyuen,* Piers Plowm. OF. *reçoivre,* MF. *recevoir.* Likewise *decĭpere* > AN. *deceivre,* Jos. 958, 963, *decevre,* PP. 1636 > E. *deceive, decĕpit* > AN. *deceit,* SD. 1878 ; also *conceive, perceive; conceit, receipt.*

ceil, ceiling. Lat. *cēlum* > ME. *syll, cyll, seile,* a canopy > MOD.E. *ceil, ceiling.* This is the only French word in which Lat. *ē* is represented by *ie,* for the *ie* in the two other words given by Brachet, *cimetière* and *chantier,* is due to metathesis.

manor. Lat. *manēre* > ME. *maneir, manere,* Piers Plowm., changed under French influence (F. *manoir*) > MOD.E. *manor.*

purpess. This spelling is etymologically more correct than *porpoise.* Lat. *porcus piscis* gives in AN. *purpeis,* or *purpes,* comp. *peissun* (*piscis*), SD. 396, ME. *purpeys,* Prompt. Parvulorum. F. *poisson.*

In all these words the Norman *ei* (Lat. *ē* or *ĭ*) is rendered in English by an *e* or *i* sound. We come now to the consideration of some real or apparent exceptions.

void. Lat. *vĭduus.* This is only an apparent exception. Lat. *vĭduus* gives us in Old French two forms : (1) *void,* by the regular diphthongization of $\bar{\imath} = fidem > foid, foit$; (2) *vuid*, by a transposition of the *u*. The E. *void* may come either from *void*, for the latter is found in Norman (Chanson de Roland, CXIII.), or from *vuid*, just as *destroy* from *destruire*, *annoy* from *ennuyer*. The MF. *vide* is a "mot savant."

coy. Lat. *quietum*. This is a more difficult case. *coy* is a decidedly French form; the Norman form is *quei:* "Icels d'Alverne . . . . se cuntiennent plus *quei*," Chanson de Rol. 3797. The English form should therefore be *quei* or *quay*.

Before nasals Lat. *ē* becomes *ei* in common Old French and remains so in Modern French; e. g. *vēna*, F. *veine*, E. *vein;* *rēnes*, F. *rein*, E. *reins*, etc.

b. Latin Pretonic *ē* and *ĭ* in Open Syllables.

Generally the same rule holds good as for *tonic ē* and *ĭ*.

convey. Lat. *convĭā're* > AN. *conveier, conveer* (*enveier, enveer* occur in Jos. 988, SD. 367) > ME. *conveien*, and under French influence *convoien*, hence MOD.E. *convoy* and *envoy*.

leisure. · Lat. *lĭcē're* > AN. *leisir*, PP. 703 > ME. *leyser, leysere*. OF. and MF. *loisir*.

purvey. Lat. *provĭdē're* > AN. *purveier, purveer*, SD. 439, 1427 > ME. *purveien* > MOD.E. *purvey*, doublet *provide*. Derivative: AN. *purveance*, PP. 941 > E. *purveyance*, doublet *providence*. AN. *purveiur* > E. *purveyor*. Thus also *survey, super-vĭdēre*.

covet. Lat. *cupĭtā're* (Skeat's *cupiditare* is an impossibility) > AN. *cuveiter, cuveter*, SD. 1861, PP. 1412 > ME. *coueiten, cuveten*. Derivative: AN. *cuveitus*, PP. 35 > E. *covetous*. OF. *co(n)voiter*, MF. *convoiter*.

tourney. Lat. **tornĭare* > AN. *turneier, turneer* > ME. *turneyen*. Derivative: *tournament* (for *turnement*, AR. p. 390). OF. *tournoi, tournoiement, tournoyer*. ·

ME. **viage**, Chaucer; *veage*, Rob. of Gl. Lat. *vĭáticum*, AN. *veage*, Jos. 2856. The etymologically correct ME. form has been crowded out by the F. form *voyage*.

ME. **real.** Lat. *rēgā'lem* > ME. *real*, Chaucer, C. T. 1020. Crowded out by the F. *royal,* probably to avoid confusion with E. *real,* from L. *realis*, but survives in the derivative *realm*, L. *rēgālimen*, F *royaume*, doublet *real*, a Spanish coin. Thus also L. *lēgā'lem* > E. *leal*, doublet *loyal*.

The Latin infinitive termination -*ĭare* becomes -*y* in English: *varĭā're* > *vary*, **studĭā're* > *study*, etc.

Only one word in this class has a decidedly French form, viz.: —

poise. Lat. *pēsā're* (for *pensare*). The Norman form is *peiser:*
"d'Oliver li *peiset* mult forment," Chanson de Roland, 2514;
and *peisen* actually occurs in Piers Plowm. Hence, if no
French influence had been brought to bear on it, the Middle
English form would be *peise* (or *peese, pease*).

Just as the common Old French *ei* resulting from Lat. *ē* or *ĭ*
becomes *oi* in the French proper, and remains *ei* in Norman, so
does the *ei* coming from other sources change to *oi* in French
proper, but remains *ei* in Norman. The other most important
source of *ei* is a Latin *e* attracting a following *i* or a guttural
or palatal vocalized to *i;* e. g. L. *mĕdiā'num* > N. *meien, meen,* OF.
moien, MF. *moyen.* The Norman form gives us the English *mean.*

Other examples : —

ME. **peitrel.** Lat. *pectorale* > ME. *peitrel, petrel,* Chaucer. The F.
form *poitrel* is also found.

bennet (proper name and botany *Geum Urbanum*). Lat. *benedictum*
> AN. *beneit, benet* Jos. 406, SD. 1688, PP. 406 > E. *bennet.* OF.
benoit, MF. *benoît.* Derivative : *beneiçun, beneisun,* Jos. 1588, PP.
54, 1535 > ME. *beneisun,* Havelock > ME. *benison.*

pray. Lat. *prĕcā'ri* > AN. *preier, preer* Jos. 2647, but also *prier* SD.
1716 > ME. *preien, preyen,* KH. 769, 1200 > MOD.E. *pray.* OF.
proper *proier,* but also (under Norman influence ?) *preier,* contracted > *prier.* Derivative : AN. *preere,* Jos. 1382, SD. 1720,
1841 > ME. *preiere, preyere,* Chaucer > MOD.E. *prayer.*

praise. Lat. *prĕtiā're* > AN. *preiser,* SD. 1084, PP. 898 > ME. *preisen,* AR. pp. 64, 74, 144, etc. > MOD.E. *praise.*

defeat. Lat. *disfectum* > AN. *defeit, defet* > ME. *defeiten, defeten,*
Chaucer. Likewise *discomfit, discomfiture.*

strait. Lat. *strictum* > *strectum* > N. *estreit, streit,* Chanson de
Roland, 1001, 2202 > ME. *streit,* Lay. 22270 > MOD.E. *strait.*
OF. *estroit,* MF. *étroit.*

dean. Lat. *dĕcā'num* > AN. *deien, deen* > ME. *den, deen, dene,* Piers
Plowm. > MOD.E. *dean.* OF. *doien,* MF. *doyen.*

The diphthong *oi* is found only in words of decidedly later introduction, — for instance, *adroit,* according to the Dictionary of the
English Philological Society first used by Evelyn, A. D. 1652. Had
the word been introduced during the Anglo-Norman period, it would
be *adreit,* comp. Jos. 3 : "la *dreite* veie de salu."

The terminations -*erium* and -*eria* which appear in French as -*ier* and -*ière* are in Norman regularly represented by -*er* and -*ere*, and in this form they also appear in English : —

manner. Lat. **maneria* > AN. *manere*, SD. 79 > ME. *manere*, Lay. *b*, II. 373, AR. 6, 136 > MOD.E. *manner*. F. *manière*.

matter. Lat. *materia* > AN. *matere* > E. *matter*. F. *matière*.

mystery, or **mistery**, (a trade,) corrupted from ME. *mester*. Lat. *ministerum* > AN. *mester*, Jos. 302, 1827, PP. 1125 > ME. *meister*, AR. 70, 212, *mester*, AR. 72, 210, etc., *mistere*, Chaucer. The later form *mistery* may have been brought about by confusion with AN. *mestrie*, Jos. 768, 2191, SD. 1224, which comes from L. *magisteria*.

The "terminaison savante" -*erie* is occasionally found, e. g. *materie*, AR. p. 270, and it survives in a few Modern English words of later introduction, as in *cemetery*, F. *cimetière*.

B. *Latin ĕ in Open Syllables (ĕ "libre").*

a. TONIC.

Latin ĕ, which in common Old French is usually diphthongized, is as a rule retained in Anglo-Norman as a simple vowel ; e. g. *bref*, SD. 475, *sege*, SD. 1871, etc. Middle English orthography generally agrees with the Anglo-Norman ; but in Modern English *ie* is often written, although it is pronounced as a simple vowel. We give some examples : —

brief. Lat. *brĕvem* > AN. *bref*, SD. 475 > ME. *bref*, *breef*, Piers Plowm., AR. p. 344, etc. > MOD.E. *brief*. Compound : ME. *embreven*, AR. p. 344.

siege. Lat. **sĕdium* > AN. *sege*, SD. 1871 > ME. *sege* = seat, throne, AR. p. 238 > MOD.E. *siege*. F. *siège*.

rear. Lat. *rĕtro* > AN. *rere* (*arere*, SD. 1484, PP. 200) > ME. (*ar*)*rere*, Piers Plowm. F. *arrière*.

fierce. *fĕrus* > AN. *fers* (adv. *ferement*, SD. 951) > ME. *fers*, Chaucer, C. T. 1598 > MOD.E. *fierce*. F. *fier.* — This is a very curious word, in that it is the only Norman adjective which has been taken into the English language in its nominative form, *fierce* standing of course for *fier-s ;* and this is the more remarkable because it exists in French as an original accusative.

piece. Low Lat. *pĕtium* > AN. *pece*, SD. 1504 > ME. *pece*, Robert of Gl. > MOD.E. *piece*. F. *pièce*, etc.

b. Pretonic.

Latin pretonic *ĕ* in open syllables is usually preserved in French as well as in Anglo-Norman and English : —

tenant. Lat. *tenentem* > N. *tenant.* F. id.

precious. Lat. *prĕtiosum* > AN. *precius*, Jos. 720 > ME. *precius, precious*, Piers Plowm. F. *précieux.*

congeal. Lat. *congĕlā're* > ME. *congelen*, Gower, etc.

In one case the pretonic *ĕ* has become *i* : *ĕbŏrea* > ME. *ivory, ivorie*, also *every* (Prov. *evori*, Bartsch, 33. 22). F. *ivoire.*

Latin pretonic *ĕ* and *ĭ*, if accented in English, are treated like *ē* : *ord'inā're* > AN. *ordener* > ME. *ordeynen*, Piers Plowm. > MOD.E. *ordain.* Likewise all the compounds with *tĕnē're* : AN. *meintenir*, Jos. 1730, SD. 16 > ME. *mainteinen, maintenen*, King Alisaunder ; *contain, obtain, sustain, abstain, retain, entertain.*

C. *Latin ī in Open Syllables* (*ī* "libre ").

Preserved in French as well as in Anglo-Norman and English : Lat. *pīca* > F. *pie*, E. *pie ;* Lat. *diffīdā're* > F. *défier*, E. *defy*, etc. The termination -*ī'a* is always unaccented in English : *phantasī'a* > ME. *fantasie*, Chaucer, C. T. 6098 > MOD.E. *fancy.*

D. *Latin e and i entravé.*

A vowel is called *entravé* when it is followed by any two consonants, except (1.) *pr, br, tr, dr*, in which cases it is considered to stand in open syllables; and (2.) *cr, gr, pl, bl*, or any consonant + a palatal, in which cases it is called variable. (Romania, x. p. 37.) In common Old French, and also in Norman, every *i entravé* becomes *e;* e. g. *firmum* > *ferme*, *mittere* > *mettre*, etc. Hence for our purpose *i entravé* and *e entravé* amount to the same thing, and may be treated under one head. As a rule, the *e entravé* of the common Old French and of the Norman remains in Middle English, but in later English it is subject to the same change of pronunciation as every other ME. *e.* Hence : —

beast. Lat. *bestia* > OF. *beste* > ME. *best*, AR. pp. 120, 128, 134, etc. > MOD.E. *beast.* MF. *bête.*

feast. Lat. *festa* > OF. *feste* > ME. *feste*, AR. p. 22, etc. > MOD.E. *feast.* MF. *fête.*

seal. Lat. *sigillum* > *sigellum* > OF. *seel* > ME. *seel* > MOD.E. *seal.* MF. *sceau.*

search. Lat. *circare* > AN. *cercher*, PP. 1334 > ME. *serchen, cerchen* > MOD.E. *search, research*, etc. F. *chercher*.

preach. Lat. *prēdicare* > AN. *precher*, SD. 87, 1824 > ME. *prechen*, AR. pp. 70, 260. Likewise Lat. **impĕdicare* > ME. *empechen, apechen*, > MOD.E. *impeach*, etc.

conquer. Lat. *conquī'rere* > AN. *cunquerre*, Jos 2249, PP. 404 > ME. *cunqueren, cunqueren*, Rob. of Gl. > MOD.E. *conquer.* MF. *conquérir.*

acquire and require are treated in Anglo-Norman and in Middle English just like the preceding ; e. g. AN. *requerre*, Jos. 1021, ME. *requeren*, Chaucer, C. T. 6634, etc.; but they were afterwards remodelled after the Latin ; *aquire*, according to the Dictionary of the E. P. S., about 1600 (Shakespeare's Hamlet).

The Latin combinations *ng* and *gn* are represented in Norman by a single or double nasal; e. g. *feinnez*, Jos. 1484 (2d plur. pres. from *feindre*, L. *fingere*), F. *feignez; cumpainnie, cumpainnun*, Jos. 317, 2346, SD. 277, 443, etc. The *e* and *i* are then treated as usually before nasals. In Middle English the Anglo-Norman model is followed, but in Modern English orthography the original *g* is often restored, though it is never pronounced. Thus we have *dignare*, N. *deinen*, ME. *deinen*, Gower, Rob. of Gl., MOD.E. *deign*, but *disdain*, F. *deigner*. Similarly : *reign* (L. *regnare*), *feign* (L. *fingere*), but p. part. *faint, attain* (L. *attingere*), *restrain* (L. *restringere*), *taint* (p. part. L. *tingere*), *paint* (p. part. formed by analogy to *taint*), *refrain* (L. *refringere*, perhaps confused with *refrenare*), etc.

The word *sue*, which belongs to this class, is rather troublesome, but no more so than in French itself. Lat. **sequere* gives us in OF. *sevre, sivre*, and, probably by a double influence of the *v*, *suivre*. In ME. we have *sewen, siwen, suwen*, Lay. *b*, I. 59, II. 264, AR. p. 208. It is not impossible that the noun *suite* may have influenced the English verb ; *suite* comes of course from *secuta, s'cuta*, not from *secta*, as Skeat absurdly proposes. The latter would have given us *seat* in English, just as *disfectum* gives us *defeat*.

There was a tendency in the Anglo-Norman dialect, as well as in the Old French proper, to change the sound of *e* before *r* + consonant into *a*. This was probably due to the nature of the *r*, but the greatest irregularity prevails. Thus we have in French: *par* (L. *per*), *lézard* (L. *lacerta*), *lucarne* (L. *lucerna*), *parchemin* (L. *pergamenum*), *marchand* (L. *mercatantem*), *appartenir* (L. *appertinere*), etc.; but on the other hand : *personne* (L. *persona*), *clerc* (L. *clericum*), *aper-*

cevoir (L. *ad* + *percipere*), etc.   In Anglo-Norman we find the same inconsistency: *sarmuner*, PP. 182 (L. **sermonare*), *aparcevre*, Jos. 2471, PP. 428, 435, etc., *marchant, marchandise*, Jos. 697, 713, etc., *parfit*, PP. 513, etc.; but on the other hand: *rehercer*, Jos. 941, *mervillus*, SD. 1235, *certein*, PP. 32, etc. In English this phonetic tendency has left many traces, and the best evidence of the irregularity with which it works is the fact that sometimes those words which in Anglo-Norman and French appear with *a* have *e* in English, and *vice versa*; e. g., N. and F. *marchand*, E. *merchant;* F. *merveilleux*, N. *mervillus*, E. *marvellous;* E. *parsley*, F. *persil;* E. *partridge*, F. *perdrix.* Other examples of -*ar*- in English are *parson* (doublet of *person*), *garland, war, parrot, garner, tarnish, varnish, quarrel*, etc. There are certainly many more words occasionally pronounced with -*ar*- instead of -*er*-, and -*ar*- is often written in proper names, e. g. *Sargent, Clark*, etc.

II. The Vowel a.

A. *In Open Syllables (except before n).*

In French the Latin *a*, whether long or short, is usually represented by an *e* sound, written *e* or *ai*, in a few cases also by *ie*: *căput* > F. *chef; nāsum* > F. *nez; măre* > F. *mer; amārum* > *amèr; tālem* > F. *tel; cārum* > F. *cher; clārum* > F. *clair; pār* > F. *pair; cănem* > F. *chien; grăvem* > F. *grief.* The Anglo-Norman dialect prefers as a rule simple vowels to diphthongs; hence we find: *per* (L. *pār*): "truver ne pout l'em sun *per*," Jos. 170, 2935, SD. 323, PP. 1424, etc.; *cler* (L. *clārum*), PP. 58. In Middle English we find *e* in most cases, but in Modern English some differences in pronunciation and spelling exist.   Thus we have:—

peer. Lat. *pār* > AN. *per* (cited above) > ME. *pere*, Chaucer > MOD.E. *peer.* Doublets: *pair*, a French form, and *par*, a Latin form. With irregular change of vowel: *non* + *par* (meaning impartial) > ME. (*n*)*umpere*, (*n*)*ompere* > MOD.E. *umpire.*

cheer. Lat. *cara* > *chere*, Jos. 1502 > ME. *chere*, AR. pp. 88, 192, 212, etc.; Lay. *b*, II. 371, "þat al sculen þine *cheres* — iwurðen swulc þes eorles " > MOD.E. *cheer*, F. *chère:* "fair chère lie."

friar. Lat. *frātrem* > N. *frere*, Chanson de Roland, 1214, etc. > ME. *frere*, Chaucer > MOD.E. *friar*, probably through *frère.*

clef. Lat. *clāvem* > E. *clef*, formerly also *cliff.*

degree. Lat. *de* + *grădum* > ME. *degre, degree*, Chaucer.

die. Lat. *dătum* > ME. *dee, die,* Chaucer > MOD.E. *die, dice.* The
E. form *die* looks as though it were due to an OF. form *diet*
instead of *det;* but it may also be nothing but an irregular
vowel change, just like *umpire* for *umpeer,* above.

agree. Lat. *ad + grātum* > AN. *a gre,* Jos. 2561, v. *agreer* > ME.
agreën, Chaucer. Etc.

In the case of suffixes the language is of course more regular.

-tātem gives us in AN. regularly *-te,* the same in ME., and *-ty* in
MOD.E. : Lat. *pietatem* > AN. *pite,* SD. 360 > ME. *pite,* AR. p.
368 > MOD.E. *pity,* MF. *pitié; civitātem* > AN. *cite,* SD. 85 > ME.
cite, AR. p. 228 ; *amicitātem* > E. *amity,* F. *amitié.*

-ā'lem occurs in AN. both as *-al* and *-el:* par *igal,* SD. 897, *com-
munal,* PP. 722, are found by the side of *mortel,* Jos. 2007, *ostel,*
Jos. 2067. Both terminations occur in ME. ; but in MOD.E. —
doubtless under the influence of the many words in *-al* belonging to the period of the revival of learning — the termination
-el has been superseded by *-al,* although pronunciation could
hardly distinguish between them.

-ā'ta is usually *-ee* or *-eie* in AN., the same in ME., and *-ey* or *-y* in
MOD.E.: L. *diurnā'ta** > AN. *journee,* Jos. 292 > ME. *journeie,*
AR. p. 352 > MOD.E. *journey;* similarly L. *gelā'ta* > E. *jelly;*
armā'ta > E. *army; caminata* > E. *chimney.* To this class belongs *galley,* ME. *galeie,* KH. 185, 1020, OF. *galie,* which is generally supposed to go back to L. *galea,* although the termination
seems to have caused trouble. Vid. Burguy, Grammaire de
la Langue d'Oïl, III. p. 178. The OF. form *galic* might perhaps
be considered as the contract feminine of the participle *galié*
(comp. F. "faire chère *lie*" = *laeta*), standing thus for *navis
galiata, galeata.*

Latin pretonic *a* is subject to weakening: *căballárium* > AN.
chevalier, Jos. 279, PP. 1268 > ME. *chivalr(ie),* King Alis. > MOD.E.
chivalry; L. *căminā'ta* > E. *chimney; lăcerta* > E. *lizard; canī'le* >
E. *kennel; salī're* > E. *sally.* In English this cannot of course be
the case whenever the word becomes an oxytonon: L. *dilatā're* >
E. *delay; tradī're* (for *tradē're,* for *trádere*) > E. *(be)tray,* etc.

Just as the Anglo-Norman shows a preference for *ei* over against
the *oi* of the French proper, so it has a decided predilection for
ei over against the French *ai,* from whatever source the last may
come; *ai* occurs indeed, but the general tendency is decidedly

in favor of *ei*, which is then often contracted into *e*. The Middle English forms agree in the majority of cases with the Anglo-Norman.

feat. Lat. *factum* > AN. *feit, fet,* SD. 420 (F. *fait*) > ME. *feite, fete* > MOD.E. *feat.* Similarly: *factura* > AN. *feiture,* Jos. 29, SD. 353 > ME. *feture* > MOD.E. *feature;* *foris-factum > AN. *forfet,* Jos. 467 > E. *forfeit;* also *counterfeit, surfeit, feasible,* etc.; over against which we have with the French diphthong *ai* only *affair,* which according to the D. E. Th. S. is spelt *affere* until Shakespeare's time.

plead. Lat. *placitare > AN. *pleider, pleder,* Jos. 1003 > ME. *pleden,* Piers Plowm. > MOD.E. *plead.* OF. *plaider.*

lease. Lat. *lacsare (laxare)* > AN. *lesser,* Jos. 2514, PP. 1419 > ME. *lessen* > MOD.E. *lease.* Derivative: *lessor, lessee.* OF. *laissier,* etc.

treat. Lat. *tractare* > AN. *treiter, treter* > ME. *treten* > MOD.E. *treat.* Derivatives: AN. *tretiz,* PP. 12 > ME. *tretis* > MOD.E. *treatise.* Similarly, E. *treatment, treaty.* F. *traiter.*

peace. Lat. *pacs (pax)* > AN. *peis, pes,* Jos. 902 > ME. *peis,* AR. 22, 166, 172, etc. > MOD.E. *peace.* F. *paix.* Compound: ME. *apeisen, apesen* > MOD.E. *appease.* F. *apaiser.*

please. Lat. *placere* > AN. *pleisir,* PP. 267, 523 > ME. *plesen,* Piers Plowm. > MOD.E. *please.* F. *plaisir.* Verbal noun *pleasure,* ME. *plesure,* just as *leisure,* from *leisir.*

seize. OHG. *sazjan* (> LL. *sacire) > AN. *seiser, sesir,* Jos. 2340 > ME. *seysen,* Havelock > MOD.E. *seize.* F. *saisir.* Derivatives: *seizure,* etc.; also *seizin,* a law term, ME. *seizine.*

eager. Lat. *acrem* > AN. *eigre, egre* > ME. *egre,* Chaucer > MOD.E. *eager.* F. *aigre.*

meager. Lat. *macrum* > AN. *megre,* Jos. 858 > ME. *megre,* Piers Plowm. > MOD.E. *meagre.* F. *maigre.*

heinous. AN. *heinus* > ME. *heinous, heinus,* Chaucer. OF. *haïnous.*

reason. Lat. *rationem* > AN. *resun,* SD. 230 > ME. *reisun, resun,* AR. 78, 112, 156, etc. > MOD.E. *reason.* F. *raison.*

season. Lat. *sationem* > AN. *sesun,* PP. 138 > ME. *seysun, sesoun,* etc., Chaucer > MOD.E. *season.* F. *saison.*

treason. Lat. *tra(d)itionem* > AN. *treisun, tresun* > ME. *treisun, tresun,* AR. 56, 220, etc. > MOD.E. *treason.*

orison. Lat. *orationem* > AN. *ureisun, uresun,* Jos. 1357, SD. 228 > ME. *oreisun, ureisun,* AR. pp. 16, 22, 36, etc. Doublet: Lat. *oration,* F. *oraison.* Similarly other nouns in *-ationem: comparison,* F. *comparaison; venison,* F. *venaison,* etc.

Those words which become oxytona in English usually preserve the original *ai* with the same sound as in *ray :* —

aid. Lat. *adjutare* > AN. *eider*, SD. 316 > ME. *aiden*, MOD.E. *aid.*

flail. Lat. *flagellum* > ME. *flail*, Piers Plowm.

frail. Lat. *fragilem* > ME. *frail, freel*, Chaucer. Similarly : *abbatia* > E. *abbey; badium* > *bay* (= brown) ; *bacca* > *bay* (laurel tree) ; *laicus* > *lay; radium* > *ray*, etc. The only exception seems to be *sagēna* > *seine* or *sean*, MF. *seine.*

This peculiarity of the Anglo-Norman of running Lat. *a + i* (F. *ai*) into *ei* and then contracting it into simple *e* accounts for the doublet *master* and *mister*, which seems to have given Mr. Skeat some trouble. He says : "It is difficult to trace the first use of *mister*, but it does not appear to be at all of early use, and is certainly nothing but a corruption of *master* or *maister*, due to the corresponding title of *mistress.*" It seems to me that in this case Mr. Skeat should tell us how we get *mistress*, and why we do not say *mastress.* The explanation is not difficult. According to the rule stated above, *magistrum* has to become *maister* in Old French proper, but *meister* or *mester* in Anglo-Norman ; and the latter form is found in Jos. 448, 1386, 2835, etc. The form *maister* does not occur in any of Chardry's poems. Besides *mester*, we have the abstract noun *mestrie* in Jos. 768, 2191, SD. 1224, etc. The Middle English form must then be *meister*, found in AR. pp. 56, 64, 182, etc., which in accordance with the above cited Anglo-Norman form may be contracted into *mester*, found in the abstract noun *mesterie*, AR. p. 108. To get from this ME. *mester* the MOD.E. *mister* is surely not difficult : we have precisely the same change in the case of Lat. *ministerium* > AN. *mester*, Jos. 302, 1827 > ME. *meister*, AR. pp. 70, 212, *mester*, Ib. pp. 72, 549 > MOD.E. *mister*(*y*), *myster*(*y*), (q. v. in Skeat, p. 386). By the side of the properly AN. form *mester* we find in later ME. — doubtless under French influence — *maister*, KH. 621, 642, etc. ; and our conclusion is then that the MOD.E. *mister* is not only no "corruption," as Mr. Skeat calls it, but the regular AN. > ME. development of the word, while *master* is a rather "frenchified" form of it (comp. *cash* from F. *caisse*).

B. *Entravé (except before Nasals).*

Latin *a entravé* is usually preserved in French as well as in Norman and English, best of all before *r* + consonant: *partem* > *part; artem* > *art.* Similarly : *marble, alarm*, etc. ; Lat. *damnaticum* >

damage; mansionem > *mansion*, etc. If not protected by surrounding consonants, the ME. *a* follows the usual mutation of pronunciation common to most English words; hence MOD.E. *āgent, nāture, chāste*, etc.

In a few words Lat. *a entravé* becomes *ai* in Old French and in Norman, and hence in English: *captivum* > OF. *caitif* > E. *caitiff; aquila* > F. *aigle* > ME. *egle*, Chaucer > MOD.E. *eagle*.

In Anglo-Norman Lat. -*al* before consonants becomes -*au*, just as in French, and many English words give evidence of it; e. g. Lat. *alburnum* > ME. *awburn, auburn*, Prompt. Parv. > MOD.E. *auburn; calciata* (sc. *via*) > ME. *cawsee, causee*, Barbour's Bruce > MOD.E. *causeway*, etc. In a few cases, however, we find double forms in ME.; e. g. Lat. *altare* > ME. *auter, alter* > MOD.E. *altar*, doubtless under Latin influence. There must also have existed in Anglo-Norman a tendency to drop the *l* before consonants entirely; e. g. *mut*, PP. 739, for *mult*, etc. This tendency produced such English words as *savę* from *salvare*, F. *sauver; chafe* from *cal'fare** (for *caleficare**), F. *chauffer*, etc.

C. *Before Nasals.*

Latin *a* before simple *n* becomes in French either *ai*, for instance, *manum* > *main, romanum* > *romain, nanum* > *nain*; or *e*, for instance, *christianum* > *chrétien, paganum* > *païen*, etc. In AN. *a* before *n* or *m* becomes *ei*; e. g. *plānum* > *plein*, Jos. 1266; *clamare* > *cleimer*, SD. 1119. In ME. we find as a rule *ei* as in AN., but in MOD.E. *ai* is usually written. Thus we have ME. *plein, pleyn, plain* > MOD.E. *plain;* ME. *vein, veyn*, Chaucer > MOD.E. *vain*. Similarly, MOD.E. *claim, exclaim, proclaim, grain*, etc. In unaccented syllables we sometimes find the old *ei* contracted into *e* and so written in MOD.E.: AN. *sudein*, PP. 1081 > ME. *sodein, sudein*, Chaucer > MOD.E. *sudden*, F. *soudain*. Similarly, MOD.E. *mittens*, F. *mitaine*, etc. But as a rule the French spelling prevails in English; e. g. *villain* (AN. *vilein*, SD. 186), *certain* (AN. *certein*, SD. 2, PP. 32, etc.), *fountain, chaplain, captain, chieftain* (AN. *chevetein*, SD. 1855), etc. Popular etymology has curiously changed the orthography of *foreign* and *sovereign*, making them appear as though they were connected with *reign* (Lat. *regnum*), while their true Latin types are *superanum** and *foranum**.

Before a fortified nasal (*n* or *m* + consonant) *a* must have had in Anglo-Norman a decidedly nasal pronunciation. This appears from its peculiar graphic representation by -*aun*- common with Anglo-

Norman and English writers, and preserved in some words up to the present time. This representation gives us a clue to the phonetic nature of the nasalization: *aun* must have been pronounced somewhat like the Portuguese *ão*, which is an *a* sound followed by a nasal, and not like the French *an*, which is an *a* sound itself nasalized. In later English the original sound gradually wore down to a simple long *a*, as in MOD.E. *vaunt;* but in most words even this pronunciation, and with it its peculiar graphic representation, had to give away to such sounds as we have in *change, chance,* etc. Oxytona show themselves of course more conservative than other words ; hence we have still *aunt* (L. *amita*), *vaunt* (L. *vanitare*), *avaunt* (L. *ab-ante*), *haunt* (OF. *hanter*), *daunt* (OF. *danter*, L. *domitare*). Similarly, *haunch, launch, paunch, staunch,* etc. On the other hand, we have *grange, strange, ample, grant, chant,* etc., all of which are found in ME. with *aun.* The only non-oxytonon which has preserved the *aun* is *gauntlet;* all others have *an: giant, servant, tyrant, substance, advance, enhance,* etc., ME. *geaunt, servaunt, tiraunt, substaunce, avaunce, enhaunsen,* etc.

III. The Vowels o and u.

A. *Latin ō and ŭ* ("libres").

Latin *ō* and *ŭ* pass in Low Latin into one sound, generally denoted by *ó* (*o fermé*), and believed to have been the same as the French *o* in *côte, pot,* etc. If *libre,* this sound then passes in French proper into *eu* ; e. g., L. *hōra* > F. *heure;* if *entravé,* it passes into *ou* ; e. g., L. *currit* > *court.* The Norman shows in both cases a preference for *u.* In Middle English we have likewise *u* as a rule, but this soon passes into *ou* or *ow.* Hence we have : —

hour. Lat. *hōra* > AN. *ure,* PP. 548 > ME. *ure,* AR. pp. 6, 8, 20, etc., later *houre,* Chaucer > MOD.E. *hour.* F. *heure.*

flour, flower. Lat. *flōrem* > AN. *flur,* PP. 64, SD. 1554 > ME. *flur,* AR. p. 340, KH. 14 > MOD.E. *flower.* F. *fleur.*

crown. Lat. *corōna* > AN. *corune, curune* > ME. *crune,* Lay. 4252, etc., KH. 475, etc., AR. p. 40, etc. ; *croune* only in Lay. Ms. *b* > MOD.E. *crown.* F. *couronne.*

spouse. Lat. *spōsus* (for *sponsus*) > AN. *espus(e),* PP. 1183 > ME. *spus,* AR. pp. 2, 10, etc., *spus-bruche* = *adultery,* AR. 56 > MOD.E. *spouse.* Derivative v. ME. *spusen, i-spused,* KH. 1050, etc. > MOD.E. *to espouse.* F. *époux, épouser.*

Several suffixes with $\bar{o}'$ are of importance : —

-ō'rem gives us regularly *ur* in AN. : *valur* SD. 429, *vigur* 939, *culur* 947, etc. In later AN. we find *our* and *or* by the side of *ur*; e. g. Vie de S. Gr. *amor* 327, *amour* 1741, *labor* 9, *colour* 705, etc., probably either under French or under Latin influence. In the earliest Modern English we find *ur*, e. g. *colur*, KH. 16; later also *our*, and under Latin influence *-or;* hence MOD.E. *valour* (*valor*), *honour* (*honor*), *vigor*, *conqueror*, etc ; F. *valeur*, *honneur*, *rigueur*, etc.

-ō'sum is treated very similarly. AN. *-us:* *vigerus* PP. 576, *precius* Jos. 720, *mervillus* SD. 678, 1235, etc.; later *amorous* Vie de S. Gr. 86, *desirous* 122, *merveillouse* 639, *vigrous* 65, etc., and *pretioses* 219. ME. *-us:* *gracius*, AR. 366, etc. ; later *-ous* as in MOD.E. *gracious, vicious, marvellous*, etc. F. *-eux:* *gracieux, merveilleux*, etc.

-ō'nem. AN. *passiun* SD. 372, 1717, *garisun* Jos. 270, *peissun* SD. 396, etc.; ME. *passiun* AR. 116, 188, etc., *devociun* 286, 368, *contemplaciun* 142 ; but MOD.E. *-on.*

In unaccented syllables *u* is also common in Anglo-Norman ; e. g. *curage*, SD. 43, *cuardement*, 1031, *uresun*, 228, Jos. 1357, etc. ; and the same is found in Middle English, but later the change of the English accent brings about differentiation ; hence MOD.E. *courage, solemn, orison*, but *endow, coward*, etc. Modern English is here so whimsical that it is absolutely impossible to formulate any rule ; e. g. *ŏdō'rem > odour, cŏlō'rem > colour*, etc.

B. *Entravés (except before Nasals).*

Latin *o entravé* is usually preserved in French as well as in Norman ; hence L. *cotta >* E. *coat ;* L. *costa >* E. *coast ;* L. *tosta >* E. *toast ;* L. *concha >* E. *coach ;* L. *appropiare* * *>* E. *approach ;* L. *repropiare >* E. *reproach*, etc. All of these are spelled with simple *o* in Middle English.

Latin *u entravé* generally becomes *o* in Old French, and later *ou ;* e. g. L. *turrem >* OF. *tor*, later *tour*, MF. *tour.* The Norman, having a predilection for *u*, retains it, of course, and as such it passes into Middle English, where it later follows the regular mutation to *ou ;* e. g. AN. *tur*, Jos. 261 > ME. *tur*, Lay. *a, b*, I. 258, AR. p. 226, KH. 1103 > MOD.E. *tower ;* L. *dubitare >* AN. *duter*, SD. 950 > ME. *duten*, AR. 244, KH. 344 ; L. *gutta >* E. *gout*, etc. Before *r*, however, this change to the *ou* pronunciation does not take place, although it is sometimes written : L. *diurnā'ta* > E. *journey;* L. *incurrere* > E. *incur;* L. *nutricem* > E. *nurse;* L. *cohortem* > E. *court* (AN. *curt,* DS. 223, ME. *curt, kurt,* AR. 210, 212, etc., KH. 245).

C. *Latin ŏ, tonic.*

Latin *ŏ* in the tonic syllable is regularly diphthongized to *oe* in Anglo-Norman; e. g. *quoer, foer, hoem, proeve, moert, voelent,* etc. This *oe* must be supposed to represent some kind of an *o umlaut.* In Middle English it is at first represented by an *e* or *ee,* sometimes *oe,* which is then subject to the regular mutation of pronunciation; hence, ME. *retreven* > MOD.E. *retrieve,* and in two words at least, viz. *choir* and *contrive,* the mutation has gone one step further yet. The words belonging to this class are : —

beef. Lat. *bŏvem* > N. *boef,* Kelham > ME. *beef,* Chaucer. F. *bœuf.*

people. Lat. *pŏpulum* > N. *poeple* > ME. *peple, poeple,* Piers Plowm. > MOD.E. *people.* F. *peuple.* (Comp. the Rhaetian *pievel.*)

jeopardy. Lat. *jŏcum-partitum* > ME. *jeopardy, jepardy, jopardy, jupartie,* etc., Chaucer. Possibly at various times confounded with *jeu perdu* and *j'ai perdu.*

affeer. Lat. *ad* + *fŏrum* > AN. *afeoren,* Kelham > ME. *aferen* > MOD.E. *affeer,* preserved in legal language = to reduce or assess, as an arbitrary penalty or amercement, to a precise sum; to reduce to a sum certain, according to the circumstances of the case. Blackstone. MF. "au *fur* et à mesure."

proof, prove. Lat. *prŏbā're* > AN. *pruver,* SD. 1250, but as tonic syllable, 3d pers. plur. *proevent,* SD. 1394 > ME. *preoven, preven,* AR. p. 390, Piers Plowm. In Modern English the vowel has been changed under Latin influence, but it is preserved in the compound *reprieve,* ME. *repreven,* a doublet of *reprove.*

retrieve. AN. *truver,* SD. 1269, but accented *troē've,* SD. 1857 > ME. (*re*)*treven* > MOD.E. *retrieve.* Similarly, we should have *contrieve,* but for some unknown reason the vowel has here shifted once more to *contrive,* just as in

choir. Lat. *chŏrus;* it should be *queer,* which form is actually found in Barbour's Bruce, xx. 293, and in the Prompt. Parv. p. 420, *queere* = *chorus.*

move. Lat. *mŏvē're* > ME. *moeven, meven,* Piers Plowm. and Chaucer, changed through Latin or French influence to MOD.E. *move.* Similarly, ME. *remeven, ameven.*

This treatment of Latin *ŏ* in Anglo-Norman and Middle English, illustrated by the above examples, will clear up the etymology of *inveigle,* which Mr. Skeat considers doubtful. He would like to take it from *in-ab-ocul-are*,* which indeed looks reasonable enough, but he objects to this etymology on account of the "spelling." English orthography is of course altogether below scientific criticism ; hence it must be the pronunciation, and particularly that of the tonic syllable, which gives the trouble. Mr. Skeat cannot account for the *i* (Continental) sound arising from a Latin *o*. The matter is easy enough : Latin *ŏ* gives us, according to the rule cited above, *oe* or *eo* in Anglo-Norman ; hence the form *enveogler* cited in Kelham's Norman Glossary ; *enveogler* gives us the ME. *enveglen,* which then takes part in the regular mutation of vowel sounds, *ei* being chosen to represent the *i* sound. This matter of spelling is indeed non-essential, for in Richardson's Dictionary we find a number of other spellings of this same word, but all representing the same sound, which is the essential point.

D. *Latin ū, tonic.*

Latin *ū* in accented syllables is preserved in French as a *u* umlaut. In Norman it is always *u*, but its Modern English pronunciation shows that even in Norman it must have partaken of the *umlaut sound*. We have L. *pūrum* > E. *pure;* L. *mūtum* > E. *mute;* L. *ūsum* > E. *use;* L. *adventura > E. *adventure*, etc.

As a pretonic we have it in L. *glūtī're* > E. *glut*, which has doubtless been influenced by *glutton*.

E. *Latin o, u + i, or palatal.*

In French a Latin *o* unites with a following *i* or a palatalized guttural to form *oi*, and this is later changed to *ui* ; e. g. *noctem* > *noit* > *nuit;* *oleum* > *oile* > *huile*, etc. On the other hand, *u* under the same circumstances becomes *oi*, and does not change again ; e. g. *fusionem* > *foison*. In Anglo-Norman the same process takes place, except that the *oi* never changes to *ui;* thus *oi* is also the rule for Middle English, and likewise for Modern English. Hence L. *jungĕre* > E. *join*, F. *joindre;* L. *junctum* > E. *joint; punctum* > *point; fusionem* > *foison*, etc.; L. *oleum* > E. *oil*, F. *huile;* L. *molliare** > E. *moil*, F. *mouiller; spoliare* > *spoil*, F. *(de)pouiller;* L. *inodiare** > E. *annoy*, F. *ennuyer*, etc.

F. *Before Nasals.*

Before nasals Latin *o* is retained in French; e. g. *nomen* > *nom*, *montem* > *mont;* Lat. *u* becomes *o* before a fortified nasal; e. g. *fundum* > *fond*, *abundare* > *abonder.* In Norman we have in both cases *u*, likewise in the early Middle English, later in the accented syllables *ou.* Hence L. *nomen* > AN. *nun*, SD. 208 > ME. *nun*, *num* > MOD.E. *noun;* L. *otundum* > AN. *rund*, PP. 1334 > ME. *rund*, *round*, MOD.E. *round.* Similarly : L. *montem* > E. *mount;* L. *comitem* > E. *count;* L. *computare* > E. *count;* L. *fundere* > E. *found;* L. *componère* > E. *compound;* L. *consilium* > E. *counsel;* L. *adnuntiare* > E. *announce*, *renounce*, *pronounce*, but in the unaccented syllable of course *-nunciation*, etc. In French we have simple *o;* e. g. *rond*, *nom*, *mont*, *conter*, *prononcer*, etc.

CONCLUSION.

It will be seen that in a general way the phonology of the Norman words in English can be traced back to that of the Anglo-Norman dialect. Irregularities are mostly due to the influence which was exercised by Romance words introduced at other times, and belonging to other stages of linguistic development.

ANGLO-NORMAN TEXTS.

Jós.   Josaphaz   ⎫ All by Chardry (twelfth century), edited by John Koch,
SD.   Set Dormanz ⎬   Förster's Altfranzösische Bibliothek, Vol. I., Heilbronn,
PP.   Petit Plet   ⎭   Henninger, 1879.
Vie de S. Gr. — La Vie de S. Grégoire, par Frère Angier (beginning of the thirteenth century), edited by P. Meyer, Romania, xii. p. 145.

MIDDLE-ENGLISH TEXTS.

Lay.   Layamon's Brut. ed. F. Madden, London, 1847, 3 vols.
        Text *a*, about A. D. 1205.
        Text *b*, about A. D. 1255.
AR.   The Ancren Riwle, ed. Morton : about A. D. 1200.
KH.   The Romance of King Horn in Morris's Specimens : about A. D. 1300.

Other Middle English texts cited after Skeat's Dictionary.

VI. — *The Ablaut in High German.*

By BENJAMIN W. WELLS, Ph. D.,

FRIENDS' SCHOOL, PROVIDENCE, R. I.

CONTENTS.

THERE is hardly a modern language which presents so faithful a picture of its former state as the German. Both consonants and vowels are preserved with infrequent, and in great part unimportant changes, and both the inflexional and ablaut systems have suffered less than in the older Germanic dialects. The article, the adjective, the pronoun, and the noun retain their earlier declension with few alterations; the verb has preserved many of its personal endings; and the ablaut, which has survived in barely a quarter of the Old English verbs, and even in these with such irregularities as to make the study fruitless, except from an historical point of view, is found in German in one half the older verbs, and with a fulness and a regularity in its formation that are hardly paralleled.

In a study of the strong verbs, what questions present themselves to be solved, and how should our work be di-vided ? We must first classify them. This has been sufficiently spoken of in previous papers. Within each class the growth and decay of the ablaut must be shown during the three periods which make up historical High German, — the old, the middle, and the new periods; the first extending up to about 1100, the second to 1500, and the third to our own day.   Here, however, a difficulty presents itself; for in OHG. almost every document has a different system of spelling, and the MHG. is by no means uniform, even in the same district and century.   It would be impossible in the limits of this essay to give every form, and therefore the normal and usual forms have as a rule alone been given, though others have been noticed wherever they possessed any historic value.   This analysis of the ablaut is accompanied by complete lists of all verbs belonging to it at each stage of the language.   But the study of these lists suggests several other questions.   Whence come the additions that appear first in MHG., and even in NHG.?   The history of these intruders must be examined, and their source discovered.   And we find also many that have become wholly or partially weak. We ask ourselves when and why these verbs became so; and when this question is disposed of, there remains the long list of verbs that have fallen from the ranks in MHG. and NHG., and we ask when and why they were discarded.

Such is the scope of this study.   Tabulated results have been added, and summarize the scattered details.   Frequent comparisons with the history of the English ablaut, taken from my paper in the Transactions of 1882, will show some interesting results for the comparative grammar of these languages.

SECTION I. — THE STRONG VERBS.

Class I. a.

The Old Germanic ablaut was *e, a, ā, e;* and this remained unchanged in OHG., though this class, which originally comprised all verbs whose stems contained *a* followed by a mute, has in OHG. suffered considerable loss to Class I. b., where the past participle is with the vowel *o*.   This change embraces all stems ending in *hh* (*brehhan, rehhan, sprehhan, stehhan, trekhan, swehhan*), and *trefan;* but *swehhan* has occasionally a participle in *e*. These verbs therefore appear under I. b. This change from I. a. to I. b. goes still further in MHG., occurring sometimes in *lesen, kneten, pflegen, stechen, wegen, weben,* and always in *rœchen, schrecken,* which two are therefore listed under I. b. NHG. adds to the list *weben, wegen,* and *gären,* while *pflegen* vacillates between I. a. and I. b.

Grammatic change of *s* to *r*, *d* to *t*, and *h* to *g*, occurs after the third and fourth ablaut vowels regularly in OHG. In MHG. it is less common, and in NHG. survives only in the deflective *war* : *gewesen*, and in *gären*, where it has got into the present also.

The present vowel *e* becomes *i* in OHG. in the *ja* stems (*bittan, liggan, sizzan*), which is retained in MHG. and in NHG. (*bitten, liegen, sitzen*). *E* is also changed to *i* in the indic. sing. present (*sihu, sihst, siht,* from *sehan*). This change becomes irregular in MHG., and is now confined to the 2d and 3d pers. sing. of verbs with the ablaut *e, a, e,* while those with *e, o, o* have no change. In NHG., however, the *i* becomes *ie* before sonants, e. g. *liest, geschieht, giebt, liegt.*

In MHG. the regular ablaut undergoes no change. The passing of verbs to I. b. has been noted above. Isolated peculiarities are *ō* for *ue*, and *ū* for *ui*, in OHG. *quedan* (*kōden, kūde*), and *wuog* for *wag*, as a past to *wegan*, by the analogy of Class IV.

In NHG. the regular ablaut is *e, a, e.* The *a* of the singular finds its way into the plural. Four verbs have forms like I. b., *e, o, o ; weben, bewegen, pflegen, gären.* Of these *pflegen* is sometimes weak, and has sometimes *e, a, e; wegen* appears also as *wägen* and *wiegen,* and *gären* is often weak. The *ä* for *e* is due to the *r ;* see I. b. *bären* or *bähren.*

The verbs belonging to this class are : —

OHG.	MHG.	NHG.
bittan, *bid*	bitten	bitten
	brehen, *shine*	
ezzan (frezzan), *eat*	ezzen	essen
fehan, *rejoice*		
geban, *give*	geben	geben
gezzan, *get*	gezzen	ver-gessen
jehan, *say*	jehan, s. and w.	

OHG.	MHG.	NHG.
jesan, *ferment*	jesan, geren	gären, gähren, *o, o,* and w.
jetan, *weed*	jeten	gäten, w.
knetan, *knead*	kneten	kneten, w.
lechan, *lick*	lechen	lechen, w.
kresan, *creep*	kresen	
lesan, *read, pick*	lesen	lesen
liggan, *lie*	liggen	liegen
mezzan, *mete*	mezzen	messen
nesan, *recover*	nesen	ge-nesen
pflegan, *care for*	pflegen, s. and w.	pflegen, *a, e ; o, o ;* and w.
quedan, *speak*	queden, kōden	
redan, *sift*	reden	
	regen, *rise*	
scehan, *happen*	schehen, s. and w.	ge-schehen
sehan, *see*	sehen	sehen
sizzan, *sit*	sizzen	sitzen
stredan, *glow*	streden	
swedan, *burn*		
tretan, *step*	treten	treten
weban, *weave*	weben	weben, *o, o*
wegan, *move*	wegen	be-wegen, wägen, wiegen; *o, o,* and w.
wesan, *be*	wesen	*wesen, war, gewesen
wetan, *bind*	weten	

SUMMARY.—Strong in OHG., 28; MHG., 28; NHG., 17. Weakened in MHG., always none, sometimes 3; in NHG., always 3, sometimes 3. Absent from OHG., 2; MHG., 2; NHG., 10. Total number of stems, 30.

Class I. b.

The Old Germanic ablaut was *e, a, ā, o.* Originally confined to stems with *a* followed by *l, m, n, r,* this class contained many additions from I. a. in OHG., and still more in MHG., as well as some from I. c.; the *ā* taking the place of *u* always in *dehsen* and *lesken,* which are therefore listed here, and often in *bresten, flechten, fechten.* *Vice versa,* we have *e* for the regular *o* in the past participles of *stemen, zemen,* but not regularly. See Class I. a. and I. c.

In MHG. the ablaut is preserved intact.

In NHG. the regular ablaut is *e, a, o ; e, o, o* occurs in *scheren, rächen.* Before, and sometimes after *r, ä* is used for *e,* as in *gären* I. a.; e.g. *bären.* The *ö* for *e* in *löschen* and *schwören* is irregular and unexplained. The *ue* in *queman* becomes *o* usually in MHG., and always in NHG. Two verbs of Class IV. have come to have the ablaut *e, o, o* in NHG., *heben* and *schwören*. We find, however, the older pasts *hub, schwur,* and also the adj. *erhaben*.

The verbs belonging to this class are : —

OHG.	MHG.	NHG.
beran, *bear*	beren	bären, bähren
brehhan, *break*	brehhen	brechen
breman, *hum*	bremen	
	dehsen, *beat*	
dweran, *twirl*	dweren	
helan, *conceal*	helen	ver-hehlen, w.
leskan, *extinguish*	leschen	löschen, *o, o,* and w.
neman, *take*	nemen	nehmen
quelan, *kill*	quelen	quälen, w.
queman, koman, *come*	komen, s. and w.	kommen
	rechen, *gather*	
rehhan, *avenge*	rehhen	rächen, *o, o,* and w.
sceran, *cut*	scheren	scheren, *o, o*
	schrecken, *frighten*	schrecken
sprehhan, *speak*	sprehhen	sprechen
stehhan, *prick*	stehhen	stechen
	stemen, *hinder*	
stelan, *steal*	stelen	stelen, stehlen
sweran, *hurt*	sweren	schwären, -schweren, w.
swehhan, *gush*	swehhen	
trehhan, *push*	trehhen	
trefan, *meet*	trefen	treffen
	tremen, *endure*	
twelan, *be stiff*	twelen	
zeman, *befit*	zemen	
zeran, *tear*	zeren	zären, -zehren, w.

SUMMARY.—Strong in OHG., 21 ; in MHG., 26 ; in NHG., 12. Weakened in MHG., always none, sometimes 1 ; in NHG., always 4, sometimes 2. Absent from OHG., 5 ; from MHG., none ; from NHG., 10. Total number of stems, 26.

Class I. c.

In old Germanic the ablaut was *e, a, u, o.* In OHG. this remains, except before nasals, where it becomes *e, a, u, u.* In the indic. sing. present *e* becomes *i* in OHG.; this becomes

irregular in MHG., and in NHG. is confined to 2d and 3d persons ; e. g. *wird,* O. M. NHG. 3d. sing. of *werden.*

MHG. loses a few verbs from this class to I. b.; which see.
Here also the *a* and *o* sometimes become *u.* In NHG. *a*
occasionally appears as *u,* but *o* never does.

In NHG. the regular *ablaut* is *e, a, o,* or *e, o, o,* except before
nasals. Before *n* + mute, the ablaut is *i, a, u;* before *nn,*
i, a, o; before *mm, i, o, o;* and in *schwimmen,* usually *i, a, o.*
Werden alone has preserved the original four vowels ; *u* is regular in the past plural and subjunctive (as *ü*), and sometimes
in the past singular, *werden, ward (wurde), wurden, worden.*
Occasionally *u* appears for *a* in the singular indic., and oftener
as *ü* in the subjunctive ; examples are *dung, rung, schund,*
schwund, stunk, trunk, klünge. In the verbs with *e, a, o,* we
find *ö* sometimes in the past subjunctive, e. g. *böre, gölte,*
schölte; and sometimes *ü,* e. g. *bürge, hülfe, stürbe, verdürbe.*
In verbs with *i, a, o,* we find *ö* in the subj. in *begönne, ge-*
wönne, rönne, sönne, spönne. Isolated is the present *schallen*
strong and weak, for *schellen;* this form is from a MHG.
weak *schallen,* but the remainder of the verb is the old
strong one.

With *e, a, o: bersten, bergen, verderben, dreschen, fehlen,*
gelten, helfen, schelten, sterben, werben, werden, werfen (12).

With *e, o, o: flechten, flechten, melken, quellen, schallen, schmel-*
zen, schwellen (7).

With *i, a, o: beginnen, rinnen, sinnen, spinnen, schwimmen,*
winnen (6).

With *i, o, o : glimmen, klimmen ;* rarely *schwimmen* (2).

With *i, a, u: binden, dingen, dringen, finden, klingen, ge-*
lingen, ringen, singen, sinken, slingen, springen, stinken,
schwinden, schwingen, trinken, winden, zwingen (17).

With *i, u, u : schinden,* and rarely *schwinden, ringen,*
dingen (1).

The verbs belonging to this class are : —

OHG.	MHG.	NHG.
belgan, *swell*	belgen	
bellan, *bell*	bellen	bellen, w.
berstan, *burst*	bersten, bresten	bersten, *a, o,* and w.

OHG.	MHG.	NHG.
bergan, *hide*	bergen	bergen, *a, o*
bindan, *bind*	binden	binden, *a, u*
brettan, *bind*	bretten	
	brimmen, *hum*	
brinnan, *burn*	brinnen	
	delhen, *delve*	
	derben, *spoil*	ver-derben, *a, o,* and w.
	dimpfen, *smoke*	
		dingen, *a, u ; u, u ;* and w.,
		[*hire.*
dinsan, *pull*	dinsen	
	drellen, *turn*	
drescan, *thresh*	dreschen	dreschen, *a, o,* and w.
	drinden, *swell*	
dringan, *push*	dringen	dringen, *a, u*
dwingan, *compel*	twingen	zwingen, *a, u*
fehtan, *fight*	fehten	fechten, *o, o*
flehtan, *braid*	flehten	flechten, *o, o*
felhan, *conceal*	felhen s. and w.	fehlen, w., empfehlen, *a, o*
ferzan, L. *pedere*	ferzen	ferzen, w.
findan, *find*	finden	finden, *a, u*
	gelfen, *boast*	
gellan, *yell*	gellen	
geltan, *be worth*	gelten	gelten, *a, o*
ginnan, *begin*	ginnen	be-ginnen, *a, o*
	glimmen, *glimmer*	glimmen, *o, o* and w.
helfan, *help*	helfen	helfen, *a, o*
hellan, *sound*	hellen	
hinkan, *limp*	hinken	hinken, w.
hrespan, *pluck*		
kerran, *cry*	kerren	
klimman, *climb*	klimmen	klimmen, *o, o,* and w.
	klimpfen, *squeeze*	
klingan, *clink*	klingen	klingen, *a, u,* and w.
klinnan, *smear*		
	knellen, *ring*	
krimman, *press*	grimmen, grinnen	
krimpfan, *crumple*	krimpfen	
limman, *snarl*	limmen	
limpfan, *befit*	limpfen	
lingan, *attain*	lingen	gelingen, *a, u*
linnan, *yield*		
melkan, *milk*	melken	melken, *o, o,* and w.
nindan, *dare*		
quellan, *gush*	quellen	quellen, *o, o,* and w.
rimpfan, *wrinkle*	rimpfen	
ringan, *fight*	ringen	ringen, *a, u,* and *u, u*
rinnan (trinnan), *run*	rinnen	rinnen, *a, o*
scellan, *sound*	schellen	schallen, *a, o,* and w.

OHG.	MHG.	NHG.
sceltan, *scold*	schelten	schelten, *a, o*
scerran, *scratch* ·	scherren	
	schinden, s. and w., *skin*	schinden, *u, u*
scrindan, *crack*	schrinden	
	selken, *drip*	
singan, *sing*	singen	singen, *a, u*
sinkan, *sink*	sinken	sinken, *a, u*
sinnan, *think*	sinnen, s. and w.	sinnen, *a, o*
slindan, *devour*	slinden	= *schlingen*
smelzan, *melt*	smelzen	schmelzen, *o, o,* and w.
slingan, *devour*	slingen	schlingen, *a, u*
spinnan, *spin*	spinnen	spinnen, *a, o*
smerzan, *hurt*	smerzen, s. and w.	schmerzen, w.
springan, *spring*	springen	springen, *a, u*
snerfan, *pull together*	snerfen	
snerhan, *tie*	snerhen	
sterban, *die*	sterben	sterben, *a, o*
	sterzen, *project*	
stinkan, *stink*	stinken	stinken, *a, u*
swelhan, *swallow*	swelhen	schwelgen, w.
swellan, *swell*	swellen	schwellen, *o, o,* and w.
swelzan, *be consumed*	swelzen	
swerban, *hover*	swerben	
swimman, *swim*	swimmen	schwimmen, *a, o*
swindan, *vanish*	swinden	schwinden, *a, u,* and *u, u*
swingán, *swing*	swingen	schwingen, *a, u*
telban, *dig*	telben	
trinkan, *drink*	trinken	trinken, *a, u*
wellan, *roll*	wellen	·
werban, *obtain*	werben	werben, *a, o*
werdan, *become*	werden	werden, *a, u, o*
werfan, *throw*	werfen	werfen, *a, o*
werran, *confuse*	werren	wirren, w.
windan, *wind*	winden	winden, *a, u*
winkan, *wink*	winken	winken, w.
winnan, *win*	winnen	ge-winnen, *a, o*

SUMMARY.—Strong in OHG., 73; MHG., 82; NHG., 45. Weakened in MHG., always none, sometimes 4; in NHG., always 7, sometimes 13. Absent from OHG., 14; from MHG., 5; from NHG., 35. Total number of stems, 87.

Class II.

The Old Germanic ablaut was *ei, ai, i, i,* which in OHG. became *ī, ei, i, i;* and, before *h, ī, ē, i, i.*

In OHG. grammatic change substituted *t* for *d, r* for *s,* and *g* for *h*, after the third and fourth ablaut vowels. In MHG. this change was also regular; but in NHG. it occurs only in *leiden, schneiden.*

In MHG. the ablaut is unaltered; *e* occurs sometimes for *i*, and *ei* for *ē*. In stems ending in a vowel or *w*, *scrīen, spīwen, glīen*, and in *līhen* (Gothic *leihvan*), we have *ei* or *ē* in the past sing.; and in the plural, for *iw*, either *iuw* or *ūw*; thus, *schriwen, schriuwen, schrūwen; spūen, lūwen*, are not uncommon forms. Occasionally we find *r* for *w*, as for instance in *spirn, schirn*, especially in Bavaria. Gradually the *e* of the past plural and participle begins to appear in the singular also. The earliest example is in Schonebek, Das Hohe Lied, which is dated by Weinhold A. D. 1276.

In NHG. the ablaut is *ei, i, i,* before surds, and *ei, ie, ie,* before sonants. This change of *i* to *ie* before sonants occurs also in I. a. in 2d and 3d singular pres. indic. *Leiden, schneiden,* have *i, i,* owing to the change of *d* to *t* in the past and participle.

With *ei, i, i: beissen, bleichen, befleissen, gleichen, gleiten, greifen, keifen, kneifen, kneipen, leiden, pfeifen, reissen, reiten, scheissen, schleichen, schleifen, schleissen, schmeissen, schneiden, schreiten, spleissen, streichen, streiten, weichen* (24). Final consonants, *ch, f, p, ss, t*, and *d = t*.

With *ei, ie, ie: bleiben, gedeihen, leihen, meiden, preisen, reiben, scheiden, scheinen, schreiben, schreien, schweigen, speien, steigen, treiben, weisen, zeihen* (16). Final consonants, *b, d, g, h, n, s,* and final vowel.

The verbs belonging to this class are: —

OHG.	MHG.	NHG.
bītan, *bite*	bīten, s. and w.	
bīzan, *bite*	bīzen	beissen, *i, i*
blīcan, *pale*	blīchen	bleichen, *i, i,* and w.
	brīsen, *tie*	
	brīten, *weave*	
dīhan, *flourish*	dīhen	ge-deihen, *ie, ie*
flīzan, *be zealous*	flīzen, s. and w.	be-fleissen, *i, i*
	glīfen, *slant*	
	glīen, *cry*	
	glīten, *slip*	gleiten, *i, i,* and w.
glīzan, *glisten*	glīzen	gleissen, w.
gnītan, *rub*		
grīfan, *gripe*	grīfen	greifen, *i, i*

OHG.	MHG.	NHG.
grīnan, *grin*	grīnen	greinen, w.
		keifen, *i, i,* and w., *chide*
kīnan, *bud*	kīnen, chīnen	
klīban, *cling*	chlīben	
		kneifen, *i, i,* and w., *nip*
		kneipen, *i, i,* and w., *nip*
	krīgen, s. and w., *get*	kriegen, w.
līban, *leave*	līben	b-leiben, *ie, ie*
līdan, *suffer*	līden	leiden, litt, litten
līhan, *lend*	līhen	leihen, *ie, ie*
līchen, s. and w., *be like*	g-leichen, *i, i,* and w.	
	līmen, *snare*	
mīdan, *avoid*	mīden	meiden, *ie, ie*
	nīden, s. and w., *envy*	be-neiden, w.
nīgan, *bend*	nīgen	neigen, w.
pfīfan, *pipe*	pfīfen, s. and w.	pfeifen, *i, i*
		preisen, *ie, ie, praise*
rīban, *rub*	rīben	reiben, *ie, ie*
rīdan, *twist*	rīden	
rīhhan, *rule*		
rīhan, *set in order*	rīhen	
rīnan, *touch*		
rīsan, *rise*	rīsen	
rītan, *ride*	rīten	reiten, *i, i*
rizan, *tear*	rīzen	reissen, *i, i*
scīnan, *shine*	schīnen	scheinen, *ie, ie*
scīzan, L. *cacare*	schīzen	scheissen, *i, i*
scrīban, *write*	schrīben	schreiben, *ie, ie*
scrīan, *cry*	schrīen, s. and w.	schreien, *ie, ie*
scrītan, *stride*	schrīten	schreiten, *i, i*
sīgan, *sag*	sīgen	
sīhan, *sift*	sīhen	
	schīben, *roll*	
	schīden, *divide*	scheiden, *ie, ie,* and w.
	schīten, s. and w., *split*	
slīcan, *crawl*	slīchen	schleichen, *i, i*
slīfan, *drag*	slīfen	schleifen, *i, i,* and w.
slītan, *slide*	slīten	
slīzan, *slit*	slīzen	schleissen, *i, i*
smīzan, *smite*	smīzen	schmeissen, *i, i*
snīdan, *cut*	snīden	schneiden, *ie, ie*
spīwan, *spew*	spīwen, s. and w.	speien, *ie, ie,* and w.
	splīzen, *split*	spleissen, *i, i,* and w.
	sprīten, *bend*	
sprīzan, *split*		
stīgan, *mount*	stīgen	steigen, *ie, ie*
strīhhan, *stroke*	strīchen	streichen, *i, i*
strītan, *quarrel*	strīten	streiten, *i, i*

OHG.	MHG.	NHG.
	swīfen, *rove*	schweifen, w.
	swīgen, s. and w., *be still*	schweigen, *ie, ie*
swīhhan, *deceive*	swīchen	
swīnan, *vanish*	swīnen	
	tīchen, *try*	
tīban, *drive*	trīben	treiben, *ie, ie*
wīhhan, *yield*	wīchen	weichen, *i, i*
wīfan, *wind*	wīfen	
wīhan, *fight*	wīhen, s. and w.	
wīzan, *show*	wīzen	weisen, *ie, ie*
zīhan, *accuse*	zīhen, s. and w.	zeihen, *ie, ie*

SUMMARY.—Strong OHG., 51; MHG., 64; NHG., 40. Strong and weak in MHG., 12, always weak, none; in NHG., always 6, sometimes 11. Absent from OHG., 21; from MHG., 8; from NHG., 26. Total number of stems, 72.

Class III.

In Old Germanic the ablaut was *eu, au, u, u*, which in OHG. becomes regularly *io, ou, u, o;* but before *w*, and always in the indic. sing. present, we have *iu* for *io*. A few verbs had *ū* for *eu* in Old Germanic; these retain *ū* in OHG. See Schmidt, Vocalismus, I. 140 ff. In the past, *o* occurs for *ou* before the dentals *t, s, z,* and *h*. The third vowel, *u*, is retained, but in the participle *u* becomes *o*.

In MHG. *io* becomes *ie; iu* and *ū* remain, though in MG. we find *ū* sometimes for *iu*. Gradually *ie* takes the place of *iu*, especially in the first person sing. In the past, MHG. sometimes uses *ou* for *o* before *h*, but usually keeps the OHG. forms. In late MHG. *o* appears in the singular, coming from MG., where *o* is regular in the plural. The oldest example is in Jeroshin, A. D. 1340. In the past plural, *u* is usually retained, but before *w* we find *ū, iu, ou;* e. g. from *fliohan* we find *flūwen, flouwen, flūn*. Compare the effect of *w* in Class II. In MG. *o* regularly takes the place of *u*, and this appears in late MHG., and is now regular. From the plural *o* made its way into the singular, especially in verbs which had *ō* in the singular, and this *ō* appears also in the plural. The participle in MHG. is always *o* except before *w*, where *u, ō, iu, ou* occur.

In NHG. the ablaut is *ie, o, o*. For *ū* we have *au*, and in

2nd and 3d pres. ind. sing. *eu* for OHG. *iu* occurs rarely.   Two
verbs have *ü* in the present (*lügen, küren*), perhaps by metathesis of *iu* to *ui* = *ü*.

Grammatic change of *d* to *t, h* to *g*, and *s* to *r*, is regular
after the third and fourth ablaut vowels in OHG. and MHG.
In NHG. this is confined to *sieden* : *sott; ziehen* : *zog. Flie-
hen* : *floh, kiesen* : *kos*, retain the present consonants, while
küren : *kor, frieren* : *fror, verlieren* : *verlor*, bring the *r* into
the present also.

The verbs belonging to this class are : —

OHG.	MHG.	NHG.
biogan, *bow*	biegen	biegen
biotan, *offer*	bieten	bieten
bliuwan, *blow*	bliuwen	bläuen, w.
	briezen, *burst out*	
briuwan, *brew*	briuwen, s. and w.	brauen, w.
diozan, *roar*	diezen	
driozan, *annoy*	driezen	ver-driessen
fliogan, *flee*	fliegen	fliegen
fliohan, *fly*	fliehen	fliehen
fliozan, *flow*	fliezen	fliessen
friozan, *freeze*	friezen	frieren
giozan, *pour*	giezen	giessen
hliozan, *cast lots*	liezen	
hniotan, *fasten*		
kiosan, *choose*	kiesen	kiesen, küren, s. and w.
kiuwan, *chew*	kiuwen, s. and w.	kauen, w.
klioban, *cleave*	klieben	klieben
kriochan, *creep*	kriechen	kriechen
liogan, *lie*	liegen	lügen
liosan, *lose*	liesen	ver-lieren
liotan, *grow*		
lūhhan, s. and w., *lock*	lūhhen	
niosan, *sneeze*	niesen	niesen, w.
niozan, *enjoy*	niezen	ge-niessen
niuwan, *renew*	niuwen	
riohhan, *smell*	riechen	riechen, s. and w.
riozan, *drip*	riezen	
riuwan, *repent*	riuwen	reuen, w.
scioban, *shove*	schieben	schieben
sciozan, *shoot*	schiezen	schiessen
		schrauben, s. and w., *screw*
siodan, *seethe*	sieden	sieden, s. and w.
sliofan, *glide*	sliefen	schliefen
sliozan, *shut*	sliezen	schliessen
	smiegen, *bend*	schmiegen, w.

OHG.	MHG.	NHG.
	spriezen, *sprout*	spriessen
	snūfen, *snort*	schnaufen, schnauben, s. [and w.
stioban, *fly about*	stieben	stieben
sūfan, *drink*	sūfen	saufen
sūgan, *suck*	sūgen	saugen, s. and w.
triogan, *betray*	triegen	betriegen, s., betrügen, w.
triofan, *drip*	triefen	triefen, s. and w.
ziohan, *draw*	ziehen	ziehen

SUMMARY. — Strong in OHG., 38; in MHG., 40; in NHG., 29. Weakened in MHG., always none, sometimes 2; in NHG., always 6, sometimes 8. Absent from OHG., 5; from MHG., 3; from NHG., 8. Total number of stems, 43.

Class IV.

In Old Germanic the ablaut was *a, ō, ō, a,* which in OHG. became *a, uo, uo, a.* Verbs that had *ja-* stems take umlaut of *a* to *e* in the present in late OHG. and MHG., which change usually occurs also in 2d and 3d pres. indic. sing. of all verbs of this class; in NHG. this is written *ä* (*fährt, mählt,* &c.).

MHG. keeps the ablaut unchanged; MG. has *ū* and *ō* for *uo.* Occasionally we find irregular pasts of this class in verbs of other classes; thus *swuor, swūr,* from *swern,* I. b; *wuoc, wūc,* from *wegen,* I. a.; *bluonden,* from *blanden,* V. Rarely in MHG. *a* becomes *o* in the participle; e. g. *sworn* for *swarn,* from *swern.* This causes a change in NHG. to I. b. in *schwören* and *heben.*

In NHG. the ablaut is *a, u, a,* except in *heben, schwören,* I. b.

Grammatic change of *h* to *g* is regular in OHG. and later. In MG. *h* is elided between vowels; e. g. *slān, twān.*

Stān is anomalous; the forms are: OHG. *stān* (*standan*), *stuont* (*stōnt*), *standen* (*stān*); MHG. *stān* (*stēn, standen*), *stuont* (*stūnt, stōnt, stuot*), *standen* (*stan*); NHG. *stehen, stand, standen.*

The verbs belonging to this class are: —

OHG.	MHG.	NHG.
bachan, *bake*	bachen	backen
	blappen (participle)	
dwahan, *wash*	twahen	
faran, *fare*	faren	faren, fahren

OHG.	MHG.	NHG.
		fragen, s. and w., *ask*
galan, *sing*		
graban, *dig*	graben	graben
hefjan, *lift*	hebban, s. and w.	heben, *o, o.* See I. b.
hladan, *load*	laden, s. and w.	laden, s. and w.
hlahhan, *laugh*	lahhen, w.	lachen, w.
laffan, *lick*	laffen	
lahan, *blame*		
malan, *grind*	malen	malen, mahlen, s. and w.
nagan, *gnaw*	nagen	nagen, w.
sahhan, *quarrel*	sachen, w.	
scafan, *make*	schaffen, s. and w.	schaffen, s. and w.
scaban, *shave*	schaben	schaben, w.
sebban, *notice*	sebben	
slahan, *slay*	slahen	schlagen
spanan, *stretch*	spanen	
stān (irr.), *stand*	stan (irr.)	stehen (irr.)
sweran, *swear*	swern	swören, *o, o.* See I. b.
tragan, *bear*	tragen	tragen
wahan, *call*	wahen	
wahsan, *wax*	wahsen	wachsen
waskan, *wash*	wasken	waschen
watan, *wade*	waten	waten, w.

SUMMARY. — Strong in OHG., 25; in MHG., 22; in NHG., 14. Weakened in MHG., always 2, sometimes 3; in NHG., always 4, sometimes 4. Absent from OHG., 2; from MHG., 3; from NHG, 9. Total number of stems, 27.

Class V.

In Old Germanic the preterit was formed by reduplication, but in OHG. the reduplication coalesced with the stem syllable, and, where this had *a*, produced *ia* or *ē;* where the stem had *ā, ei*, the result was *ia* (*ea*); where it was *uo, ou* (*ō*), the contraction gave *io* (*eo*). All these became *ie* in MHG. except where final, when we have *iu*. In NHG. *ie* is invariable, though sometimes contracted to *i* before *ng;* e. g. *hing* or *hieng.* Umlaut of *a, ā* to *e, ǣ*, occurs in 2d and 3d pres. indic. sing. in late OHG. and MHG. There are five subclasses. In V. a. the OHG. ablaut is *a, ia* (*ē*), *a;* in V. b. *ā, ia* (*ea*), *ā;* in V. d. *ei, ia* (*ea*), *ei;* in V. c. *uo* (*ua, oa, ō*), *io* (*eo, ia*), *uo* (*ua, oa, ō*); V. e. *ou* (*ō, au, oa, ū*), *io* (*ia, ie, iu, eu, eo*), *ou* (*ō, au, oa, ū*). Beside these

we find in V. c. e. forms with euphonic *r* between the vowels of the past; e. g. *steroz*, V. e.; *pleruz*, V. c. Anomalous
forms are *ern*, V. a., with umlaut in the present; *fāhan, hāhan*,
V. a., with *ā* for *an*, and past and participle with *ng* (*hēng, fēng,
hangen, fangen*).

In MHG. the ablaut is in the main the same. All pasts have
become *ie* except in V. e. before *w*, where we find *iu, eu*, and *i*.
MG. has *ī, ē* in these cases. In the present and participle MHG.
has often *ū* for *ou* and *ō* in V. e. Elisions are more common
in MHG. than in OHG. We have *hie, fie*, for *hieng, fieng*, and in
MG. *hān, fān*, for *hahan, fahan*. *Lāzan* became *lān* in late OHG.,
and here has the past *lie*, by analogy of which is formed *hie* for
hiez; hizzen, MG. from the same verb, is by analogy of Class II.
OHG. *gangan* has a secondary stem *gān*, whence come a great
variety of forms in MHG. Many verbs of V. c. show a tendency
to Class III.; e. g. *hiuwen, hou, gehūwen; loffen, luffen; gebū-
wen; biozan;* and others.

In NHG. the ablaut is *a* (*ei, u, au, o*), *ie* (*i*), *a* (*ei, u, au, o*).
Gehen has a present from a different stem; otherwise it is
regular. *Hangen, fangen*, have taken the *ng* of the other forms
into the present also.

The verbs belonging to this class are:—

OHG.	MHG.	NHG.
V.a. bannan, *banish*	bannen	bannen, w.
blandan, *mix*	blanden	
ern, *plough*	ern, s. and w.	
fāhan, *catch*	fahen, fān	fangen
fallan, *fall*	fallen	fallen
faltan, *fold*	falten	falten, w.
gān (irr.), *go*	gangen, gān (irr.)	gehen (irr.)
hāhan, *hang*	hāhan, hān	hangen
	halsen, s. and w., *embrace*	halsen, w.
haltan, *hold*	halten	halten
halzan, s. and w., *limp*	halzen, w.	
salzan, *salt*	salzen	salzen, w.
scaltan, *dispose*	schalten	schalten, w.
spaltan, *split*	spalten	spalten, w., Part. s.
spannan, *stretch*	spannen	spannen, w.
walkan, *full, walk*	walken	walken, w.
waltan, *rule*	walten, s. and w.	walten, w.
walzan, *roll*	walzen	walzen, w.

OHG.	MHG.	NHG.
V.b. bāgan, *fight*	bāgen, w.	
blāhan, s. and w., *blow*	blǣjen, w., Part. s.	blähen, w.
blāsan, *blow*	blāsen	blasen
brātan, *roast*	brāten	braten, s. and w.
lāzan, *let*	lāzan, lān	lassen
rātan, *advise*	rāten	raten
slāfan, *sleep*	slāfen	schlaffen
trātan, *dread*	trāten	
wāzan, *blow*	wāzen	
V.d.	eischen, s. and w., *ask*	heischen, w.
heizan, *be called*	heizen	heissen
	leichen, s. and w., *dance*	
meizan, *cut*	meizen	
sceidan, *divide*	scheiden	= *scheiden*, II.
sweifan, *roam*	sweifen	schweifen, w.
zeisan, *tease*	zeisen, s. and w.	
blōzan, s. and w., *sacrifice*		
V.c. ruofan, s. and w., *call*	ruofen, s. and w.	rufen
fluohhan, s. and w., *curse*	fluochōn, w.	fluchen, w.
wuofan, s. and w., *weep*	wuofen, s. and w.	
V.e. bōzan, s. and w., *beat*	bōzen, s. and w.	
bouwan, s. and w., *dwell*	bouwen, s. and w.	bauen, w.
houwan, *hew*	houwen, s. and w.	hauen, s. and w.
loufan, *run*	loufen, s. and w.	laufen
scrōtan, *bruise*	schrōten	schroten, w.
stōzan, *push*	stōzen	stossen

SUMMARY. — Strong in OHG., 41; in MHG., 39; in NHG., 15. Weakened in MHG., always 4, sometimes 12; in NHG., always 16, sometimes 2. Absent from OHG., 3; MHG., 1; NHG., 13. Total number of stems, 44.

SECTION II. — THE NEW STRONG VERBS.

There are 45 additions to the strong verbs in MHG., and 7 in NHG. Some of these verbs are from Old Germanic strong verbs, for they have strong verbs corresponding to them in other Germanic dialects, and were doubtless present in OHG., though they fail to occur there in Mss.; others have probably the same origin, for we find ablaut derivatives in Germanic and other European dialects. Several, however, are produced from older weak verbs, and some appear without any related forms in the older dialects by which we can trace their

origin.   Others are derived from foreign languages, or owe
their present ablaut to a change of class.   The analogy of
words with similar sound has been often the cause of the
change, and sometimes a sort of imitation of the meaning of
the word by the sound seems to have been sought, as in our
kling, klang; ding, dong.

There are a number of strong forms sporadically developed
from weak verbs in MHG. to meet the exigencies of rhyme.
These are merely personal idiosyncrasies, and I have passed
them over hitherto.   I will notice here those cases which are
known to me, with citations according to Lexer's abbreviations : —

I. c. fürchten : forchten, Nib. 1723. 4, and elsewhere.
      kunnen : kunnen (part.), Kindh. 70 and elsewhere.
      wurchen : worchen, Lieds. 8. 74.
      schenken : schank, Heldenbuch 547. 34.

II.   glīchen : gleich, glichen, Virg. 289. 10, Wolfd. D. V. 59. 4.
      krītzen : kreis, Koditz 78. 17.
      prīsen : preis, prisen, Wolfd. 301. 4, Virg. 886. 3.

III. drouwen : drouwen, (part.), Fol. 158. 19 ; but see Schade
      Altdeutsches Wörterbuch, 2d ed., p. 960.

IV. jagen : jagen (part.), Karlem 206. 8.
      laben : laben (part.), Boner. 54. 40.
      laden : luot, Myst. I. 241, Otack. 363.
      machen : machen (part.), Hugo v. Montf.
      schaden : schuod, Ad. Eva 1289, Zimmersche Kr. IV. 225,
         31, 35.
      schamen : schamen (part.), Weinhold's MHG. Grammar.

V.   begrāben : begrāben (part.), Teichner.
      denen : dannen, Mart. 37. 60.
      drāgen : drān, Weinhold's Allem. Grammar.
      pfenden : pfenden (part.), Teichner.
      salben : sielb, Gundack. 751.
      weln : wiel, Schonebek 7097.
      welben : wielb, Anzeiger 8. 481.

A reference to the list in Section I. will show that, of the
MHG. 45 new strong verbs, NHG. keeps 11, weakens 6, and dis-
cards 28 ; NHG. adds 7, and has therefore 18 strong verbs not
OHG.

The following 11 MHG. verbs are old, though not found in OHG. The arrangement is by classes : —

dehsen : cp. Lat. texo, Gk. τέκτων, Skr. taksh ; Fick 3. 129.

rechen, Gothic rikan, I. a. ; cp. also Fick 3. 249.

dimpfen : cp. OHG. dampf, dumpf, OE. damp, and Kluge, Wörterbuch 46.

drinden, OE. þrindan.

gelfen, OE. gíelpan, ON. gialpa.

selken, OE. séolcan.

gliten, OE. glīdan.

briezen, OE. brēotan, OS. brētan ; Schade, Wb. 84.

smiegen, OE. smūgan, ON. smiuga ; Schade, Wb. 832.

spriezen, OE. sprēotan ; derivatives in OHG.

leichen, ON. leika, G. leikan, OE. lācan.

The following 15 are from older weak verbs : —

MHG.   schrecken, OHG. scricchen, screcchōn, screcken w.

stemen, OHG. stemmen w.   All derivatives have *mm;* e. g.
stammeln, stumm.

delhen, OHG. delhan w. : cp. Scherer, Deutsche Spr. 241.

schinden, OHG. scintan w. : cp. ON. skinn ; stem *skinþa-.

sterzen, OHG. starzen w. : *e* is here umlaut of *a.*

lichen, OHG. līchan, līchēn w., OE. līcjan w., G. leikan w.

nīden, OHG. nīden, nīdōn w., from OHG. nīd.

schīben, OHG. scīben w.

sprīten, OHG. spreitan w., OE. sprædan w.   See Kluge,
Wörterb. 324, but note the irregularity in the vowels ;
OGH. *ei* remains unchanged in MHG.

swīgen, OHG. swīgēn, OE. swīgian w.

halsen, OHG. halsēn, halsōn, halsan, halsen w.

eischen, OHG. eiscōn w., OE. āscian w.

NHG.   dingen, MHG. dingen w., OHG. dingōn w., OE. þingian w.

preisen, MHG. preisen w., from O. French prīser.

fragen, MHG. vragen w., OHG. fragēn w. ; cp. OE. frig-
nan, Ic.

The following 5 are from nouns : —

MHG.   brīsen, from MHG. brīse.   The stem is isolated in MHG.

krīgen, kriegen MG. strong and weak, but LG. strong.   From
kriec, *war.*

līmen, from MHG. līm ; cp. OHG. līmjan w.

schīten, from MHG. schīt, OHG. scīt, MG. schiten w.

NHG. schrauben, from NHG. schraube, MHG. schrūbe.

The following 4 are from strong verbs of other classes :

MHG. brimmen I. c. is from OHG. breman I. b., as is also MHG. brummen w.

glimmen I. c. is from OHG. glīman II.   All old forms have *m*, but modern developments have *m* and *mm*.   See Kluge, Wb. 110.

schīden II., from OHG. sceidan V., and scīdōn w.

swīfen II., from OHG. sweifan V.   See Schade, Wb. 914.

The following 5 are borrowed from the LG. : —

MHG. splīzen, from LG. splītan for an older *splintan I. c.; cp. OHG. sprīzan.   Here, as often, *l* = *r*.

snūfen, snūben, from LG. snūven.   NHG. schnaufen, schnauben, and schnupfen w.   The stem is not found elsewhere.

NHG. keifen, from LG. kīven II. ; cp. ON. kīfa, s. and w.

kneifen is originally identical with kneipen, from LG. knīpen II. : cp. ME. nīpen w.

There remain 12 isolated developments in MHG., the origin of which is still more or less doubtful.

MHG. brehen (to sparkle) : cp. G. braho (twinkling), 1 Cor. 15. 52.   No connection with ON. brā.   See Fick 3. 216.

regen : cp. MHG. regen w., ragen w., but no forms are older than MHG.

tremen : Schade, Wb. 952.   Hardly to cp. trimz MHG.

derben : confined to MHG., NHG.   The root is the same as that of sterben ; starbh = starb and þarb.

drellen, from dræjen : cp. Scherer, Deutsche Spr. 241.

klimpfen, from krimpfen.   All Germanic and Slavic derivatives have *r*.   This stem is isolated.

knellen.   An onomatopoetic word ; cp. OE. cnfell.

brīten.   Perhaps cp. brīttel.   Else wholly alone.

glīfen stands alone.

glīen stands alone.

tīchen stands alone.

blappen occurs only in Frauenl. **447. 20**, and stands
alone.

It will be observed that, of the 45 MHG. new strong verbs, but
11 remain strong in NHG., while 6 are weak, and 28 wholly discarded. This, when compared with the OHG. verbs, shows
clearly that these new verbs rarely obtained a secure footing
in the language. They remained strange to the popular ear,
and usually soon fell into disuse.

Section III. — The Weakened Verbs.

Many verbs which were strong in Old Germanic had become weak in OHG. These were noted in my paper in the
Transactions of last year. The tendency grew in force in
the MHG. and NHG. periods, though now it is greatly checked.
Usually those verbs developed weak forms in MHG. which by
the action of regular phonetic laws got a peculiar vowel in the
present, which thus became more like a weak verb, and so followed their analogy. Verbs of Classes IV. and V. are pecu-
liarly susceptible. Thus may be explained the regular weak
forms of *lachen, sachen ; halzen, bāgen, blǣjen, fluochōn;* and the
occasional weak forms of *komen; briuwen, kiuwen; heben, laden,
schaffen; ern, halsen, walten, eischen, leichen, zeisen, ruofen,
wuofen, bōzen, bouwen, houwen, loufen.* There remain, however,
to be explained the occasional weak forms in the following :
*jehen, schehen, pflegen ; felhen, schinden, sinnen, smerzen; bīten,
flīzen, krīgen, līchen, nīden, pfīfen, schrīen, schwīgen, schīten,
spīwen, wīhen, zīhen.* Of these *schinden, līchen, nīden, swīgen,* were originally weak, which accounts for their weak
forms. It will be seen also that the semivowels *h, w,* and a
vocalic stem, favor weak forms, but several verbs still remain
unaccounted for.

The verbs sometimes weak are distributed as follows :
I. a. 3; I. b. 1; I. c. 4; II. 12; III. 2; IV. 3 ; V. 12. Always
weak are 2 of IV., and 4 of V. In all, 37 sometimes, and 6
always, weak.

In NHG. the verbs which are weak in MHG. are either weak or
obsolete; but of those sometimes weak in MHG., 9 are obsolete;
9 are always weak (*schmerzen; kriegen, neiden; brauen, kauen;
walten, bauen, halsen, heischen*); 6 are strong and weak (*pflegen; ·fehlen; speien; laden, schaffen; hauen*); and the remain-
ing 13 are always strong; and yet NHG. has far more wholly and
partially weak verbs than MHG. The weakening must therefore have been guided by other motives than in MHG. Though
peculiar presents will account for a considerable number,
many seem to become weak for the lack of derivatives, that
by their various vowels might keep alive the consciousness of
the ablaut. As long as *binde, band,* and *bund* remain in common use as nouns, the verb *binden* will be strong, while *hinken*
with no such sustaining words may become weak.

Forty-six verbs are always weakened in NHG. They are:
*gäten, kneten, lechen; hehlen, quälen, schwären, zehren; bellen,
ferzen, hinken, schwelgen, schmerzen, winken, wirren; gleissen,
greinen, neigen, sweifen, kriegen, neiden; brauen, bläuen, kauen,
niesen, reuen, smiegen; lachen, nagen, schaben, waten; bannen,
falten, salzen, schalten, spalten, spannen, walken, walten, wal-
zen, blähen, sweifen, halsen, heischen; fluchen, bauen, schroten.*
I. a. 3; I. b. 4; I. c. 7; II. 6; III. 6; IV. 4; V. 16. In
all, 46.

Forty-two verbs are sometimes found with weak forms in
NHG., though they are originally strong. These are: *gären,
pflegen; rächen, löschen; bersten, derben, dingen, dreschen,
-fehlen, glimmen, klimmen, klingen, melken, quellen, schallen,
schnellen, schmelzen; bleichen, gleichen, gleiten, scheiden, schleifen, speien, spleissen, weichen, keifen, kneifen, kneipen; kiesen
(küren), sieden, riechen, saugen, schnauben, schrauben, triefen,
-trügen (-triegen); fragen, laden, mahlen, schaffen; braten;
hauen.* I. a. 2; I. b. 2; I. c. 13; II. 11; III. 8; IV. 4; V. 2.
In all, 42.

If we contrast these results with those in English, we find
that ME. has 51 sometimes, and 9 always, weak, against 37
sometimes, and 6 always, weak in MHG.; while NE. has 81
always weak, and 14 weak with strong participial adjectives,
against 45 always, and 42 sometimes, weak in NHG.

Section IV.— The Obsolete Verbs.

Only a few words need be added in regard to the verbs that have dropped by the wayside. There seems no other cause for their passing away than that they were not needed and grew unfamiliar, because they had no group of derivatives to rely upon for support. This could be shown in detail by an examination of the obsolete verbs as they appear in the lists in Section I. From these lists it appears that 15 OHG. verbs have disappeared in MHG. These are divided among the classes as follows: I. a. 2; I. c. 4; II. 4; III. 2; IV. 2; V. 1. Beside these 15, the NHG. loses 69 OHG. verbs and 28 of the MHG. additions, making in all 111, distributed as follows: I. a. 10; I. b. 10; I. c. 35; II. 26; III. 8; IV. 9; V. 13.

Here too, though NHG. has lost more than a third, the NE. is more surprising in its changes. Out of 309 verbs, NE. has lost 155, or more than half; while ME. has lost 67, more than four times as many as MHG.

The numerical results of the foregoing study may be summarized in the annexed table. The first column contains the total number of stems which occur during the period covered; the second, those which are found in OHG. The third contains the number of MHG. verbs, while in the following column may be seen the number of those that are not found in OHG. but occur first at the MHG. stage. The next column shows how many of the MHG. strong verbs are found also with weak forms, and the following column gives the number of the OHG. strong verbs which are always weak in MHG. The same arrangement is preserved in the NHG. division of the table.

CLASS	Total strong stems	OHG strong	MHG strong	MHG additions	MHG strong and weak	MHG weak	MHG absent	NHG strong	NHG additions	NHG strong and weak	NHG weak	NHG absent	CLASS
I. a.	30	28	28	2	3	0	2	17	0	2	3	10	I. a.
I. b.	26	21	26	5	1	0	0	22	0	2	4	10	I. b.
I. c.	87	73	82	13	4	0	5	45	1	13	7	35	I. c.
II.	72	51	64	17	12	0	8	40	4	1	6	26	II.
III.	43	38	40	4	2	0	3	29	1	8	6	8	III.
IV.	27	25	22	1	3	2	3	14	1	4	4	9	IV.
V. a, b, d.	34	31	31	3	6	3	0	11	0	1	13	10	V. a, b, d.
V. c. e.	10	10	8	0	6	1	1	4	0	1	3	3	V. c, e.
Total,	339	277	301	45	37	6	22	172	7	42	46	111	Total.

The following table summarizes the regular phonetic development of the ablaut. The first vowel is that of the present stem; the second is the vowel of the 1st and 3d person of the present singular; the third is the vowel of the 2d person singular and the plural of the present; the fourth is the vowel of the passive participle. The vowels placed in parentheses are modifications of those that precede, due to consonant influence. Where the NHG. ablaut has dropped one of the OHG. series, the gap is indicated by an *x*.

	OHG.	MHG.	NHG.			OHG.	MHG.	NHG.
I. a. 1st	e (i)	e (i)	e (i)	III. 1st		io (iu, ū)	ie (iu, ū)	ie (au, ü)
2d	a	a	a (o)	2d		ou (ō)	uo, (ō, o)	o
3d	ā	ā	*x*	3d		u	u (o)	*x*
4th	e	e	e (o)	4th		o	o	o
I. b. 1st	e	e	e (ä)	IV. 1st		a	a (e)	a (e)
2d	a	a	a (o)	2d, 3d . . .		uo	uo	u
3d	ā	ā	*x*	4th		a	a (o)	a (o)
4th	o	o	o	V. a, a, b. 1st, 4th		a, ā, ei	a, ā, ei	a, ei
I. c. 1st	e (i)	e (i)	e (i)	2d, 3d		ia (ea, ē)	ie (iu)	ie (i)
2d	a	a (u)	a (u)	V. c, e. 1st, 4th		uo, ō, ou	uo ō, ou	u, o, au
3d	u	u	*x*	2d, 3d		io (ia)	ie	ie
4th	o (u)	o (u)	o (u)					
II. 1st	i	i	ei					
2d	ei (ē)	ei (ē, i)	i (ie)					
3d	i	i	*x*					
4th	i	i	i (ie)					

VII. — *On Combination and Adaptation, as illustrated by the Exchanges of Primary and Secondary Suffixes.*

By W. D. WHITNEY,

PROFESSOR IN YALE COLLEGE.

ALL building-up of grammatical structure in language, all production of forms, or of words having a radical part and a formative part, is carried on by the joint means of combination and adaptation. The beginnings of human speech are roots, or elements possessing no grammatical character—not being one part of speech more than another, nor exhibiting any of those distinctions of office which we mark by inflectional and derivative endings ; and this absence of grammatical character is all that makes a root, in the view of the historian of language. No advance beyond the root-condition is, then, possible except by combination : unless, indeed, we are to regard formative endings as having sprouted out from roots ; and this involves a theory of language so grossly physical that it may be simply set aside as absurd by those who refuse such a theory. It is also flatly opposed to all observation of the growth of linguistic forms during the recorded periods of language-history. These show by abundant examples how a word originally independent can enter into combination with another word, and finally become a mere modifying element in the structure of the latter ; and they do not show that words win new elements of structure in any other way. It ought to be clearly seen and acknowledged, therefore, that those who reject this explanation of structural growth do it in virtue of denying the scientific principle that, in a continuous history of development, the earlier steps of development are to be explained by studying the later and observable steps, and reasoning back from these, with due caution and allowance for the difference of conditions, into the obscurer past. All real progress in linguistic science, however, seems plainly enough dependent on the acceptance of this principle and its rigorous application. If it be abandoned, one man's guess in matters of language is as good as another's, and the pet theories of one period may be succeeded by those of a following one, without any prospect of an end.

But while there can be no form-making without combina-tion and adaptation working together, their co-operation does not necessarily and always issue in forms. The combina-tions of roots may still be roots, modified or differentiated in meaning, increasing the vocabulary of a language, but not enriching its grammar, or giving it even the beginnings of a grammar, if it have had none before. In order to make a form, the process of combination must have a peculiar history. There must be a word of specially adaptable meaning, added to and combined with a whole body of other words, and im-pressing upon the latter an identical and apprehensible modi-fication of meaning ; then there is created the possibility that this common added element will retain its separateness while losing its independence, and so will assume the *status* of a formative affix, making a class of words or of inflectional forms to which it gives a common grammatical character. This is the plainly traceable process by which have been made in later times the most recent accessions to the stock of forma-tive elements, in languages of which we can follow the history: familiar and especially accesssible examples are our English *-ly* (adverb), the French *-ai* (future) and *-ment* (adverb), the Germanic *-d* (preterit), and so on. And our own languages offer abundant examples of processes of combination and adaptation that seem on the way to suffix-making, without actually reaching that end. No one would suspect the word *road* of any formative capabilities, in however many compound words it may be used — as *railroad, tramroad,* and so on ; the almost equivalent *way,* however, comes perceptibly nearer to a formative office, in *straightway, alway, lengthways,* etc., as does *wise* in *likewise, otherwise, crosswise, nowise,* etc. : either of these last might be said to have had antecedently a better chance of becoming an adverbial suffix than the adjective *like,* out of which our *ly* is actually made ; but the chances of linguistic history did not so bring it about. Moreover, out of the different combinations of the same element may be illustrated both the suffix-making and the non-suffix-making processes of combination. Our *like* is formative in words like *manly* and *friendly*, and in words like *truly* and *ably ;* but in *such* and *which* (from *so-like* and *who-like*) it is present without any formative value. So *pre* is an English formative, in such words as *pre-existence, prejudge, pre-adamitic,* and *con* in *conjoin, conjuror,* and the like ; but they have no shadow of formative force in *preach (pre-dicare), cost (con-stare), count (con-putare),* of which they are equally a part. Words like *such* and *which* and *preach* and *cost* are, in the proper sense of the term, radical in English speech, just as much as *this* and *mine* and *speak* and *love ;* for the fact that our historical knowledge chances to put it within our power to analyze the former set one stage further back, pointing out the last process of combination and fusion they have undergone, makes no essential difference ; no reasonable person will hold that the other set go back as roots to the ultimate period of human speech-history, or that they too are not the products of a combination, only of one that lies too far in the past for us to trace out. Many (perhaps even most) linguistic scholars appear to be under the impression that, when they have dissected out and demonstrated the roots of a given language, they have come to the foundation, and established something really original. But that is far enough from being the case. In all probability, there lies behind us in the history of language such an immeasurable unknown past, that between the roots of English and the Indo-European roots there is but a trifling difference in point of originality. In every language, new roots are constantly being wrought out or brought in, and invested with just that amount of formal variation (if any) which the language has at the moment at its disposal ; the new material is assimilated to the old ; and, after a time, no one can tell which is new and which is old.

Indistinct views upon such points as these lead to serious errors in regard to linguistic history. For example : a philologist of high rank and great achievements (Lepsius), some

years ago, recalled and urged attention to the fact, not unknown before, that evidence preserved in the literature and
dialects of Chinese proved the monosyllabic root-words (as they
had been generally viewed) of that language to have once had
a fuller phonetic form, showing plentiful signs of final consonants where now there are none, which final consonants might
perhaps be the relics of second syllables ; and he proceeded
at once to draw the inference that the Chinese is not a root-
language, that it has behind it a career of grammatical development, and that its words of one syllable are only worn-out
forms, like those, for example, of which the English is so
largely made up.   And these conclusions have been taken up
and pressed since by other scholars, some of whom have
even appeared to think that in them lay the final and irrecov-
erable overthrow of the root-theory of language. Yet nothing
can be plainer than that they find no sufficient support in the
facts on which they profess to be founded. To give them any
substantial value, it must be shown, first, that there are no
languages having final vowels or even second syllables to their
roots while yet destitute of grammatical structure ; or, secondly, that the Chinese finals have a demonstrable formative
value ; or, thirdly, that the grammatical character and use of
Chinese monosyllables is so closely analogous with that of
English monosyllables as to compel us to postulate behind the
former a formal development such as we know to have preceded the latter.   Those who comfortably accept and repeat
the Lepsian theory without concerning themselves about these
three difficulties that lie in its way, or trying to remove them,
cannot expect that their advocacy will count for much in its
favor.   Any real and seriously conducted argument to show
that the Chinese was not always so jejune as it now appears,
but once possessed a system, however scanty, of formally expressed grammatical distinctions, will be received with respect
and a hearty welcome by all who are interested in the history
of language ; I am not aware that any one has ever attempted
such an argument.   Of a language possessing in its roots
final consonants and second syllables in which no grammatical
value has been found traceable, we could not well have a more

striking and more dignified example than the ancient Egyptian, the language of the hieroglyphs; if nevertheless they are roots, why should the Chinese elements of similar phonetic constitution be assumed, in anticipation of any proof to that effect, to be grammatical forms? There are very fair phonetic reasons for holding the theory that all dissyllabic roots, or roots even with final consonants only, are and must be the result of combination; the theory may be some day raised to the value of an established principle; but it will then still remain to be determined in any particular case, by evidence, whether the combination was or was not of a grammatical nature.

Again, while adaptation is a necessary aid to combination in the process of form-making, since mere agglutination can never make forms, it is by no means limited to this department of action. On the contrary, it is an element of universal presence and efficiency in all language-history, in languages of every period and grade of development, and in every part and parcel of their material. Accompanying combination, it sometimes leads to the possession of forms; acting by itself, it sometimes provides means of another kind by which the purposes of forms are answered. The same element, meaning 'set' or 'make,' which in combination yields the *d* of *loved*, in independent adaptation becomes the *did* of *did love;* the same element, meaning 'seize' and 'possess,' which in combination becomes the *ai* of *monterai*, 'shall mount,' in independent adaptation takes the two very diverse offices instanced in *ai à monter*, 'have to mount,' and *ai monté*, 'have mounted.' The whole store of auxiliaries and form-words is won in no other way than this, whether used, as in our family of languages, to supplement the resources of formal expression, or, as in some other families, to supply their place. Grammatical classes of words are thus made, which may rise, and in fact not seldom do rise, to the value of "parts of speech." Thus certain demonstratives and numerals (either with the fortuitous aid of phonetic divarication of form, as in English, or without it, as in French and German) are turned into "articles"; thus interrogatives and demonstratives become "relatives"; thus adverbs either add or substitute the value of "prepositions"; thus "conjunctions" are made, out of materials of no small variety—and so on through a long catalogue. The same adaptation is seen in phrase-making, of every period, from what is obsolescently formal, like *come to pass*, down to colloquialisms and slang, like *knock under* and *give away;* it is seen in the elaboration of a moral and intellectual vocabulary out of the physical; it is seen in the whole refining process by which a language is made throughout capable of other, higher, and more varied uses. Its possibility rests on the fundamental character of language as a body of conventional signs, which can be indefinitely turned to new purposes by its users, and which must be so turned, if its users have any new purposes to serve. It is inseparable from the life of all language, and is the most pervading and intimate expression of that life. In a language without structure, like the Chinese, it gives the distinction of "full" and "empty" words (which is what in Chinese comes nearest to the distinctions of inflective speech), and it supplies the immense variety of meaning and application out of which the general make-up of the sentence allows the intended meaning in the given case to be selected by the quickly apprehending mind.

To imagine that, because adaptation thus performs an important part along with combination in developing the structure of an inflective language, and because in a structureless language it produces a sort of *succedaneum* for structure, it therefore is by itself capable of producing structure — so that, for example, the question can be raised whether "agglutination or adaptation" is the efficient principle in Indo-European development — is wholly wrong, and argues a most imperfect comprehension of the facts of language. Form-making by simple adaptation is an absurdity; adaptation can only assign the products of combination to new and further differentiated uses, even as it exercises this power over the radical elements themselves in such cases as that just referred to. It is easy to sketch the main features of its action to this effect in Indo-European language-history. The earliest probable example is the distinction of pronominal from so-called verbal roots; this appears to have been the result of a gradual attenuation and dissimilation of meaning, prior to all formal development, and analogous with the Chinese distinction of " empty " from " full " words. Of much later examples, one of especial importance is the gradual differentiation of the noun into noun-substantive and noun-adjective, or noun and adjective ; for their distinction has no formal foundation, and is posterior to the complete establishment of noun-inflection. Hence comes the "concord" of the adjective with its substantive ; this is no result of a specially delicate " sense of form " in Indo-European speakers — as, indeed, any such explanation of language-facts is mere sentimental fancy ; there is always something concrete and palpable at the base of them. Another example is the distinction of adverbs from case-forms (as explained by the author before the Association two years ago : see the Transactions for 1882). Others are the distinction of infinitives and participles from ordinary nouns and adjectives, and those already referred to above, of conjunctions, of articles, of relatives, and the like. When these are subtracted, there remains of the formal structure of the languages of our family only verb-inflection, noun-inflection, and the apparatus of stem-making suffixes. Original identities and gradual differentiations by usage are to be suspected here also, and even back to the very beginning, when predicative forms or verbs were first made. The difference even of noun and verb, the most fundamentally important in Indo-European grammar, may be a matter of differentiated use, in combinations of originally identical value : as in some languages of less developed structure, like Egyptian and Turkish, in one and the same combination, the pronominal ending is now possessive, conditioning a noun, and now subjective, making a verb. Nor is it at all improbable that the earliest suffixes of derivation and of inflection were the same thing, with two faces or aspects of value, little as we may be able to do in the way of proving it. Upon all such points, light is to be expected rather from the study of ruder tongues than from any perfecting of the processes of historical analysis as applied to our own tongues ; because, in the latter, original processes are too much covered up under later accretions.

When the roots of a language have once been clothed throughout with formative elements, or made into forms, no further provision of formative elements is possible except by additions to such forms — that is to say, all new endings will be of secondary character. Thus, for example, such a form as *monterai* can be made only by combining the auxiliary *ai* with the form *monter*, not with the root itself ; and here, throughout the whole formation, the infinitive *r* happens to remain, to betray the origin of the tense. A like thing is unquestionably true of the combination with *did* which makes *love-d*, though even in the earliest Germanic nothing is left to show clearly what the form was to which the auxiliary was added. But *monterai* has come to seem to the users of the language as direct a formation from the root *mont*, with added tense-sign and endings, as, for example, *montasse* — which, indeed, is in all probability by origin another case of the same kind, only so much older that the historical student of language can no longer trace its genesis with anything like the same confidence. When the secondary character of a combination is lost sight of, the combination becomes to all intents and purposes primary, and may be propagated as such. In this way, reduction to primary value becomes possible in formative, as well as in radical elements ; and the semblance of root and immediately added ending, both made out of material of later date, is kept up throughout the whole history of a language. Hence it appears that the distinction of primary and secondary suffixes, however well marked in the main, is after all of the same doubtful and changeable character, dependent on shifting usage, which belongs to grammatical distinctions in general, as abundantly instanced above. This point admits of interesting illustration by a series of secondary formations in Sanskrit, which have won the aspect of primary formations, and are so used in the later or classical Sanskrit.

The most prominent example is that of the gerundives, or future passive participles, corresponding in use quite closely with the Latin formation in *-ndus*. The native Hindu grammar, with its usual carelessness of historical accuracy, describes them as made directly from the root, with the suffixes *anīya*, *tavya*, and *ya*, and gives rules for the treatment of the root before them : thus, from root *kṛ*, 'do or make,' come *kar-aṇīya*, *kar-tavyà*, and *kār-yà*, all alike meaning 'faciendus.' But such forms as *karaṇīya* are entirely wanting in the oldest Sanskrit, that of the Rig-Veda; they begin to appear, but sparingly, in the second period, that of the Brāhmaṇas (there are two rather doubtful cases in the Atharva-Veda), and grow somewhat more common later, without ever attaining real frequency — although, taking the whole literature together, a respectable list of them can be quoted. And at the start they are palpably and undeniably a secondary formation from the extremely common *nomen actionis* in *ana*, with the added adjective suffix *īya*, making adjectives that signify general pertinence or concernment. Such is the value of no small part of them throughout ; and the line between the gerundival and the more ordinary adjective use is in other cases not always easy to draw. Beyond all question, *karaṇīya* is properly to be divided *karaṇ-īya*. The history of the gerundive in *tavyà* is nearly parallel with this : it is unknown in the Rig-Veda, begins with two examples in the Atharva-Veda, and then gains rapidly in frequency, becoming much more common than the formation in *anīya ;* it differs from this also in never having any other than a gerundival meaning. It is really made from the verbal noun in *tu* (the same from which comes also the ordinary infinitive in *tum*), by addition of the secondary suffix *ya*, before which the final *u* of *tu* is strengthened to *o* (*ău*), and this converted to *av*, as is usual with that final : compare the ordinary adjectives *hanavyà* from *hánu*, *madhavyà* from *mádhu*, *paçavyà* from *paçú*, and the like. The accent *tavyà* (all the examples accented *távya* in the Petersburg lexicons, larger and smaller, are errors) shows that the real form of the secondary suffix is *ta* ; and it is, in fact, in all probability originally identical with the *ī'ya* (or, as it appears in other formations, *íya*) which makes *karaṇī'ya* etc. In the Rig-Veda, which (as already noticed) lacks both these formations, their place is in good measure taken by similar secondary derivatives with simple *a* from the same *nomen actionis* in *tu* from which the words in *tavya* come : thus, *kártva*

(i. e. *kártu-a*, and, in fact, requiring so to be pronounced in Rig-Veda verse) = *kartavyà*, 'faciendus.'

The case of the gerundives in *ya* is not so clear, and I have treated it as doubtful in my Sanskrit Grammar; but I am more and more inclined to believe that, as this suffix is palpably secondary in character in the great body of words made by it, so it is also in the rest; and that even where it has most of a primary aspect, this is only illusive. To classify and discuss here its diversified uses is unnecessary; the other examples are enough to establish the point desired to be made: that the gerundive formation in Sanskrit is in the main, if not wholly, a secondary one, and of comparatively recent development. In the later or classical language, however, these endings of compound and secondary origin are treated as primary; and derivatives with *anīya* and *tavya*[1] are made directly from the root, as much as those in *ya*, which have a less demonstrably secondary character, or as those in *ana* and *tu*, which perhaps are after all equally secondary, could we only trace out their history a little further.

Another notable example is that of the suffix *in*. This is, through the whole history of the Sanskrit language, one of the commonest secondary adjective suffixes, signifying possession: thus, *bala*, 'strength,' *balin*, 'possessing strength, strong'; *pucha*, 'tail,' *puchin*, 'having a tail, tailed.' Like several other conspicuous suffixes, and like the great class of possessive compounds, it has won this particular meaning doubtless by specialization from the more general sense of appurtenance. But there is also a considerable class of words made with it, and that even from the earliest period, which are reckoned as primary, and have that aspect, being the grammatical equivalents of present participles, and governing participially an accusative: e. g. *kāmin*, 'loving,' *kānkṣin*, 'desiring,' *abhibhāṣin*, 'addressing,' *satya-vādin*, 'truth-speaking.' But it is entirely evident that the suffix is the same in both uses, and that *kāmin*, for example, really means 'having love,'

---

[1] Of course it follows that Sanskrit derivatives in *tavya* are not to be compared with Greek verbals in τεος, as if they were an Indo-European formation — unless, indeed, a like development can be demonstrated for the words in τεος.

being made from *kāma*, 'love'; that it admits a participial construction is in accordance with numerous facts in the Sanskrit language, where the distinction between ordinary adjectives and verbal adjectives or participles is much less marked than in most of its kindred, and words of the former class are constantly stepping over into the other. The derivatives *kāmin* and *vādin* and their like can be made, artificially, to come directly from the roots *kam* and *vad*, with suffix *in* and second-grade strengthening of the radical vowel; and in later Sanskrit they are actually so made, because to the users of the language they seem so; the suffix has won a primary value and application; but there are numerous instances in the older language to which that explanation will not apply: for example, *vighanin*, 'slaying,' which can come from the root *han* only through the derivative noun *ghana*; and *garbhin*, ' pregnant with' (also governing an accusative), from *garbha*, ' foetus.'

Again, a well-defined and much-used *nomen agentis* in later Sanskrit is made with the suffix *aka*: thus, *kār-aka*, 'a doer or maker,' from the same root *kṛ*, ' make,' which has been used in illustration above; it, too, occasionally has an accusative object, like a participle: for example, *mithilām avarodhakas*, 'besieging Mithilā.' But here, again, the formation is altogether wanting in the older language; and as it makes its appearance, one sees clearly that it is produced by adding the general (secondary) adjective-suffix *ka* to a derivative noun in *a*: that is to say, *kāraka* is not *kār-aka*, but *kāra-ka*, 'concerned with making'; and *avarodhaka* is *avarodha-ka*, 'concerned with siege.' [1]

Another case quite analogous with the last is presented by the nearly equivalent suffix *uka*. This is, however, peculiar in regard to its range in the history of the language. Wanting in the earliest period (there is a single example of it in the Atharva-Veda), it is also quite rare in the later language, while it is a frequent and characteristic formation of the in-

---

[1] Hence is seen the worthlessness of Müller's explanation of the Germanic word *king* etc. as the correspondent of Sanskrit *jan-aka*, 'father': as if *aka*, which is not even so old as early Sanskrit, could be dealt with as an Indo-European suffix! The anachronism it involves is so palpable, that the etymology can only be called a blunder.

termediate or Brāhmaṇa literature, being made from over
sixty roots there, and not at all infrequent of occurrence, with
the value of a present participle. That it is, however, of secondary and compound structure, is not to be questioned ; it
comes by addition of *ka* (the same as seen in *aka*) to a derivative in *u*. Adjectives in *u*, with the same participial value,
are made in Sanskrit in considerable numbers ; but, by a peculiar limitation of use, they come in the main from secondary
conjugation-stems, especially desiderative ; whereas the words
in *uka* are made from the base of primary conjugation, and
those in *u* from which they are made can only in a few instances be pointed out in independent use.

Other examples of the same kind could be brought forward,
yet less clear and instructive than these — which, then, may
suffice for their purpose. They show that the analysis of suffixes into simpler elements, in which comparative philologists
often indulge, has a historical basis and justification ; they
show, also, in what way compound suffixes are made : by the
addition, namely, of one suffix to a form already ending in
another, and then the fusion of the two into one.

Since the general tendency in language is toward fusion
and the disguise and loss of original value, it is much easier
to illustrate the conversion of secondary suffixes into primary
than that of primary into secondary. Yet there are instances
of the latter conversion also, more or less completely carried
out. In Sanskrit, the suffixes *īyas* and *iṣṭha* make directly
from roots comparative and superlative adjectives which have
in general no connection except that of association of meaning with any positives ; and the agreement in this respect
with the corresponding Greek ιων and ιστος shows that the
restriction was a pre-historic one. Yet, as the one of these
has become in Latin the ordinary comparative ending, making
secondary derivatives from adjectives of every kind, so there
are beginnings of such use in Sanskrit also — which might
have ended in the same way, if another pair of equivalent
endings, *tara* and *tama*, had not by their growing popularity
crowded the *īyas* and *iṣṭha* quite out of use as means of making new words.

Another case is that of the suffix *ta*, forming past or passive participles through the whole history of Indo-European language; in later Sanskrit it may be added as secondary suffix to almost any noun or adjective, making derivatives meaning 'possessed of, affected by,' and the like: thus, *gharmita*, 'heated' (*gharma*, 'warmth'); *durbalita*, 'weakened' (*durbala*, 'of little strength'), etc. This use is precisely analogous to that of our own participial suffix *ed* in such words as *blear-eyed, four-sided, three-tined;* and it has plainly come, in the one case as in the other, through the medium of a much used denominative-verb formation, especially common in its participles, which then have made it seem that any noun-stem may be turned into participial form, whether there be or be not a denominative verb made from that particular stem. But the suggestion of a possible denominative formation lies so near that the conversion to secondary value can hardly be regarded as complete. Such examples merely help to show the uncertain and shifting nature of the distinction between primary and secondary suffixes, as of so many other of the grammatical distinctions of language, all growing together out of the nature of the material of which language itself is composed, as arbitrary and conventional sign-material, ever convertible to new purposes under the exigencies and in obedience to the suggestions of practical use. This is an instance of minor consequence, but it illustrates a truth of widest and deepest significance in the history of human speech.

VIII. — *On Latin Glossaries, with especial reference to the Codex Sangallensis 912.*

By MINTON WARREN,

ASSOCIATE PROFESSOR IN THE JOHNS HOPKINS UNIVERSITY.

DURING the past ten years there has been a marked increase of attention paid in Germany and elsewhere to the problems of Latin lexicography. In this connection the old Latin glossaries have assumed a fresh importance, as containing a mine of new and old words not yet sufficiently explored. This renewed interest is largely due to the efforts of the late Dr. Gustav Loewe, who published in 1876 his masterly Prodromus Corporis Glossariorum Latinorum, and up to the time of his death was diligently engaged in collecting materials for a grand corpus. . These collections have now passed into the hands of Loewe's colleague, Prof. Georg Goetz of Jena; and the Königliche Sächsische Gesellschaft der Wissenschaften is to furnish the means for the further prosecution of the undertaking.

One of the most remarkable features in the history of Roman literature is the surprising activity with which grammatical studies were carried on in the last century of the republic and the first two centuries of the empire. When Verrius Flaccus composed his work, De Verborum Significatu, he must already have had a large stock of material to draw from, and his alphabetical lexicon doubtless resembled in its fulness an encyclopædia rather than a common dictionary. Upon this work later writers drew when they wished to make a show of learning. Nettleship [1] has shown the dependence of Aulus Gellius, Nonius Marcellus, Macrobius, and Servius upon Verrius, and has done much to indicate the lines upon which a partial reconstruction of the work of Verrius must proceed. The relation of the Placidus glosses to Verrius has been pointed out by Loewe; and they have been well edited by Deuerling,[2] although

[1] Cf. American Journal of Philology, Vol. II. pp. 253–270, Vol. III. pp. 1–17, 170–192.

[2] Luctatii Placidi Grammatici Glossae, rec. et illust. A. Deuerling, Leipsic, 1875, and Glossae quae Placido non adscribuntur nisi in Libro Glossarum, A. Deuerling, Munich, 1876.

many still remain to be reclaimed from the older glossaries. Loewe shows that where Paulus in his epitome of Festus gives only the nominative of a substantive, or the first person singular of a verb, Placidus often gives the exact form used ; so that, in the collection of the fragments of early authors, much more weight must be attached to the testimony of Placidus than has been the case hitherto. E. g. Varro L. L., V. 153 says, "In circo *carceres* unde emittuntur equi, nunc dicuntur *carceres*. Naevius *oppidum* appellat." Placidus p. 57 gives *iuxta oppidum : prope carceres*. Hence we may be almost certain that Naevius wrote *iuxta oppidum*. So where Paulus 89 says that Cato used *futare* in the sense of *saepius fuisse*, Placidus has 44 and 45 *futavit : fuit, futavere : fuere*, which definite forms may doubtless be referred to Cato.[1] So nearly all glossaries compiled from different sources contain oblique cases of substantives, or verb-forms not in the first pers. sing. of the present indicative or in the present infinitive, which we may be certain actually occurred ; and although we may not be able to assign them to any definite author, they have their value for the study of forms.

For example, Georges cites for the use of *abstare* Horace, Ars P. 362 (*abstes*) and Plaut. Trin. 264 (*abstandus*). Loewe, Glossae Nominum, p. 204, cites glosses containing the forms *abstat, apstant*, and *absto*. To these must be added from the Sangallensis 912 *abstans : distans* A 44. Vergil, Æn. IV. 606, uses the form *extinxem*. So we find E. 255 *extixe : extincsisse*, which would prove the existence of the form *extinxe*, unless indeed we suppose that the gloss originally referred to the Vergilian passage, and that the final *m*, as frequently, has been lost.

Nearly every large library in Europe has its old Latin glossaries. They range in date from the seventh century down to the fourteenth and fifteenth. The Bibliothèque Nationale in Paris is especially rich in manuscripts of this sort, many of which I have examined. In the Vatican, at Leyden, Munich, Milan, St. Gall, Berne, Vienna, and elsewhere are found valuable glossaries, most of which have never been edited, although in some cases large excerpts have been made. The character of the results which may be expected from a careful editing of the more important of these glossaries I hope to illustrate by some remarks upon the Codex Sangallensis 912, which I afterwards print in full. Of this codex Loewe, Prodromus, p. 139, says : "Cum codicibus Vaticano (3320, saec. IX.) Vindobonensique (2404) consentit etiam codicis Sangallensis 912 praecipua glossa-

---

[1] Cf. Loewe, Glossae Nominum, p. 95 ff.

rum materia. Sangallensis praeter Vaticanum 3321 omnium codicum quotquot hac usque noti sunt vetustissimus." It belongs to
the latter part of the seventh or the beginning of the eighth century. In form duodecimo it contains three hundred and twenty
pages (of which pp. 1–3, 159, 160, 196, 230 are left blank), with an
average of about sixteen glosses to the page. Altogether it has
about five thousand one hundred and fifty glosses, of which the
largest number for any one letter (six hundred and twenty-two) fall
to C, while P has five hundred and twenty-six and S four hundred
and fifty-seven. Most of the words are Latin. Not a few Hebrew words and proper names, however, occur, due to ecclesiastical
sources ; and there are numerous Greek words in Latin transliteration. Singularly enough, one Gothic word is found. B 38 *baltha :
audax. Gothice* is written on the margin. The glossary begins with
abba : pater, and closes with *Zipherus : ventus* EXPL. ERMENEU-
MATA DŌ GRATIAS AMEN.

The orthography of the Codex deserves our careful consideration ; for it throws light upon the pronunciation and phonetic
changes of a comparatively late period, and has a value for the
student of the Romance languages.

Moreover, a conspectus of the bad spellings which are common
is often helpful for the emendation of difficult glosses. There is,
of course, danger of referring to a phonetic cause mistakes which
are purely palæographical in their origin, as the confusion of *c* and *t,*
of *c* and *g,* of *s* and *r,* of *a* and *u,* etc., due to a resemblance in the
form of the letters ; but where a bad spelling is constant or frequently repeated, it usually has a phonetic significance. I can only
give here comparatively few instances under each head ; but the
examples given by Schuchardt in his Vokalismus des Vulgär-
lateins might be largely increased from this codex.

CONSONANTS.

d for *t,* very frequent : [1] *aboditur* A 40, *abscondida* 58,[2] *amicidia* 62,
padior 173, *nodrix* 267, *appedit* 320, *pudridum* C 195, *consuedudo* 553,
penades P 212, *odiosi* R 96, *scadit* S 60, *solidudo* 291, *todidem* T 164,
aequides 178.

t for *d,*[3] much less frequent : *innotata* A 122, *multituto* 189, *stopite*

---

[1] Cf. Schuchardt, I. 124 ; Seelmann, Die Aussprache des Latein, 309.

[2] Where no letter is added, the word occurs under the same letter as the
word preceding.

[3] Cf. Schuchardt, II. 257 ; Seelmann, 309.

B 53, *canditi* 60, *bipetalis* 118, *complutere* C 430, *metriatrix* I 360, *Atri-atici* L 102, *splenditum* 139, *sorditum* 175, *sorditus* O 43, *palutamenta* P 30, *cupitidas* S 3.

g for *c*:[1] *agonita* A 203, *praefugat = praefocat* 283, *simulagra* 347, *belligusa* B 73, *belligare = vellicare* D 84, *verrugas* M 96, *mulgatores* 143, *negromantia* N 54, *pupligatum* P 438, *progatia* 439, *trages* T 32, *truges* 208. One of the earliest examples of this change of surd to sonant, which was persistent, is furnished by *negotium;* so, too, *neglegens.* The prox-imity of *l* or *r* favors it; as G. 71 *gremia* for *cremia*, although Mommsen, Ulp. dig. 32, 55, 4, retains *gremia.* Compare also *sagrarium* B 9 (cf. It. *sagramento*). Interesting is *grotalus* O 121 (cf. It. *agrotto*, Sp. *ocroto*, both derived from *onocrotalus* by G. Baist, Romanische Forschungen, I. 445).

c for *g.* These cases are to be received with caution, as it is often diffi-cult to decide whether the Ms. has *c* or *g.* *G* being differentiated from *c* only by a slight stroke, some of these cases may be due to the carelessness of scribes. It is probable, however, that as *c* was often pronounced *g*, so *c* was often written for *g*, but pronounced *g* ("Umgekehrte Schreib-weise"). Schuchardt, 1I. 413, says, "Die Verwandlung des *g* in *c* ist zwischen Vokalen unmöglich." *abiucassere* A 16, *abgreco* 50, *agacula* 192, *navicio* 220, *antaconista* 279, *locobris* 397, *clanco* C 148, *coaculatum* 467, *elivicata* E 46, *prodicus* P 442, *repacula* R 91, *propaco* S 265, *tecula* T 28.

b for *p*:[2] *aborreas* A 27, *abricum* 67, *crebindia* C 263, *crebido* 265, *scabum* S 64, *obtima* 217.

p for *b*,[3] infrequent : *puplica* A 444, *pupligatum* P 438, *puplice* 467. Cf. *Puplicus* in inscriptions, *opproprium* O 149, *vipurna* V 105.

b for *v*.[4] The vulgar confusion of *b* and *v*, from the second century on, is well known. Examples very numerous. *Ababus* A 2, *abita = avida* A 24, *flubius* 80, *bispillus* B 106, *bobinatores* 130, *obserba* C 122, *silbas* 222, *fabor* F 1, *serbus* M 42, *prelibabimus* P 129, *quibi* Q 30.

v for *b* : *duvium* A 61, *acevitas = acerbitas* 73, *duvitanti* 218, *caval-lares* 253, *sivi* 269, *vaccae* B 43, *cavallus* C 7, *cavallarius* P 356, *biven-dum* S 191, *lividinantes* 362.

ti for *ci*:[5] *dilitias* A 133, *apitiosus* 301, *sotius* C 369, 382, 431, 544, *commertio* 394, *sotietate* 427, *caltiamentum* 589, *untias* D 242, *homuntio* H 133, *mendatium* I 212, *sautio* M 179, *fallatia* P 118, *audatia* 439, *sautius* S 52.

ci for *ti* : *precium*, O 127.

c dropped before *t*:[6] *autionarius* A 433, *autio* 444, *contratus* C

---

[1] Cf. Corssen, I. 77 ; Schuchardt, I. 124 ff.; Seelmann, 346.
[2] Cf. Schuchardt, I. 124, 127, 144 ff.; Seelmann, 299.
[3] Cf. Seelmann, 299.
[4] Cf. Schuchardt, I. 131 ; Seelmann, 239 f.
[5] Cf. Seelmann, 323.
[6] Cf. Seelmann, 278, 348.

542, *defunturium* D 119, *funtio* F 240, *iunturi* R 148, *coniuntum* S 38.

n dropped before *t :*[1] *cantates* A 163, *ardetes* 353, *hydromates* H 66, *laterna*[2] L 18, *fulgetes* 27.

n dropped before *d :*[3] *compedium* C 545.

Perhaps in D 68 *depenendi : reddendi, n* is for *nn = nd dependendi.* Compare *dispennite distennite,* Plaut. Mil. 1407.[4]

ss for *ns* : *condessat* A 84.

ns for *ss : consensus* C 133, *defensus* D 83.

n inserted before *s :*[5] *pertensum* P 300.

n dropped before final *s :*[6] *freques* C 198, S 91, 98, *flagras* F 82, *ingeminas* I 227, *obnites* O 56, *loques* 166.

s for final *x : arupes* A 348, *senes* D 6, G 65, *mermis* M 76.

s for *sc :*[7] *resiscere* R 103.

Dropping of final *m*, frequent : *aliena* A 14, *lege* 58, *aliena terra* 102, *arcu* F 198, *ad ira* P 486, *pala* V 159.

Dropping of final *t: aberunca* A 9, *tolle =: tollit* 14, *demitti* M 105, *peiera* P 199. So often in verb-forms.

H is very frequently omitted or falsely added : *abitudo* A 15, *actenus* 81, *achademia* 86.

f for *ph* is very frequent. Cf. F 23, 58, 65, etc.

l for *d* is found in *apoliterium* A 317.[8]

g for *i = j* in *degerat*[9] D 150.

g dropped between vowels [10] in *frius* H 113. Cf. *panorum* for *paganorum* P 55.

Worthy of mention is G 53 *gneumon : dicitur pulmo,* which may be accounted for in this way. The scribe found *neumon* for *pneumon,* just as in Pliny, N. H. XIX. 60, certain Mss. have *neumaticis.* Having a consciousness of some silent letter, he prefixed *g,* after the analogy of *gnatus, gnavus, gnosco,* and *gnomon.* Compare the " Umgekehrte Schreibung," cited by Schuchardt, I. 144, *pturmae* for *turmae,* from an inscription of about 200 A. D.

VOWELS.

o for *ū :*[11] *aboditur* A 40, *nodrix* 267, *degostat* D 156, *fotiles* F 187, *gostata* H 9.

o for *ŭ,* very frequent:[12] *colmine* (cf. *columen*) A 103, *intolit* 108, *oc-*

---

[1] Cf. Seelmann, 283.
[2] Cf. Saalfeld, Tensaurus Italograecus for *lanterna.*
[3] Cf. Seelmann, 283.
[4] Cf. Seelmann, 312.
[5] Cf. Seelmann, 285; Corssen, I. 255.
[6] Cf. Seelmann, 284.
[7] Cf. Schuchardt, I. 145; III. 75.
[8] Cf. Seelmann, 310.
[9] Cf. Schuchardt, I. 72.
[10] Cf. Seelmann, 349.
[11] Cf. Schuchardt, II. 181 ff.
[12] Cf. Seelmann, 216; Schuchardt, II. 149 ff.

corro 114, *aemolo* 134, *locrum* 140, *aercolus* 162, *volocres* 228, *stopite* B 53, *copidus* 75, *oxore* C 206, *foturum* F 189, *iovenalis* I 178, *doplans* 227, *orbanitas* S 15, *simolat* 207, *sporca* 319.[1]

u for *ō* :[2] *furmula* D 297, *cupiosus* F 102, *ferux* 113, *futa* 172, *verbusitas* G 11, *custudia* 13, *nubeli* 69, *murio* H 35, *fluritum* 112, *pucula* I 369, *immubilis* O 53, *cognuscere* R 103, *suspis* S 442, *lurica* T 169.

u for *ŏ* :[3] *accula* A 102, *cognitur* C 574, *curtina* 596, *superinspectur* E 106, *interpulavit* I 342, *balneatur* M 78, 79. So frequently nouns in *-tor*, which Schuchardt claims had *ō* " vulgärlateinisch." *obturpuit* O 49, *pulluta* P 427.

i for *ē* : *acidia* A 91, *vinditio vindunt* 429. (Schuchardt[4] compares wal. *vinde*, sizil. *vinniri*) *bisteis* B 69 (cf. It. *biscia*), *biluae* 99, and P 239, *delivit* D 108, *disperatus* 183, *disidem* 185, *fistinanter* P 135, *filicitas* 494, *criscet* 364, *signities* S 193, *signes* 196.

i for *ĕ* :[5] *inergumina* I 169,[6] *innomirum, innomirabilem* 282, *numirus* M 20, *nimpe* N 92, *quatinus* Q 2, Cf. Festus 258, *quatenus significat qua fine, at quatinus quoniam.*

e for *ī* :[7] *fermandi* Q 43 (cf. Fr. *fermer*) *ceccum* C 217. Gröber, Archiv für Lat. Lex., I. 545, shows that Span. *chico,* Fr. *chiche,* It. *cica,* prove the *i* to be long.

e for *ĭ* :[8] *proicet* A 13, *tollet* 25, *abluet* 51, and so frequently in the 3d pers. sing.: *addedit* 108, *adepiscitur* 110, *semile* 144, *vectimae* 198, *vicessim* 216, *aletus* 237, *engens* B 122 (cf. Fr. *engen* < *ingenium*), *minester* C 40, P 43, S 53, *spessavit* C 266 (cf. It. *spesso*) *sinester* S 114, *pegritia* 198.

Prosthetic *i*[9] is seen in I 407 *istromates* and 416 *istromatheas* = *stromateus.* I inserted L 133 *linchine*[10] = *lychni.*

Examples of *ae* for *e,* and *e* or *ę* for *ae* will be found on every page.

a for *au* :[11] *agusta, agustum, agustorum, agustius* A 184–187, *actius* A 96, *cadices* C 119, *ladis* F 1, *lade* H 63. Cf *latomus* L 61, and Saalfeld, Tensaurus *lautumiae.* Perhaps *caudalocus* = *catalogus* C 62 may be regarded as an instance of "Umgekehrte Schreibung."

Other phonetic peculiarities will be touched upon in the notes. I will only mention here as deserving attention, if my reading is correct, a single case of *ie* for *ĕ* for *ĭ* :[12] *biviera* for *bivira* B 101. In Plautus Mss. *veri* and

---

[1] Cf. Schuchardt, II. 355; Isid. Or. XII. 1, 25: "*porcus* quasi *spurcus* (Var. *sporcus*).

[2] Cf. Seelmann, 214; Schuchardt, II. 91 ff.

[3] Cf. Seelmann, 211 f.; Schuchardt, II. 101.

[4] Cf. Schuchardt, I. 343 f.; Seelmann, 189 f.

[5] Cf. Seelmann, 183, 186.   [6] Cf. Schuchardt, III. 140.

[7] Cf. Seelmann, 191.   [8] Cf. Seelmann, 200.

[9] Cf. Seelmann, 317.

[10] Cf. Schuchardt, II. 410, and Saalfeld, Tensaurus.

[11] Cf. Schuchardt, II. 306–320; Seelmann, 223.

[12] Cf. Schuchardt, II. 332 f.

vero are frequently found for *viri* and *viro* (cf. Loewe, Prod., p. 75).
Compare Fr. *fier, miel, fiel,* from *ferum, mel, fel.*

To inspire respect for the miscellaneous contents of these glossaries, it is only necessary to show that many of the unusual words
and forms found in them go back to the most excellent sources.
This I shall endeavor to do by a few illustrations taken from the
Sangallensis.

nis : nobis N 86. Neither Loewe nor De Vit in his Glossarium cites
this gloss, although doubtless it will be found in other glossaries. The
only other evidence for the existence of a form *nis* is a remark of Paulus
under the world *calim* 47, " Antiqui dicebant pro *clam,* ut *nis* pro *nobis,
sam* pro *suam, im* pro *eum.*"

anxati : vocati nominati A 276. Compare with this Paulus 8, *axare :
nominare. Axare* seems to be required by *axamenta* Paulus 3, and the
derivation from the root seen in *negare, adagium.* But, as Mueller
remarks, the alphabetical order seems to require *anxare,* standing, as it
does, between *antarium* and *antipagmenta.* See also Gloss. Labb. *anax-
ant :* ὀνομάζουσιν. De Vit gives a gloss *anxiati : nominatim vocati.*

exanclare : exaurire E 287. Compare Paulus 80, *exanclare : exhaurire.* Placidus 38, *exanclare, exhaurire, a Graeco veniens, quod quidem
verbum Plautus, saecularis poeta comicus posuit in Sticho :* " ne iste ede-
pol vinum poculo pauxillulo saepe exanclavit."

*oppidanus : civis ex oppida nam oppidaneus Latinum est, apud anti-
quos oppida dicta sunt quod opem dare* (*nt*) O 131. Paulus 203, *oppidum
dictum est quod opem praebet.* The *dare,* however, is as much a part of
the etymology as *opem;* and so Festus 202, quoting from Cicero de Gloria,
has " quod *opem darent.*" This is lost in the *praebet* of Paulus. Other
explanations are given by Varro, L. L., V. 32, and Servius ad Æn. IX. 608.

remilus : repando R 73. Compare Paulus 276, *remillum dicitur quasi
repandum.*

sarissa : genus tèli Macidonici S 36. Festus 318, *Sarissa est hastae
Macedonicae genus.*

sucerda : stercus uvile S 378. Paulus 303, *Sucerda stercus suillum,*
etc. To make sense, *uvile* should be emended to *suillum* (*suile* ?) An
easier emendation, however, is *ovile* (*u* for *o,* cf. *opilio* and *upilio*). And
as, according to the conjecture of Mueller .Festus 302, Verrius Flaccus
must have treated of *ovicerda = stercus ovile* in the same connection,
ovile may have arisen from some confusion of two glosses.

tagax : forunculus T 3. Festus 359 *Tagax furunculus ā tangendo
cuius vocabuli Lucilius meminit* " et mutonis manum perscribere posse
tagem." (*tagacem* Paulus). Goetz Rheinisches Museum Bd. XL. p. 327
cites from Vaticanus (1469) "*tagax : fugax*" where *furax* is to be written. Cf. Loewe Prod. p. 317.

nusciosus : qui plus vepere videt N 133, is a corrupt remnant of what is found in Paulus 171. *Nusciciosus, qui parum videt propter vitium oculorum, quique plus videt vesperi, quam meridie.* From the fuller statement of Festus 173, we learn that Aelius Stilo explained the word thus, *qui plus videret vesperi, quam meridie, nec cognosceret, nisi quod usque ad oculos admovisset.* Cf. Loewe Prod. pp. 17 and 121.

lixa: aqua dicebant antiqui unde elixare dicitur L 148. Compare Nonius Marcellus p. 62, *lixam namque aquam veteres vocaverunt, unde elixum dicimus aqua coctum;* and p. 48, *elixum quicquid ex aqua mollitur vel decoquitur nam lixem aquam veteres dixerunt.* In the latter passage Quicherat reads *lixem* with the Mss., but in the former against the Mss. corrects *lixam* to *lixem.* The evidence of the glossaries, as Loewe points out (Prod. p. 404), would rather favor the correction of *lixem* to *lixam.* The gloss, while not derived from Nonius directly, may go back to the same source.

alcitellus: alte evocatus A 256, *altellus: terra nutritus* 258 (not *terrae*, as Loewe reads Prod. p. 12, where other forms of this gloss are given). *Altellus* as a surname of Romulus is known to us only from Paulus 7. Whether the form *alcitellus* is anything more than a corruption, it would be difficult to say. It has some support in *acitella*, Frag. Vindob. 2404 (Loewe l. c.).

exaustant: exauriunt E 234, confirms Paulus 82, *exhaustant: efferunt.* Although the lexica furnish no example of this verb, we may be sure that this exact form occurred.

taura: sterelis T 17, is an example of a gloss reduced to its lowest terms. Compare Paulus 353. *Tauras vaccas steriles dici existimatur hac de causa, quod non magis pariant quam tauri,* see also Festus 352.

aeneatores: corno vel calamo cantates A 163, contains, with slight emendation, the same information as Paulus 20, *aeneatores: cornicines dicuntur, id est cornu canentes.*

ceccum: cortex maligranati C 217. Paulus 42, *Ciccum membrana tenuis malorum punicorum.* For a full discussion of this gloss see Loewe Prod. p. 274.

bibinare: inquinare sanguine muliebri minstruum B 154. The alphabetic order requires *bubinare.* Paulus 32, *Bubinare est menstruo mulierum sanguine inquinari.* Lucilius: "Haec" inquit "te imbubinat, at contra te imbulbitat." Placidus p. 13, *bibinare, sanguine inquinare. Inquinare* should be read in Paulus, cf. Loewe Prod. pp. 250 and 313 f.

campae: equi marini C 17. Paulus 44, *Cappas marinos equos Graeci a flexu posteriorum partium appellant.* If we compare *Hippocampi, equi marini, a flexu caudarum, quae piscosae sunt,* Nonius p. 120, we can hardly doubt that *campas* should be read for *cappas.*

carisa: faba C 69. Paulus 44, *Carissam apud Lucilium vafram significat.* Hence for *faba* we must read *vafra.* According to Loewe Glossae Nominum, p. 150, Codex Casinensis 439[5] has *carissa: paba.* For fuller glosses of this word see Prod. p. 304.

For other glosses which go back to equally good ancient sources, see the notes on *abellum* A 11, *acerlis* 82, *alux* 224, *arceria* 361, *bispillus* B 106, *boa* 121, *camuribus* C 22, *cannar* 116 and 44, *ceritus* 234, *cocula* 341, *compernens* 402, *gentiunt* G 49, *hostit* H 124, *hostimentum* 128, *intercapito* I 352, *investis* 384, *macilentus* M 30, *mapalia* 33, *metacastor* 80, *lapite* L 60, *opniparum* O 154, *saccella* S 12, *taxat* T 7, *trabica* 23, *transtres* 24, *tragula* 27, *tesqua* 88, *tybicines* 112, *vola* V 146.

Sometimes it is possible to refer a word glossed with more or less probability to a definite author.

Thus A 287 and 288, *anfracta : intertortuosa, anfracta : et difficilia* undoubtedly refer to a passage quoted by Varro, L. L. VII. 15, and after him more fully by Nonius, p. 192, from the Eurysaces of Attius, —

> *Super Óceani stagna álta patris*
> *Terrárum anfracta revísam.*

Varro's explanation is somewhat different, *anfractum est flexum, ab origine duplici dictum, ab ambitu et frangendo.*

A 157, *aetatula : aetate modica*, shows that the gloss refers to some passage where the word occurred in the ablative. Such a passage is quoted by Aulus Gellius II. 23, 10, from Caecilius, *Quis vestrarum fuit integra aetatula ?*

C 93, *caliotur : fallit*, corrupt for *calvitur*, which may go back to the Laws of the XII. Tables. "Si calvitur pedemve struit manum endoiacito," quoted by Festus 313. Placidus, p. 25, has *Calvitur, frustratur. decipit*, which more resembles the explanation of Nonius, p. 6. *Calvitur dictum est frustratur; tractum a calvis mimicis, quod sint omnibus frustratui.* Plautus in Casina (II. 2, 3)

> Nam ubi domi sola sum
> Sopor manus calvitur.

It is better, therefore, to refer the gloss to this passage. It is worthy of notice that Servius ad Æn. I. 720, explains *calvio* by *fallo*, "Alii *calvam*, quod corda amantum *calviat* id est *fallat* atque eludat." For other glosses see Prod. p. 366.

C 316, *circumfundimur : circumdamur.* No one can doubt that the reference here is to Verg. Æn. II. 383, —

> Inruimus, densis et circumfundimur armis.

A 380, *ast ego : ego autem* probably refers to Æn. I. 46, —

> Ast ego, quae divom incedo regina, Iovisque (cf. VII. 308),

in commenting on which Servius compares Sallust's use of *vos autem.*

A 220, *allabi : navigio duci* refers, I think, to Æn. III. 131, —

> Et tandem antiquis Curetum adlabimur oris.

The form *adlabi* occurs Æn. X. 269.

A 248, *allavitur: leviter decurit* may refer to Æn. X. 292, —

> Sed mare inoffensum crescenti adlabitur aestu.

C 382, *compotrix: sotia ad bibendum,* may refer to Terence, And. 232,

> Quia compotrix eius est. di, date facultatem obsecro.

A 244, *aliorsum : altera in parte* may refer to Ter. Eun. I. 2, 2, where Donatus explains it *in aliam partem.* In a Terence glossary found in Cod. Vaticanus 1471, recently edited by Goetz, occurs *aliorsum : aliter dicit.*

Many other cases of this sort will be found in the notes. I will only call attention to *bobinatores* B 130, *bucones* 153, *catax* C 34, *cassibus* 52, *carinantes* 114, *calcitrones* 135, *conbibiones* 543, *consuetio* 553, *discerniculum* D 227, *libare* L 99, *perpexa* P 307, *persolla* 310, *senta* S 106, *serpit* 150, *semicem* 157, *subtemine* 353, *suffecet* 398, *tresoli* T 83, *tumulus* 196, *undantia* U 189.

Now, a good source having been established for so many of these glosses, it stands to reason that other rare and difficult words go back to equally good sources, although we may not be able to appeal to any ancient authority for their use. While the evidence of a glossary as corrupt in its orthography as the Sangallensis may be regarded as insufficient to establish a form or word otherwise unknown, the comparison of several related glossaries may enable us to arrive at the true form, and to assign to it its right meaning; and words thus established, if supported by good analogies, ought to be looked upon as the property of the language, and received into our dictionaries. A few examples will illustrate this.

helitores: ortolani (= *hortulani*) H 40. Loewe Prod., p. 339, cites four other glosses in support of *helitores.* Doubtless the word was contained in the fuller discussion of Verrius Flaccus, from which Paulus 100 has preserved "*Helus* et *helusa* antiqui dicebant, quod nunc *holus* et *holera.*" In this case, therefore, we are not only certain of the form, but we can assign it to a very early period of the language. Plaut. Trin. 407, already uses *holitores,* and Placidus, p. 51, gives *Holitores, holerum distractores.*

dilargus: multum donans D 172. *Dilargus,* which according to Loewe Prod., p. 382, and Hildebrand, p. 105, is found in several glossaries, has already been received into the dictionaries of De Vit and Du Cange. It is supported by the use of *dilargiri,* although after the analogy of *deparcus* (Suetonius) we might rather have expected *delargus* as its opposite.

exumptuavi: pauper factus sum E 236 (cf. Hildebrand, p. 136, and Loewe Prod., p. 425, who also gives *exsumptuavit: pauperavit*). Both De Vit and Du Cange give *exsumptuare,* and the latter cites Baldricus lib. I. Chr. Camerac, cap. 120, *Domesticos sane exsumptuabat locupleta-bat alienigenas.* Before assigning the word, however, to a late period, it will be well to remember that Lucilius uses *deargentare,* and Plautus has *expeculiatus.*

aequalentiae : semile (similis) divisio A 144. This word is doubtless of late origin. Du Cange defines it as " Divisio hereditatis vel bonorum per aequales partes," and gives several examples of its use. ·

baulat: latrat B 14, we might be inclined to emend to *baubat. Bau-bantur* occurs in Lucretius V. 1070, and Isidorus Diff., I. 607, gives *canis baubat vel latrat,* while Codex Casinensis 439 has *baubantur catuli* (cf. Loewe Glossae Nominum, p. 249); but in an onomatopoetic word the termination may easily vary. We may well compare the English *bawl,* of which the *baw* is the essential part, and Gr. βαύζειν. According to Du Cange, Ugutio, in giving the names for the cries of different animals, has " Canum latrare seu baulare." Du Cange and Diefenbach both recognize *baulare.*

abiuga : a iugo semota vel dissociata A 18 seems to prove the existence of an adjective *abiugus.* De Vit cites a gloss *Abiugus : θυσίαι, ζώγεαι,* which must be compared with *abiuges hostiae: iugum non expertae* also given by Du Cange. So we have both *biiugus* and *biiugis, quadriiugus* and *quadriiugis.* Vergil speaks of such *hostiae* in Georg. IV. 540, as *intacta cervice iuvencas.* Cf. Ovid Met. III. 12, *bos — nullum passa iugum.*

omnopere: omni virtute O 111, also found in Ambr. B 31 (cf. Loewe Glossae Nominum, p. 168). *Omnopere* is formed regularly after the analogy of *tantopere, magnopere.*

elapidavit: distruxit E 40. Pliny uses *elapidatus* = freed from stones. Hildebrand, p. 134, gives this gloss, *expilat, occulte exterminat vel elapidat. Dilapidet* in Terence Phorm. v. 8, 4, is explained by Donatus as *disperdat.*

bidendo: fodio B 94 (cf. Du Cange under *bidendare* and *bidentare*). The substantive *bidentatio* shows that there must have been a verb *bidento,* although it seems not to occur in any author.

cinnus : tortio oris, unde dictus est cicinnus C 327. Loewe gives in addition the following glosses, Prod., p. 393 : *cinnus : torti oris ; cinnus : tortio oris ; cinus : torciores inde cinnus ; cinos : tortiones indecentes* (corruption for *cinnus : tortio oris ; inde cincinnus*). He conjectures that the full gloss once read *cinnus : tortio oris, inde dictus est cincinnus* [*tortus capillus*], and that we may explain *Cinna* as *homo torti oris.* Furthermore he cites *cinnus : nutus ; cinnus : νεῦμα* (gloss. Philoxeni, p. 38, 29); *nutu : voluntate sive cinno vel aspectu ; nictare : cinnum facere, id est oculo annuere ; cinnavit : innuit promisit.* Nothing could illustrate better the assistance to be derived from a comparison of many glossaries. No one can doubt the existence of *cinnus,* at least in vulgar Latin,—and Gröber Archiv I. 545, without referring to the proof of Loewe, posits *cinnum* in sense of " Stirnrunzeln, Winken nach : span. *ceño*, aspan. *aceñar* winken, port. *cenho*, prov. *cenn-ar*, winken, afrz. *cener*, *acener*, rät. *cin*, Wink, ital. *cenno, acennare.*"

For other new, rare, or difficult words, some of which still wait for a satisfactory explanation, see the following glosses with their notes : —

acrore A 94, *recertatur* 279, *intertortuosa* 287, *belligeratores* B 71, *castalitati* C 43, *carpacus* 75, *canier* 115, *recrastinatio* 395, *conlibiscet* 480, *conclasare* 504, *abinvicem* 623, *desitescere* D 48, *verruculatus* D 132, *divale* 190, *discipulati* 210, *dispernit* 244, *diplumatarius* 249, *extestinum* E 286, *eloquus* F 2, *fassiloquax* 18, *famicus* 48, *favisio* 62, *furfuraculum* 241, *gastromargia* G 15, *grumat* 82, *glevo* 87, *hestispicus* H 36, *heculaneus* 51, *iacturarius* I 10, *impopulavile* 66, *insuetare* 307, *interminia* 360, *daemoniosa* L 5, *leptopyria* 90, *manicat* M 23, *mermis* 76, *minsare* 95, *monachosmum* 127, *musitanter* 173, *musia* 174, *mutturci* 181, *olitana* O 105, *gravosum* 124, *oridurius* 166, *pactorium* P 7, *parasituli* 33, *panera* 67, *prestigiaverunt* 139, *deambulatorium* 238, *imaginarie* 253, *pergenuat* 270, *persum* 271, *clustellum* 312, *ramen* R 18, *refoculat* 52, *ronannis* 168, *rustu*, 192, *sarga* S 35, *saures* 45, *sconna* 311, *scrupulatur* 388, *superaria* 415, *taria* T 6, *pertusorium* V 74, *vicissitur* 97, *unicuba* 197, *ypinx* Y 8.

Finally, I wish to illustrate by a few examples the value which these glossaries have for the student of late and vulgar Latin. In the interpretations one may find many words which were unknown in the classical period, or which were used in a different sense. In some cases it may be assumed that the correct classical word had fallen into disuse, and that the word used in the interpretation was ordinarily employed in its place. Compare with C 175 *cliens : susceptus*, what Servius says, ad Æn. VI. 609, "*clientium* quos nunc *susceptos* vocamus.*"

Rönsch, Itala and Vulgata, p. 334, gives a great many instances of *modicus* = "klein, gering, unbedeutend," and says " *modicus* in dieser Bedeutung ist ein fast nie fehlendes Charakteristicum der Itala und Volkssprache welches nur hier und da durch *pusillus* sich ersetzt findet." Loewe Prod., p. 414, ff. gives twenty-seven examples from glossaries, only one of which is cited from the Sangallensis, although some from the Cod. Amplonianus are identical with those found in our glossary. I have collected twenty examples.

A 157 *aetatula : aetate modica.*
A 233 *allec : pisciculus modicus.*
C 221 *cercilus : navicula modica.*
C 613 *cumba : navicula modica.*
E 75 *emuniles : modice eminentibus.*

F 202 *frusta : particula modica.*
L 137 *linter : navicula modica.*
M 62 *meliusculum : modicum meliorem.*
M 160 *munusculum : modica donatio.*
N 55 *nequiquam : nec modicum.*
P 14 *pauxillum : paulolum modicum.*
P 87 *papiliones : tenturia modica.*
P 167 *prelus : modicus.*
P 326 *pixides : vasa modica,* etc.
Q 7 *quantolum : modicum.*
Q 42 *quiddam : modicum aliquid.*
Q 47 *quippiam : aliquid modicum.*
S 73 *scafa : navicula modica.*
S 140 *sensim : paulatim modice.*
V 129 *virguncula : virgo modica.*

The frequent use of *minutus* for *parvus* in Cassius Felix has been noticed by Wölfflin. Cf. "Ueber die Latinität des Afrikaners Cassius Felix," Berichte d. bayer. Akad. der Wissenschaften, 1880, p. 403. I have noted the following instances of *minutus* thus used : —

C 210 *caementum : minidorum lapidum congregatio.*
D 270 *dispicatis : minutis partibus.*
L 90 *leptopyria : minute febris.*
M 107 *migma : palea minutarum.*
Q 45 *quisquilias : paleas minutissimas.*
V 105 *vipurna : silva minuta.*
V 110 *virecta : loca quaevis sint in agris arboribus minutis fron-
            dentibus.*
V 114 *virgulta : silva minuta.*

Summitas, according to Krebs-Allgayer, Antibarbarus, is late Latin for *altitudo, cacumen, fastigium.* De Vit cites several passages from the Vulgate. Compare the following glosses : —

C 82 *cacumen : summitas.*
C 265 *crebido : rima summita.*
C 594 *culmmen : summitas.*
C 612 *cuspis : summitas aste.*
D 77 *de vertice : de summitate.*
I 24 *iuga : capita et summitatis montium.*
S 64 *scabum : summitas cacumen.*
V 79 *vertex : summitas capitis et cacumen montis.*

Of *circumquaque* the Antibarbarus says "spät Latein und nur einmal kommt *circumquaque* vor für *circum*." Other examples, however, will be found in Georges and in Paucker, Supplementum Lexicorum Latinorum. Compare C 300, *circumquaque : undique,* and C 500, *conlustrare : cir-*

cumquaque conspiciens. The word occurs in a Latin hymn of the eleventh century. (Cf. Mélanges Lat. et bas-Latins, par A. Boucherie, Montpellier, 1875, p. 34), —

> Salve tu, inclita,
> Circumquaque septa
> Clusione mirifica! Deus.

The fact that in the Romance languages *ferre* was supplanted by *portare* makes the following glosses significant : —

A 372 *armiger : armiportatur.*
B 106 *bispillus : ubi mortuos portant* (Paulus 369 *efferunt*)
D 115 *devectus : deportatus.*
E 144 *evehit : transportat.*
F 111 *ferunt : portant.*
F 112 *feretrum : lectus in quo mortui portantur.*
(Cf. Varro L. L. v. 167, *ubi lectus mortui fertur,* and Servius ad Æn. XI. 64, locus ubi mortui *feruntur.*)
F 179 *fosforus : lucem portans.*
G 46 *gestat : portat.*
I 392 *invehit : infert portat.*
I 397 *invectus : inportatus.*
L 35 *latur : portatur.*
L 44 *laurigeris : laurum portantes.*
L 71 *lectica : qua consoles portantur.*
R 65 *relatum : reportatum.*
R 67 *regerit : reportat.*
R 126 *revehit : reportat.*
R 135 *revicta : reportata.*
S 32 *sandapila : ubi portantur gladiatoris.*
S 190 *signifer : qui signum portat in bello.*
V 36 *vectitat : frequenter portat.*
V 41 *vehiculum : iumentum, carrum vel omnem quod a portandum utilem est.*
V 42 *vehit : portat.*
V 45 *vectus : portatus.*

S 279 *stricto pungione (pugione) : evaginato glatio (gladio).* The same gloss is given by Loewe Prod., p. 106, from Cod. Leidensis 67 F[1]. Suetonius uses *strictis pugionibus,* Julius Cæsar c. 82. *Evaginare* seems to be vulgar and late. *Evaginato gladio* is found in the Vulgate, Mark xiv. 47, Acts xvi. 27. See Georges and Rönsch p. 190. Add Hegesippus I. 28, 3, IV. 30, and Ambrosius de fide III. 125. (Cf. Romanische Forschungen I. 271 and 415.)

G 12 *garrit : verbosatur.* The verb *verbosari* belongs to ecclesiastical Latin. See examples in Rönsch Itala und Vulgata, p. 171, and compare especially Augustin. Serm. 251, "in ecclesia *garriunt,* ita *verbosantur* ut lectiones divinas nec ipsae audiant."

D 140 *deverticulum: ubi camsatur.* Compare D 250 *diverticolum: quod brevi loco divertitur.* The verb *camsare* in the one gloss takes the place of *di-* = *devertere* in the other. Ennius wrote *Leucatam campsant* (cf. Priscian K. I. p. 541, where DH have *camsant*) in place of which Cicero ad Att. V. 9, uses *Leucatem flecte. e.* The word, however, seems to have continued in the vulgar idiom. I quote Du Cange. "*Camsare, Flectere iter* in Glossar. Vatican. sec. XI. ap. Maium Classic. auct. tom. 7, p. 534; *plectere iter* in cod. reg. 7644; *Item flectere* in Papiae cod. 7609. Regula Magistri c. 56, 'Cum fratres spiritales sine laico ambulant iuncti ad se, *campsantes* modice de via, flectant genua.' Hinc *cansare* pro *cedere, locum dare, flectere, deflectere,* apud Dantem Infer. can. 12, in Purgat. can. 15, et Matth. Villaneum lib. 1, c. 1."

L 58 *latibulum: defensaculum,* — Neither Harpers' nor De Vit gives *defensaculum;* but it is used by Servius ad Verg. ecl. VII. 6; Augustinus ep. 102, 35, and ps. 67, 21, umbra ista *defensaculum* intelligitur, etc. Vulgar forms in *-aculum* must have been very common. See Rönsch p. 37 f.

To the examples of *pos* given by Loewe Glossae Nominum p. 210 f. and Prod. p. 137, may be added —

D 105 *denique: pos modum, deinde.*

P 263 *perendie: pus cras.*

R 129 *revinxit: pos tergum ligavit.*

For the use of *sero* in sense of *vesper* (cf. fr. *soir,* it. *sera*) we have interesting testimony in H 62 *hesperus: stella quę primos sero apparit.* See Wölfflin, ueber die Latinität des Cassius Felix p. 396.

In the same article Wölfflin, p. 410, says: "*Saepe,* welches in den romanischen Sprachen verloren gegangen und in Italiänischen durch *sovente (subinde,* frnz. *souvent), spesso, frequentemente* ersetzt worden ist, findet sich zwar bei Caelius ziemlich häufig, verhältnissmässig selten dagegen bei Cassius, nämlich nur 179, 16. und in den Formeln *saepe memoratus* 37, 8, und *ut saepe dixi* 38, 7, wogegen sich die längern Formen *saepius* und *saepissime* leichter behauptet haben. Das absterbende *saepe* wird bei Cassius mehr als unterstützt durch das etwa 70 mal gebrauchte *frequenter,* ein Missverhältniss, welches um so mehr auffällt, wenn man sich erinnert dass *frequenter* ein von Cäsar, Sallust und mehreren andern Autoren der guten Zeit nicht verwendetes Wort ist," etc., (cf. Archiv. I. p. 4). From this point of view the following glosses will be found interesting: —

C 264 *crebo* (= *crebro*): *spissum, subinde.*

C 124 *capessere: capere, invadere f r e q u e n t e r* (Servius ad Æn. I. 77, *saepe capere*).

D 203 *dictitat: frequenter dicit.*
F   8 *factitat: frequenter facio.*
F   12 *facesso: ———— frequenter facio.*
I   10 *iacturarius: qui frequenter patitur damnum,* etc.
I 105 *imperitat: frequenter imperat.*
I 370 *interdum: frequenter.*
M 103 *missitat: frequenter mittit.*
M 177 *musitat: frequenter murmurat.*
P 43 *parentat: umbris vel tumulis mortuorum frequenter paret,* etc.
P 257 *perpesitius: qui frequenter aliquem patitur.*
P 379 *potitur: frequenter utitur vel fruitur.*
V 16 *valetuderius: qui frequenter egrotat.*
V 36 *vectitat: frequenter portat.*

The positive *saepe* occurs only once, P 146; pressant: sepe precedunt; *saepius* occurs four times, —

C 159 *clamitat: sepius clamat.*
M 95 *minsare: sepius mingere.*
O 82 *occursat: saepius occurrit.*
R 156 *rogitat: saepius rogat.*

Assidue occurs M 88 *minitatur: assidue minatur.*

One would suppose that in the definition of " verba frequentativa " a writer might be tempted by the etymology to use *frequenter*, even if elsewhere he used *saepe*. It is worthy of notice, therefore, that of the Grammarians included by Keil, who treat of frequentatives, *saepe* is used by Servius (IV. 413), Pompeius (V. 220), Macrobius (V. 626), and Sergius (Anecd. Hel. 152); *saepius* by Charisius (I. 255), and Diomedes (I. 344); *frequenter* by Cledonius (V..16), and Augustinus (V. 516); while the Commentum Einsiedlense has, p. 207, *saepe lego;* p. 253, quod *crebro* fit ut *lectito, saepe lego ;* and on the same page, *volitat, frequenter volat.* Verrius Flaccus undoubtedly used *saepe* in conformity with the usage of his time, and this is preserved in Festus and Paulus. See under *adnictat, abnutare, auditavi, futare* (here *saepius*), *mantare, meritavere, obsonitavere, ostentas, occisitantur, quassare.*

A profitable treatment of syntactical usage could hardly be based on a single glossary, and I shall not undertake it here. Many mistakes that appear are doubtless due to the sheer carelessness of scribes. Others represent laxity of usage in the language as actually spoken at the time when the glossary was written, or even at some earlier period. Thus we find *sine dubium* P 440, N 94, and Q 46; *sine consilium* E 201; *sine spem* E 241; *sine sensum* F 32; *sine barbas* I 62; *de adulterium* N 111; *ex intervallum* E 195; *ex totum* P 306; *ex matrem nubilem* S 428; *de quo scribitur* S 257 (instrumental for the simple ablative; cf. Rönsch Itala und Vulgata p. 393); *cum ventum* N 78; *cum III pedes* T 129; *per manu* M 23; *per otio* U 23; *ad pugna* M 28; *ad gloria* P 63; *ante sole* A 435; *ante luce* L 170; *post captivitate* P 394; *in unum volumine* C 525; *qui in provintia proficiscunt* P 43; *circa uva* T 153; *sine arma* I 164; *sine effectum* I 401; *incircumscriptus: terminum carens* I 133. Compare Rönsch Itala und Vulgata, pp. 406–412 and 414.

Enough illustrations have I trust been given to show the extreme value of these glossaries for the study of Latin in its earlier and later periods. Many others under each category will be found in the notes. Romance scholars will doubtless find many forms and orthographical peculiarities of interest on which I have failed to comment. A very interesting example is furnished by V 82, *Vernum: prima vir* (= *ver*). We have here apparently a forerunner of the Italian *primavera*. Not until, however, a great many of these glossaries have been edited can the best results be realized, and the gain may be expected to be almost as great for the Romance languages as for the study of Latin.

AN OLD LATIN GLOSSARY.

CODEX SANGALLENSIS 912.

P. 4. Abba: pater
ababus: tritavi pater
abacta: immolata
abactus: ab acto remotus
5 abantes: mortui
abaso: infirma domus
abest: deest
abit: discedit
aberunca: abstirpat
10 abemcat: eradicat
abellum: agnus recens natus
abiit: discessit
abicit: proicet, minat
abigeius: qui tolleremaliena
15 P. 5. abitudo: abitus corporis vel vestitus
abiucassere: disiungere
abiungere: dissociare
abiuga: a iugo semota vel dissociata
abissus: profundum
20 abiungit: seiungit
abincursu: ab inpugnatione
abingruentis: abinmittentis
abiurat: negat
abita: insatiata
25 abolet: tollet
abolere: dememoria excludere
aborreas: manatio
abonat: repudiat
aboris: a finibus vel ab initiis
30 abolitio: res semota et oblivione perducta
P. 6. aborsus: ab eo quod est ordior
abortus: ex eo quod est orior
aborrit: dissonat, discrepat
abunde: satis
35 abunda: panici et millei follicoli
abusive: abuso tracta
abusi: male usi
abluta: diligenter lota
abusitatus: minus instructus scientia
40 aboditur: recusat
abdixit: ammovit
abligurire: plurima consumere id suspensis degitis leviaescebum tangere
abnegat: plusquam negat
abstans: distans
45 abrepticius: furiosus
P. 7. absono: non simili sono
abdicat: a re alienat
ablutum: absconsum
abdidit: occultavit
50 abgreco: reparo et egreco
abluet: emundat
ablegatur: condemnatur
abnuit: rennuit
abniso: nolo, veto

55 abnenepus: qui nascitur de pronepote
abrogans: humiles
abrogare: lege tollere
abstrusa: abscondida
abstemius: sobrius
60 absistit: loge est
P. 8. absurdum: turpe, duuium
absque foedere: sine amicidia
abstote: recedite, abite
absedeto: longe sedeto
65 abtra: folia vitae
abricum: locus temperativus sine rigore
abset: longe
acapis: caritas
acapitus: dilectus
70 acathe: genus lapidis
acantes: genus floris quo vestes inficiuntur
acentus: sonu vocis coreptae vel productae
P. 9. acevitas: crudelitas
acervuus: tumulus
75 acerbum: inmaturum
acceptatur: auctor, conscriptur
accersit: vocat
acer: durus
acertio: vocatio
80 acero: flubius aput inferus
atenus: usque nunc
acerlis: securis quam flaminei subpontificis habebant
acersa: arculatoreania
accevat: condessat, constipat, quoadunat
85 achademicus: phylosophus
achademia: locus ubi Plato tractavat
P. 10. acrimonia: sevitia
acidiatur: stomachatur
acie: turba
90 aciem: ocolorum aut vim ferri
acidia: tędium animi
accitur: advocatur
accito: evocato
acidus: ab acrore
95 acepitrem: aceptore
actius: amplius uberis
aconito: genus veneni
acononitus: qui nulli communicat
acroceria: ligatura articolorum
100 hic acinus: et huacini generis masculi
P. 11. acuum: diathema
accula: qui aliena terra colit
a colmine: ab alto
actutom est: statim, confestim
105 actuarius: acta qui facit
adeas: accedas

adonai : dominus significans
addedit : intolit
adeptus : consecutus
110 adepiscitur : consquitur
adest : presto est
adesto : auxiliare
addida : adiucta
adero : auxiliabor vel occorro
115 P. 12. adulta : matura
adnectens : nodans vel ligans
adserens : disputans, adfirmá
adsertio : disputatio
adsertor : confirmator
120 adseverat : adfirmat
adminiculum : auxilium, adiutorium
adnixa : innotata, adiucnta
adtonitus : intentus
adstipulatus : adiucntus
125 adstipulatos : idoneus testes
adstipulatio : professio
adstipulatione : adsponsione
adfinis : proximus
P. 13. adluricum : res ad lumen
apta
130 ad summum : ad novissimum aut ad
primum
aephyphama : apparatio, ostensio
aelam : porticum
aeden : dilitias
aemolo : invido
135 aemolus : imitatur
aemola : imitatrix seu adversa
aemolatio : zelus, contentio, invidia
aestuat : anxiat
aestus : calor
140 aemolumentum : locrum vel quęstum
ęquiperat : ęquant, conpensant, semi-
lant
ęquargentus : am
P. 14. aequae : iustae
aequalentiae : semiledivisio
145 aequora : maria ab aequalitate
aequora : campi
aestus : calor
aevum : aestas vel tempus
aevo gravis : sexus vel aetate infirmus
150 aevitas : aetas
aeternum : perenne, perpetuo
aer : inter caelum et terra
aerarium : tesaurum
aestu : turbaţione, calore
155 aethra : rota cęli
aethon : aquila
aetatula : aetate modica
aenenitores : tui cenes
aeneade : coniuratio
160 aequevus : unius ętatis
P. 15. aethera cálestia vel possesio
caeliignea
aercolus : genus arboris
aeneatores : corno vel calamo cantates
Aeneades : Romam vel Troiam

165 aeviterum : aeternum
aeſunnę : aestimationis
aerumna : labori nopia
aes : ęramentum
aeneum : aereum
170 aepos : versus
aedituus : custus domorum et templorum
aſrodin : spumam sanguinis gerante
afficior : tedium padior
a fectum : studium
175 adfectio : voluntas
affatim : abundanter
apthas : oris ulceratio
P. 16. affatibus : allocutionibus
afuit : defuit
180 affluentia : habundantia
aformas : occasionis
agios : sañtus s̄c̄s
agaso : domesticus
agusta : pulchra vel sancta
185 agustum : amplificum
agustorum : sanctorum
agustius : magnificentius
agrestis : rusticus vel fęrus
agmen : multituto
190 agone : pugna, certamen
agutus : velox, agilis
agacula : lenocinatur
agricola : colonus
agason : minester officialis
195 agaron : qui negotia aliena anteambolat
P. 17. Agrippa : qui in pedibus nascitur
agnati : liberi qui per adobtione veniunt in tantum đ cognati, adfinis
agoniae : hostiae, vectimae
agonitheta : qui ipse est in bello
200 agonia : alacritas, amor vel vigor
Agracas : nomen montis in Sicilia
agiographa : sancta scriptura
agonita : herba venenaria
aggeres : terre congeries
205 aggerat : congregat
agon : certamen
ait : dicit
ais : dicis
aio : dico
210 aisti : dixisti
ain : ergo
Alcides : Hercules a virtute appellatus, alce grece virtus dicit
alioquin : nam si non
P. 18. alacer : laętus, gaudens, ex-
pedī
215 algor : frigus
alternantim : vicessim
alternanti : duvitanti
alabastrum : genus marmoris pretioso
allabione : inundatione *aquarum*
220 allabi : navicio duci
alogia : convivium grece

allicula : genus vestis
alucinatio : lucis alienatio
alux : pollex in pede
225 alſeus : deus marinus
alma : virgo sancta, Hebreum est
aalma : virgo
alites : volocres
altilia : studiosaginata
230 altilia : volatilia
alatis : pinnatis
altercatur : litigat, obiurgat
*allec : pisciculus ex mare modicus ap-
    tusatium liquuminibus*
P. 19. alveus : profundus vel torrens
235 alvus : venter
aletus : nutritus
aliendum : nutriendu
alleluia : laudate dominum
alias : aliter
240 altricem . nutricem
allectu : electum
alienigena : alterius generis
alumnus : quem quis aluit, id est nu-
    tritus
aliorsum : altera in parte
245 alea : ludum, tabulae a quodam mago
    alea nomine qui hoc adinvenit lu-
    sum
alimentum : nutrimentum
alnum : lignum agnetano idest vernum
allavitur : leviter decurit
alligorit : aliud pro aliod significans
    similidudo id est
250 altrinsecus : abinvicem, hinc et inde
aliquantisper : aliquandiu
ala : pars multitudinis exercitus
alacres : cavallares
alebre : polchrum, bene educatum,
255 *allubione : quae ripis aquarum pē . . . ex
    alia parte aderiscent arenas*
P. 20. alcitellus : alte evocatus
altibuans : in alto, ex alto sonans
altellus : terra nutritus
albet : splendit
260 alacrimonia : laetitia
alteruter : alter et ambo
allectat : spectat .
alit : nutrit
alimonia : aesca
265 alsosus : frigorosus
albus praetoris : ubi sunt conscripti
    qui recitandi sunt, tabū ē in albis
    litteris
altrix : nodrix
alvearia : vasa apium
alluvium : quotiens flumen alium sivi
    meatu facit
270 allapsus : sensim veniens
altematur : variator
Amen : fiat vel sive fideliter
ambrosiae : divinae pulchre
amoenum : dilictuvile, iocundum

275 P. 21. anquirit : inquirit
anxati : vocati, nominati
anxilites : aves volocres
ancurata : genus furiae
antaconista : recertatur
280 anethematus : abuminatus, perdidus
anxiferis : misteficis
antra : obscura loca
anget : praefugat, solicitat, stimulat
annuus : anniversarius
285 anniculus : unius anni
anquisit : valde scrutat vel quir ? ?
anfracta : intertortuosa
anfracta : et difficilia
anasceve : adstructio
290 anathema : abuminatio
anarscis : mansionis, grę
antecellet : antecedet, praecellit
anethema : maranatha, prodicio in ad-
    vento domini
P. 22. antitheta : aposita vel contra-
    posita
295 annales : libri qui totius anni ordine
    continet
aoma : Rediaterra
aonii : populi
aona : circuitus, tractus, clima
apostolus : missus
300 apostata : refuga
apitiosus : calbus
aptet : impleat
aptam : congruam
aptamus : adiungimus
305 apex : distinctio notę aut summa pars
    teli vel cuiuscumque re
aperet : ostendit
apostrofat : transitum facit
apostēsis : constantes, animosi
aplistia : saturitas, crapulat
310 apocalypsis : revelatio
apodixen : ostensio, provatio vel exem-
    plum
aperetos : sine febre
P. 23. apocrifa : recundita vel oc-
    culta
aplustria : navis ornamenta
315 apiternus : qui his rebus caret
apocrisis : depulsio
apoliterium : ubi ponuntur res laban-
    tio
appolit : vetat, proiget
apostrofa : conversio quando ad alias
    rem sobito commutatione facit
320 appedit : desiderat
arcanum : secretum
arcarius : dispensatur
arces : aedificia summa vel palata
arcis : luca summa muntium
325 arcitectus : qui domum tegit vel cope-
    rit
arbata : modiatrea
arcet : vetat, prohibet

arcire : repellere
arctus : stellae septemtrionalis vel situs in caelo
330 artus : membra, degita, noda
P. 24. arta : stricta, angusta
artat : stringet
arrogantes : aelatę
arrogantia : iactantia
335 arduus : altus, grevis
ara : altares
arva : terra, agrs et semenibus apta
arbiter : iudex aduobus electus
arvina : adeps vel axungia
340 arundine : canna vera vel calamum
arguet : increpat vel docet
artutim : membrati
arthemeticus : numerarius
aruntius : nomen stellae
345 Arcivi : Greci vel Mędi
ardalio : glutto
argi : simulagra
arupes : qui adara sacrificat
ariolu : vatis qui et fariolus
350 P. 25. area : ubi granum triturātur
argumentum : quod rei fidem dat
ardens : flagrans
ardetes : festinantes
aries : genus machinae ad expugnationemurorum
355 arrepet : adpreendi
ariopagita : curialis
aripus : gladius falcatus
Arar : flubius Germanię
arbusta : vineae fructuosae rei
360 Argus : civitas Gręciae qûlevis
arceria : vas vinarium cum quo vinum ad aras ferebat
arx : emenentissimus locus
arcera : plaustrum
arcessit : incusat
365 aruspices : qui intendunt signa corporis
arbitrerium : collegio arbitrorum multorum id est ipsa consensio ipsorum.
arguit : accusat
P. 26. armonia : conpetens coniunctio vel ex multis vocabolis aptę modolatio aut duplex sonus
Argolica : Greganiga
370 aridum : siccum
arentia : siccantia
armiger : armiportatur
arida : terra sicca vel sterelis
arcum : secretum vel incurvum aliquid
375 (a)quilicum : ventriculum
aquilum : fuscum, nigrum
astra : stellae
astrologus : aestimatur siderum et lunae cursus
ascemo : inunestus
380 astego : ego autem
asper : durus

aspernatur : contempnit, dispicet
astarium : ubi venduntur bona
asilum : locus confugientium
385 P. 27. asparagus : quia virgas habet asperas
asotus : luxuriosus
assem : quod unum dicimus
aspectare : voluptose intueri
aspirat : aflat
390 atnenses : ianitores
athomi : tenuissimi pulveris qui in radiis apparet solis et dividi non possunt
atra : nigra, tenebrosa
ater : niger
atrocĕ : amarus
395 atrox : crudelis, amarus, pessimus
atavus : proavi pater
atratus : locobris
athomus : indivisio
atrox : orrivilis
400 P. 28. atlum, athla : unumquoque opus palestricum quod ad victoria pertinet
atria : aedes
attollit : aggerat
atnepus : abnepotis filius, pronepotis nepus
atquin : adque ideo
405 aula : domus grecia
aulice : minester regis
auspicia : somnia
auspicei sunt : consecuti sunt
aucupat : capit
410 aucupatur : venatur
audet : ausus est
audacter : audaciter
audenter : confidenter
autumant : dicunt, aestimant
415 austri : nymbae, venti
P. 29. avitus : anticus
austeritas : amaritudo
avidus : avarus, copidus
augus : qui aves colliget
420 avia : extra via
avium : secretum avia
avellit : tollit
avulsa : subtracta
austa : putta
425 ausat : gustavat
aureax : neque solitarius
austrare : humidum facere
auctoritas : meritis aliquibus confirmata persona
aucturatio : vinditio, nam subauctoñ est qui rem vindunt
430 auctoramentum : ipsa res vinditionis
auspicio : in avis nuntium quod in aves aspiciatur
augurium : signa avium volantium
P. 30. autionarius : qui emet
aurifodina : metallum

435 aurora: nubes rosea ante sole
auleum et aulea: straclum genus cor-
　tinę regalis
augustum venerbilisancto
avidium: antiquitus vel ababibus re-
　lictum
augustrius: sanctius, pulcrius
440 ausim: audeo
aucta: superposita
aurire: sumere, implere
auspicare: somnia inquirere
autio: puplica vinditio
445 auceps: avium venatur
avunculos: frater matris
aunculus: magnus frater aviae
auriga: agitatur

B.

Bachum: vinum pro eo quia inventus
　est
bacht: sacrificat

P. 31. bachi: antiqui
bacatum: gemmis ornatum in modo
　bacarum
5 bacchatur: discurrit
batis: nomen serpentis
batus: aurora
bacchar: floris genus
baccanal: quod paganis agrarium Li-
　beris patris dicebant
10 bacerus: baro factus
baligera: stulta vel bruda
Baccanalia: vacationis fures
bace: genus mulierum
baulat: latrat
15 bacapulus: in quo mortui efferuntur
bassas: oves
basum: non altum
basileus: rex
basilea: regina
20 P. 32. basilica: regula
basilicus: regolus
babil: confusio
bardus: stultus
babigera: stulta
25 barginę: peregrinę
blasto: cuvicularius
baccilatix: vinum
bacchatio: discursio, furor
baxem: quas buccellas dicunt
30 baratrum: gurgugite, fovea vel terrę
　hiatus
basilicus: serpens
balantes: oves
babtismum: lavacrum
barbitus: lyra maior sonus ut orcunum
35 bautride: vaccae
barduni: neptuniani
barbarostomus: homo qui barbarismis

plenum profert verba
baltha: audax. Gothice
barcus: tardus, sine lingua
40 barriton: genus organi
　P. 33. barnicum: alefanti vox
balista: genus machinae unde excu-
　tiuntur sagitte
bassarides: vaccae
beat: beatum facit
45 beabo: beatum faciat
bariona: filius colombę
Bartholomeus: filiùs scs pendentes
　aquas
bravium: palma id est manus victoriae
bracata: caleata
50 brabeuta: qui palmas dat
blax: stupidus, insipiens
blattet: perstupitę loquitur
blapere: stopite et sine causa loqui
blatta: genus porporę
55 beati: filices
beatitas: beatitudo
belzebub: vir muscarum
benificus: benefactor
　P. 34. *benivolus: benignus*
60 berillus: genus lapidis canditi
bellum: pugna
belligerat: pugnat
belliger: bellator
bellum civile: bellum domesticum
　quando una civitas inter se pugnat
65 betere: vade, proficiscere
Belſecor: simulacru Priapi
bellum navale: pugna in navibus mari
beto: avesqꞏ in auspicio servatus
beluuri: bisteis marinis
70 Belide: abillo patre
Bessi: homines Tracie belligeratores
bestiarius: venatur bestiarum
Bellona: belligusa dea, belli dea infe-
　riori
belos: gratiosus
75 bellicosus: pugnandi copidus est locus
　bellicosus
　P. 35. beluae: bestiae
benivolentia: bona volontas
breſotroſium: locus venerabilis in quo
　infantes alontur
blenones: pudedi autercosi
80 blesus: qui aliosono corrupit litteras
benignus: satis bonus
bibliothica: ubi libri reconduntur
bibliopula: qui codicem vendit
bivulus: valde bevitur
85 biblum: funes denave ex buda facta
bialcis: nomen gigantis
biceps: duorum capitum
bicepiti: duplici
bicamus: qui duas habuit vel havit
　oxores
90 bicliniom: duas habet cellas
bicellium: quasi duas habet cellas

biblioticarius : qui codices resecat
bifarius : bilinguis
P. 36. bidendo : fodio
95 biditum : biforme
bipertitum : duabus partibus partitus
bidentis : oves
bilis : ira, comutio
biluae : bestiae marinae
100 bissui : sirico torto
biviera : secunda coniux vel quod duos habuit maritus
bifores : duplices ianuae
bilis : fel
bitire : ire
105 bigene : e duobus gentibus natum
bispillus : ubi mortuos portant
bimalcus : liber pater
bithalasum : peculum duarum navium
bimembres : centauri
110 Bitemon : nomen gigantes
P. 37. bisulcum : divisum ut ungulae
bivium : via duplex
bitet : vadit
bissam : corium bubolum
115 Briareus : gigans tentimanus
biti : proficisci
bimatur : doplatur
bipetalis : duorum pedum
bipertit : duobus erogat
120 bipennis : securis amazonica penum dicebant antiqui bis acuto
boa : sopor vehimens
boas : serpens engens et tumor in cruore suffusio sanguine
boriro : rubus, niger
Boreas : ventus Aquilo
125 borre : (*rasura*)
boare : damare, sonare, mugire
bona caduca : pecunia sine eredem
Borforus : transitus maris ponte in Asia
Bromius : Liber pater
130 bobinatores : inconstanter
P. 38. bomus : sonus aut vox tumidus
brocca : labrosa
bolus : iactus
Boetes : Septemtrionalis stella comis
135 bombus : sonus
boatus : sonus vocis
boantes : strepentes, sonantes
boves Lucaniae : elefanti
buda : storia
140 bucula : vaccula
bumbum : sorbillum
busta : ignis
bumboso : sonoro furibudum
bustum : ubi homines comburuntur ad sepulturam mortuorum
145 buceta : pascua
bursa : cloaca

bucerum : pecus bubulum
buceria : armenta
bunde : sonus tympani
150 bullonium : luto quod lacerarii salsamentum dixerunt
butrus : uva
buxus : tibiole et genus ligni
bucones : stulti, rustici
P. 39. bibinare : inquinare sanguine muliebri minstruum
155 bustuarii : qui corpora humana cremant
bubo : nomen aves nucturne
bruma : tempus hiemis
bruda : solida
burgus : castra
160 burrum : rufum
busticeta : sepultura in agro
bullantes : bullas emittentes
budus : incipiens
brutus : stultus

C.

catholicus : rectus
calumnia : falsa accusatio
catholica : universalis
cassiculum : reticulum
5 caticuminus : instructus vel audiens
catazizat : edocit, redarguit
cabo : cavallus
cannon : regula
P. 40. cacinnus : ridiculum, inutile
10 caplosus : inlisus
callere : scire, intellegere
caudex : rubor vel radix
capido : spatium inter parietes
cathecorias : adscriptionis
15 calathis : canistris
calestir : ubi vespe nascuntur
campae : equi marini
catasta : genus suplicii egolio semile
Causten : flubius Tracie
20 calleo : novi, intellego
calip : fornax ferri
camuribus : brevibus cornibus
cautris : cordis
calce : fine
25 carcesia : genus pucoli
cavillum : locum, convitio
carptus : discessus
P. 41. caleon : quasi humiles leo
catapota : genus calicis
30 canamala : canna de qua canetur
caritius : marmor
canditus : veste regia
caries : vetustas
catax : clodus a coxa
35 cartarinum : velanterior
calos : ovus, avis
catasceue : distructio

capite census: qui de capitebis sub
corona vel sub asta vindibatur
carcer: locus inclusionis
40 calator: minester sacrorom
caducarius: heres qui in alterius bona
succedit
calamalarius: ipse qui de canna canet
castalitati: de elocutione
P. 42. *caserserescaptivigene ex captivo*
nate
45 casu: eventum pro eventum
casus: pericula
cancalum: dubium
cassa: vana
canamala: lanugine habente id est ci-
donia
50 caterva: multitudo
cassabundus: instavilis
cassibus: retibus vel telas araneorum
cartallum: canistrum
caterva: multitudo
55 catirvatum: multepliciter
carpit: detrait, fruitur
calculus: gladius lapideus et victoria
id est iudicu
caule: ovile
calcolum: numerum
60 carmen: canticum
caupo: qui vinum vindit
caudalocus: ordo, series
caupones: stabularii vel tabernarii
cantabrum: cantare
65 P. 43. catuceum: virga Mercuri
clandestina: latentia
capidinis: eo quod manu capit
cano: canto
carisa: faba
70 caulae: ubi sunt avocati
cathaplum: conventus navium vel ad-
ventus
canora: cantu gruia vel suavia
cana: vetusta, antiqua
callidus: durus, malitiosus
75 carpacus: pistor
catus: sacer
carisma: donum spiritalem
carismata: dona spiritalia divine gra-
tie
calabris: ventis siccis
80 P. 44. cataclismum: dilubium
careo: nolo
cacumen: summitas
cados: anfora semis
capacitas: amplitudo
85 cancer: forceps
carcire: abicere
calico: tenebre
capit: accepit
cacule: servae militum
90 cacula: ligna arida
capax: continens memoria
cataver: corpus mortuum a cadendo

caliotur: fallit
capissat: tenit, liventer accepet
ç.
95 catmea: vitorie non bone
P. 45. cavillatur: locatur, deridet,
sed non simplici corde, et calumnia facit
caminus: fornax
capillacis: capillis prorictus
capite census: taxatio possesionum
vel qui in capite tegerint corona
100 captura: detentio
calimbum: ferrum
capitilinus: capitulium serviens
caducus: demuniacus, inanis, deiectus
cancri: cancelli
105 candit: splendit
capite solutus: capite periclo liberatus
castimonium: sanctimonium
capes: galeae militum
caristia: dies festus inter cognatos
110 catulum: ubi mortui feruntur
candes: vasa fictilia
capulum: manubrium gladii, id est
spata
caperata: contracta rugosa
P. 46. carinantes: inludentes
115 canier: leno
cannar: senes
calamischos: calamos
cariscos: quasi in modo nocis formatus
cadices: arborum radicis
120 cauponalia: tabernaria
calamistratus: capillosus, compositus
vel crispus
cave: obserba
canacem: gladium
capessere: capere, invadere frequenter
125 cautes: (ras.) pula et saxa in mare latentia
callidus: astutia
cautus: sulecitus
cavillatio: derisio vel calumnia
canicularius: medio aestatis vel hiemis
130 P. 47. camene: musae
caracter: signum vel nota
cauteriata: sucensa
cavea: consensus spectaculi
caduca: peritura
135 calcitrones: qui infestant calcibus
casnomia: musca venenosa
caris: nomen saxi
calone: calearii militum
cantus: cantellena
140 caule: cavellum ante iudicem
cameleon: quasi humiles leo
capparis: frutecti genus est lintis co-
semile
calta: genus floris
clanculum: mane
145 claudies: claudi

classicus : celeuma navis
 P. 48. classica : navigia militum
clanco : sonus tubarum
clam : ocultae
150 casu : titixi
clandire : cladicare
clanculum : diminutive
classicat : tuba sonat
chaus : profundum vel confusio rerum
155 crappulat : aebrietas
claricatio : clara actio
cladis : pestis vel calamitas
claustra : portę aut serratur[ę]
clamitat : sepius clamat
160 amicum ton filon
clausula : finitio, conclusio, firmi ser-
 mones
kaiper : super que
claba : fustis
clanculę : ocultessime
165 clandestina : latentia
 P. 49. chelis : cithara
clericus : sors dei
clerimonus : heres
clemens : pius
170 clepit : rapit
clementia : pietas
cliscet : crescet
clypeum : scutum
clinicus : paraliticus
175 cliens : susceptus
clivus : ascensus
chirogus : funibus
cloes : pluvia
clepsedra : per quo ore colleguntur
180 clientella : officium clientis
clunes : coxae
clivanus : formus vel festus
chirografum : cautio propia manu
 scripta
clues : polles
185 clivanar : quasi tunica ferrea
climactera : tractus vel spatium mundi
clima : circuitus tractus vel aona
clupeum : ubi imagines proponuntur
 P. 50. caeleps : virgo vel vir sine
 semine
190 caelitus : calestis
cęrine : aqua, nymfa
caelibem : solitarium
cęlata : sculpta
caelotes : voloces
195 cęnum : stercus pudridum
caelonites : caelestis
cęroleus : viridis
caeleber : freques
cęcunia : noctua
200 caeleber : sanctus
cęsaries : capilli
caelebre : solemne
cęlebritas : solemnitas
cęleberrimus : venerabilis

205 cęlebritas : solemnitas, vel conventus
caelibatus : sine oxore eo quod caelus
 sit dignus
caerates : serpens cornutus
caeles : qui et caelicolae
caeronomio : sacrum deorum
210 caementum : minidorum lapidum congregatio
chamaneus : possidens sive possessio
 ita autem dictus simo navicocharia
 P. 51. celsa : excelsa, sublimis
celsus : altus
cerula : nigra
215 censura : discriptio, sententia
ceruleus : bistea marina
ceccum : cortex maligranati
cei : iudicatores
cere : frumentum
220 celidon : erundo, grę
cercilus : navicula modica
cemerias : silbas obscuras
cenum : loti voragum
certiscar : certior fiat
225 Cecropide : Atheniensis
cetron : tenebre
Cea : nomen insule
cerealia : arma pistoria
ceram : tabula vel imaginem
230 census : facultates
censetur : statuitur
 P. 52. cerata : cornuta
ceraster : serpens cornuta
ceritus : subinsanus ex comutione ce-
 ribri
235 censura : sententia
censet : statuit, iovet
censor : iudex
ceu : axi, quasi
cecennit : cantavit
240 cernet : videt
crevit : vidit
censeo : iudico, statuo
censuet : deliberabit
cerebrosus : qui in cerebrum vitium
 abet
245 celidrus : serpens aquaticus
cernuus : in capite ruens
cenodoxus : vane gloriae copidus
certatim : stutiosim
cenodoxia : vana gloria
250 cedit : concedit vel socubet
 P. 53. cessit : victus est
cespis : frutex
celer : velox
cementum : mendatium, cogitatum
255 celebrat : frequentat
celoces : navicolę
celox : navicula
ceterum : alia fabula
crateras : vasa vinaria
260 crapulam : inibriatet nausia oppotum
crabro : vespa longa

cretus: generatus
crebindia: signa vel indicia
crebo: spissum subinde
265 crebido: rima summita
crebruit: spessavit
creat: gerat
crepere: in corpore dubitare
crepusculum: finem noctis et initio
diei
270 P. 54. creperum: dubium
CRISTVS: unctus
crispans: concutiens, vibrans
crisma: unctio
crismatus: galeatus
275 crinidior: crine prolixior
cruccitus: clamor corvi
crura: ossa tibiae anterioris
Crustumenus: populus
Crustumia: regio
280 cigneum: album
citam: velocem
Cintia: luna
citato tramite: curso veloci
cis vel citra: id est de ista parte
285 circumspectus: circumcinctus
circum pletus: circumdatus
civicā: civem facet
circiter: plus minusve
P. 55. Cilix: pirata
290 cirsum: carpentum
circumscripsit: concluset, in praeiu-
dicio misit
ciroxere: circumdare
citaxus: similes taxo
cirsus: vehiculi genus
295 ciparisus: cypressus
citissum: frutectum
citimum: citra omnia, proxumum
circum lectus: circumventus
cymbia: poculorum genera
300 circumquaque: ūndique
cicatrice: vestigium vulneris
ciliarcus: tribunus qui mille contribus
ulibus
cicni: poete dicti a suavitate cantico-
rum
circumvallat: circumdat
305 civitas: a conversatione multorum
dictaest, quia multos contenet in
una vita
P. 56. ciet: citat, vocat.   voco
cicor: prudens, mansuetus
cicurare: militare, exorare, mansue-
facere
citro: proximo
310 civivica: corona
citra: extra
Cillinius: Mercurius
circumvenit: fallit, decepit
circiae: radiis solis
315 circumvolat: circumdat
circumfundimur: circumdamur

citroque: et ulterius
citerius: exterius
citerior: exterior
320 cymera: bestia
circuitus: girus
ciere: concitare
citreus: pomerius
civita: ut frequentia maior
325 civis patricius: senatus
P. 57. circus: girus
cinnus: tortio oris, unde dictus est cicinnus
Cymbri: Galli
citro: hunc adnos   .
330 circopeticus: animalest semile simie
caudati
ciritat: populum adloquitur
cinici: philosophi sunt a canibus vita
ducentes
cinus: canis, Gre
chidaris: pallius sacerdotalis ex bisso
hunc Greci et nostrithiarum vocant
335 cynocephalus: ipsi sunt homines qui
capita canina habent
copolo: coniungo
copola: coniunctio
coęvum: coętaneum
coturnum: superbum
340 cosmum: summa potestas
P. 58. cocula: ligna arida vel vasa ęrea
coibet: conpescit, contenet
coercet: refrenat
coacerbat: colliget
345 conpescit: ponit
cognati: a fines sed per feminas
cogiorum: donatio imperatoris
coalescit: congluttinat
coacti: provocati, conpulsi
350 coetus: collectio multitudinis
coit: convenit, ambulat
coiit: ambulabit
coitus: concubitus, commextio maris et
feminae
coitio: genitura
355 coiit: concubuit
coepit: inchoavet, initiabit
coepti: incoati, initiati
P. 59. cooritur: simul nascitur
coeunt: conveniunt
360 coarto: constringo
coerco: conpesco
chors: militum castra
coalescet: simul nutritus vel crescit
chor: multitudo rusticorum
365 collegium: conventus, societas
columes: salvus
collatio: conferentia
colaphus: pugnus
colega: sotius
370 calapisat: pugno cedit
coloni: incolae, inquilini

colluvio: commixtio
(c)oline: coquinẹ
coltax: clodus a coxa
375 colus: virga q' per cochea vulvitur
comit: ordinat, ornat, componit
comptus: conpositus, ornatus
comis: ornatus, subtilis
    P. 60. compus: consimilis, magna-
    nimis
380 commentum: argumentum, similitudo
compotem: partecipem, semile
compotrix: sotia adbibendum
compilat: spoliat
complosus: inlisus
385 comoratio: havitatio
comedia: historia comidi, grec.
comperi: cognovi
compages: coniunctionis
commolatius: uberius, amplius
390 commessatio: conviummeretrico
complus mentis: desiderii sui conple-
    tur
comminus: prope, iuxta, et simul in se
commessatio: commextio
commertio: mutatio
395 comperendinatio: recrastinatio vel di-
    latio
commeat: iter agit
commeare: iter agere
    P. 61. comat: frondet
commeat: simul ambulat
400 comiter: benigne
commessat: manducat
compernens: qui infestant callidibus
commessatio: commestio
commissatur: turpiter convivatur
405 commude: honeste
commedius: utelius
commentario: expositio vel adinventio
commentatias: adinventitias
commeatum: viaticum aut commite in
    teneris id est oratione et gradia
410 commentator: praecipuus disputator
comitium: tempora onorum quando
    dantur
comidium: locus ubi dantur honores
comitate: benignitate vel umanitate
    P. 62. competa: fines, bivia, trivia,
    quatrivia
415 comparat: adsimilat
cõmulcat: conculcat
componet: ordinat
comenta: fraudes
comma: brevis dictio
420 comminiscit: mentitur, simulat
commentatus est: mentitus est
comminiscitur: commemoratur
commodat: ad tempus prestat
commentum: commune mendatio et
    librorum expositio
425 competitur: amicus
compulit: coegit

comitatum: sotietate
complectitur: continet
commode: utilis
430 complutere: repercutere
comes: sotius in via vel onos vel honor
comedia: signifigidio morum
    P. 63. singolorum cum detractus quis
    fit in cerco
commulcat: conculcat, conturbat
consercrat: sanctificat
435 contuitus: contemplatus
contuimur: conspicimus
conpescere: pariter comedere
conpertum: conlatum, plenum
contumax: contemptor
440 confit: perfecet
conitio: aestimatio
condedit: edeficavit
connectit: coniungit
conplectit: conprehendit
445 consultum: iudicio senodale
conicit: consimulavit
contritio: mota plaga
consitum: contextum
conditus: sepultus
450   P. 64. confestim: mox, continu·
    statim
condet: servat, reponet
connicita: coniectura, argumentum
convulsa: eradicata
congesta: coadunata
455 coniestio: collectio
conixe: coniuncte
conbentia: conspiratio vel consensio
contribuli: consanguinei quasi ex una
    tribo participes
contagio: morbum
460 contigus: proximus
contio: conventus populi
contitionatur: aloquitur
consulat: consilio dat
consoluit: consilium petivit
465 condensa: secreta
constipata: repleta
concretum: cummixtum, coaculatum
    P. 65. conubi: coniugia
confertum: contextum
470 confutatus: convictus
conticuit: tacuit
convexa: declinata et cumportata
contaminatum: inquinatum
coniectore: arbitratore
475 coniectura: ingenium, argumentum
contemplatio: consideratio
concintus: simul in unum convocatus
concinnaverunt: ficta lŏcuti sunt
concilia: amicum facit
480 conlibiscet: conplacet, delectatur
condiarium: domus stipendii
consuet facit: consuescere facit
conticuere: tacuere, tacuerunt
conspicuus: pulcher, altus

485 conibentibus: faventibus, consentien-
    tibus
consternatus: prostratus, abstupiscens
    et territus
confligit: luctatur, certat
    P. 66. consulte: provide
consors: particeps
490 consultus: in consilio abitus
contabiscet: exsiccat
conversa: mutata
controversa: iurgium, lis vel causa
concinent: consonat a cantandum
495 concrepant: concinunt, resonant
convoli: concordes
conflagravit: concremavit, exuset
conditio: potestas, lex inposita
conpilavit: furatus est
500 congluttinavit: copolavit, convinxit
conlustrare: circumquaque conspi-
    ciens
conclave: interior cubiculus
conluvione: conlectionim sordium
conclasare: adiugere classem
505 convicium: sermo iniuriae
conpatior: misereor
colivium: genus pecuniae
    P. 67. confectus: debilitatus, ma-
    ceratus
conserar: conpungar
510 conserit: interponit
conlabuntur: corruunt
cor: consentanens
consumimus: expendimus
consumpta: trasacta, expensa
515 concors: unius concordiae
coierat: simul cum citeris iurat
conari: temptari
conatus: temtatus, adgressus
consistorium: rupis alta
520 conpacta: coniuncta, conposita
continuatur: periuratur, congregator
condensati: consiti in uno
conlocati: collecti
constipati: collecti, condensati
525 conglobati: in unum volumine densi
conspirati: unianimes coniurati
conseremor: per ordinem facimus
    P. 68. congeriaria: quod in populo
    erogat
conticuus: coniunctus, proximus
530 conum: summa pars galeae
confusa: conturbata
confundit: conmiscit
concilium: conventum
conlapsa: dibilia
535 contraimus: collegimus
convia: declivis
confore: futurum esse
concrepuit: sonuit
confieri: effici
540 concidit: simul cecidit
conlinati: mensurati

contratus: cauto placitus
conbibiones: a bibendo dicti
conplices: sotii
545 conpedium: locrum
conticinium: primum tempus noctis
    com omnia quiescunt
conticescere: quiescere
consumat: finet, explicat, conplet
conpertum: conportatum, plenum
550 conpertum: cognitum
    P. 69. conperi: cognovi
conpererant: cognoverant
consuetio: consuedudo
confuse: permixte
555 coniector: interpres
confossus: vulneratus
coniectus: in vinculis missus, inpul-
    sus
congeries: congregatio
congerit: congregat
560 conserere: conferrere
contactus: inquinatus
contra fas: contra ius, damnum
contra nefas: scelus contra
conclivum: crematum
565 concitus: festinans
congruit: convenit
contagies: contactu in culturis
conflixerunt: concertati sunt
convexo litore: rotundo
570 conlibuit: conplacuit
conspicatur: intendunt
constans: animum firmus
constantia: animi firmitas
    P. 70. cognitur: curiosus
575 conpanipularis: conscius, collega
consubrini: qui ex duobus sororebus
    procreantur
contumelia: iniuria clamoris
consciscunt: coniungunt, consonant
chornus: tempus
580 corda: animus
color:
coram: presentibus
corilus: avellanas
corpulentus: corpore plenus
585 cornua: fortia vel potentia significans
cornipides: equos
corax: corvus
corsam: divinans
corturnum: caltiamentum
590 corscum: crispum
corimbata: nabis
coruscatio: speldor
culpat: infama, vitoperat
culmmen: summitas
595 cunabulis: initiis vel ab infantiis
curtina: respunsum
cruor: sanguis
    P. 71. curriculum: cuncti temporis
    cursum
curio: pronuntiat populum

600 cuncur : densus populus turma homi-
　　num
　　cunctatio : dubitatio
　　cudit : sculpit
　　culix : zinzala
　　cur : quare
605 cudietur : inpellitur, percutitur
　　cuiuspiam : cuiuscumque
　　cudere : studiose agere, facere, scalpire
　　curalisella : ubi consules sedent
　　cultur : vestitus, ornatus
610 cunctanter : difficulter
　　cupido : amor, cupitidas
　　cuspis : summitas aste
　　cumba : navicula modica
　　culmus : calamus frumentorum
615 curvato gurgite : ericto fluctuo
　　P. 72. cursi : citius
　　culmen : gilionibus
　　cuniculum : degestio aquarum
　　culmo : arista gillone
620 cuinam : interrogatio de persona
　　cuidam : cuiquam, alicui
　　celeus : tunica ex partu in modo ero-
　　　nis facta qua liniaebantur pice et
　　　bitumine, et in ea includebantur
　　　umicidę cum simia serpentę et uno
　　　capone, ac insuta mittibantur in
　　　mari, contendentibus se animalibus
　　　quo ire se dicuntur abinvicem homo
　　　maioribus poenis aficiebatur

D.

　　danus : feneratur
　　danista : feveratus
　　Danai : Greci
　　Dardani : Troiani
　5 P. 73. draconia : gemma ex cerebro
　　　piscium
　　Davus : senes discinctus
　　dapsilis : largus dapibus
　　dapes : epulę
　　damare : capere
　10 dat venum : vendit
　　davir : draculum
　　damma : genus capreę similis
　　decalocum : dece verba legis
　　decus : gloria
　15 dedecus : crimen
　　dilibo : immolo
　　deluit : labit
　　delibutus : untus, perfusus
　　delinquet : peccat
　20 delituit : latuit
　　delitescet : latet
　　deliquum : defectum
　　delitescere : diu latere
　　delinitus : depagatus, unctus
　25 delicat : probat
　　delata : in longo ducta

　　delubra : templum, ara, idolon
　　delusit : circumvenit
　　debella : ex pugna
　30 delabunt : deficiunt
　　P. 74. delicuum : defectio
　　devotus : dicatus
　　delictum : peccatum
　　dedicatus : promissus
　35 deléberat : cogitat
　　densitas : spissitudo
　　deiscens : aperiens, ianuis patefaciens
　　dedunt : tradunt
　　denique : postremo
　40 degit : habitat, vivit, agit
　　dedicat : consecrat
　　devotio : distenatio
　　devota : distanata
　　defeneꝶ : vindidavit
　45 devinctissimo : inseperavilem
　　demum : postremum
　　deinceps : deinde, postea
　　desitescere : necligenter agere, con-
　　　temnere
　　dependere : pro alio solvere
　50 decenturius : ingeniosus
　　P. 75. deterremum : de malo peiore
　　depromunt : proferunt
　　decipula : laqueus
　　depromuerunt : protulerunt
　55 deviat : errat
　　depopulatus : devastatus
　　dedicius : qui de sua provintia ad alia
　　　se tradet
　　declivis : inclitus locus
　　deflat : inridet, dedignat
　60 dedegit : denutat, manifestat, provedit
　　devium : extra via
　　dedo : trado
　　deditus : traditus, sublectus
　　dedita : opera valde data
　65 dedas : tradas, des
　　devito : diverto
　　deserta : direlecta, disoluta
　　depenendi : reddendi
　　decuria : numerus decem hominum
　70 decretum : definitum, statutum
　　depeculato : defurto puplico, deo
　　　demptato
　　P. 76. decrepitus : valde sónis
　　deriguit : obꞇ stipuit
　　deflet : lugit
　75 demicat : pugnat
　　detestabilis : abuminabilis, pessimus
　　devertice : de summitate
　　desipiens : amens
　　dementicus : insanus, amenticus
　80 desistere : desinere, cessare
　　dementia : insania, amentia
　　devinctus : legatus
　　defensus : fatigatus
　　deglubere : belligare
　85 dependit : reddit

dextrum : prosperum
derogans : detraens, vitoperat
detracta : valde detractat, contemnit
detrectare : recusare
90 demolitur : exterminatur
defluunt : cadunt
   P. 77. depascet : comedet, non con-
   sumet sed degestat
defreta : disperata
deplet : evacuat
95 defunctus : mortuos
deplene : de pleno docere
depalata : manifestẽ divulgata
debellio : bellatur
desidia : pegritia
100 demiror : dispicio
denus : nomen pecuniae unde et nummus denarius dicitur
demet : tollet
degenerat : a genere suo dissimulat
detectus : nudatus, deopertus
105 denique : pos modum, deinde
detrusus : expulsus
devorat : glottit
demsit : tollit, delivit
desivit : cessavi
110 decedit : cecedit
decernunt : statunt
depositum : creditum
denodat : detrait
degener : ignobilis
115 P. 78. devectus : deportatus
deicet : deturbat
de more : ex consuitudine
degladiando : pugnando
defunturium : transitorium
120 derivatum : sparsum
demeda : praeceda
debellet : rumpit
devitat : spernit
devinxit : conlegavit
125 delegit : eliget
desciscere : deficere
depudiscente : inpudentem
deseͅvit : ad iracundia lenitur
deposcit : vade rogat
130 dedecet : non dedecet
dedecus : ingloriosus
delictus : veruclatum quem dicunt
defecatum : liquidum, purum, extersum
delubra : templa ideo quia in in gressû
   lacus aque fiebant ubi [P. 79.] se
   sacerdotes sacrificaturi purificabant
   et ad diluendum id est labandum
   delubra dicta sunt
135 derelictus : dimessus
decens : pulcher
deformis : fede formẹ
desuetus : inconsuetus
deiscet : os aperet
140 deverticulum : ubi camsatur
decrevit : ordinavit

deprovatum : deformatum
depraces : genus serpentis
deses : ignarus, piger
145 devulgat : puplicat
destituunt : relincunt
dedocere : de doctrina evacuare
despectat : despicet
demum : iterum, secundum
150 degerat : per deum iurat, male iurat
despirat : spiritum tollet
   P. 80. deflectit : deviat
deunce : dece untiarum
defitiscit : defricet, fatigat
155 delictum : peccatum
delivat : precepit, degostat
debaccatur : provagatur
defruet : minuet
desecto : inciso
160 delirat : cessat
destitus : relictus
detrimentum : dispendium
deditio : sui traditio
destitutus : derelectus, desertus
165 despicatis : patefactis
decumbit : infirmatur
decidium : qui cito decedet
delationis : proditiones factorum
deuterunomia ; quasi seconda lex
170 dialogus : disputatio
dialecticus : disputatur
   P. 81. dilargus : multum donans
dispectus : cumtemtus
dia : potestas
175 diathece : ˙ testamenta
dilatus : aductus
diaria : actio sed unius diei
distraxit : abstraxit
dicat : dedicat
180 discernit : deiudicat
distinat : disponit
difficulter : tarde
difisus : disperatus
dilectum : electum
185 disidem : pigrum, ignarum
disipet : sapere desine
discidium : separatio
dirimit : dividit
diripiunt : auferunt
190 divale : divinum
dilucolum : ante mane
distentus : satis plenus
dirivitorium : loci contubernii
divalis : princeps, imperator qui quasi
   deus habebatur
195 dissectus : divisus
   P. 82. divortium : repudium
dilectus : carus
discerpsit : diripuit
diermi : turpis
200 dimicat : pugnat
discolor : dissimilis
dispectabilis : contemptebilis

dictitat : frequenter dicit
disto : dissimilo, differo
205 distitet : cessabit
disceptat : disputat
discrimen : periculum
dispendium : damnum
disceptatur : litigat
210 discipulati : edocti
dilubium : lavacrum
dirus : crudelis
diversum : consentiens
discretu : divisum
215 dispalatum : dificatum
diermi : turpis
dimolire : dissipare
dipsas : serpens
diverberat : disiungit
220 diurnum : unius diei
diapsalma : spiritus pausat
dicatio : conscratio
dessidet : discordat
discors : dissimilis cordis
225 diuturnum : multi temporis
    P. 83. dypfnoicos : difficultas spi-
        randi
discerniculum : ornamentum capiti mu-
    lieri
dictator : imperator qui dictat erdinat
    exercitum
dirivat : a suo curso convertit
230 direptus : praedatus
digegitur : dissipatur
diribere : dinumerare
dirimire : separare
dispertit : patitur
235 discidium : separatio per vim facta
disetatines : disputationes
dis manibus : dis inferorum
diutinum : diuturnum
dissertum : expositum
240 distinctum : apertum, manifestum
distractum : venundatum
diuncem : undicem untias
discolus : difficilis
dispernit : contempnit
245 discidio : dispositio vel subligentia
distentus ; cibo plenus aut virgas ex-
    tensus
diplumum : duplicatum
    P. 84. disserit : disponit, narrat
diplumatarius : duplicatur
250 diverticolum : quod brevi loco diver-
    titur
distinctio : separatio
diutinum : diuturnum
diditus : divulgatus
dipulit : dispersit
255 divexum : inclinatum
displosa : divisa
divaricatus : satis separans
divesupu : locuples
diversurium : hospicium a divertendo

260 dicto citius : quam dici potes
discrepat : dissentit
dispares : dissemi
diruit : eiecit, evertit
dialis : cottidianus
265 dissecere : dissipare et in diversas se-
    care
diriguit : rigitus et frigitus est
digressus est : abiit
disparile : dissimile
disidentes : discordantes
270 dispicatis : minutis partibus
didior : dividior, doctus
    P. 85. discrevit : separavit
dissinso : discordia
dipsas : nomen serpentis
275 docitat : frequenter dicit
dilata : in longo ducta
· divinitus : quod ex divinitate fit
dogma : doctrina
dolus : fraus
280 dorcades : quadrupes capreo similis
documentum : exemplum
dorcas : caprea
dolabra : securis vel asciae Iapetaria
dolones : tela abscondita
285 Dolopes : milites fini condotati per
    manus
Densa : nomen insulę
docimentum : alterius exemplum
domata : moenia dicuntur vel certe
    superioris domus
dubium : incertum
290 dumtaxant : praecipue, sine dubio
duces : ductores
dumi : spinę
dumeta : loca silvestria, spinosa
duellium : secundum bellum

295   P. 86. dulcia : iocunda
dumus : spina
duca : furmula
duella : ? vIII
duellius : aversarius
300 duellum : bellum duorum hominum

E.

Evangilium : Bona adnuntiatio
... citas : multituto
edax : comissatum
etacitas : voracitas
5 edito : prodito
edictum : future dicisio
etacitas : multituto comessationis
educat : nutrit
effabilis : docilis
10 edemitat : dentes secludit
efatur : loquitur
eflagitat : reposcit
efferetur : funus dicitur

effeta : adaperire
15 effemeris : cottitiana res
effrenati : immoderatus vel abruptus
effeminati : mollis eviratus enervatus
    tamquam femina mollis
    P. 87. *effeminatus : stupratus*
effecit : perfecet
20 efferiebamur : superbievamur
efficet : sufficit
efflavit : exalavit
efugium : locus refugii
effetanda : disputanda
25 effeta : sine fetu
effeminat : in femina convertit
efferus : ferox, inmansuetus
effivi : aduliscentes
effebus : inverbis
30 egerimus : tollimus
egrate : exegrate
egerit : excutit, foris mittit
egre : moleste
egestio : curatio
35 eger animo : dicitur
egestio : purgatio
elatus : superbus
    P. 88. elavi : evadere
eloboro : sitro
40 elapidavit : distruxit
elegantia : pulcritudo
Elisei : Cartaginensis quando et ilisica·
    dicta est
elchere : evocare
elementum : celum, terra, sol, ignes,
    natura
45 elapsa : discussa
elivicata : purificata, deplanata
Elisius : pagani beatus nuncupavat cam-
    pos
elinguis : mutus, nullius lingę
elogia : pars carminis
50 eluxit : luctum deposuit
eclesia : congregatio
elues : ligor qidāde quod aliquid eluitur
elogium : titulum cuilibriei
elatus   ambiciosus, superbus
55 eliciens   producens suadendo, traens
    P. 89. ecudit : excudit vel producit
eculeus : genus turmenti in quo stans
    extenditur homo
emax : emptor
emaces : emptores
60 emacitas : emendi aviditas
emeritus : milis vetera
em : admiratio
emereor : conplaceor, numquid iam
    conplevit malitia
emicuit : repulsit
65 emerita : arma victricia
emolumentum : locrum
emeritum : furiarum
eminet : exta taltum est
eminens : excellens, altus

70 emolus : invidus
empurius : locus supemare
emblema : ornamenta vasorum
emfaticum : audax increpatur
empesū : empos, impatiens, amens
75 emuniles : modice eminentibus
    P. 90. *ensito : insertum*
    enervat : castrat
    enervatus : mollis, efeminatus
enitor : conor
80 encrypias : subcineritios vel occultus
    panis
enixa : conata
enisi : conati
enormis : sine mensura
enotat : explicat
85 enixius : instantius
enixe : sedule, inpense
ensicium : a secando
enodis : sine nodis
enormia : grandia
90 enucleatim : clare, manifeste
enucleo : perpendo, expono
Eolus : rex ventorum
eo minus : tantum minus
epiphania : aparatio, ostensio, mane-
    festatio
95 epithoma : adbreviatio
epithomarius : abrevicatur
    P. 91. epicrama : abreviatio
epimiris : diurnis
epilogon : narrationes et ratione
100 epithapium : carmen mortuorum
epilogus : extrema pars libri
epitalamum : carmen nuptiarum
epifora : lippitudo oculorum
epistula : scribula
105 epus : lux
episcopus : superinspectur
epotat : ebebit
epulum : convibium
ephot : quod est super humerales
    sine cucullo vestis sacerdotalis ca-
    sullę cuius vestis duo sunt genera
    unum lineum et simplex quod sa-
    cerdotis habebant, aliut diversis
    coloribus et auro gemmisq contexta
    quę solis pontificis utibantur
110   P. 92. epichrimata : conamina
equidem : ego quidem
equiperant : equidem facit
equos pegassus . alatus
ergata : vicinus vel operatur
115 eragine : e contra
era : domina
Erinis : Furia, ira magna
ermana : calamitas
ermula : statua sine manibus
120 erisibe : erugo ę̄ tribicommessio
erga illum : circa illum
erciscende : dividende
eruditus : doctus

erumna : miseria
125 ergastulum : operibus duris
ergastulum : locus ubi damnati marmoris secant nam grece metallum
dicitur
P. 93. esedum : veicolum
estrita : caput
esidat : comedet
130 esu : esca
esedarius : mulio veicoli
ethesiae : venti in certo tempore
essentia : subsistentia id est uniuscui-
que persone
Etrusci : Tusci
135 ethica : moralis sed proprietas
ethicon : proprium
Etruria : Tusca
ethnicus : gentilis
etymologia : paratum verbum
140 eugenis : nubilis
evoma : effundat
eugenia : humelitas
evum : tempus
evehit : transportat
145 evirat : castrat
evo : seculo
evitat : declinat
eventus : successus
evolvet : exponit
50 eviscerato : exempto
P. 94. *eonas : secula*
evulsit : expoliavit
evanuit : aufugit
eulilogi : versiculi
155 euychias : dilitias
eu : *laudantis est vox*
evelantur : spoliantur
evidenter : manifeste
eurus : ventus subsolanus
160 evelatus : spoliatus
evidens : aperta
evatatur : flagitat
evantes : fugentes
evistigio : statim
165 evetatus : pertritius actu privatus vel
ocisus
Euterpe : nomen musae
euripus : piscina longa
evertit : funditus movit
Eumendum : Furiarum
170 euebaristia : gratia
eus : vox inclamantis
P. 95. exta : interanea ostiarum
extat : emminet
exalat : spirat
175 exaditat : excludit ab aditis
exaustis : exacuatis
exsanguis : sine sanguine
examussi : ingredere diligenter
examinat : inquirit, discutit
180 exitus : excessio, mors
exorsus : incipit loqui

excedit : errat
exomologismum : preces vel confes-
sionis
extimus : extremus, extraneus
185 expiat : purgat, mundat
exerat : aruminat
exploratores : inquisitores
P. 96. excurat : vigilat, observat
extimuit : satis timuit
190 exprobrat : inproperat
exor : sine sorte, eretidates
extat . supereminet
exultat : exilet
exesum : cummistum
195 ex intervallum : ex inposito tempore
excidium : expugnatio
exemit : produxit, abstolit
exubite : spoliaque, ociso oste tolluntur
exertum : apertum
200 exilis : gracilis, macer
expers : sine consilium alens
exitiale : mortifirum, periculorum
experrexi : evegilavi
expertus : probatus
205 exequia : mortuorum obsequia
P. 97. exolitus : dissulutus
extulit : elavavit
explodit : expellit, vitoperat
extrinsicus : a foris visceribus et exterius
210 exuti : spoliati
extinctum : interfectum
exestimatio : cretulitas
exosus : odiosus
exorit : aperit
215 exanimis : sine anima
extimplo : statim, mox, continuo
exedent : comedent, devorant
expergefactus : a somno surgens
exordiarius : ludus theathri
220 excellens : nubilis, eminens ceteris
exitium : calumnias, periculum
exulcerat : verbis asperis vulnerat
exaustis : vacuis defectis
P. 98. exedra : hoc subselliorum id
est absida salutaria
225 exortus : natus
explodita : exclusa
exorie : nascentie
excivit : excitavit
exciturum : excitaturum
230 expromimus : exponimus
exeremus : proferemus
expilandi : nudandi, praedandi
expelatores : aliene ereditatis subtractores
exaustant : exauriunt
235 exestuat : fluctuat, fervet
exumptuavi : pauper factus sum
expergifica : suscitabilis
explodam : evertam
exomnis : vigilans

240 experiendum : experimentandum
exspes : sine spem
excors : sine corde
expectorat : extra pectus elci
exephebis : a pueritia
245   P. 99. extorris : exterminatus extra
      . terminos
experientia : prudentia
expergiscor : excutior
expediam : explicet, liberet
experire : cognoscere
250 exoptatum : disideratum
exulto : gaudeo
extrusi : expuli
extruso : expello, recludo
expiabilis : (*rasura*) inmundus
255 extixe : extincsisse
excitur : evocatur
exfretat : navigat
expertia : aliena
exagerat : provocat, explorat
260 experiar : cognoscar
experta : docta
      P. 100. eximietas : sublimitas
exuberant : profluunt, habundant
exolescit : defecet
265 exuit : deposuit
exolevit : in oblivionem venit
exemplum : formam
explet : perfecet
exuret : cremat
270 exerti : evocati
expositus : in medio positus
exempla : sublata
exemptum : explicatum
existite : perdurate
275 exemplaria : similia
exere : producere
ex coniectura : ex arbitrio
excanduit : in iracundia exilibi
exodus : exitus, egressus
280 exolidus : dissolutus
exorabilis : placabilis
exormis : inmanis
exitie : poene sententię
expressit : explanavit
285   P. 101. excautus : intentus
extestinum : extraneum
exanclare : exaurire
ex tasin : mentis excessum
expediunt : educunt, proferunt
290 exvito : diverto, divido
extespices : aruspices
exidium : divortium, repudium
exinuat : exemplat, exaperit
exlex : extralege
295 excedendus : devorandus
exercita : miserabiliter sollicita
exete : evidenter, perspicue
exemptis : sublitis, conplicitis
experimentum : usum
300 exaurit : evacuat

exerti : nudi
exintervallum : exintermisso tempore
excidium : eversio urbium, separatio
expuncta : finita
305   P. 102. eximius : praeclarus, subli-
      mis
exporrectus : extinctus
extorris : exiliatus
extorrem : extra terra propria expulsus
experita : parva, vacua
310 extudit : dtundendo extorsitum
exclusit : propiam expulsus

                         F.

fabor : testimonium ladis
facitus : elegans, iocosus, eloquus
fabre : perfecte, arteficiose
facundus : abilis, gratiosus, eloquens
5 facitia : iocus, elegantia
facesie : eliganter
fatiscet : aperitur
factitat : frequenter facit
facinorosus : scelestus
10 facilitas : possibilitas, licentia
facitior : hilarior, gratiosus
      P. 103. facesso : duo significat, facet
      facesset et frequenter facio
faustus : festus
fautor : qui fuit et consentit
15 facinus : scelus, factum
factus : superbus, contemptor
facinora : crimina scelestia
fas est : ius est vel ratio
facinnat : quando laudando decepet
20 falanx : legio, lingua macido
faces : faculę
fandi : loquendi
falerare : ornare
fatus : locutus
25 fanum : templum
fatur : loquitur
fando : loqendo
fassiloquax : mendax
familiaris : domesticus amicus
30 falaria : ₁ancea magna vel genus teli
magni¹
farcire : fulcire, implere
fatuus : stultus, sine sensum
fallet : decepit
fax : facula
35   P. 104. Fascenninas : clausebiles
      vallationis
favisor : consentaneus
fanaticus : aspectus honorosus
fanatici : minestri templorum
falernum : vinum
40 faxo : inºendo
faxo : faciat, tempus futurum
famereas : mortiferas
fartores : saginatores

fameticum : a fama vel esurientem
45 farra : frumenta
fana : inlicita sacrificia
fassus : confessus
famicus : locus in urbe
fatidici : fata canente
50 fauces : angusta claustra
falcidia : quarta pars
faleras : atolator averba
fatiscunt : feriendė dissipantur
fatiosus : fallax, deceptur
55 P. 105. fariolus ı vatus
factio : coniuratio
fascinant : gravant
farus : turres speculatoria
faustus : felix, laudavilis, benignus
60 facultas : conditio, possessio
fastus et fausti : libri sunt ubi sunt
nomina consolum
favisio : suffragium
fatidicus : divinus
fasta : honores
65 farisei : divisi
faxit : fecit
fastes : honeres
fastigium : culmen
faemina : a femore
70 faetivus : letus, conpositus
faemor : quod super geniculu est
fastidum : superbia, contemptus
fateor : confiteor
fa :
75 flagitat : postulat, expetit
flagris : flagellis
P. 106. flabri : fabulosi, ventosi
flabris : ventisicci
flagitiosus : crimenosus
80 flagtium : adulterium livitum vitium
flagrantia : ardentia, suavitas odoris
flagras : ardens, fulgens
flamina : venti
flamea : virginitas
85 flammigena : de flamma natus
flammonius : honor pontificales aput
gentiles
flamen dialis : sacerdos Iovis
flagra : incendia
flavum : rureum
90 flammeo : irato
fluvidus : inpetuosus
fiabra : fysimata vel venti
fluxerunt : ceciderunt
fluxa : resoluta
95 fluidum : mollem
fluit : deducit, currit
fluxum : vanum
fluctuat : vacillat, dubitat
P. 107. flammen Martiales : sacerdos
Martis
100 flamen yrinalis : sacerdos Cyrini. Cy-
rynus enim aput Romanos deus fuit
fertilis : fructuosus

fecundus : cupiosus, fertilis
fecunda : fructifer
fere : prope, pene, forte
105 ferme : circiter, prope, propter
ferales : mortales
fer : tolle
fercula : missoria
fervidus : turpis, iracundus
110 fertur : dicitur
ferunt : portant, dicunt
feretrum : lectus in quo mortui portantur
ferux : crudelis, stevus
Fenices : Carthaginensis
115 fedant : inquinant
festivus : feriatus
P. 108. *fefellit : elusus vel inluset vel
frustratus sive concisus*
ferascit : efferum facit
fessus : fatigatus
120 Feronia : dea agrorum
feriae : cessationes ab opere
ferisne : poteris ergo ferre
fletus · lamentatio, luctus
fenus : usura
125 fenicum : coccinum
fenerat : mutuat, inpromutat
femor : dupliciter diciter, dicitur ab eo
quod est femor femor, facit ab eo
quod est ab hoc femine facit femen
et declinatur quomodo carmen
flevile : lamentabile
fiduciarius : qui re aliquam fiducia accepit
130 finum : stercus animalium
fio : efficior
fistulor : sibilor
fibras : figata, pulmones, iocinora
ficubus : corde cithare
135 P. 109. figolus : fictor
fincxit : conposuit
ficti : pravi, falsi, simulatores
fidicula : cetharedi
filargyria : avaritia, amor pecunię
140 fidicula : genera tormentorum sicut
lāminę
fibea : luna
finctus : formatus
fidicina : citharista
figmentum : similitudo
145 finitimi : vicini, confines
finget : simulat
fidiculę : cordę
fibula : ligamenta
figmenta : conpositionis adinventiones
150 fragor : sonitus, strepitus
fragosus : torrens
fremit : rugit, furet
frendit : dentibus stridet
P. 110. fretus : confisus, fiducia ha-
vens
155 fratruelis : matertere filius

fratria : fratris uxor
fribula : vasa fictilia
fragores : tonitrua
framea : asta, gladius bis acutus
160 freta : maria
fretum : mare angustum
frenat : conpescit
fremunt : strepitum facit
fribous : levis, mendax
165 fribula : imaginaria, caduca
focilat : refecit
fomes : nutrimentum
fomis : lignum aridum
fomites : initia, incitamenta
170 fotus : recreatus
fovit : nutrit, studet
      P. 111. futa : nutrita, plena
fors : fortuna, casus
forenses : qui in foro sunt
175 fores : ianuę eo quod fores ponuntur
formidor : timor
format : figurat, creat
fortunatus : felix, beatus
fosforus : lucem portans
180 fomidines : pinnę, licivę in sagittis
foederati : amicati
fornex : camera
foeda : turpia, inquinata
foebes . sol
185 focas : vitulus marinus
forceps : forcipes fabri
fotiles : inanem, vacuum
forsan : fortasse
forex : foturum esse
190 fortuitus : subitus eventus et casus
fortuita : subita vel repentina
fortuna : felicitas
      P. 112. foliatum : curvatum
foedus : amicidie pactus, iusiurandum
195 forceps : clusum carcer
formidans : timens
formidolosus : temidus
fornicem : arcutiiumpalę plateę
frugalis : abstinentia, parcitas, passi-
      monia, ubertas
200 frutecta : ramorum densitas
frustratus : deceptus, exinanitus
frusta : particula modica
fructus : usus consecutus
frugi : magnanimis vel continens sub-
      stantia
205 frutices : ramos
frustra : inanis, sine causa
fructutus : fruiturus
fruges : frumenta
fucata : tincta, colorata
210   P. 113. fucatus : tinctus, dolosus
fuco : dolo
fucus : vermicolus
fufae : interiectio mali odoris
funditus : a fundamentis
215 fungit : agit

fultus : auxiliatus
futo : amplexo
fulcit : manit, firmat
funeture : funeris instrumentum
220 fulcitus : sublevat
fulvum : rubicondum
fulciat : adiuvet, auxiliet
fulmen : fulgo, iacula
fusus : fugatus
225 fusi : iacentes
fulcitrat : fulmen pręemit
fulgidum : splenditum
fumidu : fumosa
functus : minestrans
230 fulva : rura
fundi : praedia, campi
fuma : terra
funesta : scelesta
funus : deductio mortui
235   P. 114. (f)unera : luctuus mortis
fungitur : agitur, obsequitur
funus imaginarium : tumulum sine ca-
      tavere
funestum : perniciosum
functione : misteria
240 funtio : tribulatiorů exolutio
furfuraculum : tenebras
futilis : levis et inconstans
fungimur : utimur, solvimur
furor : iracundia, temeritas
245 fundandus : rusticus qui fundicolit
furia : ira magna
furebundus : valde iratus
furiata : dolore concitata
furva : obscura, nigra

                    G.

galerum : pylleum pastoralem de iun-
      co factum
      P. 115. Gabrihel : fortitudo dei
Gallilei : volubilis
galerus : calamaucus
5 ganeo : gulosus, tabernio, propinatur
ganea : taberna
gannit : muttit
galibare : mortuorum condita corpora
ganeus : luxuriosus
10 garrula : versa
garrulitas : verbusitas
garrit : verbosatur
gazofilacium : dividiarum et tęsaurcus-
      tudia
gaza : divitie, lingua persa
15 gastromargia : ventris ingluvies
galbanus : genus medica menti id est
gamus : nuptie
garon : liquamen
ganimen : tabernarius
20 gausicum : genus pallii
      P. 116. genenealogia : linea genera-
      tionis

generalis : universalis
generaliter : universaliter
genitura : seculi posteritas
25 gentale : originale
gessit : egit
genesis : factum, discretum
geometria : mensura terrę
gestum : motus corporis
30 gestatu : potatum
genitalia : sexus virilis et feminę
genimina : generationis
generosita : nobilitas
gelidum : frigidum
35 Getoli : Afri
gerusa : notrix, conpotrix
germina : semina
genium : virgo
germen : initium floris
40 genalis : lectus qui in nuptiis sternun-
  tur
  P. 117. genuinum : initium necis et
  nature id est insertum
geniculationibus : adrationibus
geometra : suppudandi arte peritus
gerolu : baiolus
45 gerit : agit
gestat : portat
Gete : Gothi et Trace
gentica : gentilis
gentiunt : anseris
50 geniatus : gratus
genę : mala in facie id est sub oculis
gerotochomium : locum venerabilem,
  in quo pauperi set propter senectute
  sola infirmi hominis curantur vel
  pascuntur
gneumon : dicitur pulmo
gymnasium : et palestra et adiutorium
  magistrorum unum dicitur anuditate
  et alterum ab ext ?
55 gymnasiarces : qui princeps est in
  gymnasia
gymnside : lavacrum, balneum
gymnos : nudus
gorstus : faretra
gignit : genera nascitur praeluium
60 gymnasta : exercitatio est palestra ipse
  locus agon vel ubi unguntur pales-
  trę luctatores
  P. 118. gylbus : malbum et nigrum,
  medius color
gratia : donum
gretissimus : iocundissimus
gramma : littera
65 grandevus : senis
grassare : invadere, predare
gradatum : paulatim
gratitur : ambulat
grandenato : ex nubeli natus
70 gremium : sinus et praefectura sedes
gremia : sicamina lignorum
gripes : alites ferę

grus : grues
grumuli : tumuli
75 gramen : genus erbę
gratis : gratia inpensa sine merito
gratatur : gratulatur
grassatur : invasor
grumus : ageratum
80 gratutum : gratu habitum
gratificus : gratis faciens
grumat : diriget, aequat
gregariis : vulgaribus
gnuus : fortis, agilis
85 gnarus : doctus, perfectus
  P. 119. glauco : viridi, presso
glevo : rusticus, arator
gleva : cispis durus
glovus : vertices
90 glaber : calvus
glomerat : convolvet, nectit
glaucoma : offusio oculorum id est
  nebula
glosa : congregatio sermonum
globus : rotunditas, condensa volumine
95 gloria : magestas, laus
globat : acerbat
glosia : veri soror
gnsia : terra gl
gurgustium : tegurium umile et tene-
  broso
100 gurgustia : loca tabernorum tenebrosa
  ubi convivia turpia fiunt
gurges : altum in fluminibus et pro-
  fundi locus

H.

harundo : canna, kalamus
haurit : implet, bivet
haustum : epotatum
haut procul : non longe
5 hasce : as autem
  P. 120. haut frustra : non sine causa
habilis : aptus, opportunus
halat : oscitur
hausta : gostata
10 hato : mendax
hamatum : uncis circumdatum
halantes : redolentes
habitudo : compositio corporis
hausit : bivit, inplevit
15 haut secus : non aliter
haecine : ita vero
havene : frena equorum lorarum tena-
  cula
hanelat : spirat
habitus : qualitas corporis
20 herus : vir fortis vel domnus
herei : domini
here : habe
hevenum : genus ligni indici

hera : donmina
25 heliotropoli : nomen gemmę et herba
  solis equiãm
  P. 121. hebitudo : fatuitas
  heres : filius
  hesitat : dubitat
  hedor : aqua
30 hersutum : asperum, vellosum
  herugo : sanguisuga
  heroes : viri fortes
  heroes : dicuntur qui dum vivunt et
    virtute nubile sunt et post mortem
    gloriam dimittunt
  hecui : alicui
35 hebes : murio
  hestispicus : aruspix
  Herebi : inferni
  heruum : anticorum
  heremum : desertum
40 helitores : ortolani
  herbedum : herbosum
  hemenum : novum nuptus
  herenicas : antiquitas
  Heumenia : Thesalia
45 herma : castratio
  heu : gemitus
  herit : fixum est
  hebitant : stupiscunt
  helluo : glutto
50 hilaritas : lętitia
  heculaneus : eunucus
  heiulatus : ululatus, he
- hereses : sectę
  heus : ingemiscentes est
55 Hermes : Mercurius
  hermaproditus : castratus
  Hercle : vere iuratio est
  P. 122. hermafroditus : nec vir nec
    mulier
  helluantes : avide comidentes
60 hespirias : occidentales partes
  hebrei : transgressores
  hesperus : stella quę primos sero ap-
    parit
  hymnum : carmen in lade dei
  hymnum : laudem cantici
65 hymen : nuptię vel carmen nuptię
  hydromates : qui ex aqua divinant
  hypocrita : simulatur
  hylidrus : seu ytri, serpentes aquatici
  hydroplasmus : cantio quia organum
    componit
70 hiantes : os aperientes
  hiliis : intestinis
  hiulcus : pastor
  hiacintum : flos porporeae
  hianiã : margarita pretiosa
75 hirti : anni grassi
  hirta : aspera
  hippecus : navis
  P. 123. hictirici : ydropici
  Hiberia : Spania

80 hispida : spinosa
  Hisperia : Italia
  hiscor : os aperior, loquor
  hirtus : asper, setosus
  hir : ꝗ ł p̄ts vigil
85 hirta : fetosa, plena, grassa
  hispidum : asperum, orredum, pilosum
  histrio : mimo scenicus
  himeus : nuptias
  hiultum : patens, aperens, apertum,
    ians
90 hippus : navis ium*en*taria
  hiscit : apertus incidit
  hiñtes : ampliantes
  histriones : praepositi meretricum
  hircus : caper
95 hiscitur : dividitur
  Hiersolima : visio pacis
  Hyades : stellę (*ras.*) quinque in modo
    quinque littere in fronte tauri posite
  hiscine : ipsis autem
  historia : fabula
100 hirco : stupeo, miro
  hiersolima : quasi usolo mone accepit
    nomen hierisalomonia
  P. 124. historiogrofus : discriptur
    fabularum
  histrix : quadrupes spinosum
  hiat : aperit
105 hincine : hinc vero
  hirsutus : asper, vellosus
  hiverna : loca callida propteɾ hieme
    facta
  historia : rei praeteritae memoriali
  hirudinis : sanguisugę
110 hiena : epicenon est gens beluę
  hiatus : spissura, vorago
  hibleus : flos vel fluritum
  hiemis : frius, tempestas
  hiscere : desineri
115 hostia : victima
  holocaustum : totum incensum
  honos : honor
  hospitalustra : hospida, peregrina
  horror : timor, pallor
120 horridus : timidus
  horrificum : expaviscendum
  P. 125. horne : huiusˌanni
  horno : hoc anno
  hostit : aequat, planat
125 heletor : orti vel olerum cultur
  hortatur : suadet
  hortor : suadeor
  hostimentum : aquamentum
  hoscitans : flans, spiritu alans
130 horonia : inrisiva dictio ut ea vitope-
    rare intellegas
  hoscine : hos vero
  hocine : hoc verum
  homuntio : non grandis forma
  hononorat : honore munerat
135 homulus : non grandis forma

humus : terra
humatus : sepultus
humana : motalia

I.

ianuam : ostium, porta
ianitor : ostiarius, custus
iaspis : genus gemmę
iacturam : damno
5 iamdudum : iam ante
    P. 126. iacula : missilia tela, id est
    lancea vel sagitta
iactantia : superbia
Iabin : intellectus
iacit : mittit, iacta
10 iacturarius : qui frequenter patitur
    damnum aut mortalitate
iactus : iactatus
iapix : velox vel ventus
Iacobus : subplantator
ieiuna : sterelis, infructuosa
15 iecor : interanea, ficatum
ieraticas : sacerdotalis literra aput
    Egyptos
Iohannes : domini gratia
iocinora : viscera
Ioram : diaconus
20 iubar : speldor vel luciferq· ante solis
    orto apparet
iugalem : coniugem
iubilate : strepite, cantate
iuba : crista, galea
iuga : capita et summitatis montium
25 P. 127. iurisperitus : legis doctor
iugiter : asidue
iurgium : litigium
iusiurandum : foedus, id est pacis iura-
    mentum
iuglandas : noces maiores
30 iustitium : locus puplicum
iugium : fervitates, captivitates
ictus : percussus
iconisma : imago, figura fine pectore a
    caput
ideo : idcirco
35 idem : iterum atque iterum
    (*rasura*) identide : ipsum per ipsum
    idem : et de uno dicitur et de pluribus,
    ut idem mihi dixit et idem mihi dix-
    erunt
    idiota : imperitus litterarum
idioma : prophetae sermonis
40 id ipsum : hoc ipsum
idolum : ex dolo nomen accepit, id est
    dolo diabuli adinventum
    P. 128. ignovit : venia veniam dedit
ignavus : stultus, inprudens
ignarus : inscius
45 ignuminia : infamia
ignovili vulgo : ignota turba

igitur : ergo
ignavia : pigritia, dementia
ignobilis : plebeius
50 ignita : igne accensa
ignominiosus : qui damnatur et de ex-
    ilio revocatur
ignipotens : Vulcanus
ilico : mox, continuo, statim
Iliaci : Troiani
55 ilex : genus arboris
ilicet : ire licet, scilicet
illinc : de isto loco
imbres : pluvię
imbicelles : dibiles
60 P. 129. immane : acervum, crudele
immanitas : ferocitas, acervitas
impubes : pueri sine barbas
imprumtum : in presentia
inpulsor : concitatur
65 imperium : regalis potestas
impopulavile : inlęsum
impune : sine vindicta
impendum : erogatio
impolitus : ineroditus
70 impos : pusillanimus
impiare : inquinare
immolo : victimo
immotum : firmum
imburio : incurvatio
75 inmensus : sine mensura
imbutus : plenus, institutus
imus : summus, altus
    P. 130. immania : ingentia, aspera
immutilata : incontaminata, inconcussa
80 impendit : erogat
impulit : adegit, percussit
impar : inaequalis
impotens animi : elatus prosperitate
impertio : tribuo, dono
85 improcinctu : ex apparatu
impenetrabile : in interiore et inacces-
    sibile
immolat : sacrificat
improbus : inportunus et inconsidera-
    tus, inpurus
immitus : inexorabilis
90 immo : potius et quod prius est
immurice : in saxo acuto
immerens : non merito
immoderatus : praeceps
impraecelsum : inexcelsum
95 impraeceps : in imo profundo
    P. 131. imperat : accipit
implex : innexa, incorporalia
improcinctu : in expiditione
imprecor : intente precor
100 impensius : largius, uberius
imperitus : indoctus
impubis : investimentibus
imploro : rogo, invoco
improvitus : qui non providet
105 imperitat : frequenter imperat

inadibilis : inaccesibilis
inanimis : qui numquam habuit animam
inbutus : institutus
incompti : inconpositi
110 incula : peregrinus
incolomis : salvus
incunabula : initia infantię
incommoda : inutilia, damna
incolatus : peregrinatio
115 incursationis : impetu
incrementum : nutrimentum, augmentum initium ·
inclemens : iracundus, impius
     P. 132. incertum : inlicitus coitus
incestat : contaminat, violat
120 inconstans : mutabilis
incomitatus : sine comitibus
increpitans : cum ioco minatur
incessere : accusare, provocare
incubuit : appetivit, tenuit
125 inconsultando : in consilio habendo
incidit : incurrit
incidet : peccat
incutet : inicet
incessant : accusant, provocant
130 inauspicatum : sine requisitione
in animum : in mente
inbelles : qui pugnare non possunt
incircumscriptus : terminum carens
incunctanter : sine dubitatione
135 inclitum : nubilem
     P. 133. incassum : supervacuum inanem
incentores : inritatores
incelebre : deserto
increbuit : diffamatum est
140 incubat : res alienas tenet
incessere : perficescere, ambulare
inconsulti : sine consilio
incentor : stimulatur
inconditus : inornatus
145 incedit : ambulat, praecedit
inconclavi : in secreto, in penetrabili
inconvulsa : incommutabilis
incuria : necligentia
in coniectura : in similitudine
150 incessum : gressum ambulandi
indeptus : adeptus, auctor adsecutus
indefessa : infatigabili
indigina : habitatur, civis
     P. 134. indemnis : sine damno
155 indix : significatur
indagine : inquisitione
indicia : signa, testimonia
indutiae : dilationis
indoles : ingenium, natura, mores
160 individuum : inseparabile
indubies : pax bello manente
indagatio : inquisitio
ineluctabilis : invincibilis
inermis : sine arma

165 ineres : piger, sine arte
ineptia : insipientia, stultitia
inexcita : invocata
incumbet : insistet
inergumina : demuniaca
170 in excessum : in pavore
inedia : fastidium
incentiva : irritamenta, aculei vitiorum, cupiditas
     P. 135. inconsequenter : inrationabiliter
in cenoleis : in conviviis
175 incursatione : ininpeto
industria : doctrina, studium
indedit : inseruit, inmisit
indoles : ętas iovenalis qui dolore nescit
indens : inserens, indicans
180 indocilis : qui docere non potest
inductio : persuasio
indiis : mendaciis
indiferens : paratus sine dubitatione
indegestum : inconpositum, inperfectum
185 induviae : indumenta
inexorabibilis : inpacabilis
indoles : certe spei vel progenies incr mentum
inergia : pigritia
inexpertum : non probatum
190 ineffabilia : quę non place loqui
     P. 136. inexplebilis : insatia*vilis*
inedie : famis, gerinia
inextasi : in excessu
inenodabile : insolubile
195 incominus : in simul
infauta : infilicia
infastis : in ore positis
infit : incipit, dicit, dixit
infititur : negat, non fatetur
200 infidus : infidelis, incertus
infimus : inferior
infestus : iratus, inruens
infetaces : infructuose
infrenis : in reverens
205 infrendimus stringimus
infersisti : intulesti
infulfor : pervasor
infolis : dignitatibus
     P. 137. infulae : vitę sacerdotales
210 infanda : nec dicenda, *crimina*
infamis : malę famę
infitias : mendatium
infetiare : crimen inferre vel negare
inficit : tinguit et colore inmutat
215 infensus : inportunus
infectum : non factum vel tinctum, focatum, coloratum
inferie : sacrificia mortuorum
infertat : inportat, minestrat
infrequens : inofficiosus
220 informitas : inconpositio

informamur : instruimur
in furia : in furore
inclubie : gyla
initum : pactum
225 ingenium : naturalis sullicitudo
ingens : magnus
P. 138. ingeminas : iterans, doplans
ingruit : inruit inminet
incluvies : voragines, sordes
230 ingemit : indigne ferit
ingentia : grandia
incruentes : inminentes, incumbentes
ingerit : infert
inglorius : sine gloria
235 inhospita : inhabitabilis
inhians : attonᶦtus animum ut tentus
inhibet : prohibet, coibet
inhiantes : desiderantes
iniet : coepit, inchoabit
240 inimica : aversaria
inicet : imittet
iniurium est : iniustum est
iniecit : inmisit
initum : pactum
245 P. 139. inlex : seductor
inlicet : seducet, suadit
inluvies : morbus, sordes, squalor
inlivata : intacta, inviolata
inlustrare : inluminare
250 inletabibilis : tristis
inliberalis : malignus
inlustrat : clarificat
inliunt : inlicita persuadēt
inlepidum : insuave
255 innox : innoxius
inexa : amplexa
insuba : quę nulli nubet
innectitur : inligatur
innocuus : qui nulli nocet
260 innitens : incumbens, confidens
inops : pauper, plus debet quod pos-
sedet
P. 140. inopinata : subita, insoirata
inormis : inmensus
inpertit : erogat uni
265 inquilinus : peregrinus
inquam : dixi
inquilini : coloni, condititionis
inlexit : suasit
inlabere : descendere, influere
270 inlecebra : inlicitas voluntas, blandi-
tia, dolus
inlicita : prohibita
inlustra//es : nobilis, gloriosi
inludet : irridet
inlectus : seductus
275 inlictant : quod supra
inluxit : lumen apparuit
innoxius : innocens
inni : conati
innupta : incognita vero
280 innixus : incumbens

innomirum : innomirabilem
P. 141. innuit : natibus indicat
inopia : famis, paupertas
inolevit : crevit, innotuit
285 inoromata : visione
inquio : dico
inpendio : erogatio
inquis : sine quiete
insignis : nobilis, magnus, ornatus
290 instar : similitudo, magnitudo
insolens : inportunus
instigat : incendit, inmittit
insons : innocens
insedit : obtenuit
295 insitio : insertio
instipat : congerit
instimulat : invistigat
insolentia : stultitia
insolescit : mutatur
300 insitum : infixum, inherens
insinuat : indicat, nuntiat
P. 142. instantia : vigilantia
insultat : inridat
inscendit : discendit.
305 insudandum : sudore querendum
insigne pietate : valde pium
insuetare : insolenter evadere
insignit : ornat, exultat
insuescit : extra consuitudinem efficitur
310 insquitia : rusticitas, inperitia
insolevit : invaluit, inhesit
insigniri : insignem fieri
insolitus : inconsuetus
insolenter : inportune
315 insitus : insertus
insertaba : inserebam
insticnto dei : inspiratione dei
insomnis : pervigilans
instinctu : inpulsu
320 P. 143. instruit : preparat, ornat
insectatus : persecutus
instaurat : reparat, rennovat
insimulat : accusat, fingit
instat : insistit, vigilat
325 instituta : exempla dispositionis praecepta
insolescere : supervivere
insignior : sublimior, nobilior
inspicare : defendere et in modo spicarum concidere
intrinsicus : inferius
330 intestinum : domesticum
intempesta nox : media nox
interpola : revocata
intercalare : interponere
interiit : periit
335 intrinsicus : inferius
intrivera : minuaverat, contriverat
intemerata : intacta, integra, incor-
rupta
P. 144. intuitur : vidit, aspicit
interritus : sine pavore

340 internusci : cognusci
intimus : interior
interpulavit : interruppit
interlitus : interlinitus
interiit : periit
345 intenti : atoniti
integratio : untio
interceptio : deceptio, fraus
in tempore : in oportunitate
intima : pretiosa
350 intersecta : interclusa
intimabo : insinuabo
intercapito : interiectio
intestabile : sine fede testium
intiger : sanguinem plenus
355 interfabor : interlogor
interpolatus : corruptus varięq ; maculatus vel fuscatus
inteptant : inferunt
intentant : intendunt, minatur
interpellante : reluctante vel inpediente
360 P. 145. interminia : innuntia, obiectus metriatrix
intimat : nodum facit
interfata : interlocuta
intempestivo : non suo tempore
interrex : designatus rex
365 interpalor: varigare
intendando : conto da intendo, äimminandenus quando inter se obliteratur
interlunium : inter prima novissimę lunä
internuntii : qui inter partes nuntium portant
inter pucula : interępulas
370 interdum : frequenter
intonuit : insonuit
intrio : infundo
interpres : conlectur
intemperantia : ieiuna set inmoderata audacia
375 interdiu : per diem
interrecta : interclusa
P. 146. intertrimentum : si aliqua speties in medio teratur
interlocutio : iudicium
introrsus : introversus
380 internitione : mortem, interitum
interna : interiora cordis
interlitus : intercisio verbi
inultum : iniudicatum
investis : sine barbis
385 invergit : perfundit
invia : difficilior via ubi non est
invisus : qui non videtur
invenus : turpis, ingratus
inumbratur : occultatur
390 invalidus : infirmus
investibolo : in ingresso
invehit : infert, portat
invisere : visitare

P. 147. invisit : ingreditur
395 invisor : invidus
inuret : incendit
invectus : inportatus
invisant : inspiciunt
invium : sine via quod adire non potest
400 inviolatus : intiger, intactus
itritum : vanum, sine effectum
iris : arcus in nube
irritat : provocat, simulat
ironia : dirisio
405 istuc : huc
ite dacus : Danubius
istromates : commentarus scientię [um
Isaurum : Danubium Isterum Danubi-
itidem : aduerbium est temporis quasi iterum
410 itemque : iterumque
itidentidem : iter̃uat· iterum
itero : repeto
iterum : item
iter : iteneris
415 Itureus : populus
P. 148. istromatheas : opus variuse ulaciniona et varia diversitate contexto

K.

kalendae : initium mensium vel a colendo dictę
kalibem : ferrum
kalyps : forca poenalis
Karybdis : vertigo maris
5 kalnes : galeę militum
karitrius : genus avis et est albam et pinnae ius non exuritur

L.

Latio : Italia
Latini : Romani
lar : focolar intra domum
larva : malificus, incantatur
5 larvalis : daemoniosa
lacernum : stola, vestis
lavitur : cadit
labus : labor
Laverna : dea furum
10 P. 149. lanista : macellarius qui carnis ferro laniat et magister glatiatorum
lata : prolata, praedicta
laqueare : camera laqueata
lapicidina : locus ubi ceduntur
latrina : recessus
15 labe : sorde
lacerum : laniatus, dibilem
laquearia : domorum tignaria
lacunculae : laterna id est vasa lucernę fictilia

labentes : cadentes
20 lactat : decepit leniter
late : passim, ubique
lapsantem : serventem
Latio : Latinorum
lavefactare : subvertere
25 latebra : locus absconsus a latendo
lacertis : musculis braciorum aut genus
   piscium
lampene : stelle fulgetes
lactasis : metaphoras ab infantibus
   P. 150. lampas : facula
30 lamnas : animal similis pardo
latex : aqua quę latet et inveniuntur
lautumia : costudia carceris
lacessit : lacerat, provocat
lanugo : prima barba in similitudine
35 latur : portatur
lascivia : voluptas animi
laberna : ferramenta latronum vel qui
   filius alienus seducet
latura : datura
laverna : homo qui filius alienus seducet id est latro
40 lacunę : fossę
lacit : captat suadet
laciniosum : pannosum
lacunaria : pendentia luminaria
laurigeris : laurum portantes
45 lacunaria : camere
lautitie : munditię
Latium : autem dictum est locus in
   partes Italię quo Aeneas Tornus
   P. 151. lancis : missurias
larvę : umb simulacrum
50 lavillis : lubricus
lascivus : luxuriosus
larantes : arantes
lascive : fervide
laicus : popularis
55 laris : genus avis guia
laqueare : vincire, alligare
lavitur : solvitur aut cadet
latibulum : defensaculum
lances : pondera, mensurę
60 lapite : cruciat, sollicitat doliter
latomus : lapidu cęsor
legio : numerus sex milium hominum
legunt : colligunt
legale : legitimum
65 legitima : iudicia, praecepta
legata : testamenta, donata
legomartia : numirus militum quasi
   Marti consecratus
legatum : donatio defuncti
legatus : internuntius
70 Leofilus : leonis filius
   P. 152. lectica : qua consoles portantur
lebetas : caccavoseneos
lectores : apparitores
lecticalis : qui lectulum facit

75 lebissata : genus marmoris
lena : vitiorum seductrix
lenta : flexebilis
lenocinia : seductionis, persuasionis
lentetur : otiose fiat
80 lepus : blandus
leno : seductor et praepositus meretricum
lentus : tardus, lenis
lenit : pacat, blandit
lenocinium : uxoris meretricatio ma-
   riti consensu
85 lepus : blandus
lepidum : pulchrum, unestum
leporem : blanditiem, dulcidine, de-
   core
lepidum : pulchur, honestum
lepidus : tener, mollis, delicatus
90 leptopyria : minute febris
   P. 153. Lerna : paludes aquę ubi
   fuit ydra serpens, qui multa capita
   habuit
Lerneus : ut anguis in Lernatus
leargus : vitium quo conpremuntur
   egriad falsum somnum
lenicavis : lenivis, dealbabis
95 Lebbeus : circulus id est a corde ipse
   est deus ipse est et Iudas Iacubi
libo : sacrifico, offero
Lilibeus : promunturius
libertas : ingenuitas
libare : est aliquid lebiter
100 Libani : potentes sęculi et fortes
Liburnus : grandis navis
Liburne : accule Atriatici maris
libumina : sacrificia, incensa
libavit : degustavit, sacrificavit
105 libitinia : lectus mortuorum
libat : fundit, sicilę
   P. 154. libiralis : munificus, largus
librat : pensant, equant
libetima : arca ubi mortui condiuntur
110 liberalitas : donatio quę fit a divi-
   tibus
liberaliter : humaniter
lictores : qui fasces ante iudices ferunt
licitatio : proposita vinditio
licessere : licere
115 licitacio : quotiens aliquis vinditur, et
   emptores super se augmentum faciunt
licetur : de praedio contenditur
lictor : apparatio
licentiosa : maiorum mancipia quo
   multa licet
licitatio : promessio, sponsio
120 licenter : licite
lienum : vinum
ligula : arguta, loquax
Liguria : provintia Italię in qua est
   Mediolanus
ligones : rastri, bidentes

125 P. 155. ligustra: genus floris croco-
coloris
limis: finisterminus
limitata: terminata
limat: mulcet
limpido: puro
130 limnis: strabo et oblicus oculis
lymphaticus: fantasticus qui quasi ex
aqua divinant
lymbus: circuitus quoiusque rei, ut ora
maris
linchine: candelae
linquet: relinquet, deserit
135 linquuntur: defluunt
lincis: bestia varii coloris
linter: navicula modica
linquit: peccat, dimittit
liquidum: splenditum, lucidum
140 liquet: patet, claret
lyra: genus cithare
litat: sacrificat
litargus: somnulentus
lita: imitat
145 litaus: tuba longa
litigium: scandalum
litigatio: causatio
P. 156. lixa: aqua dicebant antiqui,
unde elixare dicitur
lotus: libatus
150 loquacitas: multa locutio
locavit: collocavit
longiturni: longevi
longo limite: longo ordine
logium: quod est rationale, pannus ex-
iguus ex auro gemmis coloribusque
variis qui super humerale contra
pectus pontificis utebatur
155 logica: rationalis
logisticum: cogitabilem
luculentum: luce plenum
lucus: eo quod menime luceat
luctum: planctum
160 lucar: in urbe Roma et rogatio que
solebant in lucis fieri et vectigal
lupanar: habitatio meretricum
ludificat: inludit
P. 157. Luperci: pastores qui sacra
incubi nudi colebant
lumina: oculi
165 lustrum: quinquenium
lustrat: circuit, peragrat
luis: persolvis poenas
lutenes
Lucelleum: genus marmoris albi
170 lucifer: stella quę ante luce apparit
ludibrium: dedicus et quod inluditur
vanitas
lubricus: elavescens
lupanaria: cella meretricum
Lupercalia: gentium cultura id est
sacra panis qui ipse dicitur
175 luridum: sordium, pallidum

lues: pestis, morbus, dilubius
lurconum: devoratorum, gluttonum
luscina: aves quę bene canit
luxus: pompa regia et luxuria
180 P. 158. lumine turvo: diro hae tru-
culentum vultum
ludicrum: ludibrium turpe
Lucas: ipse consurgens, sibe ipse li-
bans

M.

macte: magis aut tam magis
macies: exiguitas corporis
Maceti: Macedones
magalia: loca pastorarum
5 madet: humet
magnanimus: fortis
magnites: lapis qui ferrum rapit
maius: plus, amplius
malum punici: mala granata
10 mallatia: mollities, grę
malagrama: herba venenosa
maialis: porcus pinguis eo quod de
. his Maie sacricabantur
pp. 159 and 160 left vacant
P. 161. mancipat: manum mittit et
sociat
manua: manipula
15 mansa: comista, manducata
mandemus: cometimus
mania: furor, insania
mane: persevera
manes: inferorum anime vel sepulcra
20 manipulus: numirus militum brevis
manipulus: unde et mapuli dicti fasces
gremiorum quod manu capinantur
manuale: orarium
manicat: mane surget, per manu tenet
mansuevit: mansuetus factus est
25 manubię: pręda de hostibus
manūcapta: id est spolia
mandavi: tradedi
Maburtia: res quę ad pugna pertenit
machinatur: parat, instruit
30 macilentus: macer
maior natu: senior
P. 162. maculosus: pullutus
mapalia: ex sę pastorum
madefactus: humefactus
35 magnificus: magna faciens
magnanimitas: fortitudo banimi
maleatur: faber ferr
machinationis: commenta a studii
Maria: in luminatrix vel domina
40 marsuppium: sacellum
margine: extrema parte livere
mastia: malus serbus, serbus nequam
matertera: matri soror
mavis: magis vis
45 Maurusia: Mauritania
mavens: durans, perseverans

maranathema : in adventum domini

P. 163. maiurolit: xii. signa mathe-
matici asserunt

marcet : languet

50 martirium : testimonium

marrina : potio divina

mastigie : taurie flagella

mattus : trisus

matrinus : matri frater

55 matertera : magna soror aviae

mavisse : magis volo esse

marcus : excelsus, mandatus

Messias : unctus id est Christus

melus : dolcis sonus

60 meditulium : medius locus in campo

melotes: pelles ovinas simplix qua
monachi uduntur ex uno latere

P. 164. meliusculum : modicum meliorem

metatur : habriatur, locatur

Melopeus : quasi carminis facitor

65 mensum : mensuratum

meat : manat, decorrit, ambulat

menstrum : subaudis tempus unius
mensis

Menalias : pastoralis

meritoria : loca tabernaro ubi adulteria
comminantur

70 mero hanima : simplici, sincero

mersat : merget

metiri : mensurari

mercimonia : cummertia, negutiationis

Menedes : Balię pars

75 mergitis : fatię utspinarum

P. 165. mermis · formica

melicus : poeta carminum lyricorum

mediastinus : balneatur

medustinus : balneatur

80 metacastor : ita mihi propitius set castus

messala : agricola, messor

melops : bonus cantor

mensis commodus : September mensis

mergi : fus eꝭ quibus messis colligunt

85 melopeum : dulcem, conpositum

mercedarius : qui mercedes dat pro labore

Micepsa; vifuit Numidarum

minitatur : asidue minatur

minax : minas tendens

90 minicius : ericius

mimologus : qui mimos docet

P. 166. Milesiae : amatorię geste

minas : altitutinis propugnaculum

mitra : corona et amictus capillorum ·

95 minsare : sepius mingere

myrmiceas : verrugas corporis

mysterium : occultum praefigurado

mitis : mansuetus

missele : telum quod mittitur

100 miscelluneum : cumixtitium

miscentur : praeturbantu.·

Minotaurus : monstrum qui capite tau-
rino et cetera partis corporis homo
fuit, a Minoe rege et a tauro, quia
ex utraque mater fertur semina sus-
cipisse

P. 167. missitat : frequenter mittit

missicius : qui militia exibit

105 missos nos facit : demitti nos

miseranda : misera, infelex

migma : palea minutarum

mioparon : naviculas cava pyratarum

Mihahel : qui sicut deus

110 modifica : modolata temperata

modolatio : dolcido vocis

modestus : moderatus, rectus

modestia : verecundia

moechia : adulterium et omne inlicito
concubito

115 modus : mensura, ordo

modolatur : formatur

P. 168. modolant : librant

moderatio : temperantia

molis : magnitudo, vastitas

120 mollit : mitigat, placit

molosi : canis magni

molimina : artificia cogitationis

molles : vani

molior : dispono, excogito

125 molitur : disponit, agit

monachus : solitarius

P. 169. monachosmum : genus vehiculi quod ab uno iumentum du-
catur

monogamus : unius uxori vir

monarchus : singularis rex

130 monomentis : memoriis litterarum

mons Tarpeius : Capitulium

momentum : stilus in comenta

monumentum : memoria

monilia : ornamentum in capite molie-
rum vel pectore quorum

135 monopolium : ut ubi una res venditur

monarchia : principatus singularis

monstrum : deformitas membrorum et
prodigium adversum

P. 170. monoceron : quadrupis uni-
cornuus

monimenta : auxilia

140 monadem : unitatem

mulcet : dilectat. blanditur

mulcra : vasa ubi lac mulgitur

mulgatores : peremptores

mulosus : canis rusticus

145 mulcat : pugnis vel calcibus cedit

multatio : damnum pecunię

multatus : condemnatus

multifarie : multiloque multi sermo-
nus

mulcero : limo, plano, mitigo

150 Mulciver : Vulcanus

Mulciver : ignis dicitur eo quod omnia
mulcatur

P. **171**. munifex: munera distribu-
ens
munimen: defensio
munera: officia, bellorum tributa, firmitas
155 munificus: honorificus
mundus: celum vel terram
municipium: mansio q̄ muros
murex: regalis porpora
municeps: unicus qui accepti muneri-
bus edificatur vel princeps primus
160 munusculum: modica donatio
munitabitur: munietur
munificentia: libertas libera
munimenta: testimonia murorum
munituria: precinúturia
165 *munium: quasi manufactum sic et muri*
a monicione
P. **172**. municipium: quod iam ac-
cipiat munera id est offitia
murice: coclea marina
munia: munera qui militibus dantur
murice: frutices virgultę et saxa acuta
in montibus
170 mussim: lente
museleu: monumentum
mussat: silentium murmurat, dubitat
musitanter: leniter
musia: nidi suricum
175 muscepula: temptatio, laqueum
murquiso: marmuratur, fallax
musitat: frequenter murmurat
mutilat: placitum violat
mutilo: inmino, violo, sautio, frango
180 P. **173**. mutilum: truncatum
mutturci: stulti, inertes

N.

nabo: rescendo
nabat: natabat
nanciscitur: potitus, inventus
nare: natare
5 navarcus: navi magister
navilia: loca in qua nabis educantur
nando: natando
naviter: strenue, stutiose, fortiter, ute-
liter
Nazareus: sanctus
10 nablum: quod Graece spalateriū
nanctus: adeptus, inventus
nant: natant
P. **174**. navale proelium: nática
pugna
nauta: nauta ‧ naus ‧ obsequens
15 navales res: ad nave pertinentis
navus: vigelans, celer, industriosus,
celer·
navit: strenuit agit
napeus: navium magister
navare: strenue officio facere

20 nativum: genetivum
navatoperat: datoperat
natrix: serpens
nat: natat
natice: non est
25 nardum: pysticum
nardum: fitelem, id est sine fraude
narrat: nuntiat
P. **175**. nectar: sapor vel odor sum-
mae suavitatis, vel potio deorum
et vitam
nectarius: odorifer
30 nebulo: latro, mendax
necopinans: nec sperans
necessitudo: dilectio, amicidię
nectere: inmittere
nefas: scelus invitia
35 necromanticus: evocatur umbrarum,
aut mortuorum divinatio
nenia as: vilissimas fabulas
nequa: malus
nequivit: non potuit
nefastus: nefarius, nequissimus
40 P. **176**. Neomenia: novellionium,
Kalendę
neophitus: novella plantatio
neunt: colligunt
nentes: fila torquentes
nexus: nodus, ligatura
45 neutrum: nec illum nec hoc
nepa: vipera
necnon: sedet
nevum: macula
necue: vel non
50 nebris: corium cervi
nectit: alligat
nefastus: scelere pollutus
nefarius: sceleratus
negromantia: quotiens hanimam ab
inferis revocatur vel divinatio mon-
strorum
55 P. **177**. nequiquam: nec modicum
nequeo: non possum
ne quarta: crudelis in loquendo
nẽquaqua: nullo modum
nemus: silva
60 ne: ergo
nepos: prodignus eversor
neotrici: novicii, minores
neuter: medius
neve: ne forte
65 neque: non
Nereis: nympha marina
neerant: flaverant
nempe: certe, utique
nevet: filat
70 neto: torto
nex: mors a necandi
P. **178**. nectari: ocultorum frequentia aperiri
necti corax: noctua avis
nenia: carmen funebre

75 nepa : prius in sideribus
nibarus . splenditus
nictit : canis cum acute gannit
nimbus : tempestas, pluvia cum ventum
nimboso : tempestuoso
80 nixe : munite
nidor : splendor
nimphaticus : arreptitius
niveus : canditus
ni : nisi, non
85 nidores : odores
nis : nobis
nimborum : nubium
nidor : odor
ninnarus : murio cuius uxor adulterat et ipse tacet
90 P. 179. nititur : pugnat, conatur, temptat
nimpe : nonne, utique
nisus : conatus
nigelli : nigri
nimirum : sine dubium, certe
95 Nicolaum : stultum
nectura : genitura
Nilicula : Aegyptius
nimpha : virgo celestis vel numina
nitens : incumbens et splenditus
100 nitelle : nitores parvi
niquid : nisi quid
nympheum : silanum
nisuper : proxime
nimpha : dea aquarum
105 nixus : incumbens, curvus
nitet : splendit, lucet
P. 180. nosochomium : locum venerabilem in quo infirmi homines curantur
nostratium : nostrorum
nonnulli : aliquanti
110 Noti : venti
nothus : spurius de adulterium natus vel incertus
norat : sciebat
nos satius : nil hominus, tanto magis
noxa : culpa, peccati rea
115 nocticula : luna
noxius : nocens
norma : mensura, regula
noxius : tergiversatur
nox umada : tempestas cum pluvia
120 non potative : non dubium
nomencolatur : nomen officii
num : numquid
P. 181. nutu : voluntate
nutatio : irae minatio
125 nuncupat : nomen vocat
nuper : modo, ante tempus
nutans : vacillans, pendens, titubans
numen : potestas, magestas
nugas : inutilis, vilis
130 nugacitas : vanitas, insania

nuit : annuit, promisit
·nurus : uxor filii
nusciosus : qui plus vepere videt
nutibus : gestibus
135 numquis : numquid aliquis
nummolarius : nummorum praerogatur
P. 182. numisma : nummi percussor, id est donarius
nundinationis : mercationis
nundina : mercatum
140 nuberca : matrea id est matrima

O.

obediens : dicto parens
obsecunda : obtempora
obitus : mors
obiit : mortuus est
5 obeuntia : circumdantia
obelo : linea
obice : repelle
obices : oppositionis
obverto : in alia parte verto
10 obessus : pinguis carnibus
obolum : dimidium, scripulum
obici : repelli
P. 183. *obici : rep*
obet : moritur
15 obeundi : exequendi
obicio : oppono
ob : propter
obest : contra est
obans : gaudens
20 obiurgat : oppugna, castigat, increpat
obdat : opponet, praeligat
oblicus : non rectus vel transversus
obliteratus : oblivione obscurum
obliminat : limpidat
25 oblectat : dilectatione infundit
oblata : offerta
obliterat : oblita
oblustrans : circumspiciens
obliteratio : oblivio dilata
30 P. 184. obnixus : humiles, incumbens
obnixius : subiectus
obnixii : subditi, rei
obnubet : obteget
obnueret : obtexerat
35 obortis : subito ortis
obsinatiomentis : duritia vel intentio
obstipium : contrapositum
obstupita : mente turbata
obsolitatus : inquinatur
40 obstructum : preclusum
obsecrat : deprecar. rogat
obstinatus : disperatus, inrevocabilis, obduratus
obsilitus : sorditus
P. 185. obsecunda, obsequitur

45 obscenum: fędessimum, turpem
obsessus: circumdatus
obtestatur: adiurat
obtusa: praecessa
obturpuit: infrigitavi, obstipuit
50 obtunsus: obcecatus, clusus
obtundentes: abscondentes
obticuit: ommutuit
obtutus: aspectus inmubilis
obvallatum: undique munitum
55 obluctor: contra luctor
obnites: reluctans
obnuit: operuit, obtexuit
P. 186. obnixe: intente
obnuit: aperit
60 obnutus veste: circumdatus veste
obnuto: obluto, obterito
obnectere: conligare
obstrepit: inpetit
obsita: obtecta, circumdata
65 obsillagis: marsus
obstat: contra dicit
obstipum: oblicum, inaequalem
obsunt: contra sunt
obserat: claudit
70 obsessit: subripuit
obsistit: obviat
P. 187. *obturat: obcludit oppilat*
obstetrix obstetricis: quę parturien-
tibus praeerant
obtrunco: interficio
75 obtrectans: resistens
obtundere: prohibere
occipit: incipit
obsistet: obviat
occubuit: interiit, mortuus est
80 ocior: velocior
occasus: finis
occursat: sepius occurrit
occulit: abscondit, occultat
ocreas: tibialia
85 occipitium: posterior pars capitis
occentare: contra cantare
occulluit: occultavit
P. 188. *odas: cantatio*
odeporicum: itinerarium viatorium
90 odeum: a cantu
ode: dicitur cantatio
oe: conpellatio personę
oeconomia: dispensatio
oestrum, genus tavani quod boves habent
95 officium: obsequium, minnesterium
offa: pars frusti rotundu
officit: obstat, nocet, tinguet
olli: illi
olus: olera
100 oletores: ortolani
olfacere: odorare
olim: aliquando, antiquitus .
olimat: limpidat
olores: gigni

105 olitana: vetusta
olor: gigni
olympum: caelum et nomen montis
odas: cantatio
P. 189. olografum: totum praescrip-
tum
110 omelia: popularis tractatus, gr̃e
omnopere: omni virtute
o   : auguria
ommitto: pretereo, dimitto
omousion: unius substantia
115 omoeusion: similis substantia
omentum: mappa ventris
omen: quod homo somniatur, auspicium, auguria maiora
onera: sarcina
onestum: graviosum
120 onix: gens marmoris
ongriforum: lucta ferens
onocrotolus: genus avis est quod facie
gerat asini nam stulta facię, sed obducta grotalus dicitur
P. 190. onicinum: genus lapidis
onustum: gravosum
125 opacus: umbrosus
opem: auxilium
opere precium: necessarium
operiens: expectans
oppedum: castrum vel civitas sine murus
130 oppetere: occumbere, mori
oppidanus: civis ex oppida nam oppidaneus Latinum est, aput antiquus
oppida dicta sunt quod opem dare
operit: celat, vetat
opifex: operis factur, artifex
opimus: fertilis, saginatus
135 opitulatur: adiubatur
opido: valde, vehementer, oportune,
omnino
P. 191. optimatus: optimarum artium auctor vel princeps
opinor: existimo
opter: propter
140 opinatores: existimatores
opilio: minor pastorum pecorarius
opobalsamum: lacrima balsami
optio: electio, potestas, arbitrio
opacant: obumbrant
145 oppetit: obiit
opes: divitie
· operosa: ingentia certamina
opessulatum: clavem obserratum
opproprium: malum crimen
150 opima: ampla, magna
opitulantia: suffragia
oppidum: mansio sine curia vicina
opiter: natus avo paternon vivo post
patris morte natus
P. 192. opniparum: beatum, opu-
lentum
155 oppilat: obturat, obcludit

opitis : genus marmoris
opinatissimum : nominatissimum
oportunus : necessarius
opulentus : divis
160 optigit : sorte evenit
oro : rogo, peto
orator : eloquens
orditor : incipit
ortus : natus
165 orbitas : amissio filiorum
oridurius : aspere loques
oroma : visio somnii
orbita : vistigia rotarum instrata
oris : finibus regionis
170   P. 193. orsa : cepta, locuta
oracula : responsa, precepta
orba : sine parentibus
orbatus : filiorum amittens
ora : finis, vultus, et extrema vestis
175 oriundus : natus, ortus
orei : regionum finis
orgia : misteria secreta
Ortosegia : dolus insula
ortigo metrum : cuturnix
180 ortho doxus : rictus gloriae
ortigometra : coturnices
orosscopus : circulus signorum
oreagra : fuscinula gre.
    P. 194. osanna : salvificat vel sul-
        vum facit
185 ostentatum : monstratum
ostentum : signum quod ostenditur
osurum : oditurum
os : orii
osor : inimicus ab odio dictus
190 ostentat : ostendit
os : ossis
osus : odiosus
oscine : aves quod cantando auspicia
        faciunt
ostentatura : ostensio insolita veluti
        sifiant in nocte repentina lux

P.

pasciscit : pactum facit
pactum : decretum
pacus : collegio curiae
pabulator : pastor
5 *phalax : acies militum*
    P. 195. pactio : conibentia
pactorium : plantatorium
paganitius : ut cultus
pagmat : desiterat
10 pagus : possessio est ampla sed sine
        alique iure unde et paganos dicimus
        alienus a iure vel sacris constitutis
pagi : memoriis sine idolis
pagmentes : desiderantes
pauxillum : paulolum, modicum

palestra : exercitatio ubi athlete se ex-
        ercebant
15 palmatus : coronatus
paliurus : spina vel genus palatemas
        secari carum cardi spinosi
    P. 196 left vacant
    P. 197. palpat : fovet, blanditur
palteum : murum, fastidium
paululum : aliquantulum
20 Palea : dea qui pastores colebant
palantes : fugientes in diviso
palla : Minerva et amiotō muliebri
palmola : extrema pars navis
palare : errare
25 pala : puplice, coram
palabundi : errantes
palmas : victorias
pallantes : gaudentes
paulisper : aliquantisper, paulatim
30 palutamenta : ornamenta (cf. p. 199)
    P. 198. parilitas : aequalitas
parma : scutum parvum
parasituli : bucellatarii
pacus : cupidus, abstinens
35 parastus : paratus inuria facere et pati
parpata : copidus
parasitus : qui iocos facit ut ventrem
        impleat
parumper : per parum
paraclitum : consolatorem
40 pari : similem
paradigma : similitudo, fabula
parentia : oboedientia aperiendo
parentat : umbris vel tumulis mortuo-
        rum frequenter paret id est obsequi-
        tur aut minestrat
    P. 199. militum unde hii qui in pro-
        vintia proficiscunt paludani vo-
        cantur
palpidat : temptat
45 palantur : vagantur
paralypuminon : relico, quod restat
parsimonia : frugalitas, abstinentia,
        parcitas
parabula : similitudo
parasceue : prǫparatio grc̃
50 parta : inventa
parata : quesita
parsurus : parciturus
parumpendet : nihil iudicat
parmucupula : medicamenti vinditur
55 parentalia : dies festi panorum
particus : necutiatur ipse
Paridis iudicium : quod in tres deos
    P. 200. iononem, venerem, minerva
        Paris pastor damalo aureo iudi-
        cavit
parris : lapidis canditus
pariliter : aequaliter
60 parricida : qui parentes uo occidit
paracya : adiacens vel incolatus
Pharisei : divisi, separati

paradoxus : qui se ad gloria parat
parce : exugue, continenter
65 parochia : adiacens id est didomus
pantomimus : summus iocularis qui omnes ludus novit
panera : rapina
pansa : aperta
pantera : ritia
70 panicinum : genus vestis
pantheus : quasi omnium deus deorum
  P. 201. pandictes : omnia ferens et veterum et novorum testamento-rum
pangunt : disponunt carmina vel con-iungunt
Pan : ingibus
75 paniceum : roseum
panigerici : adolatores
panseus : qui pedibus in diverso ten-detibus alat
pastoforium : atrium templi et sacra-rium
pastinantes : plantantes
80 patrius : paternus
patibulum : crucis passio
patula : aperta, expansa
patera : fyala a patendo
patravit : perfecit aut commisit
85 patologia : passionis ratio
  P. 202. *Fratruus : frater patris papiliones : tenturia modica*
patogomo : genus morbi
pascha : transcensus
90 patruiles : filii frater
patruus magnus : frater avi
paulus : mirabilis
papilla : summa pars mammille
placito : tranquillo
95 plausum : risum stultum
platea : via spatiosa
plastrografis : falsis scriptis
plancus : pedibus latis
plagiatores : seductores
100 plagat : mitigat, sedat
plaustra : carra
plagiarius : qui peculim aut manci-pium alienum seducendum distrahit
  P. 203. plantasia : orto vel pom-aria
plaudete : iubilate
105 plaudit : manibus sonum facit
placenta : dulcia
plectitur : punitur, percutitur
plebicula : amans civis
plexus : percussus, truncatus
110 plerique : aliquanti
plebēscitat : plebem adloquitur
pleades : stelle
plectrum : percussorium cythare
plerique : alicotiens
115 plebeiu : popularis ominis sine aliqua dignitate

P. 204. *prefertat : preportat, ante la-tat*
plethora : plenitudo
prestigia : fallatia
prestolat : expectat
120 prefata : antedicta
presagus : prescius
previligium : quod iure devetur et pri-mus honor seu lex non poplica sed privata
presagium : signum quod antea deus postea venet
precordia : cor est
125 predignus : ante natus
pretervolo : volociter praetereor
preconium : praedicatio alicuius rei
  P. 205. et laus antecedens
prerogativum : beneficium ante obla-tum
prelibabimus : aliqua contolimus, ali-qua diximus
130 precelerat : antecedet
presagium : divinatio futurorum
pre se tulit : plusquam oportuit tulit
prepedit : impedit
prepetes : aves quae volantes auspicia faciunt
135 prepopere : inordinate et fistinanter
prescriptum : paesti tumi
prepos : percussor velox
pre foribus : ante ostium
prestigiaverunt : ludificaverunt
140 P. 206. presidium : auxilium
preses : iudex a presidendo
pretenta : anteposita
precavit : antecavit
prelibundo : pregustando
145 pretervehor : transnavigor
pressant : sepe praecedunt
predia : fundi, villae
prevertitur : antecedit
pretexit : celat, coperit
150 prevignus : filiaster
praefatio : prae alocutio
prestantior : melior
praeterea : extra hec
presul : princeps cuntis praepositis
155 P. 207. prediti : instructi, antepo-siti, potentes
prepes : aquila
pretores : secundi sunt consolibus
presertim : quam maxime
preus : antecedens
160 prerogans : ante inpendens
pres : fede iussor
prepoperum : antea factum quod erat postea faciendo
prelo : torcular
precipitat : ab alto deicet
165 precox : prematurus
predes : fidi iussores
prelus : modicus

prerepit : ante rapit
P. 208. prepostera : perversa, in
posterum quod ante debuit
170 praestruxit : praeordinavit
precipuus : perpinguis
praerogativa : excellentia meritorum
prepollit : eminet, supersplendet
•prequoqua : celere maturans
175 praecipue : maxime, ante omnia
praesidarius : auxilium praebens
prerupto : elevato, alto
preceps : festinus, temerarius
praetestatus : infans qui de praetestato
patre nascitur
180 prepes : praevolans
prelati : antepositi
prepetibus : antepetentibus
P. 209 pectet : pectinat
pecua : armenta et pecora
185 peculatus : qui pecunia puplica furat
pecudiarius : pastor
pecudes : oves
pedor : odor gravis
pedora : aurium sordes
190 pedagogus : eroditor puerorum
pellecti : inlecebrati, seducti
pellexit : in fraude induxit
pelica : concubina
pellectum : suasum
195 Pelorum :. promunturiorum
pellax : pervera loques
pegaso : homo iocularis
P. 210. pecuratus : habundan peco-
ribus
peiera : falsum iurat
200 pelagu : carina, navigium amnicum
pecuosus : qui multa pecura habet
pedatum : carcere
pedidatus : propagato filiorum vel nepotum
pedore : foedore
205 pelicet : inlicite circumvenit
pellace : dolosu, mendace
pellector : persuasor
pellex : succuba, quae lo alterius nubet
pelusit : distulit
210 peltat : scutum amagonicum parvum
penum : cellarium, promtuaria
penades : domus vel focus
P. 211. pendolus : elavatus
penes arbitros : aput iudices
215 penula : lacerna, stola
pendeo : fabeo, blandior
pentamerum : versus quinque pedum
penis : natura, pudenda
penitralia : interiora, secreta
220 pedere : existimare
penetrat : inrumpet intra, pertransit
pene moti : cito egressi
pentomen : circumcisio
penuceo : rubeo
225 pene : prope, iuxta, secus

pensio : praecii persulutio
penate : imago pulcerrima
pepulit : expulit, inpolit
P. 212. pepegit : pactuatus est
230 peplum : stola, vestis muliebris
pepo : melone
peplus : vestis simplex qua Minerve
simulacrum velatum est
pepones : melone
pernix : agilis, velox, celer
235 perpetes : aves, volantes
pernicibus : velocibus
permulcit : lenit
perpetimur : patimur
peribulum : deambulatorium vel bilua
marina
240 percensit : considerat
peculit : perturbavit, adicit, percussit
P. 213. perpetitur : patitur
perplexus : involutus, temidus
pertemptat : perquiret
245 perstans : praeverans
perduellio : rebellatur
perpolit : coegit
permotus : turbatus, excitatus
percunctatur : perquiret, interrogat
250 perbabitur : decurrit
perniciosus : a pernitendo qui dat operam, opera a perdendo aliquem et
pernicies dicitur
permultatum : in omnium notitia inti-
mata
perfunctorie : imaginarie, transitorie
petros : agnoscens
255 pernicitas : velocitas
P. 214. perpetrat : pe agit committit
perpesitius : qui frequenter aliquem
patitur
perper : perpetuo
peremptus : interfectus
260 persistet : perseverat
perpende : perpensa, equat
periti : docti
perendie : pus cras
perfunctus : transactus
265 perniciter : velociter
perhibet : pernuntiat
peresum : comestum
pertulit : perturbavit, perstrabit
perlustrat : pervidet
270 pergenuat : genibus pergit
persum : deorsum precipitatum
P. 215. perimet : interficet
percrebruit : personavit, puplicatus est
perspicuum : manifestum, splenditum,
pulchrum
275 perfidus : qui fidem rupit semel
perfidiosus : qui semper
peripsima : humillima atque subiecta
perduellis : rebellionibus
perosum : odiosum
280 pertinax : perseverans

perfugium : locus refugii
pervicax : valde verbosus, intentione durus et contumax
percitus : provocatus
perpetim : prolixum, continuum
285 pernoscere : tractare
perc^ulum : experimentum
pereronia : per inrisione
    P. 216. perdocilis : valde docilis
perennis : aeternus
290 perlata : tolerata
periscelide : crurum ornamenta aput feminas
percellet : pervertit, evellit
perspicace : vigilant .. rem
pertinacia : duritia
295 per .... : transitus
peripsima : purgame ... m
persulto : vocifero
perfruitur : utitur
pernox : pernoctans pervi.gelans
300 pertensum : tediosum, permodestum
perfungitur : oficium unius complet
peragrat : circuit, curat
perstromata : tignina acubitus
persuma : praecipita vel confecta
305   P. 217. perfluxum : dificile
persentisca^t : ex totum sentiat
perpexa : perligata
Pergamum : Illium et hili
perpera : prave, perverse
310 persolla : persona minor
pessum : violenter oppressum
pessolum : clustellum
pestilentia : interitum
pestis : pernicies
315 petalum : area lammina tenuessima
pia : religiosa
piare : solvere
piaculum : scelus et peccatum impie commissum
pignera : filiorum sunt
320 pilant : battunt confirmat
    P. 218. pitidine : id est prostitumatum
pipa : vicitatus, q̄ritat passer
pituita : flegma
piceo : nigro
325 piniculum : sfpongia
pixides : vasa modica argentea vel lignea quas vulgus buxides dicunt
piraticus : subaudiens ut carcer
Philippus : os lampadarum
pyrada : latro marinus
330 piabunt : placabunt
piacula : placationis mortuorüm
pilo : asta rimana
pilarius : sepulcra egyptiorum
pinna : fastidium templi, muri
335   P. 219. Pyra : ara lignis altioribus conposita quae, cum adhunc non

ardet, rogus dicitur, cum vero arde, pyra dicitur Greci pyr igne
pistrix : genus bystie marī
piacularis : hostia quae offertur pro peccatum
pictae : quibus raduntur capita et tegunt se corium crudum
pignora : creditoribus danter
340 privignus : filius uxoris alterius
primilum : numerus militię primo probatus
pristinum : priorem, antiqua
privat : subtrahit
primor : prior
345 primores : priores
privis : singulis, privatis
    P. 220. pridiae : heri
pospridię : odię
primoperum : genus officii
350 priviligium : privata est lex quae ad te pertenet tantum
prisca : antiqua
prima quies : primum somnum
primignus : primogenitus
pridem : antea, dudum
355 primordium : initium
primivirgius : cavallarius quod prima est militia ipsius in visgis
poa : genus herbe ubi vestimenta labantur
polum : caelum
poederes : sacerdotalis linea
360 pollulat : germinat
    P. 221. polluit : inquinavit
polenta : genus est liguminis
pollinctus : ultimum honore affectus, id est honoratus
pollit : criscet
365 pollens : crescens, florens vigeⁿs
polinton : ubi kadavera ponuntur
poema : carmen poeticum
poenates : dii quasi domestici
populatus : prędatus, vastatus
370 poplites : genicula concavum
portentum : signum futurarum adnuntius
porrecta : undique extensa
porro tenus : usque porro
posteritas : propagatio filiorum
375 posthabita : postposita
    P. 222. postridie : cras
postulatius : petitor rogatarius
poesi : materia totius carmi in qua poeta versatur
potitur : frequenter utitur vel fruitur
380 potius : melius, magis
pothochotropis : locus in quo pauperes et infirmi homines pascuntur
pomet : statuit
pollicetur : promittitur
pompulentus : pompa plenus
385 ponetergum : pos dorsum

pollinctores: qui mortuos sepelliunt
popularitas: multitudo populi
poples: geniculum generis masculini
podix vel podice: facedenica id est anum vel culum
390 P. 223. porro: postea, utique
portendit: significavit, longe ante ostendit
poetria: femina poeta
postulat: petit
postliminium: qui post captivitate reversus iuraque admiserat recipit
395 pomarium: ubi poma ponuntur
pomerium: locus proximus mari
poeticus: canticus
potitus: adeptus, consecutus
petior: fruor et potentior
400 potissimum: meliorem
potiri: adipisci
potor: bibutur
pondo: libras xii
P. 224. prope: bene
405 probrum: turpitudo vel malum crimen
probrosum: turpia
probitas: iustitia, bonitas
problema: propositio
proba: manifesta, optima provata
410 proci: petitores uxorum
proculus: qui patre longius peregrinante nascitur
procax: inportunus, inprobus
procerum: altum pro longum
procul: non longe
415 procas: qui post morte patris nascitur
proclivi: facere parati
proclientibus: pro sociis
P. 225. proceritas: altitudo, longitudo
procella: tempestas, venti subitu
420 proceres: primati, nobilis
proclima: adclina
proclivio: humiando adcumbet
proemium: prefatio
prodigia: signa celestia mala pronuntia
425 prodi: exi
profecto: vere, nimis, aut sine dubio
profana: pulluta, violata
profligatus: perditus
profatus: proloquitur
430 profundo: alto
profitetur: praedicat, divulgat
proles: filius, progenies
P. 226. prolapsus est: ruit
proelium: pugna
435 prolemsis: preoccupatio cum antea fit quod post te debuit
promis:
promisit: foras produxit
promulgatum: pupligatum
progatia: temeritas, audatia
440 procul dubium: sine dubium

procrastinat: differit
prodicus: nimis largus, devorat
prodigiosus: astrologus
profusus: largus
445 proficiscitur: vadit
P. 227. profanus: qui sacrum polluit alienisano
profugus: longe fugatus, exul
profectus: egressus
proflixit: prostravit
450 profluit: multum fluit
prolixa: longa promunt, proferunt
proletarius: milis capite census, milis inutilis bello relictus
promit: ostendit, loquitur
promulgare: foras praeferre, restatuere
455 promeritus: bene meritus
promunturium: eminens mons in mare
promsit: locutus est
pronuba: para nympha
P. 228. pronus: incurvus, humilis
460 pronepus: filius nepotis
propheta: predicatur
propius: propinquuus
propendens: eminens
pro matertera: soror aviae
465 pronus: inclinus
properum: proximum
propulat: valde puplice
prona: inclina
propono ordino
470 pro nefari: plusquam inlicitum
propago: linia, origo, extensio
propatruus: frater pravie
prore: prout res exegit
P. 229. properat: fistinat
475 propensius:
prorigitur: ante erigitur
prosapia: origo, generatio
propere: prope, celeriter
prostituta: meretrix
480 prosa: prior pars navis
prorsus: specialiter, certe
prospecians: prospiciens
prosiquitur: verbis profitetur
propitiatio: misericordia
P. 230 left vacant
485 P. 231. proscriptio: bonorum admissio
proritat: ad ira provocat
protinus: mox, continuo, statim
protilat: prolongat
prosa: verba sine metro
490 proveor: transporto
prostituun: proponunt
pronas: carbones vivi
prosilitus: adiunctitius de aliena gente
prosperitas: filicitas
495 prosperare: recte agere
prospice: in ante aspice
proto plaustum: primum plasmatum

protervus : supervus, inrevocabilis, vi-
tiosus
P. 232. provexit : in maius levavit
500 prudens : providens
promtuaria : cellaria
puniatur : uccitatur
puplites : genua suffraginis
pubat : crescit, incrementa
505 puberes : adulti iuvenis
pubetenus : usque ad inguina
pubertas : aduliscentia
pubescentes : gene barbamittentes
pube : virilia, verenda
510 pubiscit : barbis et testes
pudicus : castus
pudor : verecundia
P. 233. pugillare : tabulam
pugillum : pugno
515 pulvinar : locus ubi stat vastant
pululat : germinat, oritor
puerperium : cum puer inascitur
puerpera : mulier quae primo parto
puero parit
pullum : nigrum
520 pugiles : certatores
pugio : gladius parvus
pudicitia : castitas, integritas
pugna : certamen
pulvinaria : are mortuorum
525 puerperum : primo genito
putamen : testa de ovo

Q.

P. 234. quatio : concutio
quatinus : qua ratione et qualiter
quandam : aliquam
quassatum : confrat ??
5 quandoquidem : tunc omnino
quantocius : quam citius, celerius
quantolum : modicum
quadrifium : quadrifarie fissum
quamquam : quamvis
10 queso : rogo
quaestuarii : mercennarii
quaerella : culpe accusatio
quaerito : sepius rogo
quaestum : lucrum, aquesitio
15 questio : disceptatio difficilis, explica-
tio, examinatio
P. 235. quaestus est : accusavit
quaestor : iudex ad requirendo
querolus : frequenter querellas ferens
et acusatur
queverint : poterint
20 questuaria : qui quaestucocorpiris vivit
quemquam : aliquem
quemcumque : quempia
quemadmodum : quomodo, sicut
queo : valeo, posso

25 quendam : aliquem, quempiam
quempia : quemcumque
queror : iniurias meas iudico
questor : consiliarius et qui pecunia
puplica prerogant
queun : possunt
30 P. 236. quibi : potui consensi
quidnam : aliquid et quid
quidve : vel quid
quin immo : magis aetiam vel potius
quispiam : aliquis
35 qui sciam : unde sciam
quiete : silentium
quiquantus : quam magnus
quin aetiam : si aetiam magis aemagis
quid stuit : quid cogitat
40 quinam : qui vero
quidni : hoc magis et quare non
quiddam : modicum aliquid
quinni : etiam, adverbium fermandi
quiverunt : potuerunt
45 P. 237. quisquilias : paleas minutissimas
quippe : re vera, sine dubium
quippiam : aliquid modicum
quisitor : iudex
quirites : populus Romanus
50 quies : pax, silentium
Quirinus : Romulus
quousque : quamdiu
quondam : olim
quopiam : alicubi
55 quo numine : qua potestatem
quorsum : in qua parte
quodpiam : quoddam
quonam : aliquo
quoque : dinuo
60 quominus : aliter
quorundam : aliquorum
P. 238. quocirca : quapropter
quodam : quocumque
quoquam : ubicumque
65 quorsus : qua ratione qo modo

R.

ratum : certum, firmum, validum
ratus : arbitratus
rates : naves
ramnum : genus herbe spinose
5 racemum : butrionem, uvam
rapacem : violentum
raptim : cursim, subito
randum : arbitrandum
raptati : tracti, separati
10 rapidus : velox
rabies : furor, insania
P. 239. rabula : rabidam
Rama : excelsa
rancor : in via dolor
15 Raphahel : nuntius dei

Rabbi : magister syṛě
radiatus : inluminatus
ramen : pulvis qui raditur de aliqua spętię
randus : velox, celex
20 radicitus : funditus
Ramensis : tribus a Romolo constituta
Racha : inanis, vacuus, vanus
rastri : ligones
rava : rauca vel clausa
25 rabitere : redire
radiat : splendit
P. 240. redemitus : coronatus, ornatus
reticuit : taeuit
ridimicula : retinacula
30 redivivum : avetustate renovatus
redarguit : convincit et de re arguit
redibet : inpensa sibi gratia rediet
redigitur : revocatur
redactus : perductus
35 redolet : bene olet
redibutionem : retributione
reductum : retroductum
rediviva : renascentia
redamat : amantes et mutuo diligentes
40 reduvias : reliquias
reducus : salvus, incolumis, reversus
P. 241. redintegrat : integrum restituit
recludit : aperiter, recludit
recensat : recitat, recognuscit
45 recubat : adcumbet
reciprocat : reconsiderat, vel reddit vicem
reica : metri genus
refello : recuso, redarguo, dissolvo
refertum : repletọum
50 refectus : plenus
referrerunt : repleverunt
refoculat : recreat
religio : sanctitas
refricat : renovat
55 refulget : resplendit
refutat : repudiat, respuit
refragatur : adversatur
P. 242. *refello : convinco*
referciunt : inplent
60 refuga : apostata
refert : revocat, reddit
regificum : regale
regimen : guvernatione
religiositas : sanctimonia, pietas
65 relatum : reportatum
relativum : dum unus nominatur, alius, demonstratur
regerit : reportat
regessit : evomuit
regius : regalis
70 reminiscor : recordor
remur : arbitramur
remeat : regreditur

P. 243. remilus : repando
remugit : clamat
75 remotiora : secretiora
remulcunt : cum scava nave dicunt
renitet : res splendit
remes : remigatur
reor : arbitror
80 remittentibus : resistentibus
renidit : redolet
rebare : arbitrare
rebellio : qui per pacem integrat bellum
rebamini : arbitramini
85 reboat : resonat
rere : arbitrare, suspicare .
repatriat : reddit ad sua
P. 244. reppedat : redit, remeat
repentinus : subitaneus
90 repente : subito
repacula : receptiacula
reppeit : invenit
repunt : serpunt
repens : natans, subtraens se
95 reserat : aperit
resides : odiosi
repedat : revertitur
respuo : contempno, refuto
resignat : re: signat, aperit
100 reses : odiosus
respectant : recogitant
resipisco : in integro spiritum redeo
P. 245. resiscere : cognuscere
respectat : respicet
105 resibunt : reluctant
resipiscens : recolens
respexit : deorsum vel retro vidi
resultant : resiliunt
restantia : residua
110 resurrectio : restitutio
resultatio : reluctatio
restagnat : redundat, abundat
residis : requies, odiosa
resuit : dissit condisire
115 reticuit : tacuit
reticiscit : ad intellectum redit
P. 246. *redarguet : convincit*
retentant : retinet
reticulata : cancellata
120 retubans : iacens
retexit : resolvit, replecat
retrudit : recludit
retundit : repercudit
retribuit : reddedit
125 reuma : revolutio gurgitis
revehit : reportat
reverens : honorificus
revelat : aperit, demonstrat
revinxit : postergum ligavit
130 revisam : reppedam
revocat : reducit
P. 247. reus : a re dicitur quasi qui rem tenet vel culpabilis

reviso : repeto, recognusco
revulsit : retraxit, eradicavit
135 revicta : reportata
rictus : patefacti oris
rigor : duritia inflexibilis
rigibant : rigidi durique erant
rinae : iuncturȩ
140 ringitur : irascitur, indignatur
rimas : fissura
rimare : inquirere, scrutare
rivales : qui unam diligunt meretricem
    tamquam adunum rivum corentem
P. 248. ridicularius : risorius
145 rigidus : fortis, inmobilis
rigit : frigit
rigare : dirigire
rimis : iunturi stabularum
ritus : cultus et consuetudo
150 rite : recte, consuete
rinoceron : animal est in Nilo flumine
    cornu in nasu habens
robor : virtus, fortitudo
roborat : confirmat
robus : lignum spinosum
155 robustus : firmus, fortis
rogitat : sepius rogat
rovigo : gelum origo
P. 249. rogum : pirum
rogis : flammis
160 rogitans : postulans
Roma : virtus
Romani : sublimis
Romolite : Romani
rostrum : pecurum est et os hominum
165 rostra : pectora navium
rosca : pulcra
roscidum : humidum
ronannis : milis qui primo in bello
    pugna comitit
rubro : rubeo flabum
170 rubore : confusione
rufus : rubeus
ruvigo : gelum vel rugo messium
P. 250. rudia : nova
rudem : novum
175 rudentes : funes velorum in nave
rudimenta : initia, infantia
rudera : stercora
ruma : mamma aḷ pugna
ruminat : diligenter recogᶦtat
180 rupea : saxosa
ruditus : asini clamor
rumigerolus : potitor omoris
rumphea : gladius
rumusculus : rumor brevis
185 rupes : saxa ingentia
rupra : ex utraque parte cavᵃto
rutilum : splenditum, crispum
P. 251. rursus : iterum, dinuo
rurigna : ruri nato
190 rus : pacus, ager durus
rusticus : rus colens

rustu : vi et fama
rura : agri, villȩ *inculti*
ruralem : tɛrrenum
195 rues : ruina
rues : ruina
ruscus : spina longa iuncus habentes
rutilat : fulgit roseo colore
Rutili : gens q̃ sub Turno pugnarunt
200 *rura : agri inculti*

S.

Sacer : sanctus
P. 252. sacramenta : mysteria
sacra famis : execranda cupitidas
sacrilegus : sacrorum violator
5 sabiat : basiat
salamandra : hanimal quoddam in ig-
    nibus vivens
salebrosus : asper
salebra : loca lotosa
salpinta : tubicinatur
10 sacra : consecrata, divina
sacax : velox scitus an invistigandum
saccella : loca sacra
sabiatur : osculatur
saburra : arena id est onus quod vacuas
    nabes stabelliuntur
15 P. 253. sales : orbanitas
salum : mare
(*rasura*) : sanus
saltim : videlicit, nunc
salebra : loca coltuosa
20 saltus : locus incoltus, silvester
salvete : salvi estote
Salentinus : Calabriensis
sambucistra : qui in cythara rustica
    canit
sambucus : saltatur
25 sambucȩ : genus symphoniarum in
    musicis
sancit : purificat
saniem : corruptionem sanguinis
P. 254. sanctum : divinum, coltum,
    consecratum
sanxit : definivit, deiudicavit
30 sane : certe
sandaraca : auri pigmentus mundus
sandapila : ubi portantur gladiatoris
sabbatum : requies
sapabapipa : quasi dulco acitum vino
35 sarga : non idoneus cuius libeartis
sarissa : genus teli Macidonici
sarabara : linon, Persa braca
sarctum : coniuntum
sat : sufficit
40 sat agit : festinat
sata : seminata
satius : melius
P. 255. Satan : adversarius, trans-
    gressor

satrapae : perfecti Persarum
45 saures : surices
satellitium : satellita turma
Saturnia : Italia a rege Saturno dicta
satest : satis est
sator : seminatur
50 satum : modium semis
satellites : sotii latronum et regni comites
sautius : vulneratus
satillis : minester scelerum
satio : messis
55 Saducei : iusteficati
Sabaoth : exercituum sive vertutum
   P. 256. Saulus : temptatio vel scuritas
Samarite : custodes
scandit : aperit, ascendit
60 scadit : bullit
scatens : bulliens
scaturrit : ebullit
scabrum : asperum
scabum : summitas, cacumen
65 squalet : sordet
scabrosus : asper
scatebrę : cesternę, paludes vel aquarum bullitiones
Scariothes : memoria domini et memoria mortis hoc numine appellatum est iuda vico in quo natus est
   P. 257. Scaurus : cuius calex extrensicus eminet pede intortos
70 squalor : inquinatio
sicominus : sin autem, quo si non
spatiatur : deambulat
scafa : navicula modica
stater : nummus est pensa untia·l·
75 strages : mu'titudo kadaverum in bello vel mo lesi congeries
statim : mox, confestim
strangulat : susfugat
stadium : passus CXXV
stragula : varia
80 stadiodromus : stadiorum cursus
   P. 258. status : statura
statuet : censit
stagnum : lacum
secta : institutio
85 secernet : separat
secunda : prospera, propitia
seclusam : separata
secordis : stultus, fatuus
secubo : secedo
90 secretus : separatus, occultus
sedulus : freques, asiduus
sectamur : sequimur, immitamur
secus : aliter et prope
secus quam : quam aliter
95   P. 259. sectans : exercens
sector : usurpatur
secelet : untiae pondus est
sedulus : freques, asiduus

sedicio : disceptatio
100 segmenta : quod e sectura serrę cadent
sedolitas : asiduitas
sedat : mitigat
secrinat : secretum facit
semicinctum : quod dimidium cingat
105 semivero : effeminato
senta : sordida
sentetia : firma et indubitata
sepsit : circumdedit
   P. 260. serrę : unde ianuę muniuntur
110 sexus : natura
semenstria : liber in quo actiones sex mensuum continetur
scelestus : sceleris adinventus
sceleratus : qui sceleris pena patitur
scevus : sinester
115 scema : imago
sceva : prava, sinestra
scevitas : pravitas
scerpus : iuncus unde calamauci fiunt
sceptrum : virga regalis
120 scena : ludus mimicus in theatro
scemata : arena ubi athlete luctantur
   P. 261. scenophygia : templi fabricatio et cum tabernacula figitur mense septembro
serta : corona ex floribus
serenus : clarus, laetus
125 serit : seminat, dicit
seria : molestia gravis
sero : darde
seu : sive
serva : ancilla
130 semivivus : medius vivus
seruit : seminavit, dixit
severitas : integritas iudicu
severus : modestus, distrectus
sevenites : lapi praecisus cuius candor cum luna adqui minuere cernitur
135   P. 262. septimontium : dies certus urbis Romę qua super septemontes sedet
semisitium : semigladium vel dimidę spatę
semoti : separati
seorsum : divisum, separatum
senium : senectute
140 sensim : paulatim, modice
sentes : spinae
sententiosus : integrę iudicans
seponit : sequestrat
series : ordo, tenor
145 sequester : suspectur pignoris
serpit : invalescit, crescit
seminarium : semen
sertor : cultor
   P. 263. semiermis : medius armatus
150 serpit : natat, penetrat
segnis : hebes, negligens

sevet: furet
sevitia: iracundia
seviter: crudeliter
155 severitas: integritas iudicii, districtio
et rigor animi
serius: tardius
semicem: prope mortuum
serra: eo quod secatur
sescupula: et summa capitis et dimi-
dia summę
160 semiustum: medium ustum
specimen: figura, similitudo
speculatur: inspector
speciales: singularis, spetiales
P. 264. speluncis: concavis saxis
165 spera: pila ingens
speltum: telum, missele
specularia: loca alta unde adtenditur
specu: spelunca
spretus; contemptus
170 Spertheus: fluvius Thesaliae [*Spechius*
in margine]
specialiter: evidenter, omnino
strenuus: efficax, fortis
stelionatus: dicitur quando una res
duobus vińditur
strepito: tumulto
175 stemata: ornamenta regalia vel nubili-
tas
Stephanus: norma vestra
stephanus: coronatus
sibola: collectio numerorum
P. 265. sicili: sudorum
180 sica: genus gladii parvi
sidus: stella augurialis vel proprie
tempestas
sicophanta: inpostorem
sicine: taliter
Sicania: Sicilia a SI
185 sicarius: gladiatur   C
siccum: serenum   A
Sicaonium: Siciliensi   N
sidera: stillae   O
                        R
sidonia: clamide syria E
                        G
                        E
190 signifer: qui signum portat in bello
sicera: omnes cõñf ligoris convinum
imitantur et enibriat sed proprie est
ligor ad bivendum suavem qui ex
dactalis expremitur
P. 266. signa: indicia
signities: ḍardi*ias*, pigritię
signanter: evidenter
195 sigilla: minora signa
signes: ḍardus, piger
signius: tardius, negligentius
signitia: pegritia
silurus: genus picis
200 silogismus: collectio sermonum
siliqua: follicolus liguminis
silet: tacet
silentes: tacentes

silenter: tacite, latenter
205 syllaba: conprehensio litterarum vel
vocabula
P. 267. silanus: tubus
simolat: fingit
simulacrum: efigies, imago
simultates: rixę content'ones
210 simulata: fincta
simultas: dolus, lis occulta
simulatur: qui aliud loquitur, aliud
cogitat
sin: si non, sic
sinodus: congregatium senum
215 sinonima: pluri numina quę multis
vocabulis unam rem significat
singultum: subglutium
P. 268. symbulum: obtima conlatio
vel pactum quod cum deo fit
sin: portus
sinphitõ: s̄p̄u caloris vitę. grēc
220 sine: dimette
sinagoga: conventus
singulatim: per singulas vices
singraphum: cautiosus scriptio
sinistrum: contrarium
225 sinaxin: solempnia
sinciput: dimidium caput
Sirtes: vada saxosa
siromace: gladium
P. 269. Sirio: stella estuales
230 sistrum: insigne sacerdotum
sistit: statuit
situs: positio, ordinatio
sion: specula
siticolosus: qui semper sitit
235 Simon: pene merore vel obediens
scivit: sententia dedit
scribula: epistula
scilicet: re vera, sine dubio
scisma: divisio, separatio
240 Scille: saxa latentia in mare
sciniphes: culicum genus aculeis per-
mulestum
P. 270. scitum: populi decretum
scidit: dividit
scinis: tabernacula
245 sciscitatur: interrogat
scriba: legis peritus
spiris: nodis quibus elegant serpentes
spicularius: lanciarius
spicula: iacula
250 spicolum: caput sagittę
spirabile: per quod spiratur
spiravere: oluerant
stigma: poena
stigia: infernalia
255   P. 271. stigmata: poena
stiga: tunica
stilus: de quo scribitur elogium trac-
toris
stridor: sonus asper
stimma stimata: genealogia

260 stipante : spissante
stipolatores : iudicatores
stipulatus : testeficatus
stipatus : multitudine circumdatus
stipendia : munera censum
265 stirps : propaco, prosapia
stipem : quod de parvo in summa colliget sive mendicans
P. 272. stiria : stillicidia celata
stivio : tinctura
Stix : palus aput inferos
270 stino : de isto loco
stimolus : compunctio, instigatio
stimulat : incitat, admovet
stipat : congerit, conponit
stipante caterva : conpremente multitudine
275 stipis : truncus
stipendium : fructum laboris, anonam
stimulatio : promissio
stiba : manubrium aratri
stricto pungione : evaginato glatio
280 P. 273. stirania : non longe
socors : stultus, negligens
socer : patris uxoris
socrus : mater uxoris
socordia : stultitia
285 subrinus : patrui magnus filius
Socrates : primus fylosophorum
sollers : astutus, vigilans
sollicitat : suadit
solatur : consulatur
290 solidat : firmat
solidudo : heremus
solemnitas : religiosa sollicitudo
P. 274. sol ruit : sol occidit
solium : sella regia
295 solitus : consuetus
sollertia : astudia
sospis : salvus
solamen : solatium
solum : terra, pavimentum
300 solido : forti
sordere : vilescere
solensa : sacrificia annua et festa solida
sontes : nocentes
solocysmus : flexuosa et tortuosa coh-
clusio
305 sons : nocens
sonipes : equus pedibus sonans
sonoras : voces graviter sonantes
P. 275. sopitus : extinctus et somno
gravatus
sopire : conpescere
310 sopit : quiescere facit, finit
sconna : sponsa
scortum : meretrix
sodalitas : amicidia
sodales : socii latronum et amici
315 spondit : promittit
sponte : voluntate, ultro

spolia : quę occiso hoste tollitur
sponsor : promissor
sporca : ignominiosa, inmunda
320 stolidus : stultus
P. 276. storiographus : storię conscriptur
stolediosus : odiosus
stropha : praeversio fraos inpost
Stoici : philosophi severissimi
325 stronopharius : inpostor
stola : genus vestimenti candida
sublimis : altus
subnixa : subiecta, supposita
subrigens : erigens
330 subpromit : abscondit, occultat
subnixi : circumdati
subtrectatur : substituitur
subiecit : humiliavit
P. 277. suboles : progenies, filii
335 subulcus : pastor porcorum
subsannat : inridet
substituit : in loco decedentis consti-
tuit
sub sudo : sub caelo
sub pectore : in animo
340 sublatum : raptum
subsedet : sucedendo possedit vel paulolum sedit
sublimior : altior
subrigit : subsistit
subparent : supplent, parent
345 substetit : paulolum stetit
subtexsunt : opponunt
P. 278. subnixius : humilius
sub visibus : prae oculis
subegit : subdedit, devicet
350 subsidia : auxilia
subsicibus : subsequentibus
subnectens : subligans
subtemine : trama
subicet : suppone
355 sublimatus : honore exaltatus
subnixus : auxilio instructus
subeo : ascendo
subfascinatum : succinctum, harmatum
subcenturatus : adiunctus
360 subtexere : obscuravere sublustru
P. 279. sublimitas : altitudo, excellentia
subantes : lividinantes
subdicione : sub potestate
subsicius : malus vel praesubdolus
365 subrepsit : intercepit
subripuit : fraudolenter tolit
substantia : facultas, natura
subvectat : supportat
submissi : supplices
370 subequilibra : sub iusta mensura
sublapsa : diminuta
subtrecta : inclinata
subrige caput : humiliate
sublegit : subtrahit, collegit

375   P. 280. subsistentia: uniuscuiusque
            persona
      subrogatus: substitus, sortitus
      succedit: intravit
      sucerda: stercus uvile
      sudum: serenum caelum
380   suellas: porcinas
      suetus: consuetus
      suere: consuete cosire
      scrutus: lucis duritia
      scrutat: discutit, inquirit
385   scurrilitas: garrolitas
      scrupea: saxa aspera
      scupulum: saxum prominens
      scrupulatur: sollicitatur
            P. 281. sudes: tetiones, pali
390   sues: porci
      suescit: consuescit
      suffusio: vulnerato
      suffultus: munitus
      sufstagium: auxilium, patrocinium
395   suffragatur: auxiliatur
      suffraginatus: percisus cruribus
      suffectus: substitutus cum decedentes
      suffecet: subminestrat
      scrupolo: dubitatione
400   scrutenium: examinatio
      scrursula: puplicus inpostor
      scurra: vaniloquax
            P. 282. scrupulosa: suspecta
      sugilat: suffucat
405   sugerit: subministrat
      sugillare: strangullare
      sutor: cultor
      sumo tenus: usque summo
      summum: postremum, novissimum
410   suppremum: ultimum
      superstitiosus: falsus, religiosus
      superus: summus
      supercilium: typum supervię
      supplet: conplet
415   superaria: vestis quae superinduitur
            P. 283. superbus: contumax
      sumptuarius: qui erogat sumptus suum
            opere
      supellectile: res mobilis
      superstitio: superflua institutio
420   supervacuus: non necessarius
      suprestis: supervivens filius
      supplex: submissus, rogans
      suppremi: occultarium extremi
·   suppet: suppetita, subministra
425   supplosa: exclusa
      suppeo: rogo in animo
      spurius: meretricius
      spurus: qui ex matrem nubilem et
            patre infimum nascit
            P. 284. spurticia: inmundicia
430   summa: quantitas pecunię
      summatim: paulatim
      suavum: osculum luxuriosum
      sura: posterior pars tibie

      susurrat: murmurat
435   sustentant: nutriunt
      sustulit: segregavit, rursu tolit
      suscepit: veneratur
      suspicienter: venerabiliter
      suspice: surso aspice
440   sus: porcus
      suscenset: irascitur, detrahit, increpat
            vel culpat
            P. 285. suspis: sanus, incolomis
      su'pensi: dubitantes
      susurrio: sententiosus, bilinguis
445   suspiciendo: surso aspiciendo
      suspectant: aspiciunt
      sustentant: nutrit
      sutor: calicarius
      sunto: sint
450   sutores: pelliū sarsores
      stupeant: mirentur
      stuprum: fornicatio
      studio: disciplina
      struet: congestio lignorum
455   struices: constructi conpagicati
            P. 286. Syrtes: loca arenosa in mari
      suovetaurealia: sacra sunt de trebus
            animalibus de sue ove tauro

                        T.

      tabitudo: putrido
      tabentes: languentes
      tagax: foruncolus
      talionum: retributionum
5   talami: cubiculi
      taria: calciamenta
      taxat: tangit, nominat
      taxator: aestimator
      tantisper: interim
10   tantotius: tanto velociu
      talentu: centum pondus auri idest pon-
            dus lxii *id est* xxii
            P. 287. tantane: tanta ergo
      tabo: sanguine corrupto
      tabe: morbum
15   tacmata: curia seu chorus
      talio: eiusdem pene ratio vel vicissi-
            tudo
      taura: sterelis
      talatrus: colaphus
      tautologia: repetitio sermonis bis vel
            ter
20   Tartharum: infernum
      taxatio: nominatio
      tantundem: aliquando, demum
      trabica: carina tuba
      transtres: tabulę in nave ubi rimiges
            sedent
25   P. 288. tramite: via, semita trans-
            versa
      trapete: molę olivarum
      tragula: teligenus quo mittitur

trasena : teculaperta qua lumen venit
trancillus : placitus
30 trabes : vestis senatorea porporea
trages : sagitiarii primi
tragum : genus frumenti
tracopis : ut supra frum
teges : coopertorium
35 tedet : penitet et tetiupatitur
tegmen : velamen
telum : sagitta
P. 289. tellus : terra
telluerunt : genuerunt
40 tegetes : cooperturia
tedae : faces nuptiales
telonium : quasi omnium litorum fiscalis ductor
tela : arma
tellitus : festivitas
45 tempestivum : oportunum
temere : audaciter
temulentus : vinolentus
temetum : vinum
temerarius : praesumptor
50 P. 290. Tempe : silvae
tempsit : contempsit
tenus : usque
tensa : genus veicoli
tentoria : papilionis
55 tenax : avarus, perseverans
tenuis : gracilis
tenor : mensura, ordo
tenacitas : continentia
theoria : consideratio
60 thesicure : mura quinta
thesaurum : pecuniẹ depositum
theusebia : sapientia
P. 291. Theophilum : quem deus
diligit
temerator : litigatur, violator
65 terribilis : metuendus
teretri : trunci, rudundi
terretus : turbatus
tergeminam : triplicem
terret : pisat terendo pede
70 tergiversare : fugire et dicta mutare
terrigine : gigantes
tergus : tergora, pelles et coria
terminalia : dies festi pertinentes ad
terminum quem deum potaverunt
Romani
P. 292. terminus : finis
75 terrivola : formidolosus
terebrat : pertundit, forat
terretigima : rotunda gemma
terrificus : terrorem faciens
terret : confundit, terrorem incudit
80 teredo : vermis in ligno
terestrum : mavurtium quod mulieres
Arabiae utuntur
trepudiat : gaudium exultat
tresoli : triduum
tremulum : crispum

85 trenis : temptatio
P. 293. testamentum : pactum
testa : vasa fictilia et caput
tesqua : deserta, aspera
testator : testibus praesentibus loquitur
90 testinum : oportunum
testudo : densitas ramorum et coniunctio scutorum
tessarius : qui bellum nuntiat
tesus : odiosus
tetrum : obscurum
95 Teutoni : Cymbri, Galli
textrinum : locus ubi nabis fabricantur
P. 294. tetrarches : quarta partem
regni tenentes
tetricus : obscurus
tetitini .. genui ... abui
100 Teucri : Troiani
Tyarus : chorus liberi patris
thisum : sacra
thyara : galea persica et pilleum frigio-
rum
Thytis : mare
105 thiasis : laudes virginum
tybia : symphonia
typus : similitudo, figura
typice : figuraliter
tyro : ignarus, novus
110 P. 295. Tybris : tiberis a tubro rege
Tybon : insula minor ubi omnium ge-
nerum arboru folia numqua deficiunt
tybicines : abies continens, vel qui tybia
canunt
tyrocinia : initia, rudimenta
typhe : stulta superbia id est secta
115 Tyrii : Cartaginenses et ipsi qui Tyro
habitant
Titan : sol
Tinia : luna
Titantes : principis
P. 296. titulus : nota, indicium
120 Tisifon : nomen furie
titubat : dubitat, vacillat
titulat : signat
tritavus : proavus
triarcus : navigans
125 tribuli : genus spinarum
triumphum : victoria
trinepus : pro nepus nepotis generatio
triumphatum : devicto
tripodis : mensae cum III pedes
130 Trinacria : Sicilia insula dicta eo quod
III acra abeat de promunturia picin-
num, pelon, lilybeum
P. 297. *trieres magna : de qua in
Esaia nō transivit per eam*
*trieres : navis magna quas Greci
dulcones vocant*
tribus : populi divisio
Trivia : Diana et Luna
135 Trinami : Siculi

Triton : homo marinus, medius pescis
Tritonia : Minerva
Trinacria pubes : Siculi iuvenes
Triarum : partitores signorum
140 tripertiti : tribus erogat
trifauci : qui trea capita habet
triboles : curiales
triari : tervo loco in exercito
trifarium : tripertitum
145 trifaria : est tribus partibus divisum
   P. 298. thomen : sectionem id est
   que dividi potest
tholum : signum rodundum q̄ super
   culmen domus ponitur
thronus : sedis
tholum : fastidium templi rotundi
150 thorvus : intento vehementi vultu
thoracium : ornatus mimicus
thomus : divisio
tholes : membra sunt circa uva
tomix : vestes leviter torta
155 torris : fusus
torrens : flubius et pluvia
torpescit : frigiscit, stopiscit
   P. 299. toga praetexta : quae in se-
   nato induitur
torrent : siccant, tostant
160 torpet : stopet, languint
torpor : stupor animi vel corporis
torus : lectus corporis
toreomata : vasa tornatilia
todidem : tanti
165 torale : pectorale
tollet : exaltat
tostum : tumulum et quoadunatio terrę
   aut lapidum
torax : lurica
tori : lacertibus bachiorum
170 toregma : tornatura
torita : velox et sicca
   P. 300. torace : pectus
turpdus : stopidus
tollit : delet, extinguit
175 trophea : signum victorię
tropologia : morales et intellegentia
Troas : Troiani
trossoli : aequides Romani cum equis
   puplicis
trocus : rota ludentium
180 tropus : mensura dictionis et sonus
tropice : moraliter
tuba : bucinum
tublia : media vel regą
tuetur : custodit
185 tuitio : defensaculum
   P. 301. tutela : procuratio, defensio
tum : tunc demum um postea
turabulum : tymia materium
turma : certus numerus hominum
190 turbitus : iratus, perturbatus
tuitur : intuitur
turbine : tempesta nigra ventorum

turificatus : purgatus
tucellaria : maleficia quae super tegula
   faciuñ
195 tunditur : ververatur
tumulus : sepulcri dicuntur prop.. rte
   raeco ngeriem
tubicines : qui tuba canunt
tubera : genus cibi quasi fungi qui sub
   terra inveniuntur
   · P. 302. tuta : secura, munita
200 tuitus : misertus
tugurium : ospicium modico teia
turbo : vertigo et impetus venti
tumidus : superbus, iratus
turgit : tomit, inflatur
205 turbulentus : obscurus
trutina : sixtera
truculentus : ferox, inimicus
truges : gentilis, asper
trutinat : perpensat, perpendit
210 trux : crudelis
trucidat : interficit
truncus : sine capite
   P. 303. trudit : inpingit, recludit
truditur : in costudia inpellitur

U, V.

vadet : concudit
vexat : movit
vabulum : favae corium
vacillat : titubat
5 vademonia : iudicia e fideiussionis vel
   sponsionis
vadatur : litigat
vadite : ambulate
vada : terra et mari
vades : fide iussoris
10 vada dura : saxa dura
vaprum : varium
   P. 304. vagitus : ploratus
vagetatur : videnter plangit
vaius : qui genibus iunctis ambulat
15 vallata : circumdata
valetuderius : qui frequenter egrotat
valvas : ianuas, fenestras
vallas : palus acutus
vallum : fossatum circa murum
20 valens : potens, vigens
valdus : firmus
validant : sani sunt
vacurrit : per otio vacatur
varice : vitia q̄dā pedu stando nascuntur
25 vates : divini et prophetę
   P. 305. vastat, praedat
vastitas : magnitudo, amplitudo
vafer : callidus, asper
vafre : inaequaliter
30 vatus : tortis pedibus
vastat : magna, grandia

vascaudes : congas ereas
vecors : minus habens cordis
veranus : minus sanus
35 vecordia : stultitia
vectitat : frequenter portat
vectigalia : a vehendo mercibus dicta
omnium quae negutiatorum solu-
tionis
velificat : navigat
P. 306. vellunt : eradicant
40 vellera : vestes ovium linosę
veiculum : iumentum, carrum vel omnem quod a portandum utilem ęst
vehit : portat
venustus : pulcher
veneunt : vendunt
45 vectus : portatus
vectigal : tributum de capite
velant : tegunt
veluti : quasi
vellum : populum
50 vegetus : incolomis, sanus
vehementer : velociter
P. 307. venum : vinditio
veneo : vendor
veneficia : maleficia
55 venustri : campani
veneratur : honorat
veniet : vendedit
venificus : venenᵃrius hervarius
venditatibus : venale offerentibus
60 venenatus : qui venenum accepit
versat : cogitat, mutat
versutus : astutus, controversiosus
vernat : floret
vernaculus : servus in domo natus
65 versatile : tornatile, voluvile
P. 308. vertigo : aquae revolutio
verrunt : supertrahunt, aufert vel scopant
verbenę : frondes
verberat : cedit, flagellat
70 vereor : timeo
verrunt : vestiunt
vergit : declinat
vernacula : ancella domestica
veretrum : pertusorium
75 verisimile : veritati simile
verpus : circumcisus
veridicus : veri dicens
versibilis : callide artificiosus
vertix : summitas capitis et cacumen
montis
80 P. 309. veternum : antiquum, vetus-
tum
veterator : inpostor
vernum : prima vir
vervotinus : sicut dicut
ubertas : habundantia
85 ubertim : abundanter
vesperago : stilla
uberes : pinguis

vescetur : manducat
vestibolum : ingressum et prima pars
domi
90 vexillum : signum militare
viaca : vehimentia
vibrare : asta intorquere, militare
vibrat : fulgit, crispat, diriget
victimo : immolo
95 victima : ostia
P. 310. vicissim : alternatim, mutuo
vicissitur : conpensatur
victus : superatus
videlicet : sine dubio et vidire licet
100 viduatus : orbatus, fraudatus
viget : vivit, valet
vigentes : virilibus pleni
vigil : vigelans
vilicus : villae custus
105 vipurna : silva minuta
vinxit : heavit
vinnubis : mollis
virentia : frondentia
vinceas : machimmentorum gene(ra)
quae fiunt in modum torrium ad ex-
pugnandos muros
110 P. 311. virecta : loca quaevis sint
in agris arboribus minutis fron-
dentibus
virulentus : venenosus
viritim : sintillatim, paulatim, semi-
gratati
virgo : a vigore aetatis dicet
virgulta : silva minuta
115 virus : odor ferarum
vis : usrtis
vis hanimi : sapientia
vis corporis : fortitudo
virere : visitare
120 vita : mores, natura
vituperat : accusat
vitulans : lascivus, gaudens, cum exul-
tatione ledans
P. 312. vincla : vincula
vividus : fortis
125 vindix : ultor, iudex
virus : venenum
viriosus : austerus
virgo : fortes femina
virguncula : virgo modica
130 virtus : animi est
vires : corporis
virendo : vescendo, vivendo
viribus : obtatibus
viscera : loca membrorum vitalia
135 vitat : declinat
vitricus : secundus maritus
vitigilat : vituperat
P. 313. volumen : liber a volvendo
dicet
voluntas : mens
140 vorat : sorbet
volvit : pectore cogitat

voluilitas : mentis veritas
voluptas : concupiscentia
volutabra : loca in quibus se porci vu-
　lutantur
145 volucres : veloces
vola : manus cava in medio unde invo-
　lare dicimus
vorago : obsorsio et fosso profunda et
　terrę iatus
vormet : vos ipsos
vociferatur : clamat
150 vovit : promittit
vuetema : adiutoria
voti compos : memor explī de v̄o
　P. 314. uberius : abundantius
uberus : abundantia
155 ubertimi : abundanter
uberes : pinguis, fructuosus
uberrima : fructuosa
vulsum : vi abstracto
vulgo : pala, passim
160 vultuosus : qui semper vulto mutat
vulgus : vilis populus aut plebs ex
vulgata : in notitia data
vultus : contemplatio
ulli : aliqui
165 ulciscor : vindico
ultor, ultrix : vindix
　P. 315. ultro : sponte
ultra : supra
ulcus : quod intus nascitur, vulnus
170 ulcera : vulnera
ultericri : posterior, inferior
ultus : vindicatus
ultatus : damnatus
ullus : aliquis
175 ulciscimur : vindicamur
ululae : aves nocturnę
ulto cetroque : intus vel foras
ultrices : vindices
ultio : vindicta
180 uligo : humor terrę perpetuus
ulna : cubitus et extensio manus ad
　gremio
　P. 316. ultimus : novissimus
ultosus : tristes
ulva : genus hervę, paludis
185 umbo : extrema pars
umbrosum : contectum
umbris : tenebris
umqua : aliquando
undantia : ebullentia
190 unco : curvo
unorum : multorum
unchus : anchora
uniginę : geminae
uncire : alligare
195 unice : prime, optime
　P. 317. unguine : unctione adipem
undique : ex omni parte
unicuba : vidua qui uni cubit
unguis : cuius diminutio ū ē ungula

200 urbs : dicitur civitas ędificium, civitas
　autem populus est, non paries
uros : bos silvaticus
urvum : quod bovules tenet in aratro
ur : incendium
urna : unde ducunt sortes, quasi quarta
205 urit : accendit
usus : consuetudo
usto : incenso, ustolato
usquam : alicubi
　P. 318. usura : faenus
210 ustrima : locus ubi conburuntur cor-
　pora
usitato : consuedudine
usquequaque : per omnia
uspiam : ullum locum
usurpat : inlicite utitur, praesumet
215 uterque : ambo, utri
utrisque : ambobus
utrubique : utrique parte
uti : frui
utensilia : usibus necessaria
220 utpote : ut aestimet
utique : manifeste, ideo
utrubi : ubicunque
utrum : potans
　P. 319. uter : unus ex altero
225 utire : fruiri
ut reor : ut arbitror
utroque : et hoc et illud
utrius : et huius et illius

X.

Xenodocium : locum venirabilem in
　quo peregrini suscipī

Y.

uberbolice : elate
ymnum : laus
ydria : situla
ydrus : aquaticus
5 yades : stel*lae*
ypotica : huniversa substantia
pliada : s̄ex̄ *stillae insimul*
　P. 320. ypinx : animal quasi ad si-
　militudinem pardorum quas alii
　lamminas dicunt

Z.

Zernam : inpetigo
zelus : emolatio
zizania : lolium
zirotha : series
5 zima : olla
zipherus : ventus
EXPL. ERMENEUMATA
DŌ GRATIAS AMEN.

PRELIMINARY STATEMENT.

The glossary, which I have here printed, was copied by me at the suggestion of Dr. Loewe, who in a letter dated July 27, 1881, wrote me as follows: "Entschieden einer der ältesten Glossarcodices ist der Sangallensis 912. Wenn man den ganz und gar publicierte, so wäre schon viel gewonnen. Jede Glosse darin ist ja mindestens aus dem achten Jahrhundert, und unter diesem Gesichtpunkt gewinnen auch die trivialen Glossen ihren Werth. Ich habe nun aus dieser HS. sehr bedeutende Excerpte, ausserdem die vollständige Copie einer parallelen HS. und sonst sehr viel was in diese Sammlung einschlägt. Wie wäre es wenn Sie diese HS. aufs genauste copirten und wir sie dann zusammen edirten." Accordingly I made a careful copy of the manuscript in August, 1881, but other duties prevented my attempting immediately the proposed edition.

In the summer of 1883 I had planned to go to St. Gall to revise my copy, and afterwards to consult with Dr. Loewe about its publication; but this plan was sadly interrupted, and I had no further correspondence with Dr. Loewe on the subject up to the time of his sudden death. He is therefore in no way responsible for the present edition. When requested by the Association's Committee of Publication to print my paper, including the glossary, I consented to do so, provided I could secure previously an accurate collation of my copy with the original. To facilitate the work of collation, which Professor Adolf Kaegi of Zürich kindly offered to do for me, I had the glossary printed at once, which must account for the notes following the text, instead of occupying the more convenient position at the foot of the page.

Early in July, 1884, I wrote to Professor Goetz, my former teacher, telling him of my plans, and inquiring about the parallel glossary mentioned by Loewe. Unfortunately, he was absent at the time in Copenhagen, and his very kind letter, dated August 25, did not reach me until the Glossary was in type as far as the letter S. I quote a part of his letter. "Loewe besass noch keine Collation der ganzen Handschrift. Mittlerweile hatte ich den Codex in Jena, und habe ihn sehr sorgfältig abgeschrieben. Auch besitze ich die Abschriften von acht verwandten Glossaren. Ein Parallel-glossar ist jedoch nicht darunter; sie sind alle mehr oder weniger verwandt. Loewe scheint sich geirrt zu haben, eben weil er den Sangallensis noch nicht vor sich hatte ausser einigen Excerpten von Usener. Ich bin jetzt gerade mit diesen Glossaren beschäftigt, weil sie den ersten Band des Corpus Glossariorum bilden sollen." Had I known earlier that an editor so much more experienced, possessed of a critical apparatus so much more complete, was about to undertake the same task, I should hardly have ventured upon it.

I regret that I have not been able, for typographical reasons, to represent the abbreviations of the manuscript, especially the very common ones for final *us, m,* for *pro, per, prae, id est, vel,* and the like; but as I particularly requested Professor Kaegi, wherever he disagreed with my resolution of an abbreviation, to indicate it, I hope that not many mistakes have arisen in this way. In other respects I have striven to follow closely the orthography of the manuscript.

I have felt obliged to make my notes as brief as possible, and often, where I might have added much confirmatory evidence from other glossaries, I have contented myself with giving simply the correct reading. Often where the correct reading must suggest itself at once, as in the case of *aemolus* for *aemulus,* I have made no note whatever. I have thought it wise, too, in view of Professor Goetz's forthcoming edition, not to indulge too freely in conjectures, which might be completely overturned by actual manuscript readings. Where no note is found, therefore, on a puzzling gloss, it may be concluded that I have not solved the puzzle to my own satisfaction. With all its imperfections, I still hope that this edition will do something to stimulate the interest on this side of the Atlantic in the subject of Latin Glossaries, and will increase the appreciation of the difficult undertaking to which

Professor Goetz has addressed himself with so much vigor in the place of his departed and honored friend.

My sincere thanks are due to Professor Goetz, who has generously furnished me with some of his own readings on glosses where I was in doubt, to Professor Kaegi for his careful collation, and to Professor Robinson Ellis, who has very kindly sent me numerous parallel glosses taken from two glossaries in Oxford. One of these is in the Balliol Library (155) and is of the fourteenth or fifteenth century; and the other is in the Bodleian (Auct. T II 24), of the eighth or ninth century. He has also sent me a few from a glossary in the Phillips Library. These will be found indicated in the notes by Ball., Bod., Phill.

Glosses which have been added by a second hand are given in the text in italics. Aside from these, three hands can be distinguished in the manuscript. *a.* The greater part is written in half-uncial belonging to the seventh or eighth century. *b.* Pages 189, 190, 225, and 226 are written in a somewhat larger, and probably later, hand (uncial), not earlier than the eighth or ninth century. *c.* Page 201 is written in an entirely different hand, of the ninth or tenth century, resembling the Merovingian.

I have referred to the following works in the notes by the abbreviations herewith given :

Loewe Prodromus, Leipzig, 1876. (Prod.) Glossae Nominum, Leipzig, 1884. (Loewe G. N.)

De Vit's Glossarium. (De Vit.)

Hildebrand Glossarium Latinum, Goettingen, 1854. (Hild.)

Placidi Glossae. A. Deuerling, Leipzig, 1875. (Plac.)

Glossae quae Placido non adscribuntur nisi in libro glossarum, A. Deuerling, München, 1876. (Plac. L. G.)

Epinal Glossary, ed. Sweet, 1883. (Epin.)

Three Erfurt Glossaries published by Dr. F. Oehler in Jahn's Jahrbücher, 1847, pp. 257–297 and 325–387. (Amplon.)

Lateinisches Glossar des 9. Jahrhunderts aus cod. Mon. 6210, G. M. Thomas, München, 1868. (Mon. 6210.)

De Genere Neutro intereunte in Lingua Latina, E. Appel, Erlangen, 1883. (Appel.)

De Differentiarum Scriptoribus Latinis, J. W. Beck, Groningen, 1883. (Beck.)

Archiv für Lateinische Lexikographie und Grammatik. (Archiv.)

Addenda Lexicis Latinis, L. Quicherat, Paris, 1862. (Quicherat.)

Itala und Vulgata, H. Rönsch, Marburg, 1875. (Rönsch.)

Auctores Classici edidit Ang. Maius, Rome, of which volumes VI., VII., and VIII. contain glosses. (Mai. VI., VII., VIII.)

Of Du Cange I have been able to use the new edition as far as F.

Words printed in small capitals will be found in the Forcellini De Vit Lexicon or in Georges.

NOTES.

A.

2. Loewe, **G. N.** p. 4, gives from Amplon. *abavus: tertius pater;* but *tritavi pater* is more correct. Verg. Aen. X. 619 has *quartus pater,* explained by Servius as *abavus.* The spelling *ababus* occurs in inscriptions. — **3.** lege involata. So Epin. 3, E 35; cf. Prod. 174; *abacta: involuta furata,* Bern. 178; *abigiata: involata,* Goetz, Archiv für Lat. Lex. I. p. 560. — **4.** l. actu; cf. Plac. 1, 12, and Goetz, l. c. "Ich fasse *actus* als den bekannten juristischen Terminus (Übertrift)." — **5.** Cf. Prod. 139, *abantes: mortui quos Graeci alibantes appellant.* "In margine manus rec. *alibantes* et aliudquid quod legi nequit, adscripsit" (Goetz). — **6.** Cf. De Vit and Hild. A 1. — **9.** l. averruncat, *abstirpat* in sense of *exstirpat*. — **10.** Perhaps corruption of *averruncat;* see, however, De Vit and Hild. A 160. Epin. 5, C 9 has *avenicat: eradicat;* cf. Amplon. 271, 351, *avenat: eradicat.* — **11.** l. avillus; cf. Paul. 14, 7, *avillas agnus recentis partus,* and Prod. 349. — **13.** l. abigit : proicit; cf. Goetz, Archiv, I. 560. — **14.** l. tollit rem alienam. — **16.** l. abiugassere; cf. Plac. 9, 13, *abiugassere: abiungere, abducere.* — **18.** "*remota r* in rasura" (Goetz). — **22.** Cf. I. 232, *incruentes: imminentes.* — **23.** l. avida; Ball. *abita: desiderata cognita.* — **27.** l. aporria; cf. Cael. Aurel. 121, *corporis defluxiones quas Graeci* ἀπορροίας *vocant ;* Plac. 4, 5 ; Bod. *aborrea: manatio;* Epin. 2, A 9, *apporia defluens.* — **28.** l. abominat. — **33.** l. abhorret. — **35.** l. apluda; cf. Plac. 8, 13, *Apluda, furfuribus milii pannicique,* where G. has *ablundam,* and Paulus 10, 14. — **36.** l. ab usu; cf. De Vit. — **39.** Cf. De Vit and Hild. A 17. — **40.** l. abutitur. — **41.** l. amovit; cf. Tertull. adv. Marcion. 4, 15, Totum quod ab homine captatur, *abdixit* Creator. — **42.** l. non plurima consumere sed suspensis digitis leviter cibum tangere; cf. De Vit. — **45.** l. arrepticius. — **48.** l. abditum; cf. Prod. 148. — **50.** l. abgrego: separo, segrego. Kaegi reads *et egreco,* Goetz *segreco.* — **53.** l. renuit. — **54.** l. abnuo, *abniso* is Goetz's reading. I read *abviso;* so Ball. *abviso: veto, nolo.* — **55.** l. abnepos. Cf. Ball. *abnepos: filius nepotis, abnepos dicitur quia seiungitur a nepote, est enim inter illum et nepotem pronepos.* — **56.** l. humilis ; Ball. *abrogans humilis dicitur, arrogans superbus.* — **60.** l. longe. — **61.** l. dubium. — **63.** l. abitote; cf. Loewe, G. N. 205. — **65.** l. aptra: folia vitis; cf. Prod. 143, and Titinius Ribbeck Frag. p. 159. — **66.** l. apricum. — **67.** Perhaps abest: longe est, or a corruption of 64. — **68.** l. agape. — **69.** Cf. AGAPETAE. — **70.** l. Achates ; cf. Plac. 3, 22. — **71.** l. acanthus; conficiuntur; cf. ACANTHION. — **72.** l. accentus . . . sonus . . . correptae. — **73.** l. acerbitas. — **74.** l. acervus. — **79.** accersitio. — **80.** l. Acheron: fluvius aput inferos. — **81.** l. hactenus. — **82.** l. acieris ; flamines aut pontifices; cf. Prod. 257, and Paulus 10, 1. — **83.** l. acerra : arcula turea (turaria?); cf. Bod. *acerra arcatura;* Epin. 1, C 1, *accerra: arcaturis;* and glosses cited by De Vit. — **84.** l. acervat : condensat . . . coadunat. — **86.** l. ubi tractabat. — **87.** l. saevitia. — **88.** l. acediatur. — **91.** l. acedia. — **95.** l. accipitrem: acceptorem, ascribed to Placidus in Liber Glossarum ; cf. Bod. *acceptorem : accipitrem,* and Lucilius, 1130 Lach. *exta acceptoris.* — **96.** Cf. Ball. *actius: amplius vel verius.* l. auctius: amplius, uberius. — **97.** l. aconitum. — **98.** = ἀκοινώνητος, which Jahn reads Juv. VII. 218. — **99.** l. acroteria; cf. Bod. *acrocheria ligamenta articulum;* Ball. *achrocheria ligatura articulorum.* — **100.** l. hic acinus et huius acini. Cf. *acini* dicuntur proiecti uvarum reliquie et ideo corripit penultimam quoniam non de nomine sed de verbo dirivatur hoc nomen *hic acinus, huius acini.* Acinum vero neutraliter dicitur aqua, qua lavantur uve post expressum vinum, *acinum* dictum quasi aquidum vocaturque vinum secundum et est potus servorum (Gloss. Phillipp.). — **101.** Perhaps acuum = aginam; cf. Paulus 10, 4, *Agina* est, quo inseritur scapus trutinae, id est, in quo *foramine* trutina se vertit; in that case l. diatrema (διάτρημα) = foramen (cf. Schol. Luciani, vol. 1, p. 579 and 597), — **102.** l. accola . . . alienam terram. — **103.** l. culmine. — **104.** l. actutum. — **108.** Cf. Isid. Or. VII. 1, 14, *Adonai* quod generaliter interpretatur *Dominus.* — **110.** l. consequitur. — **111.** The MS. has *adtest* with *t* deleted. — **113.** l. addita: adiuncta. — **117.** "adfirma et ligatura quam non intellego. an adfirmans?" (Goetz). — **122.** l. innodata, adiuncta; cf. Verg. Aen. XII. 92. — **124.** l. adiunctus. — **125.** Cf. De Vit, Astipulatus : idoneus testis adprobatus. — **127.** *adsponsio* is not given by the Lexica, but De Vit gives a gloss *adsponsio: testificatio.* — **129.** Cf. *ad luricum: res ad usum apta,* Bod. and cod. Reg. 7641. Hild. emends to *ad ludicrum; res ad ludum apta.* — **131.** l. Epiphania. — **132.** Hebrew word; cf. Prod. 140. — **133.** l. Eden: delicias. — **140.** l. emolumentum : lucrum vel quaestum. — **141.** l. aequiperant : aequant . . . simulant. — **142.** Kaegi reads *equargentus;* but for *ę* Goetz reads *a* or *ae.* After *am* nothing more can now be read. — **145.** Cf. Servius, Verg. Aen. II. 69. — **148.** l. aetas. — **149.** l. sexu ; cf. Tacitus Ann. I. 56 — **153.** l. thesaurum. — **155.** Cf. Epin. 4, A 36, *aera: rota caeli.* — **156.** = ἀετός; cf. Serv. Verg. Aen. I. 394. — **158.** aeneatores: tubicines; cf. Paulus 20, 7, and Epin. 1, C 20, *aneatores: tubicines.* — **159.** Cf. Epin. 4, C 2, *aeneada: coniurati aenea,* and Ball. *aeneator: enee coniuratio.* — **161.** Cf. Epin. 4, A. 37, *aethera : possessio caeli ignea.* — **162.** l. aesculus. — **163.** Cf. 158. l. cornu . . . cantantes. Ball. *aenitatores: cornu canentes.* — **164.** Cf. Serv. Verg. Aen. I. 157, "Aeneadae, nunc Troiani, aliquando Romani." — **165**. l. aeviternum. — **166**. Cf. Prod. 15, l. aestimiae ; cf. Paulus 26, 8, aestimias : aestimationes. — **167**. l. labor inopia. — **170**. l. epos. — **171**. Cf. Porphyrion Hor. Ep. 2. 1, 230, and Placid. 1, 15. — **172**. Cf. APHRODES and Pliny XX. 207, alterum e silvestribus genus heraclion vocatur, ab aliis *aphron . . . semine spumeo*, for gerante l. gerentem. — **173**. l. taedium patior. — **174**. l. affectum. — **177**. Cf. APHTHAE. — **181**. = ἀφορμή. — **182**. = ἅγιος. — **184** ff. l. augusta, etc. — **191**. l. argutus ; cf. Servius Ec. IV. 34, Sane quidam *Argo* a *celeritate* dictam volunt, unde verso in Latinum verbo *argutos celeres* dici. — **192**. l. agagula. — **194** and **195**. l. agaso, and cf. **183**. — **196**. Cf. Prod. 396 f., Plac. 10, 8. — **197**. Cf. *Agnati liberi, qui per adoptionem veniunt: interdum cognati* (De Vit). — **198**. Cf. Plac. 12, 8. — **199**. Cf. AGONOTHETA. — **200**. Cf. Paulus 10, 5 ff. Hildebrand, A 67, *agga: festivitas*, which H. emends to *agonia*. **202**. Cf. HAGIOGRAPHA. — **203**. l. aconita. — **208**. According to Goetz *is, a* not in MS. — **212**. l. dicitur ; cf. Servius Aen. VI. 392. — **214**. So Kaegi. Goetz reads *expediens;* perhaps for *expeditus*. — **216**. l. alternatim : vicissim. — **217**. l. dubitanti ; cf. Verg. Aen. IV. 287. — **218**. l. pretiosum. — **219**. l. alluvione ; cf. Prod. 160. — **220**. l. navigio. — **221**. Cf. ALOGIA. — **222**. l. alicula. — **224**. Cf. Prod. pp. 142, 273, and Paul. 7, 21. — **225**. l. Alpheus. **228**. "Neubauer says *aalma* is a mere repetition of the previous Hebrew word. The double *a* he thinks is introduced on account of the guttural sound of the *a*" (Ellis). — **229**. l. studio saginata ; cf. Hild. A 81. — **233**. l. alec ; cf. Isidor. Or. XII. 6, 39, *Halec pisciculus ad liquorem salsamentorum idoneus;* Ball., *allech genus piscis ad liquorem salsamentorum idoneum.* — **237**. l. alendum : nutriendum. — **245**. Cf. Isidor. Or. XVIII., 60, *Alea* id est *ludus tabulae, inventa* a Graecis in otio Troiani belli *a quodam* milite *Alea* nomine, a quo et ars nomen accepit. See De Vit. — **247**. Cf. Ball., *Alnum, lignum, .i. verna*, and see same gloss in De Vit, agnetano, perhaps for *Aquitanum* or *amne altum*. Cf. Isid. Or. XVII. 7, 42, *alnus* vocatur quod *alatur amne, Proxima* enim *aquae* nascitur. Du Cange, "*Vern* Gallis priscis et Britannis est *alnum*. In Borelli Lexico *Vergne, un aulne, arbre dit ainsi.*" — **248**. l. allabitur. —**249**. l. allegoria : aliud pro alio . . . similitudo. Kaegi notes that there is a rasura after *allegorit*, so that perhaps originally *allegorice* or *allegoriter* was written. — **250**. Cf. ABINVICEM, frequent in Vulgate. — **253**. l. alares ; cf. De Vit and Hild. A 69. Notice the form *caballares*. — **254**. Cf. Bod., *alebre: quod bene a quibus alitur*, and Loewe G. N. p. 11, under *alero: nutrimentum.* Compare Paul. 25, 4 *alebria, bene alentia.* — **255**. After *pē* there are three or four letters illegible ; cf. Isid. Or. XIV. 8, 42, *alluvium consumptio riparum ex aquis;* perhaps a gloss on Vulg. Job 14, 19, *alluvione* paulatim terra *consumitur;* l. adcrescente arena ; cf. Dig. 19, 1, 13, si decem iugera *alluvione adcreverint.* — **256** and **258**. Cf. Prod. 12. — **257**. Cf. Loewe G. N. p. 11, and Placid. 10, 12. l. altiboans. — **262**. Bod., *exspectat;* cf. Hild. A 76, who proposes " *spe citat* aut *spe lactat.*" — **264**. l. esca. — **265**. Cf. ALSIOSUS ; *frigorosus* occurs also Schol. Juv. 3, 190. Cf. Amplon. 269, 224, and 227, *alsosus: frigorosus: alsiosus: frigorosus.*— **266**. l. album ; cf. Loewe G. N. p. 127, the full gloss ended thus, *tabula est et habet albis litteris iudices et senatores.* — **267**. l. nutrix. — **269**. l. sibi meatum. .**274**. l. delectabile iucundum. — **276**. Cf. above on p. 130. — **277**. Cf. De Vit, l. axilites, which I think goes back to Verrius Flaccus. Cf. Paul. 3, 5, where *alites* follows *axit axites*, and precedes *axamenta.* — **278**. This gloss is also given by De Vit. Perhaps the word has some connection with *Anticyra* (or *Anguitia*?). — **279**. Cf. De Vit, *recertator* seems only to be found in glosses ; cf. Amplon. 264, 459, *antagonista: recertator;* re- is used as the equivalent of *anti-* as in the glosses *antidosis: retributio; antidorum: remuneratio.* — **280**. l. anathematus : abominatus, perditus ; cf. **293**. — **281**. l. maestificis.— **283**. l. angit : praefocat ; cf. De Vit and Hild. — **286**. Bod., *anqueret valde quęrit.* l. anquirit . . . quaerit, for *scrutat;* see Neue, II. 319 and 320. — **287** and **288**. Cf. ANFRACTUS ; *intertortuosa* is not given by the Lexica. Cf. *contortuosa*, Loewe G. N., p. 164. — **289**. = ἀνασκευή ; cf. Prod. 124. — **290**. l. abominatio. — **291**. Perhaps for anachoresis ; (cf. Amplon. 264, 448, *Anchoresis: recessio vel remotio vel recersio*, following *anfractus,*) or for ἀνάπαυσις, N. T. — **293**. Cf. De Vit, l. *perditio.* — **294**. l. apposita. — **297**. Aonia: Boeotia terra. Goetz reads Reoia ; cf. Isid. Or. XIV. 4, 11. — **298**. l. zona, suggested by Ellis ; cf. C 187, clima: circuitus tractus vel aona, from which this gloss was made up, hence the position under A. — **301**. l. apiciosus: calvus ; cf. Prod. 424.—

302. Cf. Epin. 3, E 30, *abtet vos: imple*[*a*]*t vos.* The gloss may refer to Vulg. Hebr.
13, 21, Deus autem pacis *aptet vos* in omni bono. — 305. Cf. De Vit, l. rei ; cf. Bod.
apex: summa pars flamme vel cuiuscumque rei. — 306. l. aperit. — 307. Cf. De Vit.
— 308. Perhaps for apostasis ; probably there is a confusion of two glosses. — 309.
= ἀπληστία. l. crapula. — 311. Cf. Prod. 159. l. probatio; cf. Epin. 1, C 22, *apo-
dixis: probatio vel exemplum.* — 312. l. apyretus. — 313. l. apocrypha ; recondita. —315.
Cf. De Vit, qui rebus caret mundanis *Ugut.* ? l. aeviternus. — 316. Cf. Prod. 159, and De
Vit. — 317. l. apodyterium…lavantium ; cf. Bod. *Apodisterium ubi ponuntur res id est in
balneum lavantium* ; Ball. *Apoleterium ubi ponuntur res lavantium ab exuendo scilicet
dictum.* — 318. ? l. prohibet; cf. 327, with which perhaps this is confused. Cf. De Vit
under *apollure.* — 319. l. apostropha ; aliam … subito … commutationem. — 320. l.
appetit. — 324. l. arces : loca summa montium. — 326. l. artaba : modii tres ; cf. Amplon.
262, 304, *artabo: modi tres.* — 329. l. sidus. — 330. l. digiti ; nodi. — 333. l. elati. —
335. l. gravis. — 337. l. ager sed seminibus aptus (?) ; cf. Serv. Georg. 1, 1, nam omnis
terra, ut etiam Varro docet, quadrifariam dividitur.   Aut enim *arvus est ager,* i. e. *satio-
nalis,* aut consitivus id est *aptus arboribus.* — 342. l. artuatim : membratim. — 343. l.
Arithmeticus. — 344. Cf. Bod. *Aruntius stelle nomen.* Perhaps for *arcturus,* or can
it refer to Arruntius Stella, the poet ? — 345. l. Argivi. — 347. l. Argei : simulacra ; cf.
Varro L. L. VII. 44. — 348. l. haruspex ; ad aras. — 349. l. hariolus, for fariolus ; cf.
Donatus Phorm. IV. 4, 28. — 353. l. ardentes. — 354. l. murorum. — 355. l. arripit :
adprehendit. — 357. Cf. Prod. 142, and Du Cange, = *harpe,* for which Sil. 3, 278,
has *ensis falcatus.* — 360. gŭlevis (?) Goetz regards as belonging to previous gloss.
— 361. Cf. ARFERIA and Prod. 13. — 365. Cf. Prod. 430, and Paul. 11, 14. — 366. Cf.
ARBITERIUM, and De Vit, l. collegium. — 368. l. harmonia … vocabulis … apta. —
372. l. armiportator. — 374. Cf. Hild. A 128. — 375. l. aqualicum. — 378. l. aestimator. —
379. l. inhonestus = ἀσχῆμων ; cf. Loewe G. N. p. 151. — 382. l. contemnit, despicit.
— 383. l. hastarium. — 385. Varro's etymology; cf. L. L. V. 21, 104, Paulus 19, 11.
— 386. = ἄσωτος. — 388. l. voluptuose. — 389. l. adflat. — 391. l. atomi … pulveres
… apparent. Cf. 398. — 397. l. lugubris. — 399. l. horribilis. — 400. l. unumquodque
palaestricum … victoriam. — 406. Cf. AULICI. — 408. l. auspicati, so Bod. — 415. l.
nimbi. — 418. l. cupidus. — 419. l. augur ; cf. Prod. 107. — 424. hausta : potata ; cf. Bod.
austa : eputata. — 425. l. hausit : gustavit. — 426. Cf. De Vit, *aureax : equus solitarius.*
— 427. Cf. Plac. 11, 10, *Austrare : humefacere, dictum ab austro, qui est pluvialis.* —
429. Cf. Gloss. Isid. *auctoratio : venditio nam sub auctione sunt gladiatores qui se
vendunt* (De Vit). — 430. l. venditionis. —433. l. auctionarius ; emit. —435. l. solem. —
436. l. aulaeum : stragulum ; cortinae in the sense of curtain, as in the Vulgate. — 437.
venerabile sanctum. — 438. l. avitum : antiquitas vel ab avis ; cf. Bod. *avitum antiquas
vel ab avis relictum.* See Hild. — 439. l. augustius. — 442. l. haurire. — 444. l. auctio ;
venditio. — 445. l. venator. — 448. l. agitator.

B.

1. Abbreviation of some fuller gloss. as in Hild. B 6, note, *Bacchum vinum et pro
vino quod a Libero patre inventum esse fingunt poetae.* — 2. l. bacchat. — 3. l. bacchi ; cf.
Bod. *bacci : antiqui,* perhaps only the beginning of a gloss *antiqui dicebant,* etc., or as
Hild. l. c. suggests from *Bacchus, vinum vetus.* — 4 refers to Verg. Aen. I. 655 ; cf. Prod.
56. — 5. refers to Verg. Aen. IV. 301. — 6. Cf. Prod. 69. — 7. Goetz reads *anfora,* but
Kaegi confirms my reading, which is of course a corruption for *amphora ;* cf. Ball. *batus
amphora una ·i· modii tres.* See Isid. Or. XVI. 26, 12. — 9. l. pagani sacrarium Liberi ;
cf. Prod. 57. — 10. A vulgar form for *bacelus* = βάκηλος; cf. Prod. 57, f. — 11. l. babigera ; cf. B 24 and Bod. *baligera stulta,* Ball. *babiger stultus,* and see Prod. 54. — 12. l.
bacchationes, furores. — 13. l. Bacchae. — 14. See above p. 134, Bod. *baubant : latrant.*
— 15. Cf. Prod. 55. Du Cange quotes from Gaufridus Grossus Vita S. Bernardi Abbat. de
Tironio, p. 62, " *Bacapulo decentissime palliato superpositus.*" Paulus 61, 12, defines
capulum as *quo mortui efferuntur.* — 16. l. obesas ; cf. Prod. VIII and 66, Vindob. 2404,
bassas : pingues aves, so that the fuller gloss was *bassas : pingues, obesas ;* cf. Martyrius
(K. VII. 176) *bassus etiam, id est grassus, in glossematibus reperi.* — 17. l. bassum, and

cf. Du Cange s. v. — **21**. l. regulus; cf. Loewe G. N. 149. — **24**. Cf. B 11. — **25**. Cf. Caper de orthographia (K. VII. 103) *Bargena, non bargina, genus cui barbaricum sit,* Martyrius de B et V. (K. VII. 175) *Bar*, cum incipit syllaba, *b* mutam habuerit positam ut *barrus* ἐλέφας *bardus* ἀναίσθητος, *bargus* ἀφυής, *barba* et quod in glossematibus inveni *bargina* ἡ προσφώνησις βαρβαρική. Hence emend Bod. *barciae: barbari.* — **26**. l. cubicularius; cf. Prod. 76. — **27**. l. Bacchi latex; cf. Serv. Aen. I. 686, *Laticemque Lyaeum latex* proprie aqua est fontium . . . sed et *vinum latet* intra uvam, unde nunc dixit *laticem.* — **28**. Cf. above B 5. — **29**. Cf. Loewe G. N. 97. Deuerling Plac. 13, 12 n. cites a gloss *baxea: genus calciamenti mulieris, quas baccheas dicunt.* Of some such gloss this is an abbreviation. Loewe quotes de dubiis nominibus (Keil V. 572) *baxeas: calciamenta feminarum ut Varro dicit.* Ellis suggests *baxellas* for *buccellas.* — **30**. A corruption of some fuller gloss referring to Verg. Aen. III. 421, *barathri ter gurgite* (hence? *gurgugite*); cf. Hild. B 13 and 14. — **33**. l. baptismum. Koffmanne Geschichte des Kirchenlatein I. p. 21, speaking of baptismus, says, " das Volk scheint *lavacrum* als Benennung für den Vorgang geliebt zu haben." — **34**. l. barbitos . . . cf. Porphyr. Hor. Car. I. 32, 3, "*barbiton organi* genus est, sed nunc pro lyra posuit." — **35**. l. Bassarides : Bacchae ; cf. **43**. — **36**.? l. Portuni : Neptuni ; cf. De Vit under *Portunus.* — **37**. l. plena ; cf. Prod. 62 and Plac. L. G. 12, 6. — **39**. l. bargus, explained by Cassiodorius and Martyrius (K. VII. 175) as ἀφυής ; cf. Buecheler Rh. Mus. 35, p. 70.— **40**. l. barbiton ; cf. Prod. 65. — **41**. l. barritus. — **43**. l. Bacchae. — **45**. l. faciam. — **46**. l. Bariona . . . columbae ; cf. De Vit Onomasticon I. p. 677. — **47**. l. Bartholomaeus : filius suspendentis aquas ; cf. Ball. *Bartholomeus filius suspendentis aquas vel filius suspendentis me, Syrum est non Hebreum.* — **48**. Cf. BRABIUM, BRABEUM, l. munus. — **49**. l. Bracata : Gallia ; cf. Bod. *Bracata gillea.* — **50**. Cf. BRABEUTA. — **51** = βλάξ ; cf. Prod. 133. — **52**. l. blatit . . . perstupide ; cf. Plac. 12, 18. — **53**. blapere for which blatire is the correct form. Wiegand (Deutsches Wörterbuch) compares *plappern, blappern* with mid. Latin *blaberare* for *blaterare.* — **54**. Cf. BLATTA l. purpurae. — **57**. l. Beelzebub ; cf. De Vit Onomasticon. — **60**. l. beryllus . . . candidi. — **65**. betere must be regarded as an imperative from bitor, biti. For a full discussion of these glosses see Loewe G. N. 196 ff. and Prod. 359. — **66**. l. Beelphegor : simulacrum ; cf. Onomasticon. — **68**. Cf. Bod. *buteo avis*, Ball. *buto genus animalis.* l. buteo : avis quae in auspicio servatur = observatur ; cf. Paulus 3, 5, *Alites volatu auspicia facientes istae putabantur: buteo, sanqualis, immusulus, aquila vulturius ;* see also Paulus 32, 7, and Pliny N. H. X. 21. — **69**. l. beluis : bestiis ; cf. **99**. — **70**. l. Belidae : a Belo patre ; cf. Serv. Aen. II. 81. — **73**. l. bellicosa . . . inferorum. — **74**. l. bellus. — **75**. l. cupidus est, *locus bellicosus* seems to be a corrupt repetition. — **78**. l. BREPHOTROPHIUM = βρεφοτροφεῖον. — **79**. l. putidi aut hircosi ; cf. Prod. 265 and Bod. *blenones : putidi hercones*, Ball. . . . *aut hircosi.* — **80**. l. BLAESUS. . . . alio sono corrumpit ; cf. Prod. 394. — **82**. l. bibliotheca. — **83**. l. bibliopola. — **84**. Abbreviation of a fuller gloss like *bibulus : bibitor qui valde bibit ;* cf. Hild. B 34, *Bibulus, bibitor qui multum bibit.* — **85**. Cf. BIBLUM. l. funis. — **86**. l. Bisaltes or? Ephialtes, corrupted into Epialtes ; Ebialces ; bialcis ; but it may be a compound of βία and ἀλκή. — **89**. l. bigamus . . . habet uxores. — **90**. l. biclinium ; cf. Loewe G. N. 150. — **91**. Cf. Hildebrand B 35 n. and Du Cange. — **92**. l. bibliothecarius ; cf. Prod. 72, where Loewe emends to *qui codices servat.* — **94**. l. bidento ; cf. Du Cange. — **95**. l. bifidum ; Cf. Prod. 75. — **98**. l. commotio. — **99**. l. beluae. — **100**. l. byssum : sericum tortum ; cf. Bod. *bissum : siricum tortum.* — **101**. l. bivira . . . maritos ; cf· Prod. 73. — **104**. Cf. above, B 65. — **105**. l. bigenerum — e duobus generibus ; cf. Paul. 33, 14, *bigenera dicuntur animalia ex diverso genere nata*, and Bod. *bigenerum e duobus generibus conceptum.* — **106**. l. vespillo(nes) : qui mortuos portant ; cf. Hild. B 44 and Paul. 368, 17, *Vespae et vespillones* dicuntur, qui funerandis corporibus officium gerunt, non a minutis volucrebus, sed quia vespertino tempore eos efferunt, etc. Georges says that the best MSS. and glosses have *vispillo.* — **107**. l. bimatus = bimater ; cf. Amplon. 278, 35, bimatur : liber pater, and Inscr. in Bollett dell' Inst. Archæol. a. 1854, p. xxxvi. Leiber pater bimatus Iovis e fulmine natus (cited by De Vit Lex.). — **108**. Cf. Glossae in Sidonium ed. Ellis in Anecdota Oxoniensia, vol. I., part V., p. 31, *Talassa* enim Graece Latine dicitur *mare.* Inde *bitalassum* .i. *duplex mare*, ubi duo .s. maria concurrunt .i. ubi quaedam terra se extendit in mare ita ut acutum terrae illius mare habeat ex utraque parte sui. Unde dicitur quod Paulus naufragatus est *in bitalasso,* and see Amplon. 276, 33, *bathilasa, ubi duo maria conveniunt;* Epin. 6, A 16, *bythalass. ubi duo maria conveniunt;* Bod. *bitalasis, periculum duorum marium,* whence emend here *bithalassum,* etc. — 110. l. gigantis. Hyginus, in his Introduction, mentions among the Giants immediately before Ephialtes (see above, 86) *Alemone,* which Munck proposes to emend to *Alcyoneus.* Perhaps it is the same word with *Bitemon,* which is not given in the Onomasticon. Otherwise one might think of Verg. Aen. V. 372, Victorem Buten immani corpore. — 113. Cf. 65 and 104. — 114. l. Byrsam . . . bubulum; cf. Serv. Aen. I. 367, Bod. *Birsum corium bubuli.* — 115. l. centimanus. — 116. Cf. 65. — 117. Cf. BIMO. l. duplatur; cf. Paulus 67, 2, *duplabis duplicabis.* — 118. l. bipedalis. — 119. *duobus* is dat. after *erogat,* as in Cic. ad Att. 8, 5. — 120. Cf. Plac. 15, 8, *bipennem,* bis *acutum, pennum* enim dicimus *acutum;* cf. Hild. B 42 and Isid. Or. XIX. 19, 11, nam *bipennis* dicitur, quod ex utraque parte habeat *acutam aciem* quasi *duas pennas. Pennum* autem antiqui *acutum* dicebant. — 121. Cf. Plac. 13, 4, *Bova* vehemens *rubor,* interdum *genus serpentis,* and Paul. 30, 14, *bova* serpens est aquatilis, quem Graeci ὕδρον vocant, a qua icti obturgescunt. Crurum quoque *tumor vias labore* collectus *bova* appellatur. — l. rubor vehemens, and 122, ingens . . . crure . suffuso; cf. Prod. 312 f. and G. N. 231. — 123. Cf. Amplon[2] 278, 72, *burrus: rufus, niger,* Amplon [1] 277, 101, *boarris, rufis, niger,* and Epin. 6, E 10, *barsis, rufus, niger.* l. burrus; but perhaps *rubus = ruber* may be retained; cf. Paul. 264, 10, *Robum rubro colore et quasi rufo significari,* etc. — 125. l. burrae; beginning of the gloss found Plac. 13, 16, *burrae varroniae, fatuae ac stupidae,* etc. — 126. l. clamare. — 127. l. herede; cf. Prod. 78. — 128. l. Bosphorus. — 130. l. bovinatores: inconstantes; cf. Plac. 13, 6. *Bovinator, tricosus et inconstans,* and Nonius, 79, 25, *bovinatores, quos nunc malitiosos et tergiversatores dicimus.* Lucilius lib. XI. Hic'st tricosu' bovinatorque, ore improbo duro; cf. Prod. 319. — 131. l. bombus; cf. 135 and Bod. *bombus sonus tumidus, imitatio vocis vel crepitus.* — 132. Cf. other glosses of *brocchus* in Prod. 80 and 391, and G. N. 144. — 134. l. Bootes; cf. these glosses cited by Loewe Prod. 84 f. *butis: stella comis qui quasi comas habet; betes: stella comites quae quasi comam habet;* and see Serv. Aen. X. 272 (Thilo, p. 422, 18) est etiam alter *cometes,* qui vere *cometes* appellatur; nam *comis* hinc inde cingitur, hic blandus esse dicitur qui si orientem attenderit, laetas res ipsi parti significat, etc. — 138. Cf. Varro L. L. VII. 39, 40, *Luca bos elephas,* . . . *Lucanam bovem quod putabant, Lucam bovem appellassent.* — 139. l. storea; cf. Prod. 82 f. — 140. Cf. Serv. Verg. Ec. 8, 86, *bucula, bovis est diminutio.* — 141. l. bombum; cf. Prod. 77 and G. N. 138, where Loewe cites from Vat. 1468, *bombum: sordidum,* and proposes to read *bombum: sordidum sonum,* but this seems to me very doubtful; cf. Hild. B 52, 53, and Bod. *Bubum: sorbellum.* I prefer to keep *sorbillum =* the sucking sound accompanying drinking. — 142. Cf. note to 144. — 143. l. bombosum: sonorum furibundum, so Bod. — 144. Cf. Paul. 32, 4, *Bustum* proprie dicitur locus, *in quo mortuus est combustus* et sepultus, diciturque *bustum,* quasi *bene ustum;* ubi vero combustus quis tantummodo, alibi vero est sepultus, is locus ab urendo ustrina vocata: sed modo busta sepulcra appellamus. Cf. Servius Verg. Aen. XI. 201. — 145. Cf. BUCETUM. — 146. Cf. Prod. 83. Bod. *Burca: clavaca;* see Du Cange, under *Burca.* — 147. Cf. BUCERUS. — 148. *buceriae* is found in Lucretius 2, 663 (Mun.) *lanigeras pecudes . . . buceriaeque greges,* but *bucera* in Ovid Met. VI. 395, *lanigerosque greges armentaque bucera* pavit; cf. Hild. B 62. — 149. Onomatopoetic word; cf. Du Cange under *bunda.* —'150. Bod. *Bulones ipsi sunt cetari qui diversa genera piscium vendunt,* so Hild. B. 66; cf. Plac. 13, 9, *Bolona,* redemptor *cetariarum* tabernarum in quibus *salsamenta* condiuntur, quas *tabernas vulgo cetarias* vocant. *Bulonium* seems to be an abstract like *mangonium* (cf. *sterquilinium*) l. lutum . . . cetarii; but perhaps there is some confusion with *bolbiton.* Loewe Prod. 77 reads *puto* for *luto.* — 151. Cf. BOTRUS = βότρυς. — 152. l. buccones refers to Plaut. Bacch. 1088, stulti, stolidi, fatui, fungi, bardi, blenni, buccones; cf. Isid. Or. X. 30, *Bucco* garrulus, quod ceteros oris loquacitate non sensu exsuperat, and Prod. 265. — 154. l. bubinare menstruo; see above, p. 131. — 155. Cf. BUSTUARII. — 156. l. avis nocturnae. — 158. l. bruta: stolida; cf. Bod. *Brunda: solida,* and Prod. 81. — 159. Cf. BURGUS. — 160. See note to 123. — 161. Cf. BUSTICETUM. — 162. Cf. BULLO. — 163. l. brutus insipiens; cf. Ball. *bruti stulti insipientes;* Bod. *Brutus, stultus gravis stupidus, hebes, insipiens.*

C.

4. Cf. Paul. 48, Plac. 30, 3, *cassiculo, reticulo, a cassibus.* — 5. l. catechumenus. — 6. l. catechizat . . . edocet. — 7. l. caballus; cf. De Vit. — 8. l. canon. — 9. l. cachinnus. — 10. l. conplosus; cf. Prod. p. XIV. Ball. *caplosus: elisus;* Bod. *inlisus.* — 12. l. robur. — 13. l. capedo. — 14. l. categorias: adscriptiones; cf. *Catagoriae: ascriptiones, accusationes* (Papias). Notice peculiar use of *adscriptiones.* — 15. Bod. *caletra;* cf. Cod. Leid. 67, E, *Caletra: ubi vespe nutriuntur,* and Amplon. 286, 62, *caloetra, ubi vespe nascuntur.* Prod. p. 46 n. = κοιλήθρα? — 17. Bod. *campe;* cf. Prod. 332 and Paul. 44, 1; see above, p. 131. — 18. l. supplicii eculeo simile. — 19. I can find no such river in Thrace. Perhaps a corruption of Causter = Cayster: fluvius Asiae. — 21. l. chalybs. — 22. l. camuris cornibus; cf. Servius and Philargyrius to Verg. Georg. III. 55. Paul. 43, 17, *Camara* et *camuri* boves a curvatione ex Graeco κάμπη dicuntur. — 23. l. canoris: chordis refers to Verg. Aen. VI. 120, *fidibusque canoris,* where Servius explains *bene sonantibus chordis.* — 24. Cf. Prod. 95 and expressions like *in calce epistulae, in calce libri.* — 25. l. carchesia . . . poculi; cf. Serv. Aen. V. 77. — 26. l. iocum convicium; cf. Paul 46, 10, and Epin. 7, C 5, *cavillatio: iocus cum vicio.* — 27. l. discissus. — 28. l. chamaeleon . . humilis; cf. Ball. *caleon: humilis leo.* — 29. Cf. Prod. 146 and Du Cange under CATAPOTA. — 30. l. calamaula = καλαμαύλης . . . canitur; cf. Phill. *calamaula canna in qua canitur.* There may have been some confusion with cana mala in C 49. — 31. l. Carystius. — 32. Cf. Plac. 20, 9, *Candys, vestis regia.* — 34. Cf. C 374. Nonius p. 25, 13, '*catax* dicitur, quem nunc *coxonem* vocant Lucilius'. . . Hostiliu' contra Festem perniciemque *catax;* cf. Prod. 308 f. — 35. l. carchesia; cf. De Vit. *Carteriae: sunt in cacumine arborum per quas funes trahuntur.* — Macrob. V. 21, Asclepiades autem . . . *carchesia* a navali re existimat dicta. ait enim navalis veli partem inferiorem πτέρναν vocari, at circa mediam ferme partem τράχηλον dici, summam vero partem *carchesium* nominari, etc. For *vel* therefore *veli* is probably to be read, and perhaps the fuller gloss had anterior pars. — 36. ? The first part is perhaps a corruption of calo: servus; cf. Acron. Hor. Ep. I. 14, 42, *Calo, servus unde calones.* — 37. Catasceue is used by Servius Aen. II. 409. — 38. l. capitibus . . . hasta vendebatur. — 40. l. minister sacrorum. — 42. Cf. Du Cange under CALAMAULARIUS. — 43. ? There is evidently some connection with Castalia, Castalis, perhaps for Castalides: deae elocutionis. — 44. This gloss added by a second hand contains a mixture of two glosses, casnar: senex = 115, and captiviginae: ex captivo natae. *captivigena* is formed like *alienigena,* but is not found in the Lexica nor in Du Cange. — 45. Cf. Mon. 6210, '*casu: eventu fortuito.* I cannot explain *pro eventum,* unless *proventu* was added as an explanation of *eventu.* — 46. So Serv. Æn. III. 265, *casum, periculum.* — 47. De Vit gives a gloss *Candaulus: γάνδαυλος; edulium ex carne elixa, pane, et caseo Phrygio cum anetho et pingui iure.* Hence read candaulus: edulium; cf. κάνδαυλος or κάνδυλος. — 49. l. cana mala: lanunigem habentes id est cydonia; cf. Serv. Ec. 2, 51. — 51. l. instabilis; cf. Prod. 4. — 52. l. tela; the first part of gloss refers to Verg. Georg. III. 371 (where Servius glosses *cassibus* with *retibus*) and the second part to Georg. IV. 248. — 53. Cf. CARTALLUS. — 55. l. catervatim; cf. Verg. Georg. III. 556. — 56. l. detrahit. — 57. Perhaps a confusion of two glosses, as calculosus: glareosus, lapideus = lapidosus, and calculus: victoria iudicum. — 58. l. caulae; cf. Paul. 46, 12, and Serv. Æn. IX. 60. — 59. l. calculum. — 62. l catalogus. Bod. *catalogus iustorum* (l. *iuxta rem,* Ellis) *numeratio ordo vel series.* — 64. Cf. following glosses cited by De Vit: *cantabrum; furfur caninum quo canes pascuntur, purgamenta tritici; cantarinum vel cantarum, equus castratus.* Du Cange gives "*cantabrum* pro *cantharus,*" which would come nearest to this gloss. — 65. l. caduceum. — 67. Cf. Gloss. Pap. *Capedines: animalia dicta, quod manu capiantur,* (alii omittunt *animalia dicta*) De Vit. — 69. l. vafra; cf. above p. 131, Phill. *carisa: vafer.* — 70. Abbreviated for Caulae; cancelli tribunales ubi sunt advocati; cf. De Vit and Hild. C 56. — 71. l. cataplum. — 72. Goetz reads *gravia,* but Kaegi *gruia* l. grata; cf. Mai. VI. 513, *canora: cantu grata.* — 75. Is the same gloss, I think, as that given by Du Cange, "*Ceragius, Cereagius, Pistor, qui ad modum cerae agit et deducit pastam.* Glossar. Provinc. Lat. ex cod. reg. 7657, *pestre,* Prov. *Ceragius, arteco-*

pus, panetarius;" or perhaps for *cereasius.* Compare De Vit under *Cerialis* and *Carensis,* both glossed as *pistor.* — 76. l. castus sacer, or perhaps catus: acer; cf. Plac. 21, 17, catus, acutus, callidus, sapiens, prudens. — 77 and 78 = χάρισμα l. spiritale . . . divinae gratiae. — 79. Cf. Lucan. V. 379, *Calabroque obnoxius Austro.* — 80. l. cataclysmum: diluvium. — 81. Cf. Bod. *careo: amitto, nolo, perdo.* — 83. l. cadus: amphora semis; cf. Bod. *cadus : amphora est habens urnas tres.* — 86 ? Cf. Mai. VIII. 142, *carrire: dividere, secernere, seiungere.* — 87. l. caligo: tenebrae. — 88. l. caculae: servi; cf. Plac. 23, 23, *Caculae, lixae aut servi militum.* — 90. l. cocula; cf. Paulus 39, 3, *Cocula: vasa aenea,* coctionibus apta, alii *cocula dicunt ligna minuta,* quibus facile decoquantur obsonia; see Loewe G. N. 206 f, and below, 341. — 92. l. cadaver. The etymology is found in Servius Æn. VI. 481. — 93. l. calvitur; see above, p. 132. — 94. l. capissit: tenet, libenter accipit. — 95. Loewe cites this gloss G. N. 151 among the *difficilia,* but as Prof. Gildersleeve has pointed out to me, it refers to καδμεία νίκη l. victoria non bona. — 96. l. iocatur . . . calumniam; cf. De Vit. — 97. Cf. Serv. Æn. III. 580, *caminis; fornacibus* Graece dixit (ἀπὸ τοῦ κάειν). — 98. l. capillatis: capillis porrectis; cf. Hild. C 37. — 101. Cf. CHALYBS. — 102. l. Capitolinus . . . capitolio. — 103. Cf. CADUCUS l. daemoniacus. — 104. Cf. Plac. 27, 15, *cancros: cancellos,* and Paulus 46, 2, *cancri dicebantur ab antiquis qui nunc per diminutionem cancelli.* — 106. Cf. Prod. 97, *capite absoluto: capitis periculo liberatus.* — 108. l. casses: nom. pl.; see Neue Formenlehre I. p. 385. — 109. Cf. CHARISTIA. — 110. l. capulum; cf. Paul. 61, 12, *Capulum* et manubrium gladii vocatur et id *quo mortui efferuntur* utrumque a capiendo dictum. See 112. Serv. Æn. XI. 64, *feretrum* locus *ubi* mortui feruntur . . . Latine *capulus* dicitur. — 111. l. capides; cf. Loewe G. N. 137. — 112. l. spathae; cf. 110 and De Vit. — 113. Cf. CAPERATA. — 114. Cf. Paul. 47, 8, *Carinantes probra obiectantes, a carina dicti quae est infima pars navis; sic illi sortis infimae;* Serv. Æn. VIII. 361, *carinare* autem est *obtrectare,* Ennius contra *carinantes* verba atque obscena profatus alibi neque me decet hanc *carinantibus* edere chartis; cf. Prod. 14. — 115. Bod. *canier leno.* Loewe Prod. 306 f, quotes this gloss from several glossaries, in some of which *leo* occurs; Cod. Leidensis 191³ has *camer leo capoleos,* where *capoleos* seems to belong to a new gloss; the liber glossarum has *caniet: leno.* Loewe's conjecture that *canierleo* or *camerleo* or *canietleno* stands for *camelleo,* i. e. χαμαιλέων, is most probable (cf. *cameleon,* 141), otherwise one might think that *canierleno* or *canietleno* was a corruption of *cantilena: cantellena;* cf. 139, cantus: cantellena, and compare Plac. 28, 6, *cantilenas, fraudes dolosque.* — 116. l. casnar senex, Bod. *canar senex;* cf. Plac. 24, 6, *casnar, senex,* 29, 8, *casnari seni, Oscorum lingua.* Paul. 47, 12. Epin. 7 A 19, cassinur: senex. — 117. = καλαμίσκος. — 118. Cf. καρυΐσκος, used in the Septuagint for καρύινα κεράμια = Lat. carenariae. The gloss given by Mai. VII. 553, *Calamostros, iscos vel cariscos quasi in nucis modum deformatos,* is evidently a confusion of this and the previous gloss. — 119. l. caudices . . radices. — 121. Cf. Serv. Æn. XII. 100. — 122. l. observa. — 123. One might be tempted to read acinacem (this form occurs Arnob. VI. 11), but by so doing we should lose a very good illustration of the way in which glosses were collected. In Servius Æn. I. 75 (Thilo.) we read errant namque qui dicunt ideo ' pulchra' dixisse propter *Canacen (canacem* L. *cavacem* M) et *Macareum (machareum* BM) in se invicem turpissimos fratres, etc. Some stupid gloss-hunter read here *canacem est machareum ;* and interpreted *machareum,* i. e. *machaerium* (cf. *macherio* Plaut. Aul. 393), by *gladium,* a more familiar word. In the same way, our very next gloss, 124, capessere: capere [invadere] frequenter, is an alteration of Servius note to Æn. I. 77, " *capessere autem est saepe capere.*" Here he substituted *frequenter* for *saepe.* — 125. l. scopula, which Hild. C 59 changes to scopuli, but the neuter was doubtless vulgar, as *puteum* and *sarcophagum;* cf. Rönsch. p. 270 f. — 126. Perhaps originally there were two glosses, *callidus: astutus* and *calliditas: astutia.* — 127. l. sollicitus. — 129. cf. CANICULARIS. — 132. l. succensa. — 133. l. consessus; cf. Serv. Aen. V. 340, *cavea consessus est populi.* — 135. Cf. Prod. 258 and Nonius 45, 28, Calcitrones, qui infestant calcibus (Plaut. Asin. I. 3, 11). — 136. l. CEONOMYIA. — 137. ? caristeum = carysteum; cf. De Vit *caristeum: marmoris genus dictum quod gratum sit scultoribus* (Gloss. Pap.). — 138. l. calones: galearii; cf. Prod. 45. — 140. l. caulae: cancellum; cf. above, 70. — 141. l. chamaeleon . humilis. — 142. l. lentis consimile. — 143. l. caltha; cf. Plac. 22, 9,

Calta, genus quoddam floris vel herbae. — **144**. So Epin. 7 A 15, and Amp. 280, 40; cf. Hild. D. 402 note, "*Duvium: clanculum ambiguum. . . .* S. Germ. *clangulum mane,* ubi lux dubia est." See, however, Censorinus 24, secundum *diluculum* vocatur *mane,* where D has δεLUCULUM. Read therefore *diluculum: mane.* — **145**. l. claudier; cf. Ter. And. 573. — **146**. Cf. Plac. 22, 2, *classicum canit, celeuma navis dicit,* Serv. Aen. VII. 637, *classicum dicimus et tubam ipsam et sonum.* For *celeuma* and *celeusma* cf. Saalfeld's Tensaurus. — **148**. l. clangor. — **149**. l. occultae. — **150**. l. τῇ τύχη (so Goetz). **151**. l. claudire: claudicare, or clandire: clandicare; cf. Prod. 357. — **153**. I doubt the existence of a verb *classicare,* perhaps for classica [sonan]t; cf. Verg. Aen. VII. 637. — **154**. l. chaos. — **155**. l. crapula: ebrietas. — **156**. l. clarigatio. — **158**. l. serraturae. — **160**. = τὸν φίλον. **160** and **163** constituted, I think, originally one gloss καίπερ τὸν φίλον: superque amicum, the *amicum* was perhaps written above the line for lack of room, and so two independent glosses sprang up. — **161**. l. finis sermonis. — **163**. l. clava. — **166**. l. chelys. — **167**. Cf. Isid. Or. VII. 12, 2, Propterea ergo dicti *clerici qui de sorte sunt domini.* — **168**. = κληρονόμος. — **170**. Cf. Nonius 20, 13. — **172**. l. gliscit: crescit, taken from Serv. Aen. XII. 9, *Gliscit crescit,* et latenter, unde et *glires* dicti sunt quos pingues efficit somnus; cf. Paul. 98, 9. — **174**. l. paralyticus. — **175**. Cf. above p. 100 — **177**. l. ceruchis; cf. Lucan VIII. 177. — **178**. Loewe Prod. 364 thinks this a corruption of **184**, clues: polles; perhaps these were the steps, *pulles, plules, pluvies, pluvia.* — **180**. l. clepsydra per quod horae colliguntur. — **182**. Cf. Ball. *clibanus fornax vel furnus,* and De Vit, *Clibanus argenteus; furnus mobilis placentis et panibus coquendis aptus, alias ex testa, ferro vel aere fiebat,* Gloss. ad Petron. Sat. 35. l. furnus testeus? cf. Isid. Or. XX. 2, 15, *clibanitius in testa coctus.* — **183**. l. CHIROGRAPHUM. — **184**. Cf. Prod. 364. — **185**. Cf. CLIBANARIUS and Hild. C 110. — **186**. Cf. CLIMACTER. — **187**. l. zona; cf. A 298. — **188**. Cf. CLYPEUS (Forcellini De Vit III.). — **189**. l. caelebs. — **191**. Cf. χέρνιψ and De Vit under chernibs. — **194**. l. celoces: veloces, used as adj. by Plautus. — **195**. l. caenum . putridum. — **196**. Perhaps a repetition of **190** or a corruption of caelestinus. — **197**. l. caeruleus. — **198**. l. celeber: frequens. — **199**. De Vit gives *Caecua et caecuma. noctua quae lucem fugit,* Müller, Ed. Festus Corollarum Glossarum p. 381, has *Cicuma avis noctua.* l. cicuma = κικύμη κίκυμος; cf. Saalfeld's Tensaurus. — **206**. l. uxore . . . caelo; cf. Paul. 44, 5, *Caelibem* dictum existimant *quod dignam caelo vitam agant.* This etymology was repeated by Donatus, Priscian, Hieronymus, Beda, and Isidorus. — **207**. l. cerastes. — **208**. l. est caelicola. — **209**. l. caerimonium. — **210**. l. minutorum. — **211**. l. Cananaeus (or Chananaeus): possidens sive possessio, ita autem dictus Simon a vico Cana; cf. Isid. Or. VII. 6, 12, *Cainam lamentatio vel possessio eorum: sicut enim Cain possessio,* etc. Cf. Onomasticon under *Cain, Cainan, Chananaei,* and *Cana.* There seems to have been a confusion of *Cana* and *Canaan.* — **214**. l. caerula; cf. Serv. Aen. III. 64, Veteres sane *caeruleum nigrum* accipiebant. — **217**. l. ciccum; cf. above p. 131. — **218**. Cf. Mai. VI. 512, *Caei; iudicatores,* and 530, *Kaii; cancelli* (an hunc spectet, viderint doctiores, De Vit). *Cei iudicatores* Gloss. Sangerm. *Kays: cancelli.* (De Vit). Diez connects fr. *quai* with *Kays.* The gloss *cancelli* would seem to point to an identification with **140**, *caule: cavellum ante iudicem,* and **70**, *caulae* [cancelli tribunalis] *ubi sunt advocati. caule* dropping the *u,* as *augustus, agustus,* would give *cale,* which, palæographically, is very nearly *caei,* = *cei;* but I think Cei may refer to Cic. Div. I. 130, and the gloss was taken from the same source as **227**. Notice that Cei is followed by cere and Cea by cerealia. — **219**. l. Ceres. — **220**. l. chelidon (χελιδών) hirundo. — **221**. l. cercurus. In Stich. 413, A has CIRCULO, B C D, *cercuro.* — **222**. l. Cimmerias, silvas. — **223**. l. caenum : luti vorago; cf. Isid. Or. XVI. 1, 2, *Coenum est vorago luti.* — **224**. l. certiscat; cf. Nonius 89, 20, *certiscant, certa fiant* Pacuvius chryse. "Atque eccos unde *certiscant,*" but Rebbeck reads *certiscent.* Perhaps *certiscat* to be read. — **225**. l. Cecropidae: Athenienses; cf. Serv. Aen. VI. 21. — **226**. l. CEDRON. — **227**. Cf. Serv. Georg. I. 14. — **232** and **233**. Cf. CERASTES, Saalfeld Tensaurus. — **234**. l. CERRITUS . . . commotione cerebri; cf. Paul. 54, 14, cerritus, furiosi. — **238**. l. ac si. — **239**. l. cecinit. — **243**. l. censuit: deliberavit. — **244**. l. cerebro . . habet. — **245**. l. chelydrus. — **246**. Cf. Serv. Aen. X. 894, *cernuus* dicitur equus qui *cadit in faciem.* — **247** and **249**. Cf. κενοδοξία. — **248**. Cf. Verg. Aen. V. 778. — **250**. l. succumbit. — **252**. l. caespes; cf. Plac.

23, 2, *caespites, frutices,* etc. — **254.** l. commentum. — **260.** Cf. **155**; cf. Amplon. 290, 279, and 298, *crapula nausia potum vel indigestio* and *crapulatus: vino obrutus.* Here we probably have a confusion of two glosses, *crapulatus: inebriatus* and *crapula(m) nausia ob potum;* but the form *crapulam* may be retained referring to Pseud. 1270, or Most. 1108; cf. Plac. 24, 8, *crapula, cruditas levis.* — **263.** l. crepundia. — **264.** l. crebro; compare It. spesso. — **265.** Cf. Bod. *crepidinem: summitatem riparum* . . Plac. 20, 3, *crepido, saxi extremitas rimata et cuiuslibet rei alterius.* Sée Hild. C 483 note, where H. emends *rima* to *ripa.* — **266.** l. spissavit. — **267.** l. generat. — **268.** Loewe Prod. 406 proposes to read *creperae: incertae, dubiae,* which he admits to be "medela audacissima." Cf. Paul. 52; 18, *Creperum: dubium unde increpitare dicimus quia maledicta fere incerta et dubia sunt.* I am inclined to think that *in corp[ore dub]itare* is in some way a corruption of *increpitare* of Paulus; cf. Hild. C. 485. — **269.** Compare the fuller gloss cited by Loewe l. c., which begins, *Crepusculum tempus inter finem noctis et initium diei.* — **270.** Cf. also Serv. Aen. I. 268, *(crepusculum) est dubia lux nam* '*creperum*' *dubium* significat. — **273.** l. chrisma. — **274.** l. cristatus; cf. Verg. Aen. I. 468, *cristatus Achilles,* but there is probably a confusion of two glosses; cf. CHRISMO. — **275.** l. crinitior. — **276.** l. crocitus; cf. Loewe G. N. 250 f. — **278.** Cf. Paulus 55, 10, *Crustumina* tribus a Tuscorum urbe *Crustumena* † *dicta est;* cf. Serv. Verg. Georg. II. 88, *Crustumina* sunt pyra . . . ab oppido *Crustumio,* and Aen. VII. 631, *Crustumerium* dicitur; cf. Onomasticon. — **280.** l. cycneum or cygneum. — **281.** So explained by Serv. Aen. VIII. 642. — **282.** l. Cynthia. — **283.** l. cito tramite: cursu refers to Aen. V. 610. — **285.** l. circumsaeptus. — **286.** l. circumplexus. — **287.** Ball. *civicans: civem faciens.* l. civicat; cf. CIVICO and Loewe G. N. 164, where, however, from Ambr. B. 31, *civitat: civem facit,* he accepts *civitare,* which Hild. C. 95 n. rightly condemns. — **289.** Cf. Lucan III. 228, Itque *Cilix* iusta iam non *pirata* carina, and Hild. C 83. — **290.** Cf. Hild. C 92. l. cisium; but perhaps *cirsium* was the original form, whence *cissium, cisium,* which would account for rhotacism not taking place. — **291.** l. praeiudicium. — **292.** ? cinxere. — **393.** l. ceu taxus, cf. De Vit. — **294.** Cf. 290. — **295.** Cf. Serv. Aen. III. 64 and 680. l. cyparissus: cupressus. — **296.** l. cytisum. — **301.** l. cicatricem. — **302.** l. CHILIARCHUS. Tribunus qui mille contribulibus praeest; cf. Epin. 6 E 25, *ciliarchus qui mille praeest,* and Ball. *ciliarchus qui mille praeest hominibus.* — **303.** l. cycni: poetae. — **305.** Cf. Isidor. Or. XV. 2, 1. — **306.** The lemma (probably *cieo*) corresponding to *voco* has dropped out. — **307.** l. cicur. — **308.** l. mitigare; cf. Hild. C 81 n. — **310.** l. civica. — **312.** l. Cyllenius. — **314.** Cf. Loewe G. N. 151, "cod. Cassinensis 439⁵ *circie: radia solis* (fort. *Circe. filia solis,* quamquam mira sane est triti vocabuli corruptela et parum congruit quod Ambros B 31 sup. *circiae radius solis* exhibet; *radii* Vat. 1468¹); cf. Verg. Aen. VII. 10, *Circaeae raduntur litora terrae,* and 19, where Servius says, *Circe autem ideo solis fingitur filia.* — **316.** See above, p. **132.** — **320.** l. Chimaera. — **321.** l. gyrus; so **326.** — **323.** l. citrarius(?): pomarius, i. e. fruit-seller. — **324.** Cf. Hild. C 96 n., who reads *civitas,* but Mai aptly compares the Ital. *civita vecchia,* etc. — **325.** l. senator. — **327.** Cf. above, p. **134.** — **329.** l. huc ad nos. — **330.** l. CERCOPITHECUS simile simiae. — **331.** l. quiritat; cf. Prod. 316 f. Nonius 21, 18, and Varro L. L. VI. 68; cf. Donatus Ter. Ad. 2, 1, 1, veteres *quiritari* dicebant, *Quirites conclamare.* — **332.** l. cynici . . . vitam; cf. Cic. Orator 3, 17. The next gloss, perhaps, ought to be joined with this. Cf. Isid. Or. VIII. 6, 14, . . . *Unde et a canibus, quorum vitam imitabantur etiam vocabulum nomenque traxerunt.* — **334.** l. cidaris for *pallius* masc.; see Appel p. 92, l. bysso . . . nostri tiaram. — **339.** l. cothurnum. — **341.** Cf. above, **90.** — **342.** l. cohibet. — **344.** l. coacervat. — **345.** l. punit. — **346** l. affines; cf. Isidor. Or. IX. 6, 2. — **347.** l. congiarium. — **352.** l. ambulavit. — **353.** l. commixtio. — **361.** l. coerceo. — **362.** l. cors, for which *chors* is later orthography; cf. Nonius 83, 14, "*chortes* sunt villarum intra maceriam spatia," and Varro L. L. V. 16. — **362.** l. nutritur. — **364.** l. c(h)ors. See Beck, p. 47, Inter *cors* et *chors: cortes* sunt *rusticorum, chortes militum castra.* — **365.** Cf. Prod. 277, Plaut. Trin. 743, *Columem te sistero.* — **369.** l. collega: socius. — **370.** l. colaphizat . . . caedit. — **373.** Cf. Nonius 55, 18, *Culinam (colinam)* veteres *coquinam* dixerunt, quoting Plaut. Most. 1. — **374.** = catax; see **34.** — **375.** l. virga quae per cochleam volvitur. — **379.** Perhaps a confusion of two glosses, compar: consimilis and compos: magnanimis, used by Tertullian (sanus-animi?). — 380. l. participem, similem; cf. 379; cf. Non. 45C 20, Compotem in bonam partem solum accipi putatur, quum et in mala positum sit, Plautus Epidico (IV. 1, 32) . . . Naevius Danae. eam nunc scis inventam probri compotem. — 382. See above, p. 133. — 385. l. commoratio; cf. Cic. ad Fam. VI. 19, et villa et amoenitas illa *commorationis*, non diversorii. — 389. l. cumulatius. — 390. Cf. Plac. 22, 16, *comesationes*, convivia et scribimus uno *m* et uno *s*; Hild. C 171 n. *comersatio* luxuria vel *convivia meretricorum* est. l. convivia meretricum. — 391. compos mentis is for compos voti. Plac. L. G. 14, 22, compos *cuius completum est desiderium.* — 391. (The reading iuxta is not certain on account of erasures in the MS. Kaegi). Cf. Hild. C 301 n. and Serv. Georg. I. 104, *Veteres enim non in tempore, sed in loco comminus ponebant, i. e. iuxta.* — 393. = 403. — 394. l. commercium. — 395. *recrastinare* is used by Pliny and Columella. *recrastinatio* is cited by De Vit Lex. from Hilarius Libell. 5, and from other glossaries. — 401. Cf. Prod. 327. *comesurus: manducaturus.* Lucilius quoted by Nonius 479, 2, uses *commanducatur* and *comest* in the same verse. Whether an active verb comesare existed may be doubted. There may be some confusion with *comisor, comessor.* — 402. Cf. Paul. 41, 1. *compernes* nominantur homines genibus plus iusto coniunctis, " Nonius 25, 25, *compernes* dicitur longis pedibus." l. calcibus, and cf. *calcitrones.* — 403. Cf. COMESTIO (De Vit). — 405. l. commode. — 406. l. commodius: utilius. — 407. Perhaps a confusion of two glosses commentum: adinventio (cf. 424) and commentarium: expositio. — 408. l. commenticias: adinventicias, which is not given by Lex. — 409. l. comites itineris id est oratio et gratia? — 411. Perhaps *comitia* is the reading of the MS. (Kaegi notes ' der Streich für *m* fast unsichtbar '). l. comitia . . . honorum; cf. Hild. C 172, n. for other similar glosses. — 412. l. comitium. — 413. l. compita . . . quadrivia. — 416. The letters are very indistinct, but the gloss evidently = 434. — 418. l. commenta. — 424. Cf. 407. l. commentatio? (but commune mendacium may be an attempt at an etymology; cf. 418 and 421. *commentum* in the sense of *commentarium* is shown by Paucker to have been used already by Columella VII. 5, 17, " Bolus Mendesius, cuius *commenta* quae appellantur Graece, ὑπομνήματα." — 425. — Hild. C 314 n. cites and defends conpertitor: amicus, but there seems to be a direct reference to Cic. de Offic. 1, 12, Dum *civi* aliter contendimus, si est *inimicus*, aliter si *competitor.* — 430. l. complodere; so Bod. — 431. l. honos = dignitas; for the various titles into which *comes* enters see Forcellini De Vit Lex. — 432. Diomedes (K. L p. 488 f.) gives a great variety of derivations for *comoedia*, which it is unnecessary to state here. Among them "ab urbana κώμη καὶ ᾠδὴ comoedia dicta est," and ' sunt qui velint Epicharmum in Co . . . hoc carmen frequentasse, et sic a Co comoediam dici." Our gloss is probably very much abridged from a fuller one. In the MS. co is written above cer I think as correction. Without much change we may read comoedia: significatio morum singulorum a come et ode tracta ῡ (vel) quia fit in Co. — 433. Cf. COMMULCO.— 434. l. consecrat; for a tendency to insert *r* in the neighborhood of another *r* see examples cited by Seelmann Aussprache des Latein p. 330, *draucus, frustrum, cretariae, Euphratre, Marcrinius* — 437. l. compascere. — 438. l. confertum; cf. CONFERTUS. — 440. confecit?). — 441. l. coniectio; cf. Bod. *coniectio, coniectura, aestimatio, arbitrium,* but *conitio* = conicio may originally have belonged to a previous gloss; cf. Bod. *conicio, arbitror aestimo reor, opinor,* and Hild. C 278 n. — 445. l. iudicium synodale. — 446. l. coniecit.— 447. Cf. Bod. *contritio: mota.* Ellis conjectures *mola.* Cf. PLAGA in its ecclesiastical use. — 448. Cf. CONSITUM = consertum in Claudian, Cons. Honor VI. 48. — 452. l. coniectio; cf. 441. — 455. l. congestio. — 456. l. CONNEXE. — 457. l. coniventia. — 458. l. tribu. — 460. l. contiguus. — 462. l. contionatur: adloquitur. — 463. consulit: consilium. — 465. Cf. CONDENSUM and De Vit. — 467. l. commixtum, coagulatum. — 468. l. conubia. — 469. *confertum* should not be changed to *consertum.* — 477. l. concitus.— 479. l. conciliat. — 480. l. conlibescit; cf. Sittl De Linguae Latinae verbis incohativis Archiv. I. p. 471.— 481. Cf. CONDIARIUM and Loewe G. N. 152. — 482. l. consuefacit.— 485. l. coniventibus. — 490. l. habitus. — 491. l. contabescit. — 493. l. controversia. — 494. l. concinunt . . . a cantando; cf. Plac. 22, 10.— 495. l. concinunt. — 496. Cf. Prod. 14 f. where conivoli: concordes, coniuncti is compared with Paul. 42, 1, Conivoli oculi sunt in angustum coacti conventibus palpebris.— 501. l. conlustrans refers to Verg. Aen. III. 651.— 502. For *cubiculus* m. cf. Appel. p. 85.— 503. l. colluvionem: collectionem. — 504. l. adiungere; cf. Plac. 20,

20, *conclassare, classem iungere.* — **507.** l. collybum; cf. COLLYBUS. — **509.** l. coniun-gar or componar? — **512.** l. concors: consentaneus; cf. **515** and Hild. C 346. — **514.** l. transacta. — **516.** l. ceteris, the form is interesting; cf. *peiero, periero, deiero.* — **521.** Cf. CONTINUO, where De Vit speaks of medical use for *purdurare.* l. perdurat(ur) congregatur. The I = J stands phonetically for *di.* — **525.** l. in unum volumen condensati. — **527.** l. conserimus. — **528.** l. congiarium quod in populum erogatur. — **529.** l. contiguus. — **534.** l. debilia. — **536.** l. convexa; cf. Paul. 58, 18, *Convexum est ex omni parte declinatum, qualis est natura coeli, quod ex omni parte ad terram versus declinatum est.* — **541.** l. conlineati. — **542.** l. contractus: cautio, pactum. — **543.** Cf. Nonius 38, 11, *Conviviones, compotores, a bibendo dicti,* Lucilius lib. XXVI. Quandoquidem repperi magnis combibonum ex copiis; cf. Prod. 320. — **545.** l. lucrum. — **546.** *com* is given in MS. with the usual abbreviation for *con,* l. quom or quo; cf. Isid. Or. V. 31, 8, Conticinium est, quando omnia silent. — **548.** l. consummat (for one *m* in Inscr. see Forcellini De Vit), finit. — **549.** Cf. De Vit. l. confertum. — **552.** l. consuetudo; cf. Prod. 257 and Plaut. Amph. I. 2, 28; cf. CONIECTUS and Ter. And. 4, 1, 44. — **560.** Hildebrand C 333 emends to *confercire,* but I think it a case of dittography. Compare such expressions as *conserere verba* and *conferre verba.* But possibly as we find vulgar forms like *feris, proferis, sufferit,* etc. (Rönsch p. 286) a vulgar infinitive *conferere* may have existed formed like *conserere.* — **564.** l. collybum: κερμάτιον, as in Gloss. Isid., so emended by Hild. C 294 n.; cf. **507.** — **567.** l. contactus; cf. Hild. C 373 n. — **568.** *concertari* occurs in Vulgate; see Lex. — **570.** Cf. Verg. Aen. I. 310. — **571.** l. conspicantur. — **574.** l. cognitor. — **575.** l. commanipularis; *mp* for *mm* seems somewhat analogous to the Romance forms *cambera, stombaco, cocombaro* (*mb* for *m*) mentioned by Schuchardt III. p. 96. — **579.** l. chronos. — **582.** Cf. Hild. C 449. — **583.** l. corylos; cf. Macrob. III. 18, 5, *Nux abellana . . . ex arbore est quae dicitur corylus;* Serv. Georg. II. 65, Sane *coryli* proprie dicuntur. Nam *avellanae ab Avellano* Campaniae oppido, etc. — **585.** Refers of course to the well known metaphorical use of horn common also in Hebrew. — **588.** Bod. *cossam: divinans.* Amplon. 288, 165, *cossam: divinam.* Loewe Prod. 342 proposes *cossens* = *consens: divinans,* but the word is Hebrew. Cf. *Cosam,* which De Vit Onomasticon derives from Hebrew kasàm h. e. *divinavit ut divinantem significet.* — **589.** l. cothurnum: calciamentum. — **590.** l. coruscum; cf. Serv. Aen. I. 164, 'silvarum *coruscarum* id est *crispantium.*' — **591.** l. corymbata; cf. De Vit and CORYMBUS. — **592.** l. splendor. — **593.** l. infamat, vituperat. — **595.** Notice use of the pl. *infantiis.* — **596.** l. cortina. — **598.** l. with Amplon. 290, 304, *curio: qui pronuntiat populo.* — **600.** l. cuneus (or concursus?): densus populus, turma hominum. — **603.** l. culex. De Vit gives only one example of *zinzala* from Cassiod. Psalm. 104 v. 31, *Ciniphes,* genus est *culicum* fixis aculeis permolestum, quas vulgus consuevit vocare *zinzalas;* but the vulgar name has survived in It. *zanzara* and Sp. *zenzalo.* — **605.** l. cuditur; cf. Paul. 62, 5, *cudere a caedendo dictum.* — **607.** l. scalpere or sculpere, perhaps a confusion of two glosses culere = colere: studiose agere, facere, and cudere: scalpere. — **608.** l. curulis sella. — **609.** l. cultus. — **611.** l. hastae. — **613.** l. cymba or cumba; cf. Saalfeld Tensaurus. — **614.** Cf. Serv. Georg. I. 321, *culmus est ipse calamus.* — **615.** Cf. Verg. Aen. III. 564, tollimur in caelum curvato gurgite, where Servius *Gurgite* pro *fluctu.* l. erecto fluctu. — **616.** l. cursim. — **617** and **619.** I do not know how to explain *gilionibus* and *gillone.* — **622.** culeus is written on the margin by second hand. l. culeus . . . ex sparto in modum aeronis quae liniebatur . . . homicidae . . . serpente . . . insuti mittebantur . . . mare . . . inter se qui odisse se dicuntur abinvicem, homo maioribus poenis afficiebatur; cf. De Vit and CULEUS.

D.

1 and **2.** Cf. glosses cited by Hild. D 8n. and DANUS = Gk. δᾶνος. I think it may still be doubted whether *danus* was used for *danista* = δανειστής. The original gloss may have been *danos: fenus id quod feneratur. danista: fenerator;* cf. Festus 68, 14, *danistae feneratores.* — **5.** l. DRACONTIA. — **6.** l. senex. — **7.** l. a dapibus; cf. Hild. D 10 f. — **9.** l. dammae; capreae; cf. **12** and Verg. Georg. III. 539. — **11.** l. Dabir: oraculum: cf. De Vit, where the Hebrew word *Dabár* is said to signify *oraculum Dei.* — **12.**

Cf. Amplon. 295, 10. *Dammam, genus ferae capreo similis.* — **13.** l. decalogum : decem verba legis. verba = λόγος ; cf. De Vit, *Decalogia: decem praecepta domini.* — **16.** l. delibo ; cf. Loewe G. N. 113. — **17.** l. lavit. — **18.** l. unctus ; cf. Plac. 34, 2 and 6. — **22.** Cf. Paul. 73, 10. *Deliquum apud Plautum significat minus* (cf. Cas. II. 2, 33) ; but here we should read *deliquium;* cf. Paul. 73, 9 ; but especially Serv. Aen. IV. 390, " Gellius Annalium *deliquium* solis et *delicionem* dicit quod Vergilii *defectus* solis." — **24.** confusion of two glosses. Delenitus : depacatus, and delibutus (delivutus) or delitus : unctus. *Depacare* is not given by Lexx. Hild. D 98 gives *deliniti, placati;* so that perhaps we should read *deplacatus.* — **25.** Cf. Loewe G. N. 150. — **25.** l. dilata : in longum. — **29.** Perhaps for debellata : expugnata (cf. Ovid Met. IV. 604 and Hor. Od. I. 18, 8), although of course *debella* might be imperative. See also *Debellum* (= *Duellum*) *bellum vel pugna,* cited by De Vit. — **30.** l. dilabunt(ur?), for an active form of this verb I have found no evidence; but compare *labascit,* and Bod. *delabere, deficere, delabunt, deficiunt.* — **31** = **22.** 35 (*e* in rasura, *i* above line). l. deliberat. — **37.** l. dehiscens . . . ianuas; cf. Verg. Aen. VI. 52. — **42.** l. destinatio. — **43.** l. destinata. — **44.** Cf. Bod. defeneravit : ditavit and Prod. 380. — **45.** l. devinctissimum. — **48.** Cf. Prod. 375 and 381, and Sittl. Archiv, I. p. 527. **50.** Cf. DECENTARIUS and DICENTARIUS. — **51.** l. deterrimium ; cf. Serv. Georg. IV. 89. *peior a malo dicitur, deterior a meliore.* — **57.** l. dediticius . . . provincia . . . aliam tradit; but perhaps *daticius;* cf. Prod. 380. — **58.** l. inclinatus. — **59.** Cf. DEFLO ; for active *dedigno* see Harpers' and Georges. — **60.** l, detegit ; cf. **104.** — **63.** l. subiectus. — **64.** Cf. Paul. 70, 5, *dedita, intelligitur valde data.* — **66.** Cf. Paul. 71, 8, *devitare: valde vitare;* but here I think *devio* should be read. — **68.** l. dependendi. — **71.**? I am doubtful whether the MS. reads deo or seo ; cf. Paul 65, 11, *depeculatus* a *pecore* dicitur. Qui enim *populum fraudat, peculatus poena tenetur.* — **72.** l. senex; the *a* above the line by second hand. — **73.** l. obstipuit. — **74.** l. luget. — **75.** l. dimicat. — **79.** Neither *dementicus* (*dementicius*?) nor *amenticus* are given by Lexx. — **82.** l. ligatus. — **83.** l. defessus. — **84.** l. vellicare. — **87.** l. detrahens, vituperans. — **88.** l. detractat (detrectat) ·valde tractat; cf. Hild. D 175 n., and Fronto ad. M. Caes. 3, 8 ; Paulus 74, 2. *detrectare est male tractare.* — **91.** l. defluunt. — **92.** l. depascit . . . degustat. — **93.** Ellis compares Ball, *defleta: plorata;* and suggests also very ingeniously, reading *desperata,* that *defleta* may be the negative of *fretus.* But compare the following glosses which I owe to him : Ball. *defretum quod defrudatur et quasi fraudem patiatur ;* Ball. *defretum dictum eo quod coquendo arescat;* Bod. *defretum saepae passum.* De Vit gives *Defreta: desperata.* Gloss. ad. Att. Polypt. p. 58. Mai. *Defrictum vinum, vocatur, sapa ut in libro antiquo.* Gloss. MS. and Hild. D 61̠ *defretum, sapa, passum.* Although *defruta* (cf. Verg. Georg. IV. 269) was doubtless the earlier orthography, derived by Vaniček from *defruere = defervere,* yet the later spelling seems to have been *defreta* after the popular etymology, from *deferveo* (cf. Georges' Lex.). So Porphy. Hor. Carm. I. 14, 19, *freta dicuntur quod semper ferveant.* Nonius, 552, 18, quotes Varro, " *Sapam* appellabant quod de musto ad mediam partem decoxerant; *defrutum* (*defretum,* Codd.) si ex duabus partibus ad tertiam redegerant *defervefaciendo.*" Possibly, therefore, we ought to read *de sa*(*pa*) *parata* for disperata. But what seems to me a more probable emendation is suggested by a note which I find in Lion's edition of Servius, Georg. IV. 269, 270, " Burm. *Defruta, vina decocta et defraudata proprio sapore.*" *Desaporata* (cf. SAPORATUS) may have been used for *defraudata sapore* (compare the earlier use of *deargentare*), and would easily be corrupted into *desiperata, disperata* (see 185 disipet); but Ellis's explanation is much simpler. — **96.** Cf. De Vit, *Deplendere: de pleno deducere,* and Hild. D 120, l. deplere : de pleno *ducere* (or *deducere.* Hild. emends to *reducere*). — **97.** l. manifesta ; cf. Ball, *depalata: manifesta;* cf. Prod. 44. — **98.** Perhaps for duellio; cf. Prod. 384, but possibly an independent word, standing in the same relation to *debellare* as *duellio* to *duellare bellare.* — **99.** l. pigritia. — **101.** cf. DENUS. — **103.** Cf. Bod. *degeneris generi suo dissimilis.* — **107.** l. gluttit. — **108.** l. delevit; *tollit* must be perfect here (unless due to confusion with 102); cf. *tollisse,* Dig. XLVI. 4, 13, 4, and perhaps in Persius, 4. 2, where the editors say the present is used for perf. — **110.** l. decidit : cecidit; cf. Verg. Aen. V. 517. — **113.** l. denudat. — **116.** l. deicit. — **118.** cf. DIGLADIOR. — **119.** l. defunctorium ; cf. Plac. 34, 3. — **120** refers to Vulgate use of *derivare* =

disperse. — **121**. l. demetam : praecidam. — **122**. l. divellit ; cf. Hor. Ep. I. 10, 18, *divellit somnos cura,* where Acron compares Georg. III. 530, *nec somnos abrumpet.* — **124**. l. conligavit. — **127**. Cf. Plac. 35, 9, *depudescentem : impudentem.* — **128**. l. desaevit . . . ab; cf. Verg. Aen. X. 569, *sic toto Aenea desaevit,* etc., where Servius *autem hic valde saevit, alias saevire desinit;* see also Lucan V. 303. — **129**. l. valde. — **130**. l. non decet ; so Plac. 33, 7. — **131**. Cf. DEDECORUS. — **132**. Cf. Bod. *delictus depulsus vel veruclatus* quod dicitur (the first part of which Loewe G. N. 115 shows to be for *delicus : depulsus*); Phill. *delictus verruclatus,* l. delectus(?) : verruculatus (so Papias); cf. Columella, 7, 6, 2, Caper cui sub maxillis *binae verruculae* collo dependent optimus habetur ; cf. Palladius Nov. 13, 7, Sed caper *eligendus,* cui sub maxillis duae videntur pendere *verruculae,* etc. Loewe l. c. errs in emending *verruclatus* to *vernula* or *vernacellus.* — **133**. l. defaecatum. — **134**. Cf. DELUBRUM, Hild. D 104 n., Serv. Aen. II. 225, and IV. 56. l. in ingressu . . . aquae . . . a deluendo id est lavando, probably an abbreviation of a much longer gloss. — **135**. l. dimissus. — **137**. l. foedae formae. — **139**. l. dehiscit : aperit. — **140**. See above, p. **138**. — **142**. l. depravatum. — **143**. Bod. *depsaces genus serpentum;* cf. Hild. D 262, perhaps the plural form was glossed here ; cf. Luc. IX. 610, l. dipsades. — **144**. l. ignavus. — **145**. l. divulgat : publicat. — **147**. Cf. EVACUARE. — **150**. l. deierat. — **151**. Is *despirat* corrupt orthography for *desperat,* and has the form influenced the etymology, or shall we keep * *de - spirat ?* — **153**. l. decuncem : decem unciarum ; cf. Hild. D 193, *Deuncem, decem uncias.* Buecheler Archiv. I. 108, quotes Agroecius (Keil VII. p. 110) *deuncem decem uncias dicimus, diuncem, undecim,* and shows that *deunx* was in regular use for *decunx* before 450. In Pers. V. 149, he thinks *deunces* is for *decunces.* — **154**. l. defetiscit : defricat ; cf. De Vit under *Defatisco.* — **156**. l. delibat : praecerpit (cf. PRAE-CERPTUS) degustat. — **158**. Cf. Bod. *defrutet. qui minuit quod frugi debuerat.* Perhaps *defruit* is to be kept despite this gloss and De Vit *defrudat, defraudat vel minuit;* cf. DEFRUO and DEFRUTUM. — **160**. *cessat* is also used for departing from the right way ; cf. Lexx. — **161**. Probably for destitutus, cf. **164**; yet *desistere* is used in active sense. Apul. Met. 4. — **165**. *despicatis,* from *spica,* is confirmed by Bod. *despicatur, decolatur.* Ellis suggests = 'strained off,' and so cleared, but compare De Vit *Dispecatis : decoriatis,* Gloss. Isid. Ball. *despicatus : apertus.* Du Cange gives *despicare, E spica educere, separare.* — **167**. l. with Bod. deciduum quod cito decidit. — **168**. l. delationes. — **172**. Cf. above, p. **133**. — **173**. l. despectus : contemptus. This enigmatical gloss is explained by Ball *Dina media potestas herbarum vis et possibilitas* nam in herbarum cura vis ipsa *dinamis* dicitur, unde et *dinamedia nuncupatur* ubi eorum medicine scribuntur ; cf. De Vit under Dynamidia, and in Lex. DYNAMIA. — **175**. Perhaps for delatus : advectus or ? adductus. — **177**. Cf. Isidor. Or. I. 63, 1, *Ephemeris* namque appellatur *unius diei gestio.* Hoc apud nos *Diarium* vocatur. *Diarium* would therefore be the more correct reading. For the plural cf. Hild. D 201, *diaria : cotidiana salaria* and *Diaria : cibus unius diei.* — **180**. l. diiudicat. — **181**. l. destinat. — **183**. l. diffisus. — **185**. l. desidem. — **186**. l. desipit : sapere desinit. — **191**. l. diluculum. — **193**. Cf. De Vit *derivatorium, castellum ex quo aquae in diversas urbis partes derivantur,* and under *diribitarium,* and *divisitorium.* Ball. *dirivatorium : locus contubernii.* l. *diribitorium;* cf. De Vit and Hild. D 269 n. contubernii emended by Oehler to Campi Martii has not yet been explained. — **199**. l. deformis, from DIFORMIS to DIERMIS, only the dropping out of the O is neccessary ; cf. Loewe G. N. 151, "Num [as] chemus : turpis ? " which seems to me highly improbable ; cf. Mon. 6210. *deformem : turpem fedum,* and Beck p. 12, "inter *deforme* et *turpe, deforme* ad corpus refertur, *turpe* ad animum." — **202**. l. despectabilis (not given by Lex. = *despicabilis*) contemptibilis, which occurs in Donatus Phorm. 2, 3, 75, and elsewhere. l. desistet. — **209**. l. disceptatur : litigat(ur). — **210**. Cf. DISCIPULOR. — **211**. l. diluvium. — **213**. l. non consentiens. — **214**. l. discretum. — **215**. l. diffugatum. — **216**. Cf. **199**. — **217**. l. demolire. — **218**. Cf. **143**. — **221**. Cf. Hierony. Ep. 28, ad Marcellum. Quidam *diapsalma* commutationem metri docuerunt esse, alii *pausationem spiritus.* l. pausatio. — **222**. l. consecratio. **223**. l. dissidet. — **226**. Cf. dyspnoea and dyspnoicus, here the adj. has taken place of noun. — **227**. Cf. Prod. 6 and 325, Mai. VI. 521, *Discerniculum ornamentum kapitis virginis.* Amplon. 296, 73, *Discerniculum, ornamentum capitis virginalis ex auro,* found in Lucilius XXX. 58, and Varro L. L. V. 129. Also called *discriminalis acus* by

Jerome; cf. Isid. Or. XIX. 31, 8, *Discriminalis capitis mulierum sunt vocata ex eo, quod caput auro discernant.* — **228.** l. ordinat. — **229.** l. derivat. — **231.** Cf. **265.** l. not digeritur, or disgregatur, but disicitur. Probably *disicitur* was written *diiecitur*, hence *diiegitur* and then *digegitur; g* for *i* as in *degerat*, **150.** — **233.** l. dirimere. — **234.** l. partitur. — **236.** l. dissertationes, or perhaps *discertationes;* cf. Georges s. v. — **241.** Cf. Nonius 287, 9, *distrahere est vendere.* — **242.** l. deuncem; cf. note on **153.** — **243.** l. dyscolus; cf. Loewe G. N. 107. — **244.** Cf. DISPERNO. — **245.** l. descriptio: dispositio vel sub licentia an abbreviation I think of a longer gloss; cf. Servius Aen. I. 159, *est in secessu topothesia est, id est fictus secundum poeticam licentiam locus . . . nam topographia est rei vera descriptio,* but Aen. I. 142, he says *sub poetica licentia,* for secundum p. l. — **246.** l. virgis. cf. Ars Am. 2, 209, *distenta suis umbracula virgis.* — **250.** Cf. **140.** — **258.** l. dives opum refers to Verg. Aen. I. 14. — **259.** l. deversorium. — **260.** Cf. Serv. Aen. I. 142, *Dicto citius . . . citius quam dici potest,* so emend. — **262.** l. dissimiles; cf. **268.** — **264.** l. cottidianus. — **265.** Two glosses confused, dissicere = disicere: dissipare and dissecare: in diversa secare. — **266.** l. deriguit (cf. Verg. Aen. III. 259) rigidus . . . frigidus, perhaps *factus* is omitted. — **269.** l. dissidentes. — **270.** *Dispicatus* must be kept I think; cf. *spicatae faces,* which De Vit explains, *ligna multi fida: h. e. in usum facum in tenues particulas aristarum modo dissecta.* — **271.** l. ditior: divitior. *doctus* is perhaps the beginning of another gloss. — **273.** l. dissensio. — **275.** l. dictitat. — **276.** l. in longum. — **280.** Fcr capreus see Prisciań (K. I. 113). — **283.** l. ascia lapidaria, dolabra; cf. Hild. D 376. — **284.** Cf. Hild. D 378 n. — **285.** Cf. Bod. *dolopes milites vel duces grecorum,* Ball. *dolopes, pyrri milites.* Serv. Aen. VII. 664, *dolones, dolo* est aut flagellum intra cuius virgam latet pugio, aut secundum Varronem *ingens contus cum ferro brevissimo.* There is evidently some confusion with previous gloss. Perhaps Dolones: conti lati per manus; Dolopes: milites pyrrhi. Kaegi notes a *rasura* above the *n* of *fini.* — **286.** l. Donusa; the MS. has *e,* but the alphabetical order requires *o.* — **288.** l. Maeniana; cf. Festus 134, *Maeniana appellata sunt a Maenio censore, qui primus in Foro ultra columnas tigna proiecit, quo ampliarentur superiora spectacula.* Amplon. *superiores domus;* cf. De Vit. — **290.** dumtaxant may have been in vulgar use. — **294.** Cf. DUELLIUM. — **298.** The abbreviation before VIII. I do not understand, but the VIII. may be due to some such grammatical gloss as we find Mai. VIII. 64 (Thesaurus), bellum componitur hoc duellum, li et duellium lii ·i· duorum bellum unde hic duellator · ris ·i· ille qui duellum peregit, etc. — **299.** Cf. Hild. D 394 n. — **300.** Cf. Plac. 76, 21, *duellum enim* dicitur quasi *duorum bellum.*

E.

1. l. evangelium. — **2.** l. edacitas, rasura in MS. = **7.** — **3.** comissatum for comissatur (tor); cf. Porphyr. Hor. Sat. 2, 1, 92, *edax; vorax, gluto.* — **4.** l. edacitas. — **6.** l. ?futuri or praetoris decisio. — **7.** Cf. Bod. etacitas *multae commestiones,* and Hild. E 10, l. edacitas: multitudo commestionis. — **10.** l. edentat. — **11.** l. effatur. — **13.** l. effertur, or ecfertur, funus ducitur. — **14.** Cf. Loewe G. N. 151, "*effica: adaperire (effeta* glossae 'asbestos' quod non dubito quin verum sit, cum in interpretamento latere videatur *pariendi* vocabulum)," but Hildebrand E 31 n. had already recognized in *effeta* the Hebrew *epheta,* which Du Cange explains by *adaperire.* — **15.** l. ephemeris: cotidiana. — **17.** Cf. EFFEMINO. — **20.** l. efferebamur: superbiebamus. — **24.** Cf. above, **14,** Loewe G. N. 151, conjectures effecanda: despumanda. — **28.** l. ephebi, adulescentes. — **29.** l. imberbis. — **31.** Cf. Mai. VI. 522, *egerate execrate,* and Phill. *egerare: spernere, detestari, execrare* read therefore eierate: execrare, or perhaps eierare: execrare. — **32.** l. foras. — **33.** l. aegre. — **34.** Cf. **36.** — **35.** l. aeger, truncated gloss. — **38.** l. elabi. — **39.** l. helleborum; cf. De Vit under Sitri, "*Sitri* pro *veratro* Anthim ep. ad Theud. 25. *Elleborum* herbam, quae latine dicitur *veratrum.* Monet Rose ad h. l. in cod. aliquo haberi. quem latini dicuntur *sitri.*" — **40.** See above, p. **134.** — **42.** l. Elissaei: Carthaginienses. For ilisica perhaps Elissa is to be read with reference to Dido; cf. Serv. Aen. I. 340, Dido vero nomine *Elissa ante dicta est.* — **43.** l. elicere. — **46.** l. elevigata. — **47.** l. Elysios: beatos nuncupabant. — **52.** l. eluvies: liquor quidam de quo aliquid eluitur; cf. Hild. E 85. — **53.** l. cuiuslibet rei; cf.

Hild. E 78. — 55. l. trahens. — 56. Cf. excudit, Verg. Aen. I. 174, and Hild. E 7. — 57.
l. tormenti. — 61 and 63. l. miles veteranus qui iam complevit militiam; cf. Bod. *Emeritus miles veteranus qui iam conplevit malitiam quia mere* (l. merere) *militare dicitur.*
The latter part of 63 belongs to 61, and is beneath it in the MS. — 64. l. refulsit. — 66.
l. lucrum.— 67. l. Eumenidum; cf. 169. — 68. l. exaltatum est. — 71. Cf. Mai.VI. 522, *empyrius, locus super mare,* Bod. *emporium, locus supra mare.* Perhaps = empyrius : locus
super aere, although in Bod. and in glosses cited by Hildebrand E 106 there is evident confusion with *emporium.* — 73. Cf. De Vit, *Empaectae; ἐμπαῖκται derisores Deorum et religionis,* with which *emphaticum* has become confused. — 74. l. empes vel empos ; cf.
IMPES and IMPOS, and Loewe G. N. 186 and 193. — 75. l. eminulis ; cf. Varro R. R. 2, 5,
genibus eminulis, 2, 9, *dentibus paulo eminulis.* — 76. l. ensitum = insitum. — 80. Cf.
ἐγκρυφίας ἄρτος. l. subcinericius ; cf. Ps. Aug. Serm. 5, 1, ' fac *subcinericios* panes ' (Genes.
18, 6) quod graece *encryphias* dicitur, *occultos* videlicet et absconditos indicans panes. —
84. l. enodat. — 87. ensicium = INSICIUM. — 90. For enucleatim see Georges. — 92. l.
Aeolus. — 95. l. epitoma ; this form for *epitome* is used by Cicero ad Att. 12, 5, 3. — 96.
l. epitomarius (of which I have found no example in use) abbreviator. — 97. l. epigramma ; cf. Bod. *ephigramma : adbreviatio scripturarum vel superscriptio tituli.* — 98. l.
ephemeris : diurnum ; the form *diurnis* seems due to the ending in *ephemeris.* — 99. l.
rationes. — 100. l. epitaphium. — 101. l. epithalamium. — 103. l. epiphora. — 104. Cf.
SCRIPULA. — 105. l. eous or eos : lux ; cf. Plac. 37, 3, *Eous* est homo de oriente. *eos*
aurora vel *lucifer.* Verg. Georg. I. 288, Aut cum sole novo terras inrorat *Eous.* — 106.
l. superinspector. — 107. l. ebibit. — 109. Cf. EPHOD and Isid. Or. XIX. 20, 5, l. superhumerale . . . casulae . . . sacerdotes . . . gemmisque contextum quo soli pontifices
utebantur. — 110. l. epichiremata. — 112. l. aequiperat, equidem may have got in from
the preceding gloss, or stand for *equitem,* a mistaken etymology or possibly for *aequiter*
= *aeque.* — 114. Hild. E 152 n., cites *ergata : vicinus aut operator* and *ergata : vicinus.* *vicinus* I do not understand ; may it not be for *oficinus* = **officinus* or **opificinus?* Compare these glosses given by De Vit, *Ergates ; ἐργάτης operarius, opifex,*
opificium : ergasterium, oppificium ; gr. *ergastulum.* (A confusion with ἀγυιᾶτις is
hardly possible.) — 115. l. e regione : econtra ; cf. ECONTRA. — 117. l. Erinys. — 118.
l. aerumna ; cf. 124. — 119. l. hermula. — 120. l. ἐρυσίβη. Du Cange gives *Erisibe :*
erugo vel rubigo messium. Here there seems to be a corruption of *erugo* (aerugo)
et rubigo messium. — 122. Cf. HERCISCO, probably refers to the phrase *familiae*
herciscundae. — 125. Cf. Hild. E 150, *ergastulis : auris* (= duris) *operibus.* —
126. l. marmor ; for fuller glosses see Prod. 147 and Plac. 37, 17. — 127. l. essedum : vehiculum. — 128. Cf. Prod. 403, where Loewe cites from Mai VI. 523 a, *Estidram : quam*
veteres canapum nominarunt. According to De Vit, Gloss. Pap. has *estrida ;* Loewe
thinks *excetra* is to be read. *Caput,* unless a corruption of *canapum, Canopum,* is very
obscure. I can only compare Serv. Aen. VI. 287, Sed latine *excetra* dicitur, quod uno
caeso tria *capita excrescebant,* and Hesychius σκύτη(?) κεφαλή. — 129. l. esitat. — 130.
Cf. ESUS. — 131. l. essedarius . . . vehiculi. — 132. l. etesiae. — 137. l. Tuscia. — 140.
Cf. eugenius and εὐγενής. — 141. l. evomat ; cf. Vulg. Levit. 18, 28. — 142. l. nobilitas.
— 143. l. aevum ; cf. 146. — 151. l. aeonas. — 154. Cf. Ball. *eulogium : divinum responsum.* Ellis says that an oracular response in verse may be referred to ; cf. Mai VIII.
193, *Eulogium, testimonium vel cantus. Marcianus : mixtis eulogium modis coaequans.* — 155. ? Cf. εὐωχίας, l. delicias. — 157. Cf. 160, Paul. 77, *Evelatum eventilatum,*
unde velabra, quibus frumenta ventilantur. Perhaps the meaning here assigned is
influenced somewhat by 152 ; *evulsit* from *evello, expoliavit ;* but why should not *evelatus*
be the opposite of *velatus?* like *exoneratus, enodatus ;* otherwise it would be easy to
emend to *enudantur.* — 162. Cf. Gloss. Isid. *evadatur · reposcit, flagitat.* — 163. Probably due to a misunderstanding of a passage like Catul. LXIV. 391, Thyadas effusis *evantes* crinibus egit. *evantes* is explained as if *evanentes : fugientes ;* Cf. above, 153, *evanuit : aufugit* and Gloss. Lat. Gr. *Evaneo :* ἀφανίζομαι. — 164. l. e vestigio. — 165. Cf.
Amplon. 329, 49, *evitatus, perterritus vel occisus aut vita privatus,* of which this seems
a corruption. — 169. l. Eumenidum. — 170. l. eucharistia. — 171. = heus. — 172. l.
hostiarum. — 174. l. exhalat. — 175. Cf. Prod. 277, *exaedituat : excludit ab adytis.*

Loewe thinks exaedituat was read in Plaut. Trin. 1127. — **176**. l. exhaustis : evacuatis. —
177. l. examussim; cf. Plac. 37, 13, *Examussim integre*, sine fraude, amussis enim dicitur regula vel mensura fabrilis. *ingredere* seems a corruption of *integre*. — **183**. Cf.
EXOMOLOGESIS. The dictionaries give no other form. — **186**. l. execrat: abominat. —
188. l. excubat. — **190**. Cf. INPROPERO, vulgar corruption of *improbro*. — **191**. l. ex(s)ors,
hereditate. — **193**. l. exilit. — **194**. l. comestum. — **195**. l. interposito. — **197**. l. abstulit.'
— **198**. l. exuviae : spolia quae occiso hoste tolluntur. — **201**. l. sine consilio (alienus ; cf.
258). Ellis suggests *agens*. — **202**. l. mortiferum, periculosum. — **206**. l. exoletus: dissolutus; cf. **280**. — **207**. l. elevavit. — **212**. l. credulitas. — **214**. l. exserit (exerit; cf. **199**). —
219. Cf. Schol. Juvenal III. 175, *Exordium, exordiarius* apud veteres in fine ludorum in-
trabat, etc. Cf. Loewe G. N. 84, note. — **220**. l. nobilis eminens (prae) ceteris. — **221**. l.
calamitas. — **224**. l. locus subselliorum, so Ball ; cf. Plac. 39, 8, *exedra absis quaedam*
separata modicum quid aut a praetorio aut a palatio. l. absida salutatoria; cf. De
Vit. — **226**. explodita I have not found in use. — **227**. ? l. exorta : nascentia. — **231**. Cf.
214. — **233**. l. expilatores : alienae hereditatis, *subtractores* not in Lexx. — **234**. Cf.
above, p. 131. — **235**. l. exaestuat. — **236**. See above, p. 133. — **237**. Cf. EXPERGIFICUS.
— **239**. l. exsomnis (exomn.). — **240**. experimentandum is supported by EXPERIMENTA-
TUS. — **243**. l. eicit ; cf. Nonius 16, 1, *expectorare* est extra pectus *eiicere*. — **248**. l.
expediat. — **249**. Neue recognizes an active form *experio*. — **250**. l. desideratum. — **253**.
Perhaps *extruso* can be kept as freq. form. — **255**. See above, p. 125. — **257**. Cf. EXFRETO,
found as yet in no author. — **259**. l. exagitat ; but there may be a confusion of two
glosses, as e. g. exacerbat: provocat, and examinat: explorat. — **260**. l. cognoscam. —
262. Cf. EXIMIETAS. — **268**. l. perficit. — **272**. l. exempta. — **276**. l. ex(s)erere. — **278**.
l. exilivit or exiluit. — **280**. l. exoletus ; cf. **266**. — **282**. = enormis, but the form EXOR-
MIS seems to have existed. — **285**. Cf. EXCAVEO. — **286**. extestinum, not in Lexx., is
formed after analogy of *intestinum*. — **287**. Cf. Paul. 80, 13, *exanclare: exhaurire.*
— **288**. Cf. ECSTASIS. — **290**. exvito = evito; cf. De Vit, l. devito. — **291**. Cf. Nonius
63, 17, Fulguratores. Ut *extispices* et *haruspices*, ita hi fulgurum inspectores. — **292**. I
think *exidium = exitium;* cf. Paul. 81, 6, *Exitium* antiqui ponebant pro *exitu ;* nunc
exitium pessimum *exitum* dicimus. Juvenal has preserved one of the formulas ' for di-
vorce, Sat. VI. 146, "collige sarcinulas" dicet libertus, "et *exi.*" Compare the expressions
domo egredi and *vade foras.* See Brisson. De Formulis p. 723 ; cf. Seneca de Beneficiis
III. 16, 2, Maritorum annos suos conputant et *exeunt* matrimonii causa, nubunt *repudii.*
This special use of *exire* supports *exitium*, of which ' probably Verrius Flaccus gave an
example in this sense ; but see **303**, excidium, where, however, *separatio* may be due to
a confusion of the two glosses. — **293**. l. exsinuat ; cf. Mai VI. 523, *exinuat, examplat,*
exaperit. exaperire is very rare. De Vit cites Augustin. Conf. 2, 10, and Interp. Ire-
naei 2, Haeres. 19, 8. Paucker adds Aug. Cassiod. in ps. 36, 6, *fulgor Dei operum nos-*
trorum qualitates exaperit. Examplat (-iat? cf. *amplo* and *amplio*) would best suit
the meaning here. — **294**. Cf. Nonius 10, 10, *Illex* et *exlex* est qui *sine lege* vivit. —
295. l. exedendus. — **297**. l. ex(s)erte ; cf. Plac. 39, 12. — **298**. l. sublatis, *conplicitis*
might be for *completis:* cf. *exemptis diebus*, etc. ; but see Bod. *exemptus sublatus, ex-*
clusus, explicitus. — **300**. l. exhaurit. — **297**. Cf. **301**. — **302**. Cf. **195**. Bod. *exinter-*
vallo. — **304**. Cf. EXPUNGO. — **306**. l. extentus; the *c* of *extinctus* was probably not
heard, so that *extentus* and *extintus* would have much the same sound; cf. Nonius 47, 3,
Exporrectum : extentum. — **307**. l. ex(s)iliatus. — **308**. Cf. Isid. Or. X. 85, *extorris* quia
extra terram suam est, quasi *exterris.* Sed proprie *extorris* cum vi expulsus sit, etc. —
309. l. expertia. — **310**. *t* is deleted in MS. and *d* is written for *t*. I now see that the
um of *extorsitum* (ū MS.) is for vel, and that *propiam expulsus* is a repetition from
308, l. extudit tundendo extorsit vel exclusit (excussit?); cf. Hild. E 333, *extudit, ex-*
tundendo extorsit.

F.

1. 1. favor . . laudis. — **2.** 1. facetus; notice that in **4** we have *eloquens.* — **4.** 1. habilis. — **5.** 1. facetia. — **6.** 1. facetiae: elegantia? — **11.** 1. facetior. — **13.** perhaps fastus; cf. Paul. 87, 19, *Fasti enim dies festi.* — **14.** 1. favet. — **16.** perhaps for *fastosus,*
or originally the same gloss as Bod. *Fastus, superbiae contemptus.* — **19.** 1. fascinat . . .
decipit; cf. De Vit. — **20.** 1. Phalanx; cf. Serv. Aen. XI. 92, *Phalanx: lingua Macedo-
num legio.* — **23.** 1. phalerare. — **28.** 1. FALSILOQUAX. — **30.** 1. falarica. — **35.** Cf. Bod.
fescennina clausibiles vel vallationes. De Vit, Lexicon, has * *Fascemina clausibilis
Vallatio circa claustra.* Gloss. Isid. n. 699, Fortasse leg. est, *fasceamina* ut sit a *fas-
ceo* vel *fascio* unde *fasceamen;* both *clausibilis* and *vallatio* are rare words. There may
be a reference to Verg. Aen.VII. 695, Hi *Fescenninas acies* Aequosque Faliscos, Hi Sorac-
tis habent arces Flaviniaque arva, where the use of *acies* has given the editors much trouble,
Peerlkamp proposing *Fescenninos colles,* and Hoffman *Fescenninos agros.* Gossrau
proposes *arces* for *acies.* — **36.** Cf. PAVISOR Georges, Loewe G. N. 173 ff. and Stowasser,
Archiv I. 440. — **37.** Cf. Bod. *fascinus: aspectus,* and Amplon. 332, 25, *fascinus aspectus honerosus.* 1. fascinus: aspectus onerosus = evil eye. — **40.** Cf. Bod. *faxo facio in-
cendo.* 1. fax: incendium. — **41.** 1. faciam; cf. Ball, *faxo faciam futuri temporis.* — **42.**
probably for *funereas;* cf. De Vit. — **44.** 1. famedicus = famelicus; cf. Donat. Ter. Eun.
II. 2, 29, A *fame* et *edendo* dictus est quasi *famedicus.* — **46.** Cf. Ball. *fana idolorum
templa.* — **48.** ? Cf. De Vit under *famicus* and *flamminicus.* — **49.** 1. canentes. — **51.**
cf. FALCIDIA. — **52.** 1. phaleras: adulatoria verba. — **53.** 1. feriendo (é in MS.); Serv. Aen.
I. 123, *fatiscunt, abundanter aperiuntur;* cf. Plac. 48, 4. — **54.** 1. factiosus; cf. Bod.
factiosus falsus vel saepe faciens deceptor fallax. (*fallaciosus* may have had some influence on this gloss, but it describes the character of a demagogue.) — **55.** Cf. HARIOLUS,
1. vates. — **57.** Cf. onerosus in 37. — **58.** 1. Pharos. — **61.** 1. fasti. — **62.** Cf. 36. — **64.**
Cf. **67,** and De Vit; probably corruptions of some case of *fasti* taken from a commentary;
but *fastes* may be for *fasces.* — **65.** 1. Pharisaei. — **69.** 1. femina. — **70.** 1. festivus: laetus;
cf. Bod. *festivus, locosus conpositus locundus, vel urbanus comptus.* — **71.**1. femor..ge-
niculum. — **72.** 1. fastidium. — **74.** cf. Bod. *Fau nihil vel subito.* — **77.** ? Cf. De Vit s. v.
— **78.** 1. ventis siccis, so Bod.; cf. Val. Flac. 6, 665. — **80.** According to Kaegi *flagtium*
in MS., Goetz *flagitium.* 1. libitum. — **81.** Notice confusion with *fragrantia.* — **82.** 1.
flagrans; so Bod. — **84.** 1. flammea; cf. FLAMMEUM. — **86.** Cf. FLAMONIUM. — **87.** 1.
rubeum. — **90.** So Bod.; cf. FLAMMEUS and FLAMMATUS. Bod. has also *flammoto
irato.* — **92.** 1. physemata. — **99.** 1. flamen Martialis. — **100.** 1. Quirinalis . . . Quirini. —
102. 1. copiosus. — **109.** Turpis belongs probably to another gloss, *foedus* (*fedus*): turpis; cf. **115** and **183,** or *fetidus· turpis.* — **113.** 1. ferox . . saevus. — **114.** 1. Phoe-
nices. — **115.** 1. foedant. — **118.** For other inchoatives with factitive meaning see Prod.
362, and G. N. 143, and Sittl. Archiv, 1, 496. Compare *efferascere.* — **122.** Bod. *ferire.*
Although *feris* is found for *fers,* I am inclined to think *ferire* correct, and taken from
some such passage as Plaut. Men. 177, *iam ferio foris?* M. *feri.* — **125.** De Vit cites
from Hilarius in Psalm. 2, n. 20, Si fuerint delicta vestra ut *phoinicium,* where the
Vulgate has *coccinum.* — **126.** ? Compare PROMUTUOR and Reichenauer Glossen,
454, *mutuo acceperam: inprūtātū habebā,* and 756, *mutuare: inprūtare.* Diez Al-
tromanische Glossare p. 37. "Impruntare ist vielleicht das älteste Zeugniss für das fr.
emprunter das im alten Provenzalischen noch nicht erscheint; entstanden durch Proclise
aus *in-promutuum,* indem sich der Accent in Verbum *impromutuare* verschob und *u* vor
der Flexion wie gewöhnlich, z. B. in *batuere,* verschwand." — **127.** Cf. Paul. 92, 2, *Femur
femoris, et femen feminis,* and Neue Formenlehre, I. 558 f. Various emendations suggest themselves. — **129.** 1. rem . . . fiducia(m), i. e. velut fiduciam. — **130.** 1. fimum. —
132. Cf. FISTULOR, and Prod. p. 386; Mart. Cap. 9, § 906, *fistula sibilatrix.* — **133.** 1.
ficata. — **134.** Cf. **138.** 1. fidibus: chordae citharae; cf. Paul. 89, 16, *Fides* genus *citharae*
dicta, quod tantum inter se *chordae* eius, quantum inter homines fides concordet; Nonius,
313, 25, *Fides chordae,* quoting Aen. VI. 120, where Servius, *Fidibusque canoris, bene
sonantibus chordis.* — **135.** 1. figulus. — **138.** Probably for fidicina: citharoeda; cf.
Hild. F, 129. — **139.** 1. PHILARGYRIA. — **140.** Cf. FIDICULAE; 1. lamminae; see **147.** —

141. l. Phoebe; cf. Mon. 6210, *feba luna*, and Serv. Verg. Aen. X. 216, *Phoebe luna sicut sol 'Phoebus.'* — **149.** Cf. Bod. *figmenta conpositiones adinventiones vel similitudo humana.* — **151.** Cf. Verg. Aen. VII. 566, medioque *fragosus* Dat sonitum . . . tor_rens. — **154.** l. fiduciam habens. — **157.** l. frivola; cf. Paul. 90, 6, *Frivola* sunt proprie *vasa fictilia quassa.* Unde dicta verba *frivola*, quae minus sunt fide subnixa. Cf. **164** and **165.** — **159.** l. hasta. — **164.** l. frivolus. — **166.** l. focillat : reficit. _ **172.** l. fota. _ **175.** Cf. Isid. Or. XV. 7, 4, *fores* dicuntur quae *foras*, valvae quae intus revolvuntur ; Serv. Aen. I. 449, *fores* proprie dicuntur quae *foras aperiuntur.* — **176.** l. formido. — **179.** l. phosphorus. — **180** ? l. FORMIDINES ; cf. Bod. *formidines pinae inligatae in quibus venatores cervos capiunt vel timores,* and Seneca de Ira, 2, 11, cum maximos ferarum greges *linea pinnis distincta* contineat et in *insidias agat.* — **184.** l. Phoebus. _ **185.** l. phocas ; cf. Verg. Geor. IV. 395. — **187.** Cf. Charisius, 94, 21, *Forfices* et *forcipes* et *forpices* quidam distingunt ut *forcipes* sint sarcinatorum a faciendo, *forcipes* fabrorum, quod *ferrum calidum capiant,* etc. ; Bod. *forceps, fabri que corruptae forfices dicitur ulcus vel cancer;* Ball, *forceps, forpicis fabri,* eo quod fortiter teneant, et *forceps ulcus aut cancer.* — **187.** l. futilem. — **189.** l. fore : futurum esse. — **193.** Cf. FOLIATUS, and Loewe, G. N. 107, who proposes *coliatum : curtatum.* The order of the letters would suggest *fornicatus;* but why not keep *foliatus,* shaped like a leaf, as *falcatus,* sickle-shaped? — **194.** l. amicitiae pactum. — **195.** See **186.** *forceps* was used of the claw of the crab, hence perhaps *cancer,* of which *ulcus* is an explanation ; so Hild. F 205. But perhaps *cancer* is a corruption of *carcer.* — **197.** l. timidus. — **198.** Cf. Serv. Aen. VI. 631, *fornice arcu.* Cicero videt ad ipsum *fornicem Fabianum ;* l. arcum triumphalem (plateae ?). — **199.** l. parsimonia. — **204.** For continens substantiae = rei familiaris. — **206.** Cf Ball, *frustra, sine causa inaniter ;* Bod. *frustra, inaniter sine causa vel in vanum.* — **207.** l. fructurus. — **212.** l. vermiculus. — **215.** For an active form of *fungo,* see Neue II. 289. — **217.** l. foto; so Bod.; cf. Ball, *fotum molliter amplexum sive calefactum,* and Verg. Aen. I. 692, where Servius *fotum, sublatum, complexum.* — **218.** l. munit ; cf. Verg. Aen. IV. 247, Atlantis duri, caelum qui vertice fulcit, where Servius *fulcit, hoc est sustinet.* — **219.** l. funebre; cf. Paul. 93, 1, *funebres tibiae dicuntur cum quibus in funere canitur,* etc. — **220.** l. sublevatus. — **223.** l. fulgor; cf. Mart. Cap. II. 151, vel sideris cursu, vel *fulminis iaculo ;* for *iacula* fem. cf. Appel, p. 60. — **226.** Perhaps for *fulgurat,* as we have Not. Tiron. p. 118 *fulgerat : infulgerat,* or it may be a verb formed from *fulgetra ;* for *preemit* perhaps *praemicat* is to be read (cf. Min. Fel. Octav. 5, *rutilare fulgura, fulmina praemicare*), or *praevenit* (= *praeaenit,* *u* for *a,* as frequently), which would be nearer the MS. reading, and the full gloss may have been fulgetra : quod fulmen praevenit, which would agree with Seneca, Q, N 2, 56, 1, Heraclitus existimat *fulgurationem* esse velut apud nos incipientium ignium conatus et primum flammam incertam modo intereuntem modo resurgentem. Haec antiqui *fulgetra* dicebant. Compare, however, Festus, 245, 22, Peremptalia, quae superiora fulgura ut † portenta peremunt, id est olunt †, and 214, 22, peremptalia fulgura Gracchus ait vocari quae superiora fulgura ut † portenta vi sua peremant, etc. — **227.** l. splendidum. — **228.** l. fumida. — **230.** l. rubra or rubea ; cf. *fulvida· rubea* De Vit, and Bod. *fulvus : rufus, rubeus.* — **232.** Cf. Prod. 106 and De Vit ; also in Bod. l. funda : rete ; cf. Serv. Georg. I. 141, *funda, genus retis dictum a fundendo,* and Amplon. 333, 114, *Fundia : retia linea et fundibus.*— **235.** *f* is not in the MS., but torn off. — **237.** Cf. IMAGINARIUS ; l. cadavere. — **239.** l. ministeria ; but the spelling *misteria* is significant; cf. O. Fr. *mistier* — **240.** So Kaegi reads, but Goetz tribulatiou ; l. functio: tributorum exsolutio : cf. Forcellini, Lex. " Saepe in Cod. Justin. dicitur *functio tributorum pensitatio ;*" and Bod. *Functio exsolutio tributorum vel possessio.* — **241.** l. terebras; cf. Georges. — **243.** l. solvimus. — **245.** Cf. *fundanus* and *fundarius* in Du Cange ; l. fundos. — **248.** Cf. Verg. Aen. II. 407. — **249.** Cf. Paul. 84, 6, *Furvum nigrum vel atrum,* and Serv. Aen. II. 18, and Georg. III. 407.

G.

1. l. pilleum cf. Mai. VI. 525; *Galeram; palleum pastorale de iunco factum* where *pallium* is a corruption of *pilleum.* — **2.** Cf. Isıd. Or. VII. 5, 10, *Gabriel* Hebraice in linguam nostram convertitur *Fortitudo Dei.* — **3.** Cf. Lagarde Onomastica Sacra, p. 58; Galilaea volubilis sive transmigratio facta. — **4.** Cf. De Vit and CALAMAUCUS; Du Cange gives *Camelaucum* as the correct form. — **5.** Propinator for popinator; cf. Isid. XV. 2, 42, *Propina* Graecus sermo est, qui apud nos corrupte *popina* dicitur. — **8.** l. GABBARAE, a name for mummies, the origin of which is obscure. — **9.** Also given by Mai. VI. 525, and placed by Loewe G. N. 165 among the new words. — **10.** l. veıbosa. — **12.** Cf. above p. 137. — **13.** l. GAZOPHYLACIUM: divitiarum et tensauri (thesauri) custodia. — **15.** l. GASTRIMARGIA, so Bod. — **16.** *Galbanus* occurs Vulg. Sir. IV. 21 ; cf. Serv. Georg. III. 415, *Galbanum species est multis apta medicaminibus;* cf. Bod. *Galbaneus genus medicamenti vel pigmentum album,* where there is confusion with *Galbineus.* — **17.** γάρον = garum. — **19.** Cf. De Vit. *Gannium; taberna;* read with Ball *ganeo: tabernarius.* — **20.** Ellis suggests *gaunacum.* Varro L. L. V. 35, speaks in the same chapter of *gaunacum* and *gausape;* cf. Not. Tiron, p. 158, *gausapum: gaunapum,* Gloss. Lat. Gr. *gausapa:* Βαρβαρικὸν πάλλιον, so that *gausapum* may have been the reading, but the alphabetical order favors *gaunacum.* — **21.** l. genealogia, but the MS. has the dittography, and in **22** I have neglected to indicate that *ne* in *generaliter* is omitted and inserted in the margin, it is doubtful whether by first or second hand. — **25.** l. genitale. — **27.** l. fatum decretum with Bod.; cf. De Vit and Prod. 118, f. — **30,** cf. **46,** l. gestatum: portatum, so *r* is dropped before *t* in **36.** — **32.** l. generationes. — **33.** l. generositas. — **35.** l. with Bod. *gerula: nutrix conportatrix;* cf. Amplon. 335, 118, *gerula nutrix quae infantes portat.* — **38.** l. vigor; cf. De Vit. — **40.** l. geniales lecti; cf. Isid. Or. VIII. 11, 88, *Genium* autem dicunt, quod quasi vim habet omnium rerum gignendarum, seu a gignendis liberis, unde et *geniales lecti* dicebantur agentibus, qui novo marito sternebantur — **41**? cf. Paul. 94, 10, *genuıni dentes,* quod a *genis* dependent (perhaps *necis* is a corruption of *genis*) ; Bod. *genuinum nature initium id est insertum vel intimum densum* (l. dentium) *vel qui interius in ore hominis nascitur;* and Hild. G. 41 n. — At least two glosses are here confused, see Mai. VIII. 261, *genius: Deus naturae,* etc., *genuinus, naturalis; genuinus, deus maxillaris;* and Hild. G. 40 and 43, *geminum, naturae, initium idem insertum.* — **42.** l. adorationibus. — **43.** l. supputandi. — **44.** l. gerulus: baiulus. — **47.** l. Getae ... Thraces. — **49.** Loewe, G. N. 248 ff., gives from different sources, *Anser: sclingit; anseres gliccire, vel sclingere; grinniunt anseres;* cf. Paul. 95, 5, *gingrire anserum vocis proprium est. Unde genus quoddam tibiarum exiguarum gingrinae.* Gloss. Philox., *Gingriunt:* χῆνες ἐκβοῶσιν, Hence read, *Gingrıunt anseres.* — **50.** Bod. *geniatus, genialıs, gratus;* cf. GENIATUS. — **51.** l. genae: malae; cf. Isid. Or. XI. 1, 43, *Genae* sunt inferiores oculorum partes, etc., and 44, *Malae* sunt eminentes *sub oculis partes.* — **52.** l. gerontocomium ... homines, for *propter* with abl., see Rönsch, 408. — **53.** l. pneumon. — **54.** The letter following *ext* is illegible. Both Kaegi and Goetz read *ext,* but Goetz thinks *t* may be *e.* I would read et palaestra et auditorium magistrorum .... alterum ab *exe(rcendo)* or *exe(rcitio)*; cf. De Vit and Plac. 49, 4, *Gymnasia* dicuntur loca, in quibus nudi homines exercentur, unde omnium prope artium *exercitia gymnasia dicuntur;* and Isid. Or. XV. 2, 30, *Gymnasium generalis exercitiorum locus.* Tamen apud Athenas erat locus ubi discebatur philosophia et sapientiae exercebatur studium. Nam γυμνάσιον Graece vocatur, quod Latine *exercitium* dicitur, hoc est meditatio. — **56.** l. gymnasia; Cf. Isid. XV. 2, 40, speaking of balnea, *Haec et gymnasia dicuntur,* etc. Amplon. 334, 7, *Gymnassis: balneis.* — **58.** l. gorytus = corytos : pharetra; cf. Serv. Aen. X. 169, *Coryti proprie* sunt *arcuum thecae;* dicitur tamen etiam sagittarum *quas et pharetras nominamus.* — **59.** ? perhaps gignit : generat, and gignitur: nascitur, but what *praeluium* (*prae* in abbreviation MS.) stands for I am uncertain. — **60.** l. gymnasia; a very confused gloss, probably from two or more glosses; cf. above **57,** and Amplon. 334, 19, *Gymnicus agon; locus ubi leguntur diversae artes,* and glosses cited by De Vit. — **61.** l. gilvus: inter album et nigrum medius color; cf. Loewe, G. N. 150,

Mai. VIII, 263, *gilnus color equi inter album et rufum quod et gilbus dicitur*, and Hild.
G. 57. But Servius Georg. III. 81, *Gilvus autem est melinus color, multum autem ita
legunt Albis et gilvo* ut non *album* vel *gilvum* sed *albo-gilvum* vituperet. Bod. *gilbus
color medius inter album et rufum.* — 63. l. gratissimus. — 65. l. grandaevus : senex. —
68. l. graditur. — 69. l. grandi nato : ex nobili natus ; cf. grandi alumno, Hor. Epod.
XIII. 11*.*: It can hardly be due to a misunderstanding of *grandis natu.* — 70. The *et* indicates that there has been a confusion of two glosses ; cf. De Vit, *Gritmanus : praetor
rusticus, praefectus pagorum,* and Du Cange, who gives " *Grietmanni et Grietania :
praefectura voces Frisionibus familiares.*" — 71. l. cremia : siccamina. — 72. l. gryphes.
75. l. herbae. — 77. Cf. Verg. Aen. V. 40 with Servius' note. — 78. Cf. GRASSATOR. —
79. Cf. Bod. *grumulus ager tractus,* Mai. VI. 526, *grumulus agger* ; Paul. 96, 16,
grumus : terrae collectio, minor tumulo ; Nonius 15, 18, *grumus* dicitur *agger* : a congerie
dictus ; *aggeratum* might be the participle, but perhaps for *agger tumulus,* cf. 74. — 80.
l. gratuitum : gratis (?) ; cf. Bod. *gratuitum non venditum id est gratia datum.* — 84. l.
gnavus. — 86. for *pressus,* see Philarg. Verg. Georg. III. 83, *neque satis diluti coloris,
neque nimium pressi;* glauci in v. 82, he explains as *subviridis albo mixtus.* — 87. l.
glebo, cf. Prod. 117, and Phill. *glebo dicitur ruricola stivarius.* — 88. l. gleba : caespes.
— 89. l. globus. — 93. l. glossa, cf. Prod. 1 f. — 95. l. maiestas. — 96. l. acervat. — 97.
l. glos : viri soror. — 98. l. Gnosia, cf. Verg. Aen. VI. 23. After *gl.* room is left for another
gloss. — 99. l. humile tenebrosum. — 100. l. tabernarum. — 101. l. profundus.

H.

1. l. arundo. — 2. l. bibit. Hild. H 26 n. says, " Pro *implet* quod ferri nequit, lege
videt," but he neglected to notice Nonius 319, 12, *Haurire* significat *exhaurire* vel *implere,* with examples from Lucretius and Lucilius ; see also 14. — 5. l. has. — 8. l. oscitat.
Bod. *halat oscitat sive olet.* — 9. l. gustata. — 10. ? = Hebrew *hato,* a sinner, suggested
through Ellis by Neubauer. I had thought of (*H*)*aretalogus,* which in Gloss. Pap. is
explained by falsidicus ; cf. Juvenal XV. 16, mendax aretalogus. — 14. Cf. 2. — 17. l.
habenae . . . lororum. For *tenaculum* Lexx. cite only Terent. Maur. Praef. 29. — 18. l.
anhelat. — 20. i. e. heros : vir fortis ; herus : dominus ; cf. 32. — 21. l. heri. — 22. Perhaps for chaere χαῖρε : ave. Cf. Lucilius (p. 135 Müll.) χαῖρε, inquam, Tite, etc., where
two MSS. have *chere;* cf. also Martial V. 51, *Ave* Latinum χαῖρε non potest Graecum. —
23. l. ebenum. — 24. l. domina. — 25. Cf. Bod. *heliotropium nomen gemme vel flores
herbe latine soliquia dicitur.* l. heliotropium : nomen gemmae et herbae, solisequia ; cf.
also HEELIOTROPIUS. — 28. l. haesitat. — 29. = ὕδωρ. — 30. l. hirsutum. — 31. l. hirudo. Helmreich Archiv I. 323 shows how *sanguisuga* supplanted *hirudo.* — 33. l.
nobiles sunt ; for the use of *dimitto* see Prod. 422, where a similar gloss is given from
Cod. Leidensis 191⁸. — 34. l. eccui. — 35. l. morio. — 36. Cf. Prod. 431, *hostispices : haruspices,* where also the form *histispices* is given from other glosses, but not *hestispicus.*
— 37. l. Erebi. — 38. l. heroum ; cf. Mai. VI. 526, *heroes ; antiqui.* — 39. l. eremum.
— 40. Cf. above p. 133, Bod. *holitor : ortolanus, orticula.* — 41. l. herbidum. — 42. l.
hymenaeum. Cf. Donat. Ter. Ad. V. 7, 7, *hymenaeum putant veluti hymnum vocari
virginalium nuptiarium.* Probably *novum nuptus* comes from a fuller gloss. — 43. ?
Cf. De Vit, *Herenicas : antiquas, heroicas,* Isid. (an Hernicas?) *Hernicus : durus ;
Hernicas : antiquas ; Herpicus : antiquus ; Heroica : antiqua ; Heroici : antiqui.* —
44. l. Haemonia. — 45. Cf. De Vit and Ball. *herma : castratio nec vir nec mulier.* — 47.
l. haesit. — 51. Cf. Bod. *herculaneus : eunuchus,* found also in numerous glossaries.
Emend, *eculiatus = excoliatus.* Cf. Petron. 44, 14, *coleos habere,* Loewe G. N. 107, and
EXCASTRATUS. — 52. l. eiulatus, *he* seems to be beginning of another gloss. — 53. l. hae-
reses : sectae. — 54. l. ingemescentis. — 56. Cf. above 45 and Hild. H 42. — 59. l. come-
dentes. — 60. l. Hesperias. — 61. Cf. HEBRAEI in Onomasticon. Bod. *haebraeorum :
transeuntium.* — 62. Cf. above p. 138. — 63. l. laude. — 66. l. hydromantes ; cf. Serv.
Aen. III. 359. — 68. Cf. Mai. VI. 537, *Hylidri : serpentes aquatici,* for ytri l. hydri. —
69. Cf. Bod. *hidroplasmus quas cantio conponit organi,* and Mai. VI. 527, *Hydroplas-*

mus; qui cantionem conponit organi. — **71.** l. iliis. — **72.** Perhaps for *bubulcus* or *subulcus;* cf. S 335, subulcus: pastor porcorum, for which *hyulcus* might be a hybrid formation (cf. ὑοπόλος). Compare Bod. *hulcus pastor;* Mai. VI. 526, *Hiticus* (also *Hiulcus*) *pastor.* — **72.** l. hyacinthum: flos purpurea. — **74.** *o* above *a*, l. unio; cf. Bod. *himo margarita preciosa.* — **75.** grassi = crassi is intelligible as a gloss for hirti, cf. 85; but I do not understand *anni.* Perhaps there is some confusion with a gloss Hete (= ἔτη) anni, or with **122,** *horne: huius anni,* or with *hippi: manni.* — **77.** l. hippagus. — **78.** Bod. *hicterici: ydropici,* Phill. *hictei* (l. hicterici) *sunt ydropici vel elephantini, hicterim enim Greci vocant elephantiam;* cf. Isid. Or. IV. 8, 12, and 13. l. icterici: hydropici. — **83.** l. hisco . . aperio. — **84.** Cf. Bod. *hyr vigel interpretator; hyr caldaico sermone latine vigil interpretator.* — **85.** l. setosa . . *plena* is perhaps an explanation of *fetosa.* — **86.** l. horridum. — **87.** l. mimus. — **88.** l. hymenaeos; cf. Verg. Aen. I. 651. — **89.** l. hiulcum . . . aperiens . . hians. — **90.** l. hippagus . . . iumentaria. — **91.** Cf. Hild. H 61 n. — **92.** l. hiantes. — **93.** Cf. De Vit and Ball. *hystriones, qui gestus impudicarum feminarum exprimebant.* — **96.** Cf. **101** and Isid. Or. XV. 1, 5, . . . *Hierusalem* quae postea *a Salomone Hierosolyma* quasi *Ierosolomonia* dicta est. . . . . *Hierusalem* autem in nostro sermone *pacifica transfertur.* — **97.** Perhaps stellę septem was first written; cf. Serv. Georg. I. 138, *Hae sunt in fronte tauri in formam Y literae. Unde etiam Yadas dici volunt. Has alii septem, alii quinque dicunt,* etc., hence read in modo Y litterae. — **100.** l. hisco: miror; but the active *miro* occurs in Reichenauer Glossen 566, *Stupebant: mirabant.* — **101.** Cf. above **96.** — **102.** l. historiographus: descriptor. — **103.** l. hystrix. — **106.** l. villosus. — **107.** l. hiberna . . . calida . . hiemem. — **108.** l. memorialia. — **109.** Cf. **31.** — **110.** l. hyaena . . . genus beluae. — **111.** l. fissura; cf. Bod. *hiatus: fisura vel apertio terrae, patefatio vel vorago.* — **112.** l. hybleus . . . floridum. — **113.** l. frigus. — **114.** l. desinere. — **118.** Two glosses confused, hostiae: lustra (or hospitia: lustra?) and hospita: peregrina. — **122.** l. horni. — **124.** Cf. **128,** and Prod. 258. — **125.** Cf. Prod. 339, l. horti; cf. Bod. *holitor horti vel olerum cultor.* — **127.** l. suadeo. — **128.** Cf. **124,** l. aequamentum; cf. Nonius 3, 26, *Hostimentum est aequamentum,* etc. Unde et *hostire* dicitur . . . id est *aequa reddere.* — **129.** l. oscitans . . . spiritum halans. — **130.** l. ironia . . vituperare. — **132.** l. vero. — **133.** l. homuncio. — **134.** l. honorat. — **135.** l. homullus. — **138.** l. mortalia.

I.

2. l. custos — **4.** l. damnum. — **8.** Cf. Lagarde Onom. Sacra, p. 32, Iabin intellegens vel sapiens. — **9.** l. iactat. — **10.** Ball. *Iacturarius qui frequenter iacturam patitur;* cf. Loewe G. N. 166; l. *mortalitatem.* — **12.** Cf. Ball. *iapex velox, agilis;* l. Iapyx. Confusion of two separate glosses. — **16.** l. Hieratica (for *hieroglyphica*) littera. — **20.** l. splendor . . . ortum; q. = quae, perhaps originally referred to stella. Cf. Serv. Aen. IV. 130 and Isid. Or. III. 70, 18, *Lucifer* . . *hic proprie et iubar dicitur eo quod iubas lucis effundat sed et splendor solis ac lunae et stellarum iubar vocatur.* — **24.** l. summitates. — **29.** l. nuces. — **30.** Cf. Ball. *Iustitium luctus publicus vel publici iuris silentium;* l. luctus publicus. — **31.** l. iugum: servitutes; cf. Bod. *Iugum servitutis servitus dominatio captivitatis.* — **33.** Cf. Hild. I 14, *Icenisma, imago sine pectore,* but *fine pectore* makes good sense; perhaps *aut caput* is to be read; cf. Bod. *iconisma imago stagma vel figura imperatoris.* — **36.** l. identidem; cf. Plac. L. G. 21, 22, *identidem idem ipsum.* — **39.** l. proprietas. — **41.** Cf. Isid. Or. VIII. 11, 14, Quidam vero Latini ignorantes Graece imperite dicunt *idolum ex dolo* sumpsisse nomen, quod *diabolus creaturae cultum divini nominis invexit.* — **45.** l. ignominia. — **46.** l. ignobili; cf. Verg. Aen. I. 149. — **59.** l. imbecilles. — **60.** l. acerbum. — **62.** l. barbis. — **94.** l. in promptu. — **66.** l. impopulabile: inlaesum; cf. Hild. I 286. — **68.** l. impendium. — **69.** l. ineruditus. — **74.** Probably *in burim;* cf. Ball. *imburim incurvatio* and *Imburim pars curva quae aratro iungitur.* It refers to Verg. Georg. I. 170, where Serv. *In burim, in curvaturam,* nam *buris* est curvamentum aratri, etc. — **85.** Bod. *in procinctu;* cf. Serv. Georg. I. 170; Ball. *In procinctu in militia, in apparatu.* — **89.** l. immitis. — **91.** l. in murice; cf. Verg. Aen. V. 205. — **94.** Probably for in praecelsum: in excelsum. — **95.**

l. in praeceps. —96. l. impetrat. —97. l. implexa; cf. Ball. *incorporata.* —97. Cf. 85.—
102. ? l. investis imberbis; cf. Hild. I 301. —104. l. improvidus. —110. l. incola. —111.
l. incolumis. —118. l. incestum. —127. l. incidit: secat; cf. Reichenauer Glossen 310,
Seccabis: incides (but perhaps for incidit in errorem). —128. l. incutit: inicit. —129.
l. incessunt. —130. requisitio, given by Lex. as α. λ., must be here taken in the sense of
examination of auspices. —135. l. nobilem. —136. Cf. Serv. Georg. III. 371, *Cassibus*
i. e. *retibus.* Hinc est quod *et incassum dicimus* i. e. *sine causa* quasi *sine cassibus*
sine quibus venatio est inanis. —138. l. desertum; cf. Bod. *incelebre, desertum desola-*
tum. —141. l. proficiscere. —152. Cf. Serv. Aen. XI. 651, *indefessa infatigabilis.* —
155. l. index: significator. —158. l. dilationes; cf. Hild. I 160. —161. l. indutiae or in-
dutias; cf. De Vit. —164. Cf. Bod. *inermis: sine armis vel debilis.* —165. l. iners. —
169. l. energumena: daemoniaca. —170. Cf. *in excessu meo,* Vulg. Ps. 115, 2.; l. excessu.
—174. l. cenulis. —175. l. in impetu. —177. l. indidit. —178. l. aetas iuvenalis quae
dolorem . . . —180. l. doceri. —182. l. infitiis; cf. 212.—184. l. indigestum.—186. l. inexorabilis. —187. Cf. Hild. I 163; l. incrementum. Cf. Bod. *Indoles certe spei vel bonae*
naturae progenies incrementum vel origo in puero vel ingenium moris. —188. l. inertia,
perhaps confused with *energia.* —190. l. placet. —191. l. insatiabilis; cf. Verg. Aen.
VIII. 559. —192. Cf. Hild. I 68, and Ball. *inedia: fames vel ieiunium;* l. inedia: fames,
ieiunia. Goetz reads in MS. geiunia, but Kaegi as I have printed. —193. l. in extasi.
Ball. has *in excessu mentis;* cf. 170. —196. l. infausta: infelicia. —197. Cf. Hild. I 189
and Bod. *Infastus in honore positus vel qui ad sacra pertinent ;* l. in fastis: in honore. —
203. l. inferaces: infructuosae; but perhaps *infetaces* can be kept; cf. Loewe G. N. 150.
—204. Ball. *Infrenis irreverens hoc est qui frenis non regitur ut Numide infreni;* cf.
Serv. Aen. X. 750.—206. l. intulisti. —207. l. impulsor: persuasor, but see Loewe G. N.
151.—208. l. infulis. —209. l. infulae: vittae sacerdotales; cf. Ball. *Infule ornamenta*
dignitatum sive vitte gentilium sacerdotum. —211. Cf. 182. —212. Cf. Bod. *Infitiae :*
mendacia vel negotiationes (l. negationes). —213. Probably a confusion of two glosses;
infamare: crimen inferre (211, infamis) and *infitiari: negare.* —215. l. fucatum. —
219. Cf. Paul. 112, 7, *infrequens appellatur miles, qui abest afuitve a signis.* —220. Cf.
INFORMITAS; *incompositio* is not in Lexx. —223. l. ingluvie: gula; cf. Paul. 112, 2,
Ingluvies a gula dicta, etc. —225. Cf. Nonius, 322, 31, *Ingenium* est *naturalis sapientia.*
—227. l. ingeminans . . duplans. —229. Confusion of two glosses, ingluvies: voragines, and inluvies : sordes; cf. 247 and Nonius, 126, 25, *Illuvies, sordes.* —230. l. fert. —
232. l. ingruentes. —235. Cf. Serv. Aen. IV. 41 f. —236. l. attonitus. *ut tentus* seems
to be for *attentus* or *intentus;* cf. Serv. Aen. IV. 64, *inhians, intenta per sollicitudinem.*
239. l. iniit, inchoavit. —240. l. adversaria. —241. l. inicit: inmittit; cf. 243. —246.
l. inlicit . . . suadet.—248. l. inlibata. —250. l. inletabilis. —253. l. inliciunt . . .
persuadent. —256. l. innexa; perhaps for *amplexa* we should read *implexa.* —257. l.
innuba. —262. l. insperata. —263. l. INNORMIS. —267. conditionis? Isid. Or. IX. 4, 37,
has *Inquilini vocati quasi incolentes aliena. Non enim habent propriam sedem sed terra*
aliena inhabitant; and in preceding paragraph, under *Coloni,* Sunt enim aliunde venien-
tes atque alienum agrum locatum colentes ac debentes *conditionem* genitali solo propter
agri culturam sub dominio possessoris, pro eo quod iis locatus est fundus, so that there may
be some connection with *conditio* or *condictio.* —269. Cf. Verg. Aen. III. 89, *Animis in-*
labere nostris. Inlabere is explained as if it were an infinitive. —270. Probably inlicita
voluptas to be read. —272. l. inlustres: nobiles. —275. Cf. 245 and 253; l. inliciant. —
278. l. innixi; cf. De Vit. —279. l. viro. —281. l. innumerum: innumerabilem. —282.
l. nutibus. —285. l. in horamate; cf. HORAMA. —288. l. inquies. —297. l. instigat. —
300. l. inhaerens. —303. l. inridet. —305. l. quaerendum. —306. l. insignem; cf. Verg.
Aen. I. 10. —307. So Hild. I 347, where *invadere* is read for *evadere.* I still think *in-*
sultare may have been the original reading. —310. l. inscitia. —311. l. inolevit . . inhae-
sit. —316. l. insertabam. —317. l. instinctu dei. —322. l. renovat. —326. l. superbire,
which was written *supervire* and then *supervivere.* —328. l. diffindere; cf. Hild. I 336.
—329. l. intrinsecus: interius; repeated 335. —331. Cf. Verg. Aen. III. 587. —332. l.
interpolata ; *revocata* is here used in the sense of *renovata.* —336. l. intriverat. *minua-*
verat in sense of crumble into small pieces is supported by *minuatim ;* cf. MINUO. —340.

l. internosci : cognosci. — 342. l. interpolavit : interrupit. — 343. Is *interlinitus* a vulgar form from *interlinere?* Cf. De Vit. — 346. l. UNITIO. — 352. l. intercapedo ; cf. Paul. 111, 3. — 353. l. fide. — 354. l. integer : sanguine. — 355. l. interloquar. — 356. l. varieque. — 357. l. intemptant = intentant. — 358. l. minantur. — 360. ? Cf. Mai. VI. 529, *intermina : internuncia obiecta vel mediatrix,* and other glosses cited by Hild. I 385 n., who proposes to read *intermedia.* — 361. l. notum. — 365. l. interpolare : variegare. — 366. The reading is doubtful, according to Goetz and Kaegi, and the emendation difficult. The first part of the gloss bears some resemblance to Hild. C 189, *Comminando, intemptando,* and the second part to Hild. I 378, *interlitus, intercessio verbi quando inter se obliterantur,* the first words of which occur at about the same place on next page ; see 382. — 367 = tempus inter primam et novissimam lunam ; cf. Isid. Or. III. 54, *Interlunium lunae est tempus illud inter deficientem et nascentem lunam.* — 369. l. inter pocula. — 372. Cf. Mai. VI. 529, *Intrio : in fundo vel tute* (followed by *intristi : parasti*). I propose for *intrio, intero;* cf. Cato R. R. 156, 6, *infundito* in catinum, uti frigescast eo *interito,* etc., and Gloss. Pap. *Intereo : infundo; Interitum : infusum.* — 372. l. coniector. — 376. Cf. 350. — 377. l. species. — 378. Cf. INTERLOCUTIO. — 380. l. internicionem. — 382. Cf. note on 366. *intercisio* seems to make better sense than *intercessio.* — 383. Perhaps for invindicatum. — 384. Cf. Paul. 368, 9. — 388. l. invenustus. — 391. l. in vestibulo : in ingressu. — 395. Cf. INVISOR. — 398. l. invisunt. — 399. l. adiri. — 401. l. irritum. — 403. l. stimulat. — 404. l. derisio. — 406. l. Ister Dacus ; cf. Verg. Georg. II. 497, *Dacus ab Histro.* — 407. l. stromatis : commentariis scientiae ; so Mai. VI. 546. — 408. The Isterum Danubium is written in fainter ink ; the proper gloss for *Isaurum* seems to have fallen out. — 411. l. iterum atque iterum. — 414. l. itineris. — 415. l. Ituraeus ; cf. Verg. Georg. II. 448. — 416. ? l. stromateus : opus varium seu lacinium (lacinia) varia diversitate contextum ; cf. De Vit.

K.

1. Cf. Isid. Or. V. 33, 13, Quidam autem *Kalendas* a *colendo* appellari exstimabant. — 2. l. chalybem. — 3. l. chalybs : furca. — 4. l. Charybdis. — 5. l. calones . . galearii ; cf. De Vit and Hild. C 20 n. — 6. l. charadrius . . alba . . prima eius ; cf. De Vit under Charadrus.

L.

3. l. FOCULARE. — 5. De Vit Lex. cites only one example of *Daemoniosus* from Rufin. 3, Recognit 3. — 6. Mai. VI. 530, has *Lacerna, stola vestis* and *Lacernum ; stola vel vestis.* — 7. l. labitur. — 8. l. labos. — 10. l. carnes . . . gladiatorum. — 13. l. caeduntur (lapides) ; cf. Paul. 118, 13, *Lapidicinae ubi exciduntur lapides.* — 16. l. debilem. — 17. Cf. TIGNARIUS. — 18. A confusion, I think, of two or more glosses, as e. g. lagunculae : vasa fictilia and laterna id est lucerna ; but see 43, and Prod. 108 and 135. — 20. l. decipit. — 22. Cf. Verg. Aen. II. 551 ; l. serpentem — 24. l. labefactare. — 26. l. bracchiorum. — 27. l. stellae fulgentus ; cf. Plac. 62, 21, *Lampenae, stellae quaedam sic dictae.* — 28. ? Perhaps for LACTARIS ; cf. Nonius 16, 13, *Lactare est inducere vel mulcere, velle decipere.* — 30. ? Cf. LAMIA and Gr. λάμνα = λάμια ; see also Y 7, *ypnix :* animal quasi ad similitudinem *pardorum* quas alii *lamminas* dicunt. — 31. Cf. Serv. Aen. I. 686, *latex ab eo quod intra terrae venas lateat.* — 35. l. lator : portator. — 37. Cf. LAVERNA ; l. filios alios seducit ; cf. Hild. L 4 and 5. — 39. See 37. — 43. Cf. De Vit and Prod. 108. — 45. l. camerae. — 47. The MS. has nothing after Tornus, but empty space is left sufficient for ten letters. — 48. l. missoria. — 49. l. umbra ; cf. De Vit, Larva : umbra exerrans, and Larva : simulacrum. — 50. l. labilis. — 52. Cf. Loewe G. N. 252, l. lirantes, so Mai. VI. 532 ; but cf. Mon. 6210, *laborat* per sincopen *larat* facit. — 55. l. LARUS . . . gavia (in marg. m. 2, add. after *guia orum* Goetz). — 57. ? Confusion of luitur : solvitur, and labitur : cadit. — 58. See above, p. 138. — 60. l. lapit . . . . dolitat ; cf. DOLITO ; cf. Paul. 118, 12, *Lapit : dolore afficit,* and Nonius 23, 7, *Lapit significat obdurefacit et lapidem facit.* — 61. Cf. LATOMUS, l. lapidum caesor. — 67. l. legio Martia : numerus. — 72. l.

caccabos aeneos. — 73. l. lictores. — 74. Cf. LECTICALIS, not found in any author ; see
Loewe G. N. 167. — 75. ? Seems to be a corruption of *Levisata genus armorum est*,
Hild. L 110; cf. Prod. 45, *Levisata: de tonica* (l. tunica) *dicit militarum;* Leid. 67, F 2.
— 76. seductrix is found in Tert. adv. Marc. 2, 2. — 78. l. seductiones, persuasiones. —
80. Cf. 85 and 87. — 86. l. honestum. — 87. l. dulcedinem, decorem. — 90. Cf. De Vit
Galen. MS. ad. Glauc. 1, 35, *Frigore et febre recedentibus sudor consequitur et leptopyria.* — 91. Cf. Verg. Aen. VI. 287. l. hydra. — 93. l. lethargus . . . comprimuntur aegri
ad. — 94. l. levigabis : lenibis. — 95. l. corculum ; cf. Isid. Or. VII. 9, 19, *Iudas Iacobi,
qui alibi vocatur Lebbeus, figuratum nomen a corde, quod nos diminutive corculum pos-
sumus appellare. Ipse in alio evangelista Thaddaeus scribitur*, etc., hence l. Thaddaeus
for *deus.* — 97. l. Lilyaeum : promontorium. — 99. Truncated ; cf. Placid. 62, 2, *Libare est
leviter aliquid contingere*, etc ; Serv. Aen. I. 256, *libavit leviter tetigit.* — 100. ? Perhaps a
corruption of Hebrew Nephilim, which occurs Gen. vi. 4, Numb. xiii. 33, and in the old version is rendered giants. In the revised version Nephilim is kept.— 101. = Liburna. — 102.
l. Liburni : accolae Adriatici. — 103. l. libamina. — 105. l. libitina. — 106. Perhaps librat
is to be read; *sicilẹ* I do not understand, unless by some mistake *libra* was glossed as *sicel.*
Cf. Isid. Or. XVI. 25, 18, or it may be for Siciliae and belong to 97; so Bod. has *lilibeum
urbs siciliae ā* (aut ?) *promontorium Syciliae.*— 107. l. liberalis. — 108. l. aequant.— 109.
Cf. 105, l. conduntur. — 113. l. venditio. — 114. Cf. LICESSIT. — 115. l. licitatio. — 116.
l. pretio. — 117. l. apparitor ; cf. above, 73. — 118. ? So Mai. VI. 521, but *quibus multa
licent.* — 119. l. promissio. — 121. l. Lyaeum. — 122. Cf. Loewe G. N. 217, l. argutus. —
123. l. provincia . . . Mediolanum. — 125. Servius however commenting on Ecl. II. 18,
Alba ligustra, says, *Ligustrum autem flos est candidus.* — 126. l. limes: finis terminus. —
130. l. limis . . obliquis ; cf. Paul. 116, 1, *limis obliquus id est transversus;* Ter. Eun. 3,
5, 53, *ego limis specto*, where Eugraphius, "Quidam intelligunt *limis obliquis* . . . . . Alii
intelligunt *limis oculis* paululum *tortis.*" — 131. *fantasticus* is here used for *fanaticus.* —
132. l. limbus. — 133. l. lychni. — 135. l. liquuntur. — 136. Cf. *maculosæ tegmine lyn-
cis*, Verg. Aen. I. 323. — 138. for this use of *dimittit* see Prod. 422. — 141. l. cytharae.
143. l. lethargus. — 144. l. litat: immolat. — 145. l. lituus. — 148. Cf. above, p. 131. —
152. l. longaevi. — 153. Cf. Verg. Aen. II. 697. — 154. *logion* is written on the margin
by second hand. Cf. Isid. Or. XIX. 21, 6, *Logion quod Latine dicitur rationale, pannus
duplex ex auro et quatuor textus coloribus ; . . . . . cui intexti erant xii. pretiosi lapides. Hic pannus superhumerali contra pectus pontificis annectebatur.* — 158. l. minime.
— 160. l. erogationes quae; cf. De Vit, and Paulus, 119, 6 and 8, *lucaris:* pecunia quae *in
luco* erat data. *Lucar* appellatur *aes* quod *ex lucis* captatur. — 163. incubi = Panis; cf.
P 74, Pan: ingibus; see 174. — 165. l. quinquennium. — 168. Left incomplete; cf. Ball.
luteres cantari vel aquarii sed cantarus graecum nomen est. — 169. l. Luculleum. —
170. l. lucem apparet. — 172. l. elabescens not in Lexx. — 174. l. dicitur (Lupercus). —
175. l. sordidum. — 176. For diluvius m. see Appel p. 85. — 178. l. luscinia: avis. —
180. l. torvo; cf. Verg. Aen. III. 677. ? diro hae (according to Goetz *hac* not *hae* in
MS.). — 182. Emend from Isid. Or. VII. 9, 23, *Lucas ipse est consurgens, sive ipse
elevans* eo quod elevaverit praedicationem Evangelii post alios.

M.

1. Cf. Mai. VI. 532, *macte: magis autem*, evidently a corruption of *magis aucte.* So
Servius Aen. IX. 641, *macte ; magis aucte, affectate gloria. Aut tam* seems to be a corruption of *autem ;* cf. De Vit. — 3. l. Macetae. — 4. l. pastorum. — 7. Cf. MAGNES. — 9.
l. Punicum. — 10. = μαλακία ; cf. MALACIA. — 11. l. mala gramina ; cf. Bod. *mala gramina, noxias herbas venenatas.* — 12. l. Maiae sacrificabant; cf. Prod. 377. — 13. cf. MANUA.
— 15. l. comesta. — 16. l. mandimus: comedimus. — 19. l. animae. — 20. l. numerus. —
21. l. manipuli (for *mapuli*) . . *cremiorum* : capiantur. — 22. *manuale* here in the
sense of napkin. *Orarium* is used by Lucilius in this sense. — 23. Cf. Hild. M 54; manicat per manum tenet vel a mane surgit. There probably was a verb formed from
manicae, as we have *manicarius.* Otherwise we might suppose *mancipat* to have been

confused with *manicat.* — **25**. l. manu-capta, evidently in connection with preceding gloss. — **28**. l. Mavortia . . . pugnam pertinent. — **30**. Cf. Paul. 125, 9, *macilenti, macie tenuati.* — **32**. l. pollutus. — **33**. l. casae; cf. Paul. 147, 16, *mapalia casae Poenicae appellantur,* etc. — **36**. l. animi. — **37**. l. malleator: faber ferri. — **38**. l. machinationes commenta astutiae. — **39**. l. illuminatrix. — **40**. l. saccellum. — **41**. l. libri. — **42**. l. mastigia . . . servus. — **43**. l. matris. — **46**. l. manens. — **47**. Cf. MARANATHA. — **48**. De Vit cites Margalet (unum ex XII. signis astronomicis), Virgil. Gramm. p. 115, Mai. — **50**. l. martyrium. — **51**. l. murrina. — **52**. l. mastigiae: taureae. — **53**. Cf. De Vit, *mattus: tristis* and *mactum est; humectum est, emollitum infectum. Mattus* occurs in Petronius in sense of intoxicated. Perhaps there has been some confusion with *maestus: tristis.* — **54**. l. matrimus: matris. — **56**.? perhaps for mavissem: magis voluissem. — **57**. Cf. Isid. Or. VII. 9, 22, *Marcus, excelsus mandato,* utique propter Evangelium altissimi, quod praedicavit. — **59**. l. melos: dulcis. — **60**. l. meditullium; cf. Plac. 65, 1. — **61**. l. pellis ovina simplex, qua monachi utuntur, ex uno latere (dependens); cf. MELOTE and Amplon. 349, 19, *merotis: pellis simplex ex uno latere dependens.* — **63**. l. metator: arbiter, locator; cf. Tert. adv. Marc. 1, 8, *tempus arbiter et metator initii et finis.* — **64**. Cf. MELOPOEUS; l. factor. — **66**. l. decurrit. — **67**. l. menstruum. — **68**. l. Maenalias(os): cf. Verg. Ecl. VIII. 21, *Incipe Maenalios.* — **69**. l. tabernarum . . . committuntur. — **70**. l. animo. — **71**. l. mergit. — **73**. l. commercia. — **74**. Kaegi reads *Bahe.* Emend Maenades: Bacchae; pars seems not to belong here. — **75**.? l. mergites: fasces spicarum; cf. Ball. *mergites: spicarum fasces,* Serv. G. II. 517, *Manipulos spicarum mergites dicimus;* cf. MERGAE. — **76**. l. myrmex. — **78**. l. balneator; cf. Porph. Hor. Ep. I. 14, 14, *mediastinus Incola mediae civitatis: an in officio balneatoris mediastinus;* see also Porph. Hor. Sat. 1, 5, 35. — **80**. l. me ita Castor: sit (siet) Castor; cf. Paul. 125, 4; *mecastor et mehercules iusiurandum erat, quasi diceretur, ita me Castor, ita me Hercules, ut subaudiatur, iuvet.* — **81**. Cf. Prod. 397. — **82**. Cf. Amplon. 351, 114 and 115, *melops, dulcissonus: melopeum, dulce conpositum.* — **83**. l. Commodus; cf. Lamprid. Commod. 11, *Menses quoque in honorem eius pro Augusto Commodum, pro Septembri Herculem,* etc., *adulatores vocabant.* — **84**. l. fustes; cf. Paul. 124, 1, *Mergae furculae quibus acervi frugum fiunt,* etc., and Hild. M 118; Bod. *merges: fustes cum quibus messes colliguntur.* — **85**. Cf. 82 and 64. — **87**. l. Micipsa: vir (?); cf. Bod. *Micipsa nomen est regis.* — **88**. l. assidue. — **90**. Cf. MINICIUS. — **92**. l. gestae. **93**. Cf. Serv. Aen. IV. 88, *minae, eminentiae murorum.* — **96**. l. μυρμηκίας (cf. myrmecias and myrmecium), verrucas. — **97**. l. praefiguratum. — **98**. l. miscellaneum: COMMIXTICIUM. — **99**. l. missile. — **101**. l. perturbantur. — **102**. l. cetera parte (or ceteras partes) . . suscepisse. — **104**. l. exivit. — **105**. l: dimittit. — **107**. l. palea minuta, so Hild. M 127. — **108**. l. myoparo = μυοπάρων: naviculas capha piratarum. — **109**. Cf. Isid. Or. VII. 5, 12, *Michael* interpretatur, *quis ut Deus?* — **110**. l. modificata. — **111**. l. modulatio: dulcedo. — **114**. l. omnis inlicitus concubitus, which seems to have been used as a neuter. — **120**. l. placat. — **121**. l. Molossi: canes. — **122**. l. cogitationes. — **127**. l. iumento . . . ducitur; cf. De Vit. — **128**. l. uxoris. — **130**. l. monumentis. — **132**. l. stilus in MOMENTANA; cf. MOMENTUM. — **134**. l. mulierum . . . equorum; cf. Gloss. Pap., *Munilia pectoralia equorum vel ornamenta in cervice mulierum;* cf. Paul. 139, 9, *monile et mulierum ornatus et equorum propendens a collo.* — **138**. Cf. MONOCEROS; l. quadrupes. — **139**. l. munimenta; cf. **153**. — **141**. l. delectat. — **142**. l. mulctra . . . mulgetur. — **143**. Cf. Plac. 65, 18, *mulcator corporis, qui corpora afficit vel cruciat.* — **144**. l. molossus. — **145**. l. caedit. — **148**. l. sermonis. — **149**.? mulceo, see **150**. — **150**. l. mulciber; cf. Paul. 144, 2, *Mulciber Vulcanus a molliendo scilicet ferro dictus. Mulcere enim mollire sive lenire est.* — **151**. l. mulceat; cf. Prod. 421. — **154**. *firmitas* perhaps goes with preceding gloss. — **156**. l. caelum, but Isid. Or. XIII. 1, 1, *mundus est caelum et terra et mare,* etc. — **157**. l. cum muris. — **159**.? l. acceptis; cf. Plac. 66, 4, *municipes, curialium maiores ex eo quod munera fisci idem accipiant,* and Isid. Or. IX. 3, 21, "Dictus *princeps a capiendo* significatione, quod *primum capiat,* sicut *municeps* ab eo quod *munia capiat."* *Princeps primus* is a corruption, I think, of some such explanation; compare, however, Bod. *municeps; princeps primus vel acceptor muneris.* — **162**.? l. liberalitas = *liberali(ber)tas.* — **163**. confusion of two glosses *monumenta: testimonia* and *moenium: murorum.* — **164**. l. munitura (= apron): praecinctorium. — **165**. l. munimen . . . munitione; cf. Isid. XV. 9, 1, *munimen vel munimentum dictum quod manu est factum.* — **166**. l. officia; cf. Isid. Or. XV. 2, 10. — **168**. l. quae. — **169**. Confusion of two glosses, *myricae: frutices virgulta* and *murice: saxa acuta in montibus* (cf. Verg. Aen. V. 205 and Ecl. VIII. 54). — **170** = **173**. — **171**. l. mausoleum. — **172**. Cf. Paul. 144, 14, *mussare murmurare;* Ennius . . . *vulgo vero pro tacere dicitur.* — **173**. Cf. Prod. 106, 121, and De Vit. — **174**. Cf. Prod. 420; l. soricum. — **175**. l. muscipula. — **176**. l. murgiso: murmurator (morator?); cf. Paul. 144, 11, *murgisonem dixerunt a mora et decisione,* Plac. 66, 18, *murgiso, irrisor, illusor,* and Hild. M 226. — **177**. l. mussitat. — **178**. Confusion of two glosses, mollitum: placidum, and mutilat: violat, Hildebrand M 230 cites Mai. VI. 533, *molitat: placitum violat,* and adds, " ubi quid pro *placidum* legendum sit non habeo;" *mollitum* was probably first corrupted to *mulitum,* and then perhaps to *mutilum.* — **179**. l. imminuo . . . saucio. — **181**. Cf. Prod. 283 and De Vit.

N.

1. ? Possibly an explanation of Hebrew proper name *Nabo* or *Nabau ;* cf. Lagarde, Onom. Sacra p. 50, Nabo sessio vel superveniens. Were it not for the alphabetical order, one might conjecture *nullo: rescindo.* De Vit cites *nullo,* as *nullum facio, muto.* — **3**. Cf. Paul. 167, 7, nancitor nactus erit (so Müller, but the MSS. *nasciscitur.* Müller adds, Fuit fortasse NANXSITOR). — **5**. l. navarchus: navis. — **6**. l. navalia . . . naves. — **8**. l. studiose . . . utiliter. — **10**. l. psalterium. — **11**. Cf. Hild. N 6. — **13**. l. nautica. — **14**. Perhaps for *navita: nauta:* l. navus: obsequens (veritatis), so Bod. in a long gloss. — **15**. l. navem. — **16**. l. vigilans; cf. Hild. N 4. — **17**. l. strenue agit; cf. Prod. 344. — **18** ? nauclerus or naupegus; cf. De Vit, *Navaretius: navargus navis magister a navis et Argus,* secundum Papiam, Gloss. Joh. de Janua. Gloss. Isid. *Nauregus: navaretius, naupicus: navis factor.* Gloss. Pap. *Naupicus: navis pater, nauregus et naurigus: navis princeps.* — **19**. l. officium. — **21**. l. navat operam: dat operam. — **22** and **24** belong together; the full gloss was, I think, natrix: serpens epicenon est, or nat*ri*ce: (ep*ice*)-non est. Cf. H **110**, hiena: epicenon est gens belue. — **25** and **26** should be printed as one gloss; l. nardum pisticum: nardum fidelem; cf. Hieronym. praef. in XII. Prophet. *nardum pisticum: id est unguentum fidelissimum.* — **27**. A second hand has repeated the gloss, *narrat: nuntiat,* at the bottom of page. — **28**. Cf. De Vit; l. vita. — **32**. l. amicitiae. — **34**. l. iniuria. — **35**. Two glosses confused, Necromanticus: evocator umbrarum, and Necromantia: mortuorum divinatio. — **36**. l. nenias. — **37**. l. nequam. — **40**. l. novilunium, Kalendae. — **41**. l. neophytus. — **47**. l. sed et. — **48**. l. naevum. — **54**. Cf. **35**; l. anima . . mortuorum. — **57**. ? perhaps for nefaria: crudelis, inloquenda; cf. *indicendus* ἄλεκτος, Gloss. Philox. — **58**. l. nequaquam: nullo modo. — **61**. l. prodigus. — **62**. l. neoterici. — **67**. l. neverant: filaverant. — **71**. l. necando. — **72**. Cf. Festus, 177, 7, *Nictare et oculorum et aliorum membrorum nisu saepe aliquid conari,* etc.; Nonius, 440, 26, . . . *nictare oculorum significantiam esse decreverint; oculorum* may be due to some such statement. It is of course easy to amend to *oculos frequenter aperire (et claudere).* — **73**. l. nycticorax. — **75**. l. scorpius; cf. Paul. 164; Fest. 165, and Placid. 70, 13. — **76**. l. nivarius: splendidus; cf. Prod. 427. — **77**. Cf. Prod. 16, and Festus, 177 a, 16; l. nictit canis, etc. — **78**. l. vento. — **82**. l. nymphaticus: arrepticius; cf. lymphaticus. — **83**. l. candidus. — **86**. See above, p. 130. — **89**. l. morio; cf. Prod. 19, for numerous similar glosses. — **91**. = nempe. — **94**. l. dubio. — **95**. l. *nictura: gannitura; cf. **77**, or perhaps natura: genitura. — **97**. l. Nilicola. — **98**. l. nympha; cf. Amplon. 355, 22, *nimpha virga caelestis vel numen aequa* (l. aqua). — **99**. l. nītens: incumbens; nītens: splendidus. — **100**. l. nitelae. — **104**. l. nympha. — **107**. l. nosocomium. — **110**. Cf. Verg. Aen. III. 268. — **111**. l. adulterio. — **113**. l. nihilo setius: nihilo minus. — **115**. l. noctiluca. — **118**. l. tergiversator. — **119**. l. umida (the *u* is corrected from *o* in MS.); cf. Verg. Aen. II. 8. — **120**. l. putativum; cf. De Vit. — **121**. l. nomenculator; cf. Prod. 404. — **128**. l. maiestas. — **133**. Cf. above, p. 130; l. nuscitiosus . . vespere. — **136**. l. nummularius: praerogator may perhaps be kept, as *praerogare* is used in the sense of pay beforehand; otherwise read PROROGATOR. — **137.** Cf. Amplon. 354, 80, *nummisca, nummi percussura calatae;* l. percussura (referring to the stamp), denarius; so Bod. *nummisma: figura quae in nummo fit vel nummi percussura id est denarium alii solidum dicunt.* — **140.** l. noverca.

O.

8. l. oppositiones; cf. Serv. Georg. IV. 422, Obice; obiectione. — **10.** l. obesus. — **11.** l. scrupulum. — **12** and **13** = **7**, added by second hand; cf. Mon. 6210, *obicem oppositionem obices repagule balbe* = repagula valvae. — **14.** l. obit. — **19.** l. ovans. — **20.** l. oppugnat. — **21.** l. opponit. — **24.** l. oblimat, in this sense apparently connected with *limare, lima,* in sense of clean off. Cf. Acron. Hor. S. I. 2, 62, *Oblimare, delere, consumere, tractum a lima qua fabri utuntur, aut certe a limo ut sit obducere, ut dicimus quaedam limo obducta, periise;* see Hild. O 21. -- **26.** offerta, late Latin; cf. *offertor* and *offertorium.* — **27.** l. obliterata. — **30.** l. obnoxius, so **31** and **32**, humilis; cf. Hild. O 30. — **33.** l. obnubit: obtegit; cf. Paul. 184, 4, obnubit, caput operit. — **34.** l. obnuberat; cf. Hild. O 31. — **37.** l. obstipum. — **38.** l. obstupida; cf. Plaut. Mil. 1254, *Quid astitisti obstupida?* — **39.** l. obsoletatus: inquinatus. — **41.** l. deprecat(ur). — **42.** l. desperatus. — **43.** l. obsoletus: sordidus. — **44.** l. obsecundat. — **45.** l foedissimum. — **48.** l. praecisa. — **49.** l. obtorpuit: infrigidavit. — **50.** l. obtensus: obcaecatus. — **51.** l. obtendentes. — **53.** l. immobilis. — **56.** l. obnitens. — **57.** l. obnubit, here glossed as if *obnupsit.* — **59.** l. obnubit: operit; cf. **33.** — **60.** l. obnuptus. — **61.** ? Perhaps two glosses confused, obruto: oblito, and obruito: obterito. — **63.** l. impedit. — **65.** ? Cf. De Vit; Mai. VI. 536, *Obisallagis: Marsusus* (Mai. adnotat " Isid. *Obsillas: marsus pro psillus: marsus* "); see Aulus Gellius, XVI. 11, 1, for the connection between Psylli and Marsi. Amplon. 357, 116, *Obsillages: marsus.* A clue to the correct reading may perhaps be found in Isid. Or. IX. 2, 88, *Marsos autem Graeci Uscos vocant* quasi ὀφιούχους *quod multos serpentes habent.* See also Gloss. Lat. Gr. Marsae: ἀσπιδοθῆραι, ὀφιοδιῶκται. Professor Gildersleeve has suggested ΟΦΙΟΜΑΧΟΣ, Φ being read as Ψ and Μ as ΛΛ. — **87.** l. occuluit. — **88.** Cf. **91.** — **89.** l. HODOEPORICON; cf. Vita Persii, et ὁδοιπορικῶν librum unum. — **94.** l. tabani. — **95.** l. ministerium. — **96.** Cf. Festus, 242, b. 26, *Antiqui autem offam vocabant abscisum globi forma, ut manu glomeratam pultem;* l. rotunda. — **97.** Cf. Hild. O 93, and Beck, p. 64, *inficit* qui colorem mutat quasi qui lanam tingit, *officit* qui *nocet.* But cf. Plac. 73, 3, *offuciarum, dictum ab offucando quod est 'furtim colorare.'* Hence perhaps there is some confusion with a gloss, *offucat: colorat, tinguit.* — **100.** l. olitores. — **103.** l. oblimat; cf. **24.** — **104.** l. cycni; cf. **106.** — **105.** OLITANA formed from *olim.* — **109.** l. holographum. — **110.** l. homilia. — **111.** Formed like magnopere; see above, p. 134. — **112.** l. omina; cf. **117.** — **114.** l. homousion. — **115.** l. homoeusion; cf. Isid. Or. VII. 2, 14, *Omousios* Patri *ab unitate substantiae* appellatur. *Substantia* enim vel essentia Graece οὐσία dicitur ὅμως unum. Utrumque ergo coniunctum sonat *una substantia,* and 16, *Omoeusios similis substantiae,* etc.; l. substantiae. — **116.** Cf. De Vit, and Hild. O 108. — **117.** Cf. Mai. VII. 571, *omentrum: auguria maiora.* — **119.** l. onustum: gravosum; cf. **124,** and Loewe G. N. 166. — **120.** l. onyx. — **121.** l. Onesiphorus: lucrum ferens; cf. Hild. O 113. — **121.** l. onocrotalus ... faciem gerit ... facies ... crotalus = κροταλος. — **123.** l. onycinum. — **127.** l. operae pretium. — **128.** l. opperiens; *p* has been added above the line by second hand (Kaegi). — **129.** l. oppidum .. muris. — **131.** See above, p. 130, and Serv. Aen. IX. 605, ... alii *oppidum* dici *ab oppositione murorum;* vel quod hominibus locus esset oppletus; vel quod *opes illo munitionis gratia congestae sunt.* — **133.** l. velat. — **134.** l. factor. — **135.** l. opitulator: adiuvator. — **136.** l. oppido, ~ opportune. — **139.** Cf. Loewe G. N. 168. — **143.** l. arbitrium. — **148.** l. oppessulatum . clave. — **149.** l. opprobrium. — **151.** Cf. OPITULOR. — **153.** l. patre non vivo . . . mortem; cf. Prod. 396. — **154.** l. opiparum; cf. Paul. 188, 8, *Opiparum magnarum copiarum apparatum.* **156.** l. ophites. — **158.** l. opportunus. — **159.** l. dives. — **163.** l. orditur. — **166.** l. loquens. — **167.** l. orama (horama). — **168.** l. vestigia .. in strata. — **170.** l. coepta. — **174.** Confusion of ora : vultus and ora : finis, extrema (pars) vestis. — **176.** Cf. **169** and **174**; possibly = Gk. ὅροι; cf. Isid. Or. XIX. 24, 20, *Fimbriae vocatae sunt orae vesti-*

mentorum, hoc est fines; ex Graeco vocabulum trahunt, Graeci enim terminum ὅρον *vocant.*
— 177. l. mysteria. — 178. l. Ortygia: Delos; cf. Serv. Aen. III. 72. — 179. l. ortygo-
metrum (a), with confusion of gender (cf. 181), coturnix. — 180. Cf. Isid. Or. X. 195, *Or-
thodoxus vir, rectae gloriae.* — 181. l. horoscopus. — 182. Cf. Isid. Or. VI. 19, 23, *dicitur
Hebraice osanna, quod interpretatur salvifica,* etc.; l. salvum. — 188. orli for oris; cf.
191. — 193. l. oscines. — 194. l. si fiat; cf. Hild. O 172, and Loewe G. N. 168.

P.

1. l. paciscit. — 2. l. pagus: collegium; cf. De Vit and PAGUS. — 5. l. phalanx. —
6. l. coniventia. — 7. Neither *Pactorium* nor *Plantatorium* appear to be found outside of glosses. *Plantarium* is common. — 8. So Amplon; cf. De Vit; Mai. VI. 538,
paganicus, ut (vir?) *occultus;* also VII. 572, *paganicius.* — 9. ? Cf. 12. Perhaps for
paginat (Cf. Du Cange): dissertat or disserit; In XI. century French, Saint Alexis
42 a, we find desirret = desiderat, so that desiterat may be an instance of 'umgekehrte
Schreibung.' — 10. aliquo .'. . alienos. — 11. ? Cf. Hild. P 6, Pagi: memoriae sine
idolis. — 14. l. palaestra. — 16. In reality two glosses, paliurus: spina vel genus cardui
spinosi, and palathe: massa caricarum; cf. Serv. Ecl. V. 39, *Carduus; spinae genus.
Paliurus herba asperrima et spinosa* [*vel ut quidam volunt, spina alba*]; cf. Hild. P
11 and 15. — 18. — De Vit cites *Palanteum: murus fastigium,* Gloss MS.; Gloss. Isid.
p. 690, Vulc. *Palteum: murum vel fastigium* (so Epin. 19, A 18; Mai. VI. 558), and
Palteum; manu vel vestigium, Gloss Isid. p. 689. (Vulcan. al. *Pluteum*). The reading
Palanteum might point to *palatium* as the original of *paltium;* cf. Isid. Or. XV. 3, 5,
and Paul. 220, 5; but there is evidently a confusion of two glosses, palatum (in sense of
taste): fastidium, and possibly pluteum: murum as suggested by Graevius; but cf. PALA-
TIO and PALATUS = palis munitus. — 20. l. Pales . . . quam. — 21. l. in diversa; cf. De
Vit. — 22. Two glosses confused, Pallas: Minerva; and palla: amictus muliebris. — 23.
l. palmula. *navis* by mistake for *remi;* cf. Servius Aen. V. 163, *palmula extrema pars
remi in modum palmae protenta;* cf. Paul. 220, 9. — 25. l. palam. — 28. Cf. Epin. 19 A,
19, *pallentes: gaudentes,* and Hild. P 10, who reads *palantes* in sense of *tripudiantes,*
whence *gaudentes;* but this is very doubtful. — 30. l. paludamenta: ornamenta militum
unde hi qui in provinciam proficiscuntur paludati vocantur; cf. Paul. 252, 1, *paludati ar-
mati, ornati. Omnia enim militaria ornamenta paludamenta dicebant.* — 33. Cf.
Prod. 419; neither of these words occurs; cf. BUCCELLARIUS. — 34. l. parcus. — 35. l.
parasitus . . . iniuriam. — 36. Cf. Bod. *parbata cupidus;* other glosses have *parabata*
=παραβάτης; cf. Hild. P 61 n. — 39. l. paraclytum. — 42. Cf. PARIENTIA, for PAREN-
TIA; the verbs *pario* and *pareo* seem to have been confused so that a *pariendo* was probably written for a *parendo.* — 44. l. palpitat. — 46. l. paralipomenon: reliquum. — 48. l.
parabola. — 49. Cf. PARASCEUE. — 51. l. quaesita. — 54. l. pharmacopola . . venditor.
55. l. paganorum. — 56. ? Cf. PARTICUS; l. negotiator. — 57. l. Iunonem, ... Mi-
nervam . . . de malo. — 58. l. Parius: lapis candidus. — 60. l. parentes suos. — 61. l.
paroecia; cf. 65. As πάροικος = Lat. inquilinus, so παροικία = incolatus. — 63. l. glori-
am; cf. Hild. P 35. — 64. l. exigue. — 65. PAROCHIA is a common corruption for PAR-
OECIA; l. dei domus; cf. Eucher. Instruct. II. 15, Paroecia: adiacens domus, scilicet Dei;
Ball. *parrochia adiacens domus aut diocesis.* — 66. l. ludos. — 67. l. Pancra; cf. Prod.
339 f. — 69. l. retia; cf. PANTHER and PANTHERA. Varro L. L. V. 100, *A quo etiam
et rete quoddam panther et leaena.* — 70. l. pannucium; cf. Isid. Or. XIX. 22, 24, *Pan-
nucia nuncupata quod sit diversis pannis obsita.* — 72. l. pandectes. — 74. l. incubus.
— 75. l. poeniceum. — 76. l. panegyrici: adulatores. — 77. Cf. Prod. 388, l. Pansa: qui
pedibus in diversa tendentibus ambulat. — 78. l. pastophorium. — 83. l. phiala. — 85. l.
pathologia. — 88. Cf. Bod. *patago,* and Paul. 221, 3, *Patagus morbi genus,* and Plautus,
cited by Macrob. Sat. V. 19, *mecum habet patagus morbus aes;* see also De Vit. — 90.
l. patruelis. — 92. l. Paulus; cf. Isid. Or. VII. 9, 8, *Paulus, quod interpretatur mirabilis
sive electus.* — 94. l. placido. — 97. l. Plastographis. — 98. Cf. Prod. 387. — 100. l. placat. — 102. l. peculium. — 103. l. plantaria: horti. — 106. Cf. Hild. P 244, *Placenta,*

dulcia vel dilicias. — **108**. l. plebicola. — **111**. l. plebem scitat : plebem adloquitur ; cf. Prod. 353. — **112**. l. Pleiades. — **114**. l. plerumque (with Bod.) aliquotiens. — **115**. l. plebeii . . hominis. — **118**. l. fallacia. — **122**. l. privilegium . . debetur . . . publica. — **123**. Something is omitted after *deus ;* cf. Velleius II. 57, cum plurima *praesagia* . . . . *Dei* immortales futuri *obtulissent* periculi ; Bod. *praesagium* : *praescium* divinum vel divinatio raticinatio vel signum quod *ante dicitur* et *post venit.* — **125**. l. privignus ; cf. De Vit under *Prevignus.* — **126**. l. praetereo. — **129**. l. praelibavimus . . contulimus. — **130**. l. antecedit. — **135**. l. praepropere . . festinanter. — **136**. l. praestitutum. — **138**. l. praepes : praecursor, velox. — **144**. l. praelibando. — **145**. l. transnavigo. — **146**. l. praecessant (not given in Lexx.) saepe, which is not elsewhere found in the glossary ; but cf. Bod. *praessant premunt exprimunt.* — **150**. l. privignus ; cf. **125**. — **151**. l. praelocutio. — **154**. l. cunctis praepositus. — **155**. l. praediti. — **159**. l. praevius ; cf. Bod. *praevius ducator antecedens precurrens, precedens.* — **160**. l. praes : fideiussor. — **162**. l. praeproperum . . faciendum. — **163**. l. prelum. — **165**. l. praematurus. — **167**. ? l. parvulus ; cf. Hild. M 162, *modicus praevalus,* hence *praelus. prælus* as here. — **168**. l. praeripit. — **173**. l. praepollét. — **174**. l. praecoqua. — **176**. l. praesidiarius. — **179**. l. praetextatus. — **183**. l. pectit. — **185**. l. peculator . . pecuniam publicam. — **186**. *pecuarius* in this sense is well known, l. Pecudarius with Ambr. B 31 ; cf. Loewe G. N. 168. **188** and **189** l. paedor and paedora ; cf. Loewe G. N. 156. — **190**. l. eruditor. — **192**. l. fraudem. — **193**. l. paelex, or perhaps PALLACA. — **195**. l. promuntorium. — **196**. l. perversa loquens. — **197**. Cf. Amplon. 365, 428, *Pesago, homo iacularis ;* Hild P 107 n. gives *pesago h. iacularis,* and *pegano : homo iacularis.* From this latter emend παίγνιος = *pegnios* = *peginos.* — **198**. l. pecoratus : abundans ; cf. Loewe G. N. 168. — **199**. l. peierat ; cf. Loewe G. N. 225. — **200**. pelagu is perhaps for pelagia, but the interpretation is like Isid. Or. XIX. 1, 24, *Pontonium navigium fluminale tardum et grave,* and 27, *Trabariae amnicae naves quae ex singulis trabibus cavantur, quae alio nomine litorariae dicuntur.* — **201**. l. pecora. — **202**. Cf. Hild. P 103, and Loewe G. N. 156, who compares Lucan II. 72 sq. *Mox vincula ferri exedere senem longusque in carcere paedor,* and thinks *pedatum carcerem* belong together, the interpretation having been lost. — **203**. ? Cf. Mai. VI. 537, and VII. 572, *Paeditatus : propagatio filiorum ac nepotum ;* perhaps Greek, cf. παιδοτόκος, παιδοτοκία ; Bod. *peditatus numerus peditum vel propagatio filiorum aut nepotum.* — **204**. l. paedore : foetore. — **205**. l. pellicit. — **206**. l. pellacem . . mendacem. — **207**. pellector, only found in glosses. — **208**. l. paelex . . quae ; cf. Hild. P 110, and Paul. 222, 3, *Pellices nunc quidem appellantur alienis succumbentes non solum feminae sed etiam mares. Antiqui proprie eam pellicem nominabant quae uxorem habenti nubebat.* — **209**. ? perlusit. — **210**. l. pelta . . Amazonizum. — **211**. l. promptuarium. — **212**. l. penates. — **213**. l. pendulus : elevatus. — **215**. l. paenula. — **216**. l. faveo. — **220**. l. pendere. — **221**. l. inrumpit. — **222**. l. paene. — **223**. l. peritomen. — **224**. l. poeniceo. — **225**. l. paene. — **226**. l. pretii persolutio. — **227**. l. pinace or pinax ; cf. Hild. P 115. — **228**. l. impulit. — **230**. l. melo. — **232**. l. Minervae. — **233**. l. melones. — **235**. l. praepetes. — **237**. l. permulcet. — **239**. l. peribolum ; the latter part of this gloss is obscure, and probably due to some confusion ; cf. Hild. P 164. — **240**. percenset. — **241**. l. perculit . . adegit. — **243**. l. timidus. — **244**. l. perquirit. — **250**. l. perlabitur ; cf. Verg. Aen. I. 147. — **251**. Cf. Hild. P 172-174. — **252**. Perhaps for pervulgatum ; Ball. *permulgatus.* — **254**. Cf. Lagarde Onom. Sacra p. 70, *Petrus agnoscens sive dissolvens.* — **256**. l. peragit. — **257**. l. PERPESSICIUS. — **258**. l. perpes : perpetuus ; so Bod. — **260**. l. perpendit : perpensat. — **263**. l. pos cras. — **268**. l. perculit, . . prostravit, with Bod. ; cf. **241**. — **270**. Cf. other similar glosses in De Vit. Pergenuare is not given by Lexx. — **271**. persum = pessum. — **272**. l. perimit. — **273**. l. personavit, publicatus. — **277**. l. PERIPSEMA. — **278**. perduellis seems to be glossed as if abl. pl. from perduellus. Cf. Hild. P 152, *Perduelles : hostes.* — **279**. Cf. Verg. Aen. VI. 435. — **286**. l. periculum. — **287**. l. per ironiam : per inrisionem. — **291**. l. periscelides. — **292**. l. percellit. — **293**. l. perspicacem : vigilantiorem ; so Bod. — **295**. ? l. pervium ; cf. Hild. P 205, *pervium, quod pertransitus, id est planum.* — **296**. l. purgamentum. — **299**. l. pervigilans. — **300**. l. pertaesum : taediosum permolestum. — **303**. l. tegmina accubitus ; cf. Prod. 347. — **304**. l. pessuma = pessumdata, Hild. P 213, Amplon. 367, 96 and 364, 412, *pe-*

suma; confracta, decrepita. — 305. l. perplexum. — 306. l. persentiscat: ex toto. — 307. l. perplexa: perplicata (?); cf. Lucr. II. 394, but see Bod. Perplexus: perligatus involutus impeditus, Hild. P 186, *perplexa, perligata,* who cites Paul. 231, 8, *plexa colligata unde perplexa,* by which analogy *perligata* may be defended. — 309. l. perperam. — 310. Cf. Plac. 74, 8, persollas: personas, and Prod. 261 (Plaut. Curc. 192). — 312. l. pessulum: clustellum (not given in Lexx.). — 315. l. aurea . . tenuissima. — 320. l. battuunt, confirmant. — 321. ? — 322. l. pipat: conviciatur, quiritat ut passer, with Loewe G. N. 219, who gives *viciatus,* as reading of San Gallensis, but Kaegi reads vicitatus. — 323. l. phlegma. — 325. l. peniculum: spongia. — 326. l. pyxides. — 328. Cf. Isid. Or. VII. 9, 16, *Philippus os lampadarum, vel os manuum.* — 329. l. pirata. — 331. l. placationes. — 332. l. hasta Romana. — 333. l. PILARIUM. — 334. l. fastigium. — 335. l. adhuc . . . ardet. — 336. l. bestiae marinae. — 337. l. peccato. — 338. l. PICTI . . et qui tegunt se corio crudo. — 339. l. dantur. — 341. l. primulum? or primipilum? cf. Bod. primolus: primorum princeps. — 344. cf. PRIMORIS. — 347. l. pridie. — 348. l. pospridie: hodie. — 349. So Hild. P 381, but not found in use. — 350. l. privilegium. — 353. l. primigenus; cf. Lucr. II. 1106. — 356. l. caballarius . . . virgis; cf. De Vit. — 357. l. herbae . . . lavantur = Gr. πόα. — 359. l. PODERES. — 360. l. pullulat. — 364. l. pollet: crescit. — 366. Cf. De Vit and Mai. VI. 540, *Politen; ubi cadavera ponuntur: Graecum est,* where Mai. notes, "Isid. *polingon.* Dic autem *polyandrion."* Very likely, however, there is some connection with *pollinctus,* see 363. — 368. l. penates. — 370. l. concava. — 377. l. postulaticius; cf. Hild. P 303, and ROGATARIUS. — 378. l. carminis. — 381. l. PTOCHOTROPHEUM. — 382. l. ponit. — 389. l. podex . . . id est anum vel culum. face-denica = φαγεδαινικός, which in some inexplicable way has crept into this gloss. — 394. l. captivitatem . . . iura quae amiserat; cf. Hild. P 277, and Varro L. L. V. 143, *pomerium locus iuxta muros.* — 399. Confusion of two glosses, *potior: fruor;* and *potior: potentior.* — 402. l. bibitor. — 404. l. probe. — 409. l. probata. — 411. for other similar glosses see Prod. 397. — 413. prolongum is perhaps to be retained; cf. PROLONGUS, or it may stand for *praelongum* or *perlongum.* — 415. Cf. Prod. 395. — 419. l. subiti. — 420. l. primates, nobiles. — 421. l. proclina. — 422. ? — 424. l. mali pronuntia for praenuntia. — 427. l. polluta. — 429. l. profatur. — 435. l. prolepsis . . . postea; cf. Pompeii Commentum; Keil V. 301, *prolempsis est praeoccupatio: sic potest latine dici, prolempsis est praeoccupatio rei futurae, pleraque quae postea fiunt sic dicimus nos, quasi antea facta sint.* — 438. l. publicatum. — 439. l. procacia . . . audacia. — 440. l. dubio. — 441. l. differt. — 442. l. prodigus and prodigit: devorat, or perhaps devorator. — 446. Cf. Mai. VII. 574, *profani: alieni a sacrificiis,* the latter part of this gloss may therefore be a corruption of *profani: alieni a fano;* cf. Isid. Or. X. 224, *profanus quasi porro a fano,* but a simpler emendation is *alieno sono.* — 454. l. restituere. — 458. l. paranympha: cf. Isid. Or. IX. 7, 8. — 462. l. propinquius. — 464. l. promatertera. — 465. Cf. 468, *inclinus* seems to be a collateral form of *inclinis.* — 466. Perhaps for *propiorem,* but see 478. — 467. l. propalam. — 470. Cf: PRONEFAS and Hild. P 465. — 472. l. proaviae. — 473. l. pro re. — 474. l. festinat. — 476. Prorigo is not found in Lexx. Possibly a corruption of *praerogatur: ante erogatur.* — 480. l. prora. — 482. l. prospectans. — 482. l. prosequitur. — 486. l. iram. — 488. l. protelat. — 490. l. provehor. — 491. l. prostituunt. — 492. l. prunas. — 493. l. proselytus. — 497. l. protoplastum. — 498. l. superbus. — 502. l. occidatur. — 503. l. poplites . . . suffragines. — 504. l. puberat . . . incrementat; cf. Hild. P 549. — 505. l. iuvenes. — 508. l. genae barbam emittentes. — 510. l. pubescit. — 513. Cf. PUGILLAR. — 514. l. pugnum. — 515. l. ubi statuae stant. — 516. l. pullulat . . . oritur. — 517. l. nascitur. — 518. l. partu puerum. — 525. Cf. 517 and 518.

Q.

4. Nothing more can be read in MS. l. confractum; cf. Vulg. Matth. 12, 20, *Arundinem quassatam non confringet.* — 6. Cf. QUANTOCIUS, and Hild. Q 14. — 7. l. quantulum. — 6. l. quadrifidum: quadrifarie. — 12. l. querela. — 14. l. acquisitio. — 15. l. quaestio. — 16. l. questus. — 17. l. ad rem quaerendam. — 18. l. querulus . . accusator. — 19. l. potuerint. — 20. l. quae quaestu corporis; cf. De Vit. According to Kaegi there

is a slight rasura in MS. between *co* and *corporis.* — **22.** l. quempiam. — **24.** l. possum. — **26.** l. quempiam. — **27.** Cf. Mai. VI. 542, *Queror: iniurias vindico* (? *indico*) *vel querellam depono.* — **28.** l. pecuniam publicam praerogat. — **29.** l. queunt. — **30.** Confusion of two glosses, quivi: potui and quievi: consensi. — **33.** l. etiam. — **36.** l. quietem. — **37.** Cf. Mai. VI. 543, *Quis quantus: quam magnus.* — **38.** l. quin etiam: si etiam magis ac magis. — **39.** l. struit. — **43.** = quid ni in **41,** or perhaps for quippini; l. firmandi. — **48.** l. quaesitor. — **55.** l. potestate. — **59.** l. denuo. — **65.** l. quomodo.

R.

4. Cf. RHAMNUS; l. herbae spinosae. — **5.** l. botryonem. — **8.** Cf. Prod. 346 and G. N. 142 for forms *randum, rabamini rabar.* — **12.** l. rabulam; cf. Paul. 272, 9, *Rabula dicitur in multis intentus negotiis paratusque ad radendum quid auferendumque vel quia est in negotiis agendis acrior quasi rabiosus,* and Nonius 60, 12, where *rabulam* is quoted from Cic. Orator 15. —**14.** l. invidia dolor; cf. Bod. *rancor invidia dolor vel odium.* — **15.** Cf. Isid. Or. VII. 5, 13, *Raphael* interpretatur *curatio vel medicina Dei.* Ubicunque enim curandi et medendi opus necessarium est; hic *angelus a Deo* mittitur inde et *medicina Dei* vocatur. — **18.** ramen, collateral form of ramentum; cf. Loewe G. N. 169; l. specie. — **19** l. rapidus . . celer; the form *randus* is perhaps due to some confusion with 8; cf. Amplon. 372, 105, *raidum: arbitrandum.* — **21.** l. Romulo. — **22.** = ῥακά, Matthew V. 22. — **24.** For clausa, cf. Isid. Or. IV. 7, 14, *Raucedo* amputatio vocis. Haec et arteriasis vocatur, eo quod *raucam* vocem *et clausam* reddat ab arteriarum iniuria; see Festus 282, Paulus 283. — **25.** l. rebitere; cf. Loewe G. N. 199. — **27.** l. redimitus. — **29.** l. redimicula. — **30.** l. a vetustate. — **32.** l. redhibet. — **36.** l. redhibitionem. — **41.** Cf. REDUX. — **43.** l. aperit; cf. Serv. Aen. I. 358, Recludit; seclusos aperit, ostendit. — **44.** l. recenset . . recognoscit. — **45.** l. adcumbit. — **47.** l. rica: mitrae genus; but the spelling *reica* may be etymological; cf. Varro L. L. V. 132, *ab reiciendo ricinium dictum.* Cf. Nonius 629, 17, *Rica, est quod nos sudarium dicimus,* and Festus 289 b, 19, *Rica est vestimentum quadratum fimbriatum pur-pureum, quo Flaminicae pro palliolo mitrave utebantur,* etc. Paulus has not preserved *mitra* in the Epitome. In Varro L. L. V. 130, *mitra* is discussed immediately after *rica.* — **49.** l. repletum. — **50.** l. refertus. — **51.** l. referserunt. — **52.** Cf. REFOCILLO. — **63.** l. gubernatio; cf. Festus 278 b, 3, *Regimen pro regimento usurpant poetae;* Ennius, L. XVI. 'Primus senex bradyn † (*ratus,* Bergk) in *regimen* bellique peritus.' — **73.** Cf. above, p. 130. — **76.** Cf. Loewe G. N. 169; l. remulcant (preserved in Sp. remolcar), used by Sisenna, quoted by Nonius, 57, 20, where Quicherat wrongly reads *remulco trahere.* See Paul. 279, 1, *Remulco est, quum scaphae remis navis magna trahitur.* l. scapha navem ducunt. — **77.** l. resplendet. — **78.** l. remex: *remigator, formed regularly from *remigo;* cf. Loewe G. N. 169. — **80.** l. renitentibus. — **81.** renidet; the explanation *redolet* is perhaps due to some association with *nidor;* cf. Hild. R 96. — **82.** l. arbitrabare. — **84.** l. arbitrabamini. — **87.** l. redit ad sua(m patriam). — **88.** l. repedat; cf. Prod. 335. — **91.** l. repagula: receptacula. — **92.** l. repperit. — **94.** l. subitaneus, due to confusion of two glosses; cf. 89, and Bod. *repens subito trahens enatans vel serpens.* — **96.** l. otiosi; cf. Serv. Aen. I. 722. — **97.** Cf. **88.** — **100.** l. otiosus. — **102.** l. integrum. — **103.** l. resciscere: cognoscere. — **105.** l. resiliunt; cf. **108.** Compare RESULTATOR, one who resists or denies, and Plac. 78, 25, *Resultatio* id est *reluctatio,* quae renititur et contra tendit, etc. — **113.** Cf. Hild. R 95, *Rendis, requies ociosa.* Hild. proposes to read *residia: requies* or *reses: quies, otiosa,* taking *quies* as an adj. See also Amplon. 371, 80, *resides, requiescendo otiosus.* — **114.** Cf. Hild. R 124, *Rescit, scit, comperit, cognoscit;* l. rescit: discit. *condisire* perhaps belongs to a gloss *rescire: condiscere.* — **116.** l. resipiscit, but the form *reticescit* had doubtless some other gloss. Cf. *Conticescit: reticescit,* Not. Tir. p. 90, and Georges under *reticesco.* — **120.** l. recubans. — **121.** l. replicat. — **123.** l. repercutit. — **125.** l. RHEUMA. — **129.** l. pos tergum. — **130.** Cf. **97.** — **133.** l. repedo; cf. **130.** — **135.** l. revecta. — **138.** l. rigebant; cf. Verg. Aen. V. 405. — **139.** l. rimae. — **140.** Cf. Nonius 165, 4, *Ringitur, irascitur.* Terentius in Phormione [II. 2, 27]. — **142.** Cf. RIMO and SCRUTO. — **143.** Cf. Nonius 32, 21, *Rivales dicti sunt quasi in unum amorem derivantes.* Teren-

tius in Eunucho [II. 3, 62]. 1. ad unum rivum currentes. — **146.** 1. riget: friget; cf.
Verg. Aen. IV. 251, where Servius, *Riget*, aut *frigida est, aut recta est* unde et *rigorem*
dicimus, *directionem.* Inde est (Georg. III. 363) vestesque *rigescunt*, et (Aen. VII. 447)
Diriguere oculi. — **147.** ? Cf. previous note. — **148.** 1. iuncturis tabularum. — **151.** 1. rhi-
noceron. — **154.** 1. rubus. — **157.** ? 1. robigo . . gelum; aerugo; see **172.** — **158.** 1. pyram.
161. = ῥώμη, etymological explanation of Roma; cf. Paul. 267, 5, *Romulus et Remus*
·*a virtute, hoc est robore appellati sunt.* — **163.** 1. Romulidae; cf. Serv. Aen. VI. 21. —
164. 1. rostrum pecorum est; os hominum = Differentia. — **166.** 1. rosea; cf. Serv. Aen.
II. 593, *roseo; pulchro. Perpetuum epitheton Veneris.* — **168.** Perhaps for *rorarius* (notice
that *roscidum* precedes); cf. Paul. 264, 8, *Rorarios* milites vocabant qui levi armatura
primi proelium committebant; Nonius 552, 31, who cites two examples of the sing.
from Lucilius. But there is some confusion with *runa;* cf. Paul. 263, 1, *Runa genus*
teli significat; Ennius, "*Runata* recedit," id est *pilata.* Why not, therefore, *Runa-*
nus = *pilanus?* Cf. **178** and Papias, *Runa: pugna.* Ugut. *Runa stipula vel pugna;*
unde runatus praeliatus. — **169.** 1. flavo, or rubro may = rubrum. — **172.** Cf. **157.**
MS. has gelum ū; 1. aerugo. — **178.** 1. alii pugna. Confusion with *runa;* see **168.** —
181. Cf. Serv. Aen. VII. 16, *ruditus* autem proprie est *clamor asinorum*, sicut grunnitus
porcorum. — **182.** 1. RUMIGERULUS: portitor rumoris. — **183.** 1. RHOMPHAEA. — **186.**
For *rupra* read *rupia*, the pure Lat. form of rhomphaea, **183**; cf. Amplon. 373, 71,
Rupia ex utraque parte acuta; so Isid. Or. XVIII. 6, 3. — **188.** 1. denuo. — **189.** The
Lexx. cite only Ov. Met. VII. 765, for rurigena. — **190.** 1. pagus. — **192.** *vi et fama* is
a corruption of βοήθημα used as in late Greek for medicine. Compare V **151**, *vuetema:*
adiutoria. rustu is for *rustum*, and goes back to Verrius Flaccus; cf. Fest. 265 a, 34,
Rustum ex (? sentex) rubus. De Vit cites Gloss. Med. MS. *Rusti* et *sentix* idem nasci-
tur ubique in campis et sepibus secundum librum antiquum *de simplici medicina.* Mai.
VII. 578, *Rusti:* arbores duri singulari numero. Mai. VI. 543, *Rusticum lignum:* fo-
liis spinosum. For the close connection of *rubus* and *sentix* cf. Isid. Or. XVII. 7, 59,
Rhamnus genus est *rubi*, quam vulgo *senticem* ursinam appellant. — **193.** inculti is
added by the same hand as **200.** — **195** and **196.** The same gloss repeated. De Vit cites
Gloss. Gr. Lat. Πτῶσις ἐπὶ οἰκοδομῆς: *ruina rues*, Gloss. Isid. *rues, ruina*, and compares
lues. — **197.** ? So Ball. Festus 262 b, 31, has a long and very corrupt note on *Ruscum*,
in the course of which he says, *Non dissimile iunco.* Cf. Mai. VIII. 509, *Ruscus: spina*
longa, and De Vit under *ruscidum.* — **198.** 1. fulget.

S.

3. 1. cupiditas; cf. Serv. Aen. III. 57, *Sacra, execrabilis.* — **5.** 1. saviat = suaviat.
Nonius 474, 10 and 12, gives two examples of active forms. — **8.** 1. lutosa; cf. Hild. S 17.
— **6.** Cf. SALPICTA, SALPINCTA. — **11.** 1. sagax . . ad; cf. Prod. 94, *satax* (= sagax):
sapiens, investigator. — **12.** 1. saccella; cf. Paul. 319, 4, *Sacella* dicunt loca diis sacrata
sine tecto. — **14.** 1. quo vacuae naves stabiliuntur; cf. Hild. S 2, and Scholia Bernensia ad.
Verg. Georg. IV. 195, *Saburram, harenam Saburra* dicitur qua naves onerantur ad
aequum opus, etc. — **15.** 1. urbanitas. — **17.** *salvus* is probably the word erased. — **19.**
Mai. VI. 544, has *locus cultosa*, which Hild. S 17 n. emends to *lutosa;* cf. **8.** Bod. has
lutosa. — **20.** 1. incultus. — **23.** Cf. SAMBUCISTRIA; cf. Mai. VI. 544, *Sambucistri;*
quae canunt cithara rustica. — **24.** 1. saltator; cf. Hild. S 27, *Sambucus, histrio, saltator.*
— **25.** 1. SAMBUCAE; cf. Paul. 324, 7. — **28.** 1. cultum. — **29.** 1. diiudicavit. — **31.** Cf.
Paul. 324, 6, 1. auripigmentum, mundus in sense of cosmetic; cf. Isid. Or. XIX. 17, 12,
Arsenicum quod Latini ob colorem *auripigmentum* vocant colligitur in Ponto ex auraria
materia ubi etiam *Sandaracha*, etc. — **34.** ? Cf. Amplon. 379, 353, *Sabapapa: unum*
quasi dulco acidum; and 379, 14, *Sabapappa, vinum quasi dulciatum;* Mai. VI. 544,
Sappapapa acidum vinum (Mai. emends *vappa*). Probably a vulgar compound of sapa +
vappa. — **35.** Cf. Gloss. Isid. *Sarga; non idoneus cuiuslibet artis professor* and several
similar glosses cited by De Vit, 1. cuiuslibet artis. Du Cange cites from Hincmarus Lau-
dun. Episc. tom. 2, p. 336, Nec recognosco me alicui parentum meorum velut *Sargae de-*

disse beneficium; compare also ARGA in Du Cange. — **36.** Cf. above, p. 130. — **37.** l. lingua Persa bracae; cf. Amplon. 378, 345, *Sarabara; braccae lingua Persarum.* — **38.** l. coniunctum; for *sarctum* see Neue Formenlehre II. 564. — **44.** l. praefecti. — **45.** l. sorices; cf. Prod. 344, f; *saures* may have been an old plural like *senes* from *senex.* — **46.** l. satellitum turma. — **50.** Cf. Isid. Or. XVI. 26, 11, *Satum . . . . unum et dimidi. um modium capiens.* Cuius nomen ex Hebraeo sermone tractum est. — **51.** Two glosses united, l. latronum; cf. Serv. Aen. XII. 7, *latrones,* quasi *laterones,* quod circa latera re. gum sunt, quos nunc *satellites* vocant; Isid. Or. X. 255, *Satelles,* quod adhaereat alteri, sive a *lateris* custodia. — **55.** Isid. Or. VIII. 4, 4, *Saducaei interpretantur iusti.* —**56.** l. virtutum; so Isid. Or. VII. 1, 7. — **57.** l. tentatio vel saturitas; cf. Isid. Or. VII. 9, 7, *Saulus* Hebraeo sermone *tentatio* dicitur eo quod prius in tentatione ecclesiae sit conversus. Persecutor enim erat, et ideo nomen habebat istud quando persequebatur Christianos. Lagarde Onom. Sacra. 71, Saulus tentatio respicientis vel saturitas. — **58.** l. Samaritae; cf. Isid. Or. VIII. 4, 9. — **59.** ? aperit, perhaps for arrepit, or is there some confusion with a gloss *scindit: aperit?* — **60.** l. scatit; so Lucr. VI. 891, or scatet. — **64.** l. SCA-PUM; so Mai. VI. 544, *Scapus: summitas aut cacumen.* — **67.** l. cisternae; cf. Mai. VII. 578, *scatae: bullitiones.* Serv. Georg. I. 110, has *Scatebris; ebullitionibus,* etc. — **68.** l. Iscariotes . . . . nomine appellatus est a Iuda vico; cf. Largarde Onom. Sacra p. 62, *Iscarioth memoriale domini.* — **69.** Cf. Prod. 389. Bod. *Scaurus cui cales retrorsum habundantius eminent pede introrsus incurvum.* — **71.** l. si quominus. — **73.** l. scapha. — **74.** Cf. STATER. — **75.** l. moles id est congeries. — **77.** l. suffocat. — **79.** Cf. STRAGULO (De Vit), and Isid. Or. XIX. 26, 1, *Stragulum* est vestis *discolor,* quod manu artificis diversa *varietate* distinguitur. *Stragula vestis,* Hor. Sat. II. 3, 118, was probably glossed as *varia vestis;* but Mai. VI. 546, and VII. 581, has *strangulat: variat.* — **88.** Cf. Paul. 292, 5, *Socordiam* quidam pro ignavia posuerunt; Cato pro *stultitia* posuit. Compositum autem videtur ex *se* quod est *sine* et corde. See Loewe G. N. 169. — **91.** l. frequens assiduus. — **93.** Originally two separate glosses, secus : aliter, and secus : prope, i. e. in its use as prep. — **97.** Cf. Isid. Or. XVI. 25, 18, *Sicel,* qui Latino sermone *siclus* corrupte appellatur, Hebraeum nomen est habens apud eos *unciae pondus,* etc. — **99.** l. seditio. — **100.** l. serrae cadunt or cadant (often after *quod* in such definitions the subj. is found). **103.** l. secernit. — **105.** l. semiviro. — **106.** Cf. Verg. Aen. VI. 462. — **107.** ? Cf. De Vit and Hild. S 137, *Sentens: sentia firma vel indubitata responsio;* with note. Isidorus has the same gloss, adding ἐπιφώνημα perhaps for Ἀποφώνημα, as Julius Rufinianus § 19, Ἀποφώνημα, *sententia responsiva,* — so that the whole gloss may have been taken from some rhetorical treatise. — **108.** l. saepsit. — **109.** l. serae. — **111.** Cf. SEMESTRIA. — **112.** l. adinventor. — **113.** l. poenam. — **114.** l. scaevus : sinister; cf. **116.** — **115.** l. schema. — **118.** l. scirpus; cf. CALAMAUCUS. — **121.** l. scammata . . . athletae. — **122.** l. SCENOPEGIA . . . . figuntur . . Septembri; cf. Amplon. 379, 24, *scenopegia: tabernaculorum fictio vel casa;* Isid. Or. XVIII. 43, *Scena* . . unde et apud Hebraeos *tabernaculorum dedicatio* a similitudine domiciliorum σκηνοπηγία appellabatur. — **127.** l. tarde. — **130.** Notice the use of medius for half; cf. **149** and **160.** — **132.** l. iudicum. — **133.** l. districtus. — **134.** l. Selenites, emend from Mai. VII. 579, *Sevenites lapis persicus cuius candor cum luna crescere atque deficere monstratur;* so here, l. crescere atque minuere; Isid. Or. XVI. 10, 7, has . . . *minui atque augeri. Nascitur in Persida.* — **135.** Septimontium is explained by Festus 340 and 348, to which our gloss, however, bears little resemblance; the latter part of the gloss must be kept distinct, quia (quae) super septem montes sedet. Perhaps *festus* should be read for *certus,* with Paulus. — **136.** Probably a corruption of *semispathium* (but perhaps of *semisicium* from *sica*); cf. Isid. Or. XVIII. 6, 5, *Semispatium gladius est a media spathae longitudine appellatum, non ut imprudens vulgus dicit sine spacio, dum sagitta velocior sit. Semigladium* seems not to occur elsewhere. — **145.** l. susceptor; cf. Hild. S 145. — **148.** Cf. SERTOR and Festus 340, 22 ff. — **150.** Cf. Verg. Aen. II. 269. — **152.** l. saevit: furit. — **155.** For *districtio* in the sense of *severitas,* see Kukula de tribus Pseudo-Acronianorum Scholiorum Recensionibus, p. 11; first so used by Cassianus (Coen. Inst. V. 38), who wrote between 425 and 450. — **157.** l. seminecem; cf. Verg. Aen. V. 275. — **158.** Cf. SESCUPLUS. — **160.** Cf. Verg. Aen. III. 578. — **165.** Cf. SPHAERA. — **166.** Cf. Reichenauer Glossen p. 12, 474, *Veru: spidus* *ferreus* and Gloss. Arab. Lat. *Verutus: qui habet spiltum;* but possibly *speltum* is a corruption of *spiclum;* see, however, Du Cange under *spedum.* — **170.** l. Sperchius. — **173.** l. STELLIONATUS . . venditur. — **175.** l. stemmata . . . . nobilitas. — **176** and **177.** Cf. Isid. Or. VII. 11, 4, *Stephanus,* qui sermone Hebraeo interpretatur *norma* quod prior fuerat in ministerio ad imitationem fidelium. . . . Idem autem ex Graeco sermone in Latinum vertitur *coronatus.* Lagarde Onom. Sacra p. 71, *Stephanum normam nostram vel* σκοπὸν *nostrum,* quo veru et iacula diriguntur. — **178.** l. symbola : collectio nummorum. — **179.** De Vit Lex. gives gloss. Lat. Gr. *Sicilum;* ξυρὸν σκυτέως (h. e. *novacula sutoris*), l. sutorum. — **181.** For sidus = tempestas, cf. Serv. Aen. XI. 259 and XII. 451. — **184.** l. a Sicano rege. — **185.** l. gladiator. — **187.** l. Sicanium. — **188.** l. stellae. — **189.** Cf. Verg. Aen. IV. 137. l. Tyria. — **191.** Cf. SICERA ; Isid. Or. XX. 3, 16, *Sicera* est omnis potio quae extra vinum inebriare potest; Amplon. 376, 209, *Sicera qui fit dactili sucu.* The MS. reading is somewhat doubtful, with several corrections by a second hand ; l. omnes conf(ectiones ?) liquoris quae vinum imitantur et inebriant, sed proprie est liquor ad bibendum suavis qui ex dactylis exprimitur. — **193.** l. segnities : tarditas, pigritia ; cf. **197** and **198.** — **200.** l. syllogismus. — **201.** l. folliculus leguminis. — **206.** So Mai. VI. 545; *tubus* = water-pipe, otherwise one might suppose connection with Festus 352, and Paul. 353, 7, *Tullios* alii dixerunt esse *silanos,* alii rivos, etc. — **214.** l. synodus : congregatio senum. — **215.** l. synonyma : plura nomina . . . . significant. — **217.** Mai. VI. 545, *singultus; suggultium;* but *subglutium* is supported by SUBGLUTIO and by *glutio.* Both forms may have existed in the vulgar pronunciation; cf. Mai. VI. 579, *singlutum; qui loquitur per singlutos* (= *singultus,* to which it is corrected by second hand). Loewe G. N. 169 accepts *subgluttus* as a new word, following Cas. 402², *singultum: subgluttum.* — **217.** Cf. SYMBOLUM in its ecclesiastical use. — **218.** l. sinus. — **219.** l. spiritum caloris vitae ; cf. Pliny XXVII. 41, *Alum quod nos vocamus,* Graeci *symphiton* petraeum . . . . utilissimum lateribus, . . . pectori, pulmonibus, sanguinem reicientibus, faucibus asperis. The meaning here given seems to be based on the Lat. *Halum* as if derived from *halo,* and differs from that of Pliny l. c. and Isid. Or. XVII. 9, 61. — **220.** l. dimitte. — **221.** l. synagoga, frequently written with an i in MSS. — **223.** l. syngraphum : cautio, suscriptio. — **225.** l. synaxin. — **228.** Cf. SIROMASTES. De Vit Lex. quotes *lanceis syromatis* as a variant in Reg. III. 18, 28. — **229.** l. aestiualis. — **233.** Cf. Isid. Or. XV. 1, 5, *Sion* quae Hebraice *speculatio* interpretatur ; cf. Lagarde Onom. Sacra p. 39, *Sion specula vel speculator sive scopulus.* — **235.** Cf. Lagarde Onom. Sacra p. 66, *Simon pone moerorem vel audi tristitiam;* p. 71, *Simonis obedientis sive ponentis tristiam aut audientis moerorem.* — **236.** l. scivit < scisco, sententiam dedit. — **239.** l. schisma. — **240.** l. Scyllae. — **241.** = σκνῖπες ; cf. CINIFES and Isid. Or. XII. 8, 14, *Cyniphes muscae minutissimae sunt, aculeis permolestae.* — **244.** Cf. SCENA, e. g. in *scena testimonii,* for σκήνη τοῦ μαρτυρίου, Exod. 27, 21, where the Vulgate has *tabernaculum.* — **247.** l. se ligant. — **248.** spicularius is not given by Lexx. — **250.** l. spiculum. — **252.** l. oluerunt ; cf. Verg. Aen. I. 404, where Servius explains by *exhaluerunt.* — **254.** l. Stygia. — **256.** Cf. STICA (Du Cange) and SPICA, and De Vit under *stigium* and *striga.* In Gr. στιχάριον is used for a variegated tunic (Eccl.). — **157.** Perhaps the latter part of the gloss is to be taken by itself = stilus : eloquium tractatoris ; for *de quo* instrumental see Rönsch 393, f. — **258.** l. stemma, stemmata. — **260.** Cf. Verg. Aen. IV. 136, and below, **274.** — **264.** *censum* is here used in sense of tribute. See De Vit Lex. IV. — **265.** l. propago. — **267.** Cf. Verg. Georg. III. 366, l. gelata ; cf. **280.** — **268.** l. stibio ; cf. Vulg. Reg. IV. 9, 30, *Iezabel . . depinxit oculos suos stibio.* — **269.** l. Styx. — **274.** See **260.** — **270.** l. stinc ; cf. Prod. 346. — **275.** l. stipes. — **277.** l. stipulatio. — **278.** l. stiva. — **279.** See above, p. 137. — **280.** ? As it is at the top of the opposite page to 267 it may be a corrupt continuation of the gloss on *stiria;* cf. Mai. VII. 581, *Stiria, spinae nomen est cujus fructus grana habet guttis similia. Ergo stiria stillicidium congelatum : et si naribus muci congeluerunt, stiria dicitur;* Ball. *stirina aqua in gelu conversa. longe* may be corrupt for *congelata.* — **282.** l. pater. — **285.** l. sobrinus ; cf. Digest. 38, 10, 3, *Patrui magnus filius ei de cuius cognatione quaeritur, propius sobrino vocatur.* — **291.** l. solitudo : EREMUS. — **296.** l. astutia. — **297.** l. sospes. — **302.** l. solennia, and perhaps solita, but see Isid. Or. VI. 18, 1, *Solennitas autem a sacris dicitur, ita suscepta*

ut mutari ob religionem non debeat *ab solito,* id est firmo atque *solido* nominata, etc. —
304. l. soloecismus. — 311. Cf. Prod. 147, and De Vit. *Sconna* seems to be formed by
assimilation from *sculna;* cf. Macrob. Sat. 2, 13, *Sponsione* contendit Antonius, dignus
sculna Munatio Planco, qui tam honesti certaminis arbiter electus est.— 319. l. spurca.—
321. Cf. HISTORIOGRAPHUS; so storię for historiae. — 322. Perhaps for stolidus: osus,
odiosus; cf. O 192; for this meaning compare Aul. Gellius XVIII, 4, 10, 'stolidos, autem vocari, non tam *stultos* et excordes, quam austeros et molestos et inlepidos, quos Graeci
'μοχθηροὺς καὶ φορτικοὺς' dicerent.' — 323. Cf. STROPHA, and Hild. S 309, l. fraus im-
postura; *praeversio* is perhaps for *perversio;* Papias cited by Hild. has *conversio.* — 325.
l. STROPHARIUS. — 328 and 331. Tertullian uses *subnixus* in sense of *subject to;* cf.
Hild. S 335, subnixus, submissus, humilis, where Hild. makes this note, L. *subnexus,*
quod magis voc. humilis respondet, sed *subnixus* quoque explicari possit *submissus ut*
Papias *subnixus, suppositus, suffultus;* and Mai. VI. 546, *subnixus, circumdatus vel*
humilis. — 332. *subtrectare* is not given by the Lexx., but the same gloss is found Mai.
VI. 547; cf. *subrogatus,* 376. — 341. Cf. Verg. Aen. XI. 268, Devicta Asia *subsedit* adulter,
where Servius, *quidam 'sub' pro 'post' accipiunt ut sit pro 'post possedit'* legitur et
devictam Asiam quod si est, ita intellegamus ut '*subsedit*' sit *dolo possedit.* l. *succeden-*
do. — 344. l. supparant . . . parant; cf. Du Cange under *Supparare* and *Supparatura.*
— 347. I have not found the comparative *subnixius* in use. — 351. l. subsicivis. — 353.
So Serv. Aen. III. 483, explains *subtemine* by *trama.* — 356. Cf. Plac. 83, 4, *Subnixus*
est instructus aliquo auxilio, item *subnixus, suffultus ex omni parte.* — 358. Probably for suffasciatus; cf. FASCIATUS, but there may be some confusion with SUFFARCINA-
TUS. — 359. l. subcenturiatus. — 360. Cf. Verg. Aen. III. 582, caelum *subtexere* fumo;
perhaps here glossed as if a perfect; *sublustru* is all that can be read in MS., perhaps for
sublustravere. De Vit cites *sublustro, as,* Atto. Polypt. p. 54, *Neque sublustrat;* cf. SUB-
LUSTRIS. — 362. l. libidinantes. — 363. l. dicione. — 364. ? l. subsicivus, but praesubdolus
or persubdolus is very doubtful; perhaps the *prae* is due to some corruption of *interpres;*
cf. Mai. VI. 546, *subcesiva: subsequentia, succedanea dolosa,* and Gloss Isid. *subcisi-*
vus: malus interpres. — 365. subrepsit = surripuit. The perfects of *surrepo* and *sur-*
ripio seem to have been confused. — 366. l. tulit. — 370. Cf. Amplon. 378, 283, *subequi-*
libra: sublibrato iudicio. aequilibra is not given by the Lexx. — 371. Cf. Verg. Aen.
II. 169. — 372. subtrecta = subtracta is perhaps in sense of *diminuta,* and so might be
glossed by *inclinata* in the sense of ' on the wane;' compare above, 332, subtrectatur. —
573. So Mai. VI. 546; but I do not understand humiliate; cf. Seneca Herc. Furens 392,
quin ipse torvum subrigens crista caput. subice or *subige caput* would make better
sense. — 376. l. substitutus. — 377. See above, p. 130, = stercus suillum. — 380. l.
suillas. — 382. l. consuere cosire. *cosire* is the later form; cf. Loewe G. N. 108. Treating of gloss *dissire: desuere,* he says, " *Sire* ist eine vulgäre Fortbildung von *suere,* die
wir noch in einem andern Compositum finden, das gleichfalls die Glossae '*abavus*' bieten.
cusire: consuere, und *consuere: cosire.* Letzteres ist dann im Italienischen zu *cucire*
geworden." — 386. Cf. Paul. 332, 4, *Scrupi dicuntur aspera saxa,* etc. — 387. l. scopu-
lum. — 388. Cf. Hild. S 89 n. and Loewe G. N. 169. No verb *Scrupulo* or noun *Scru-*
pulator is given in Lexx. De Vit cites, *Scripulor: sollicitor; Scripulatur: sollicitatur;*
scrupulator: sollicitator. Scrupulatus; curiosus et sollicitatus, etc.; so that the word
seems well attested. — 389. Cf. Hild. S 218. l. titiones, cf. Nonius 182, 18, *Titionem*
fustem ardentem, and TITIO. — 392. l. suffuso; doubtless refers to Verg. Aen. XI. 671,
where most modern editors read with Med. m. p. *suffosso;* Servius speaks of both readings. — 394. l. suffragium. — 396. Cf. Mai. VI. 547, *suffraginatus, praecisis cruribus;*
Loewe G. N. 170; Hild. S 365, *Suffraginatus, fractis cruribus vel substitus in locum*
decedentis, showing a confusion with a gloss like 397, where for *cum* accordingly read *in*
locum decedentis. — 398. l. sufficit; cf. Verg. Aen. II. 618, with Servius' note. — 400.
l. scrutinium. — 401. l. scurrula. — 404. l. sugillat: suffocat; cf. Plac. 80, 22, *Sugillare*
est gulam constringere, quomodo dicimus *strangulare.* — 405. l. suggerit. — 406. Cf.
404. — 407. l. sator or sertor; cf. 148. — 408. l. summo. — 413. l. superbiae. — 415.
Cf. SUPERARIA, and Loewe G. N. 170. — 417. Cf. SUMPTUARIUS. — 421. l. superstes.
— 423. l. occultari vel extremi; cf. Plac. 82, 11, *supremi et 'summi' significat et 'ultimi,'*

supprimi autem 'occultari.' — 424. l. supplet: suppeditat, subministrat. —425. Cf. Hild. E 226, *Exclusa, experdita vel subplosa.* —426. l. SUPPETO. De Vit Lex. under 6, says, Pro *clam* aut *alterius nomine* petere. —427. l. spurius ex matre nobili et patre infimo nascitur. —429. l. spurcitia : immunditia. —432. l. suavium ; cf. Servius Aen. I. 256, et sciendum *osculum* religionis esse, *savium* voluptatis, *quamvis quidam osculum filiis dari*, uxori basium, *scorto savium dicunt ;* and Beck p. 41, Inter *basium* et *osculum* et *savium ; basium pietatis, osculum amicitiae, savium luxuriae.* — 433. l. tibiae. —436. l. sursum tollit (or tulit). — 437. l. suspicit ; cf. Verg. Aen. I. 438, fastigia suspicit urbis, where Servius explains by *miratur.* — 438. The same gloss is given by Mai. VI. 547 and VI. 580. — 439. For *surso, suso* preserved in Italian ; see Loewe G. N. 217. — 442. l. sospes. —444. Cf. SUSURRO. *bilinguis* is here used in sense of deceptive. —448. l. caligarius. — 449.　Cf. Serv. Verg. Aen. IV. 624. — 450.　For sarsores cf. *Excerpta e Gloss. Vet.* Vulc. p. 556, *Sarsor* ῥάπτης. —454. l. strues ; cf. Festus 310, Paulus 311. — 455.　Cf. Festus l. c. *Struices : antiqui dicebant extructiones omnium rerum.* l. constructio, conpaginatio. —456. Cf. Serv. Aen. X. 678, *ubi arenosa sunt loca.* —457. l. Suovetaurilia . . . tribus.

T.

3. l. furunculus ; cf. above, p. 130. — 5. l. thalami, for cubiculus m. see Appel p. 85. — 6. De Vit gives *Tarrium quod corio tegitur in sella aut curru*, doubtless for *taurium*, of which this may be the plural ; cf. TAURINAE used for *caligae*. — 7. cf. Hild. T 25 and Festus 356 b, 17. — 10. = tanto ocius, see Terence Eun. 609 ; cf. Mai. VI. 547, *Tam tocius : tam citius.* — 11. l. talentum ; before XXII an L has dropped out ; cf. Mai. VI., *Talentum centum pondo, modo habens pondo CXX ;* Isid. Or. XVI. 25, 22, Apud Romanos enim *talentum* est LXXII librarum, sicut Plautus ostendit, qui ait *duo talenta esse CXLIV libras.* For various valuations placed on talentum see De Vit Lex. — 12. cf. Verg. Aen. X. 846, quoted by Priscian (Keil II. p. 101), under the examples of affirmative *ne*. — 12. cf. Verg. Aen. III. 29, where Servius explains *tabo* by *corrupto sanguine*. — 15. l. cuneus vel chors (= cohors). — 16. l. poenae ; cf. Hild. T 12. — 17. See above, p. 131. Servius, however, Aen. II. 140, has, quae *sterilis* autem est, *taurea* appellatur. — 18. Cf. TALITRUM and Hild. T 11, *Talatrus, colafus in talo. Talitius, talastrum, talastrus,* and *talatrus* are also found ; cf. Loewe G. N. 171. — 20. l. Tartarum. — 22. There appears to be some confusion with *tandem.* —23. Cf. Paul. 367, 2, *Trabica navis, quod sit trabibus confixa.* Pacuvius, "Labitur trabica in alveos," but what is *tuba?* Is there perhaps some confusion with a gloss *tibia = tuba?* cf. Isid. Or. XVIII, 4, 3, *Tubam* autem dictam quasi *tofam* id est *cavam.* Item *tubam,* quasi *tibiam.* — 24. l. transtris ; cf. Verg. Aen. V. 136 ; l. remiges. — 26. l. trapetes : molae. — 27. l. teli genus quod ; cf. Paul. 367, 16, *Tragula genus teli, dicta quod scuto infixa trahatur.* — 28. l. tran senna : tegula per quam lumen venit ; cf. Mai. VI. 549, *Transennam dicit tegulas per quas lumen admittitur,* Nonius 180, 15, *Transenna, non ut quidam putant, transitus, sed est fenestra.* — 29. l. tranquillus : placidus. — 30. l. trabea . . . senatoria purpurea. — 31. l. Thraces : sagittarii. — 33. l. tragoptisana. — 35. l. taedet : paenitet et taedium patitur. — 39. cf. *tollerunt : genuerunt,* Gloss. Isid. p. 696, Vulc. cited by De Vit., which seems to be another instance of the perf. *tolli ;* cf. D 108. — 40. l. coopertoria. — 41. l. taedae. —42. cf. TELONEUM.　The better form seems to be preserved in Mai. VI. 548, *Teloneum quasi omnium litorum fiscalis conductio.* — 44. l. TELETA, perhaps the abl. *teletis* occurred in passage glossed, and hence *tellitus.* — 49. cf. PRAESUMPTOR as used by Tertullian and Augustine. — 53. l. vehiculi. —54. l. papiliones. — 60. l. Terpsichore : musa quinta. — 62. l. theosebia. — 66. l. tereti, or perhaps teretes : trunci rotundi ; cf. Servius Aen. VI. 207, *Teretes truncos ; teres* est *rotundum* aliquid cum proceritate, and VIII. 633, *Tereti cervice, rotunda* cum longitudine ; cf. Hild. T 56. — 69. l. terit. — 70. l. fugere. — 71. l. terrigenae. — 73. l. Terminum quem deum putaverunt. — 75. ? cf. TERRICULA, Nonius 227, 26, Hild. T 64, and Mai. VIII. 593, *terrivola,* formidolosus tumidus, et dicitur *terrivola* quasi cum terrore *volans.* — 77. l. tereti gemma. — 79. l. incutit. — 81. l. THERISTRUM : MAVORTIUM quo. — 82. l. tripudiat. — 83. l. tris soles ; cf. Serv.

Aen. I. 745. — **85.** l. threnus: lamentatio. — **88.** cf. TESCA, TESQUA and Fest. 356, 22, Paul. 357, 4. — **89.** l. testatur. — **90.** l. tempestivum. — **92.** l. tesserarius. — **93.** l. tae-sus. — **96.** Cf. Serv. Aen. II. 16, nam ubi naves fiunt *textrinum* vocatur, and XI. 326, Graece ναυπήγια, Latine *textrina* dicuntur, quoting from Ennius. — **99.** On account of *rasurae* the reading of this gloss is very doubtful. It is probably the same gloss with Paul. 366, 11, *Tetini pro tenui.* — **101.** The MS. has Tyarus, not Tyrrus; read THIASUS . . . Liberi. — **102.** l. thiasum; cf. Mai. VII. 583, *Thyasus chorus sacra dicentium Liberi atris* (sic) *et gestamen sacrorum erat, ut vitibus uvae,* and *Thyasis: sacris,* Hild. T 74, cites Papias, *tyasi ·υ· chori, sacrae laudes virginum;* cf. **105.** — **103.** l. tiara: . . . pileum Phrygiorum. — **104.** l. Thetis. — **105.** Cf. note on **103.** — **106.** l. tibia; for sym-phonia in this sense see De Vit Lex. under § 3. — **109.** l. tiro. — **110.** l. Tybris: Tiberis a Tiberino rege; probably a corruption of Paul. 366, 2, *Tiberis fluvius dictus a Tiberino rege Albanorum . . . Tibris a Tibri rege Tuscorum;* cf. Varro, L. L. V. 29, 30, Servius Aen. III. 500, Isid. Or. XIII. 21, 27. — **111.** l. Tylos . . . arborum . numquam; cf. Pliny XII. 40, *Nulli arborum folia ibi decidunt,* etc. — **112.** l. tibicines; cf. Paul. 366, 3, *Tibicines in aedificiis dici existimantur a similitudine tibiis canentium, qui ut cantantes sustineant ita illi aedificiorum tecta; continens* is perhaps here used somewhat in sense of *sustinens.* — **113.** l. tirocinia. — **114.** Cf. TYPHE and TYPHUS, and Isid. XVII. 9, 101, *Typhus vero quae se ab aqua inflat. Unde etiam ambitiosorum et sibi placentium homi-num tumor typhus dicitur.* — **117.** l. Titania = Diana, so Serv. Aen. X. 216, *Phoebe, Luna* sicunt *sol Phoebus.* Item *Titan sol* et *Titanis Luna.* — **118.** l. Titanes: principes. — **120.** l. Tisiphone. — **124.** l. trierarchus. — **125.** So Serv. Georg. I. 153, says *tribuli, genus spinae.* — **127.** Abbreviated from a gloss like Hild. T 123, *Trinepus, pronepus pronepotis, id est sexta generatione superioris gradus.* — **128.** l. devictum. — **129.** l. tripodes. — **130.** l. ἄκρα habeat id est promunturia Pachynum, Pelorum Lilybaeum; cf. Isid. Or. XIV. 6, 32; Serv. Aen. I. 196. — **131** and **132.** Cf. Isid. Or. XIX. 1, 10, *Trieris navis magna, quam Graeci dulconem* (durconem Lindemann, durionem Cod. Zittaviensis) *vocant de qua in Esaia dicitur, Non transibit per eam trieris magna.* The passage referred to is Isaiah 33, 21, where the Vulgate reads: Non *transibit per eum* navis remi-gum, neque *trieris magna* transgredietur eum; and the Septuagint, ποταμοὶ καὶ διώρυχες πλατεῖς καὶ εὐρύχωροι· οὐ πορεύσῃ ταύτην τὴν ὁδὸν οὐδὲ πορεύσεται πλοῖον ἐλαῦνον. The read-ing *durconem* might have some connection with διώρυχες. Prof. Gildersleeve suggests that *dulcones* may stand for δίολκοι νῆες. I had thought of a possible connection with δόλιχος = kidney-bean, used like the Latin *phaselus.* — **135.** l. Trinacrii. — **136.** l. piscis; cf. Pliny N. H. 32, 144, *Tritones, Nereides, homines qui marini vocantur.* — **139.** l. Trio-num: portitores signorum. So Bootes, Stat. Theb. I. 662, is called *portitor Ursae;* cf. Gloss. Isid. Tiaries; portitores signorum; Vulcan. emends Triarii, but I think it should read *Triones.* — **140.** l. erogati, or tripertit: erogat. — **141.** Cf. Verg. Aen. VI. 417. — **142.** l. tribules. — **143.** l. triarii: tertio abbreviated from some fuller gloss like *qui in tertio loco in exercitu deponebantur;* cf. Varro L. L. V. 89, *Pilani triarii* quoque dicti *quod in acie tertio ordine* extremis subsidio deponebantur. — **146.** l. tomen. — **147** and **149.** Cf. THOLUS; l. rotundum quod and fastigium. — **150.** l. torvus. — **151.** Hild. T 71, proposed to change to *choragium: ornatus mimicus = scenicus;* as Festus 52, 10, *choragium instrumentum scenarum; thoracium* of itself is of course a perfectly good word, and occurs Ampel 8; for other glosses see De Vit under *Toragium.* — **152.** l. tomus. — **153.** Amplon. 383, 187, has *Toles membra sunt circa cavam;* cf. Festus, 356, b. 14, *Toles, tumor in faucibus quae per diminutionem tonsillae dicuntur;* l. toles: membra sunt circa uvam. — **154.** Cf. Paul. 357, 1 (Festus 356, 3), *Thomices,* Graeco nomine ap-pellantur et cannabi impolito et sparto leviter tortae restes ex quibus funes fiunt, etc.; l. restis; cf. Hild. T 97, *Torrens, fluvius ex pluvia collectus vel aqua cum impetu decur-rens.* — **155.** l. fustis. — **156.** l. fluvius, ex pluvia. — **160.** l. stupet, languet. — **163.** l. TO-REUMATA. — **164.** l. totidem. — **167** and **169.** l. torum . . . coadunatio, see Verg. Aen. VII. 674; cf. Isid. Or. XI. 1, 63. In brachiis enim *tori* lacertorum sunt, et insigne muscu-lorum robur existit. *Hi sunt tori, id est musculi: et dicti tori,* quod *illic viscera torta videantur;* tostum is perhaps for *torum,* and this may have come from some such expla-nation of *torum id est tortum.* — **168.** l. thorax: lorica. — **169.** l. lacerti bracchiorum. —

170. Cf. TORNATURA. — 171. l. torrida. — 172. l. thorace. — 173. l. torpidus: stupidus.
— 176. Cf. TROPOLOGIA. — 178. l. trossuli : equites; cf. Paul. 367, 20. — 179. l. trochus.
— 182. l. bucina. — 183. ? De Vit cites tupha: tiara regia. Here I think we should read
tupha = tufa : mitra regia; cf. Du Cange, TUFA, and τούφα in Byzantine Greek. — 187. l.
vel postea with Hild. T 148. — 188. l. turabulum : thymiamaterium. — 190. l. turbida. —
192. l. tempestas, or tempestate; cf. Verg. Aen. I. 45, *Turbine corripuit,* where Servius
explains *volubilitate ventorum.* — 193. Cf. TURIFICATUS. — 194. Cf. Prod. 378, and
TEGELLARIUS, see Du Cange under *Tectum.* — 195. l. verberatur. — 196. l. propter
terrae congeriem; cf. Serv. Verg. Aen. III. 22. — 201. l. hospitium modicum; Festus
355, 5, *Tuguria a tecto* appellantur *domicilia rusticorum* sordida, Serv. Verg. Ecl. I.
69, *Tuguri a tegendo* dictum; *teia* may be a corruption of *tecta,* or of *a tego* (cf. Sp. *teja,*
It. *tegola,* Fr. *tuile*). — 204. l. turget: tumet. — 205. l. statera. — 208. l. truces. — 213.
l. custodiam.

U, V.

1. l. incedit; cf. Hild. U 12 n. — 2. l. movet. — 3. l. valvulum: fabae corium; cf.
Festus, 375 a, 10, *Valvoli fabae folliculi appellati sunt quasi vallivoli, quia vallo facti* †
excutiantur. Cato R. R. LXII. 1, speaking of Bubus medicamentum, has *vitis albae
caules* III. *fabulos albos* III. Columella, VI. 4, 3, has *multi caulibus vitis albae et val-
vulis ervi bubus medentur;* so that possibly *vabulum* is a corruption of *fabulum.* I at
first thought there might be some connection with Plac. 43, 4, *Fabricora* (Papias, *Fabi-
cora* H va., *Favicora* C R) *proverbium in eos qui domesticis alimentis usi aliis labora-
rent, dictum ab eo quod Capitolium aedificanti Tarquinio fabros ac structores corvi
cum suo victu miserunt.* — 5. l. et fideiussiones vel sponsiones. — 6. Cf. Hild. V 6. —
8. l. mare. — 9. l. fideiussores. — 11. l. vafrum; cf. Hild. V 14, *Vafre: inaequaliter,*
varium seems to be used in the sense of *fickle, inconstant,* and is a sort of etymological
explanation, not worse· than the one given by Nonius 19, 30, *valde Afrum.* — 13. l. va-
gitatur (cf. VAGITO): violenter. — 14. l. Varus; cf. Prod. 388. — 16. l. valetudinarius . . .
aegrotat. — 18. l. vallus. — 21. = validus. — 22. l. valitant; cf. Hild. V. 26; the word
seems only to occur in glossaries. See Loewe G. N. 170. — 23. l. vagurrit: per otium
vagatur;· cf. Hild. V 17. — 24. l. varices: vitia quaedam pedum; cf. Nonius 25, 10,
Vatrax et Varicosus: pedibus vitiosis. — 28. Nonius 19, 30, *Vafrum est callidum
et quasi valde Afrum et urbanum.* *asper* is probably a corruption of *afer* (cf. corruption in Mai. VI. 550, *babis: valde, afrum est*). — 29. The explanation *inaequaliter* is probably due to *varium;* cf. 11. — 30. l. Varus as in 14. — 31. l. vasta. —
32. l. bascaudas: conchas aereas. — 34. l. vesanus. — 40. l. lanosae. — 41. l. vehiculum: . . . omne .quod ad portandum utile est. — 49. Perhaps for volgum, but
possibly from a gloss like *villum: pilum,* or *villum pro pilum dicitur* (cf. Pr. *vell,* It.
vello, Sp. *vello*). — 55. ? Perhaps for venustari : componi = comi; cf. Mai. VIII. 53,
Venustare: ornare. — 57. l. veniit: vendidit. — 58. l. venenarius: herbarius; cf. De Vit
under herbarius. — 59 l. venditantibus. — 65. l. volubile. — 67. l. auferunt; cf. Amplon.
385, 118, verrunt: subtrahunt, followed by veluti: scopant, and Hild. V 101. — 69. l. caedit. — 71. verro in sense of to hide, cover (see Lexx.), may have been glossed by *vestiunt.*
— 74. Cf. Prod. 411, and PERTUSORIUS, PERTUNDA. — 78. l. not *versabilis,* but versi-
pellis. — 82. compare Italian *primavera.* — 83. l. verbo tenus: sicut dictum or dicunt;
cf. Hild. V 94 n. — 86. l. vesperugo: stella: cf. Paul. 368, 16. — 91. Kaegi thinks that
viaea, not *viaca,* may be the reading of the MS., although the doubtful letter looks more
like *c;* l. βίαια: vehementia. — 92. l. hastam torquere. — 93. l. fulget · · · dirigit. —
95. l. hostia. — 97. Du Cange gives a verb *vicissere = per vices agere.* — 103. l. vigilans. — 104. l. custos. — 105. l. viburna; cf. Verg. Ecl. I. 25. — 106. l. ligavit. — 107.
De Vit cites Vinnolatus: lepidus, blandus, mollis; cf. Isid. Or. III. 19, 13, *Vinnolata* vox
est vox levis et *mollis* atque flexibilis. Et vinolata dicta a vinno, hoc est concinno *molliter flexo.* But *vinnubis* is rather a corruption of *vinnulus;* cf. Paul. 377, 8, Nonius 186,
10. — 109. l. vineas: machinamentorum . . . . . turrium. — 112 l. singillatim · · · * se-
migradatim. — 113. l. dicitur; cf. Isid. Or. XI. 1, 21, *Virgo a viridiori aetate dicta est.*

— **116.** Perhaps for vis: virtus; but compare De Vit, *Vors, tis,* Virgil Gramm. p. 77. Mai. *Versus* autem a quibusdam in nomine non recipitur principali sed in participio: ibi autem *vorsum* scribunt, quia *vors* ipsa pagina dicitur, Lucano dicente, *vortibus* egebant multi. — **117.** l. animi. — **119.** l. visere. — **122.** l. laetans. — **125.** l. vindex. — **127.** Cf. De Vit and VIRIOSUS. — **128.** l. virago: fortis; so Isid. Or. XI. 2, 22, *Antiqui enim fortes feminas ita vocabant.* — **133.** l. visibus: obtutibus. — **137.** l. vitilitigat; cf. Loewe G. N. 137. — **142.** l. volubilitas: mentis varietas. — **144.** Cf. Serv. Georg. III. 411. — **146.** Cf. Hild. U 218, Serv. Aen. III. 233, Isid. Or. XVII. 7, 67. — **147.** l. obsorptio et fossa et terrae hiatus. — **148.** l. vosmet. — **150.** l. vovet. — **151.** vuetema = voetema = boetema = βοήθημα (suggested by Professor Gildersleeve). — **152.** l. explendi voti. — **154.** l. ubertas. — **155.** l. ubertim. — **158.** l. abstractum. — **159.** l. palam. — **160.** l. vultum; comp. It. *volto.* — **169.** For vulnus = ulcus, see Rönsch die lexicalischen Eigenthümlichkeiten der Latinität des sogen. Hegesippus, p. 275. — **171.** l. ulterior. — **173.** De Vit cites Gloss. MS. *ultatus: dampnatus,* and Amplon. 386, 43, *Vultatus: damnatus;* perhaps corrupt for multatus. — **175.** l. vindicamus. — **177.** l. ultro citroque. — **181.** l. gremium. — **183.** Cf. Hild. V 261, Vultuosus: tristis. — **184.** l. herbae. — **188.** l. umquam. — **189.** Cf. Verg. Aen. VI. 218; l. ebullientia. — **191.** Cf. UNUS, § 2. — **192.** l. uncus. — **193.** l. unigenae. — **194.** l. vincire. — **196.** l. adipe. — **197.** l. nubit? cf. UNICUBA. — **199.** l. diminutio est. — **201.** l. urus. — **202.** Cf. URVUM, Varro L. L. V. 127 and 135. — **203.** Cf. UR, Hebrew. Isid. X. 130, "*ur enim flamma dicitur.*" — **204.** For *quarta* cf. Papias, *Quartarium: genus mensurae id est urna;* Joh. de Janua. *Quartarium, mensura quae quartam partem sextarii capit.* — **207.** l. ustulato. — **210.** l. ustrina. — **211.** l. consuetudine. — **213.** l. praesumit. — **220.** Cf. *Ut pute: nam sicut,* Prod. 175. *pute* is glossed here as if it were *putet.* — **223.** l. potius. — **225.** ? = utere: fruere. Perhaps *utere* is act. inf.; cf. UTO.

X.

1. l. XENODOCHIUM venerabilem . . . suscipiuntur.

Y.

1. l. hyperbolice. — **2.** l. hymnum. — **3.** l. hydria. — **4.** l. hydrus. — **5.** l. hyades: stellae. — **6.** l. hypotheca. — **7** belongs with **5,** Pliades. — **8.** ? *ypinx* not in Lexx.; for lamminas cf. L 30, *lamnas: animal similis pardo.*

Z.

1. Cf. Du Cange, ZERNA, and Isid. Or. IV. 8, 6, *Impetigo . . . vulgus sarnam appellant.* — **2.** l. aemulatio. — **4.** ? May have something to do with *seriatim.* — **5.** Cf. Prod. 154, and ZEMA = Gr. ζέμα. — **6.** l. Zephyrus.

APPENDIX.

MEMBERS IN ATTENDANCE AT THE SIXTEENTH ANNUAL SESSION.

Cyrus Adler, Philadelphia, Pa.
E. H. Barlow, Tilden Seminary, West Lebanon, N. H.
S. C. Bartlett, Dartmouth College, Hanover, N. H.
I. P. Bridgman, Cleveland, Ohio.
M. L. D'Ooge, University of Michigan, Ann Arbor, Mich.
Herbert M. Clarke, Syracuse, N. Y.
Albert S Cook, University of California, Berkeley, Cal.
W. W. Eaton, Middlebury College, Middlebury, Vt.
F. B. Goddard, Malden, Mass.
F. B. Gummere, Swain Free School, New Bedford, Mass.
H. C. G. von Jagemann, Earlham College, Richmond, Ind.
C. R. Lanman, Harvard College, Cambridge, Mass.
James C. Mackenzie, Lawrenceville, N. J.
F. A. March, Lafayette College, Easton, Pa.
C. K. Nelson, Brookeville Academy, Brookeville, Md.
W. B. Owen, Lafayette College, Easton, Pa.
Henry E. Parker, Dartmouth College, Hanover, N. H.
T. C. Pease, West Lebanon, N. H.
Tracy Peck, Yale College, New Haven, Conn.
B. Perrin, Adelbert College, Cleveland, Ohio.
E. D. Perry, Columbia College, N. Y.
Louis Pollens, Dartmouth College, Hanover, N. H.
Rufus B. Richardson, Dartmouth College, Hanover, N. H.
W. S. Scarborough, Wilberforce University, Wilberforce, Ohio.
C. P. G. Scott, Columbia College, New York.
T. D. Seymour, Yale College, New Haven, Conn.
J. A. Shaw, Trinity School, Tivoli-on-Hudson, N. Y.
F. B. Tarbell, Yale College, New Haven, Conn.
W. H. Treadwell, Yale College, New Haven, Conn.
Minton Warren, Johns Hopkins University, Baltimore, Md.
B. W. Wells, Friends' School, Providence, R. I.
J. W. White, Harvard College, Cambridge, Mass.
W. D. Whitney, Yale College, New Haven, Conn.
J. H. Wright, Dartmouth College, Hanover, N. H.

[Total, 34.]

AMERICAN PHILOLOGICAL ASSOCIATION.

HANOVER, N. H., Tuesday, July 8, 1884.

THE Sixteenth Annual Session was called to order at 4 P. M., in Dartmouth Hall, by the President of the Association, Professor M. L. D'Ooge, of the University of Michigan.

The Treasurer, Professor Edward S. Sheldon, of Harvard College, submitted his report for the year 1883–84, and it was read by the Secretary, Professor C. R. Lanman, of Harvard College. The summary of accounts for 1883–84 is as follows : —

RECEIPTS.

Balance on hand, July 9, 1883		$365.88
Fees, assessments, and arrears paid in	$233.00	
Sales of Transactions	66.50	
Interest on deposits	7.31	
Total receipts for the year		306.81
		$672.69

EXPENDITURES.

Postages	$26.00	
Expressages	.85	
Job printing and stationery	10.55	
Total expenditures for the year		$37.40
Balance on hand, July 3, 1884		635.29
		$672.69

On motion, the Chair appointed Dr. Edward D. Perry and Dr. Charles P. G. Scott, both of Columbia College, New York, a committee to audit the Treasurer's report.

The Secretary announced that he hoped to have the annual volume of Transactions for 1883 ready for publication in a few days.

The Secretary announced the election of a number of new members. Their names are given here, and, for convenience, those also of others elected and announced at subsequent sessions. The number of accessions is fifty-seven.

Rev. Robert Anderson, Teacher of English, Episcopal Academy, Philadelphia, Pa. (1314 Locust St.).

Robert Arrowsmith, Ph. D., 236 Degraw St., Brooklyn, N. Y.

Grove E. Barber, Professor of Latin, State University, Lincoln, Nebraska.

E. H. Barlow, Principal of Tilden Seminary, West Lebanon, N. H.

George A. Bartlett, Professor of German, Harvard University, Cambridge, Mass.

Rev. Samuel C. Bartlett, D. D., LL. D., President of Dartmouth College, Hanover, N. H.

I. T. Beckwith, Ph. D., Professor of Greek, Trinity College, Hartford, Conn.

T. S. Bettens, A. M., "The Kensington," cor. Fifty-seventh St. and Fourth Ave., New York.

Louis Bevier, Ph. D., Rutgers College, New Brunswick, N. J.

Hjalmar H. Boyesen, Ph. D., Professor of German, Columbia College, New York ("The Hetherington," cor. Park Ave. and Sixty-third St.).

Bradbury H. Cilley, Phillips Academy, Exeter, N. H.

I. P. Bridgman, Principal of the Cleveland Academy, Cleveland, Ohio.

Walter Ray Bridgman, Yale College, New Haven, Conn.

LeBaron R. Briggs, Instructor in English, Harvard University, Cambridge, Mass.

William Hand Browne, Librarian of the Johns Hopkins University, Baltimore, Md.

William H. Carpenter, Ph. D., Instructor in Icelandic, Columbia College, New York (7 East Thirty-first St.).

Herbert M. Clarke, Ph. D., 86 James St., Syracuse, N. Y.

William T. Colville, Professor of Modern Languages, Kenyon College, Gambier, Ohio.

Joseph Randolph Coolidge, Instructor in Spanish, Harvard University, Cambridge, Mass.

James G. Croswell, Professor of Greek and Latin, Harvard University, Cambridge, Mass.

Louis Dyer, Professor of Greek and Latin, Harvard University, Cambridge, Mass.

Arthur M. Elliott, Professor of the Romance Languages, Johns Hopkins University, Baltimore, Md.

Alfred Emerson, Ph. D., Instructor in Classical Archaeology, Johns Hopkins University, Baltimore, Md.

Mrs. G. W. Field, 204 Columbia Heights, Brooklyn, N. Y.

Isaac Flagg, Professor of Greek, Cornell University, Ithaca, N. Y.

W. G. Frost, Professor of Greek, Oberlin College, Oberlin, Ohio.

Albert S. Gatschet, United States Bureau of Ethnology, Smithsonian Institution, Washington, D. C.

Charles T. Gayley, Professor of Latin, University of Michigan, Ann Arbor, Mich.

Farley B. Goddard, Ph. D., Malden, Mass.

G. Stanley Hall, Professor of Psychology and Pedagogics, Johns Hopkins University, Baltimore, Md.

J. Rendell Harris, Professor of New Testament Greek, Johns Hopkins University, Baltimore, Md.

Paul Haupt, Professor of the Semitic Languages, Johns Hopkins University, Baltimore, Md.

Lucius Heritage, Instructor in Latin, University of Wisconsin, Madison, Wis.

A. V. W. Jackson, Fellow of Columbia College, Highland Ave., Yonkers, N. Y.

Frank E. Jennison, Instructor in Latin and English, Phillips Academy, Exeter, N. H.

Martin Kellogg, Professor of Latin, University of California, Berkeley, California.

George Lyman Kittredge, Instructor in Latin, Phillips Academy, Exeter, N. H.

William I. Knapp, Professor of Modern Languages, Yale College, New Haven, Conn. (75 Whitney Ave.).

Francis A. March, Jr., Lafayette College, Easton, Pa.

H. Z. McLain, Professor of Greek, Wabash College, Crawfordsville, Ind.

George McMillan, Professor of Greek, State University, Lincoln, Nebraska.

Rev. Henry A. Metcalf, Auburndale, Mass.

Rev. Hinckley G. Mitchell, Ph. D., Tutor in Latin and Hebrew, Wesleyan University, Middletown, Conn.

Charles P. Parker, Tutor in Greek and Latin, Harvard University, Cambridge, Mass.

Rev. Henry E. Parker, D. D., Daniel Webster Professor of Latin, Dartmouth College, Hanover, N. H.

Rev. Theodore C. Pease, West Lebanon, N. H.

Ezra J. Peck, Graduate Student of Philology, Cornell University, Ithaca, N. Y.

Louis Pollens, Professor of French, and Librarian, Dartmouth College, Hanover, N. H.

Horatio M. Reynolds, Tutor in Greek, Yale College, New Haven, Conn.

Alfred L. Ripley, Professor of German, Yale College, New Haven, Conn.

Arthur W. Roberts, Hughes High School, Mt. Auburn, Cincinnati, Ohio.

Edward H. Spieker, Ph. D., Instructor in Classics, Johns Hopkins University, Baltimore, Md.

Ambrose Tighe, Tutor in Latin, Yale College, New Haven, Conn.

James A. Towle, Professor of Greek, Ripon College, Ripon, Wisconsin.

Horatio Stevens White, Professor of German, Cornell University, Ithaca, N. Y.

Alexander M. Wilcox, Ph. D., Tutor in Greek, Wesleyan University, Middletown, Conn.

Henry Wood, Professor of German, Johns Hopkins University, Baltimore, Md.

[Total 57.]

At 4.20 P. M. the reading of communications was begun.

1. The Theory and Function of the Thematic Vowel in the Greek Verb, by Professor W. S. Scarborough, of Wilberforce University, Wilberforce, Ohio.

After remarking upon the agglutinative character and complexity in structure of the Greek verb, the writer defined "thematic vowel," and gave illustrations from the Greek, Latin, and Sanskrit. Explanations of the phonetic changes of the vowel, peculiar to each of these languages, were offered. The theories of Bopp, Pott, and Curtius as to the nature and origin of this vowel were passed in review and briefly discussed. Cases of apparent omission in several Greek verbs were presented, and the explanation of omission by syncopation was condemned. The conclusion was drawn that the vowel is an important element in the make-up of the verb for euphonic purposes; that its especial function is to facilitate pronunciation, and that in force it is conjunctive, serving to unite or connect the termination with the verbal base.

2. The Crastinus Episode at Palaepharsalus, by Professor B. Perrin, of Adelbert College, Cleveland, Ohio.

Caesar's account of the episode (B. C. iii. 91), and his praise of the exploit of Crastinus (iii. 99, 2–3), leave us in doubt about its precise nature from a military point of view. Subsequent writers who mention or describe the episode shed no light upon it. Cf. Lucan, Phars. vii. 470–473; Florus, ii. 13 [= iv. 2], 46; Plutarch, Caes. 44, Pomp. 71; Appian, Bell. Civ. ii. 82. The two versions of Plutarch are essentially identical, and do not vary materially from that of Caesar. Certain additions may be traced to Asinius Pollio, who was probably the principal source for Appian also.

From a comparison of all these passages the following general outline-sketch of the episode may be made. On leaving the camp Caesar hailed a centurion named Crastinus, and asked him what he thought of the prospects. Crastinus replied, "We shall conquer gloriously, Caesar, and to-day, alive or dead, I shall win your praise." Just as Caesar gave the battle signal, therefore, Crastinus made a stirring appeal to his fellow soldiers, charged foremost upon the enemy, followed by a large company, and died in the thick of the fight with a sword run through his mouth and neck.

To this general outline-sketch several specific features may be added, deduced from Caesar's words. It can be shown (1.) just what kind of a soldier Crastinus was, (2.) what special commission he had received, and (3.) what his exploit actually was.

1. Of the veteran soldiers whose terms had expired, those who had accepted

lands as a special reward for service could be called out (*evocare*) for new campaigns, and were under obligations to answer the call ; those who did not receive such lands, when called anew into service, could respond to the call or not, and if they did were *voluntarii*. The *voluntarii*, then, were a special class of *evocati*. A *voluntarius* was an *evocatus*, but not every *evocatus* was a *voluntarius*. Pompey's long career as general had made it possible for him to raise a large body of *evocati*, but Caesar had only *voluntarii*. The troop which followed Crastinus were *voluntarii*. Crastinus himself was, strictly speaking, a *voluntarius*. Caesar calls him freely an *evocatus*, either because he felt no need of making the distinction, or because *evocatus* was more often used in the singular than *voluntarius*.

2. Crastinus had been *primipilus* of the tenth legion in the preceding year, and so had directly commanded the maniple of *pilani*, the front and right of the first cohort in the front line of battle. His hortatory speech, beginning, "Sequimini me manipulares mei qui fuistis," was addressed to this body of soldiers, who stood nearest him, but no longer directly under his command. He himself commanded a special corps of one hundred and twenty *voluntarii*, stationed on the right of the front right cohort of the tenth legion, and had been commissioned to make a special charge with his troop before the regular line of battle, in order to inspire this to a bolder attack, and especially to throw the enemy's extreme left into some confusion before the tenth legion should reach and rout it.

3. The actual exploit of Crastinus was to set an inspiring example to Caesar's whole line of battle, and especially to the tenth legion, on whose success the fate of the day had been made to depend, by leading a body of re-enlisted veterans in such a fierce charge upon the enemy's extreme left, that it was thrown into some confusion, and would have been easily driven back when the shock of the onset of the regular line came, had not Crastinus fallen. But his death, and the failure of his exploit to accomplish all that had been intended, were more than made good by the exploits of the famous *quarta acies*, which not only routed Pompey's cavalry, but attacked in the rear the infantry left of Pompey, which was holding out well against the flower of Caesar's army, the pet tenth legion. To the *quarta acies*, therefore, Caesar discriminatingly gives praise for the victory ; to Crastinus, for valor.

3. **On a group of Sanskrit Derivatives (çaraṇá, çárman, çárīra, etc.), by Professor C. R. Lanman, of Harvard College, Cambridge, Mass.**

There are given by Boehtlingk and Roth, in the St. Petersburg Sanskrit Lexicon, three roots of the form çar or çṛ. The first means 'tear,' and its present is çṛ-ṇ ā´-t i (formed like δάμ-νη-μι, 'tame'); the second means 'boil,' and is used chiefly in the participial forms çṛ-t á and çr ā-t á, and in the causative. The third, say Boehtlingk and Roth, is equivalent to the root çri, 'lean upon'; it appears in no verbal forms, but is assumed on account of the derivatives çaraṇá, çárman, āçāra, çā'lā, and çárīra.

The aim of the paper was to show that the derivatives in question are not connected with the root çri, but are rather to be referred to a root çṛ with the meaning 'cover.'

çaraṇá means, 1. 'protecting, affording shelter'; 2. as a neuter substantive, 'that which affords shelter, a shed *or* hut'; and 3. in a more general and abstract sense, 'refuge, protection.'

çárman has for its principal and older meanings, 'cover, shelter, pro. tection.'

ā-çāra is a ἅπαξ λεγόμενον of the Atharva-veda, and means, as the context plainly shows, 'a cover from the rain.'

çā'lā means 'hut, house, room, stable.'

Leaving out of the question, for the present, the difficult word çárīra, let us consider the relation of the four words just defined to the root çri, 'lean upon.' To this root, as I said, they are referred by the great Sanskrit Lexicon. Grass. mann, also, in his Dictionary of the Rig-veda, follows the Lexicon in regard to the first two; the other two do not happen to occur in the Rik. Against the derivation of the words from çri there are objections which concern both the form and also the meaning.

I. First, the form. All the five derivatives point of course to a radical syllable with ar or ṛ, not to one with ri. Aside then from these derivatives, what evidence is there for a root çṛ as collateral form of çri? I find none, either direct or analogical.

1. Verbal forms and derivatives from çri are exceedingly common (çráyate, çiçrā'ya, áçret, çritá, -çrít, etc.; çrayaṇa, āçraya, etc.); but there is not a single one that can be referred to a root of the form çṛ with the sense of çri.

2 a. As for analogies — it is indeed true that ṛ sometimes comes from the contraction or samprasāraṇa of other syllables than ar or ra;[1] so from ri in tṛtī'ya, 'third,' from tritá (τρίτο-s), which in turn comes from trí, 'three.' Similarly, the root çru, 'hear,' forms the present çṛṇumás, with contraction of ru to ṛ. But these are manifestly secondary weakenings. Of such a secondarily weakened ṛ we should have to find examples of a subsequent strengthening to ar, in order to win a real parallel for the connection of çaraṇa with çri. Such a subsequent strengthening would yield, in the case of çṛ (from çru), forms like *açar[t] as equivalent of açrot, or *çaraṇa as equivalent of çravaṇa and co-ordinate with it.

2 b. If the connection of çaraṇa with çri be upheld, we shall have to find support for series somewhat like these:

çray-aṇa	: çri	: * çṛ-ta	: çar-aṇa (?)	: *açar (= açret),
çrav-aṇa	: çru	: * çṛ-ṇumas	: * çar-aṇa	: *açar (= açrot).

That is, from an unsupported çṛ as equivalent of çri we have to derive a form çaraṇa, which with the already existing çrayaṇa makes a pair of doublets which are, so far as I know, without example.

2 c. The co-existent forms of the root for 'boil,' çṛta, çrāta, and çrīta, have no bearing on this case. Here the simplest root-form is çṛ. This is related to çrā just as i to yā, pṛ to prā, and the many others discussed by Brugmann, *Morphologische Untersuchungen*, i. 1–91; see especially p. 40. The weakening of long ā to long ī is a common thing in Sanskrit. The i of çri is original (and not a weakening within the Sanskrit), as is shown by the cognates κλίνω, AS. *hlinian*, Eng. *lean*, etc.

---

[1] This phenomenon is at best sporadic: see Whitney's Grammar, § 243. It is probably explained, in the first of the cases cited (ri), by the i of the subsequent syllable, and in the other case (ru), by the u of the class-sign. The form tṛtá indeed occurs in several places of the Atharva-veda, but it is not well vouched.

II. Secondly, the meaning. The root çri does indeed mean 'lean against *or* on,' and so 'rest on, depend upon *or* betake one's self to, *especially* for refuge or protection.' Aside from the difficulty of the form, then, çaraṇa might very well mean primarily 'a leaning upon *or* taking refuge with for protection,' and, secondarily, but much less naturally and easily, by a transfer of meaning from the action to the thing acted upon, 'one's leaning, *i.e.* that on which one leans, one's support *or* protection.'

The development of meaning from 'protecting' to 'that which protects' is an example of one of the commonest of all the transitions of meaning; the reverse development (from the substantive to the adjective) is exceedingly rare. And yet we find çaraṇa, in the sense 'covering *or* protecting,' used to describe a shelter, a tree, houses, and a goddess (çarma, vṛkṣam, gṛhāsas, devī). These uses are Vedic; and, unless we leave them quite out of account, we must consider the original and primary meaning of çaraṇa to be active and transitive, 'covering, protecting,' and the development of meanings must start from this one as the first. And since çri is in all its uses most clearly intransitive, I see no way of connecting the primary meaning of çaraṇa with çri.

It may be added that çarman is described by such adjectives as uru, 'wide-extended,' saprathas, 'with breadth, *i.e.* far-reaching,' achidra, 'without a hole, *i.e.* continuous,' and so on. These show that çarman is not 'a support against which one leans,' but rather 'a cover *or* shelter spread over one.' And of course çarman is from the same root as çaraṇa.

III. The words çaraṇa, çarman, āçāra, and çālā may be more satisfactorily explained, I think, as derivatives of a root çṛ, 'cover, protect.' This root does not show any verbal forms in Sanskrit; but it is abundantly authenticated, as respects both its form and meaning, by a considerable group of words from the Sanskrit, Greek, Latin, and Germanic.

Each of the Sanskrit words, as a derivative of çṛ, 'cover,' is perfectly normal both in form and meaning. The interchange of r and l within the Sanskrit is so common that further comment on çālā is needless. The cognates from the other languages show the regular consonant-changes. Sanskrit ç represents Indo-European k^2, and this answers to κ in Greek, to c in Latin, and to the aspirate *h* in Germanic.

In Greek we have καλιά, 'hut, barn,' which agrees perfectly with çālā. Compare the Eng. phrase *get one's hay under cover,* i. e. ' into the barn.' In essentially the same sense and with corresponding form occurs the AS. *heal,* Eng. *hall.* Again κάλ-υξ (Anglicized *calyx*) is the 'cover, *i.e.* husk *or* pod'; Ger. *Hülle* means 'covering,' and the Eng. *hull* is the 'covering' of the kernel of grain. The cover of the head is called *hel-m* ('helmet *or* head-protector'), and the word is generalized in AS. poetry so as to be used of any protector, as God or Christ.

In Latin we find *oc-cul-ere,* 'cover,' and *cl-am,* 'covert-ly, secretly.' Latin *col-or,* 'color,' is strictly 'that which covers *or* envelops a thing, its outside, its external appearance.'[1] With these belong further the Latin *cēlāre,* Ger. *hehl-en,* Chaucer's *helen,* later Eng. *hele,* 'cover, *i.e.* conceal.' Finally, it may be an extended form of the root in question, which appears in $\kappa^a\lambda\upsilon\pi\text{-}\tau\text{-}\omega$, 'cover.'

---

[1] Thus the word shows the same transfer of meaning as the Sanskrit varṇa, 'color,' from vṛ, 'cover,' a transfer similar to that seen in the Eng. *coating* or *coat* (of paint).

IV. It remains to speak of çárīra, 'body.'.

1. The Hindus give several derivations for the word. The oldest are in the Nirukta, ii.16: çarīraṁ, çṛṇāteḥ, çamnāter vā, i.e. çarīra is from that root çṛ which makes its present çṛṇāti and therefore means 'tear *or* break,' or from the root çam meaning 'hurt.' The latter alternative is wholly impossible on account of the form. The traditional derivation from çṛ, 'break,' is followed hesitatingly by Grassmann, and according to it the body is conceived as 'the breakable *or* fragile part, *das Gebrechliche*.'

2 a. The later Hindu books, notably the introduction to Manu and the corresponding passage of the Mahābhārata,[1] derive the word from çri, 'lean,' and explain the body as that on which the more subtile parts of man lean or are dependent for their manifestation.

2 b. The German lexicographers quote a passage from the Aitareya Brāhmaṇa, ii. 14: açarīraṁ vāi reto, 'çarīrā vapā. yad vāi lohitaṁ yan māṅsam, tac charīram. This shows that the çarīra is distinguished from the soft viscera and inward fluid secretions. They therefore define the word as meaning 'the firm *or* solid parts of the body, *Knochen-gerüste*,' and, following the later Hindu derivation from çri, 'lean,' interpret the word etymologically as 'the support *or* prop' of the softer parts.

3. On the other hand, giving equal weight to the Brāhmaṇa passage, we see that we can no less easily interpret "the firm red flesh with the bones" as 'the hollow cover, the tegument *or* *Hülle*' of the viscera, etc. The form is easily connected with çṛ, 'cover,' being made like gabhīrá, 'deep,' and çávīra, 'strong'; see Whitney, 1188 e[2]. Even on the score of the interpretation the last view has something in its favor, while, in view of the difficulty of connecting çarīra as a *form* with çri, it is far the more acceptable.

The Vedic literature plainly distinguishes the çarīra from the vital breath or the immortal soul. Of this latter, the çarīra is the 'cover *or* envelope'; and this interpretation becomes natural and easy in view of the analogous German phrase which calls the body the *sterbliche Hülle*, 'the mortal cover *or* envelope' of the soul, 'the corporeal tegument.' In a somewhat similar manner, as Dr. Scott suggested, the Anglo-Saxon poetry calls the body the *bān-hūs*, 'bonehouse,' and *bān-fœt*, 'bone-vat.'

Remarks were made upon this paper by Professor Whitney, Dr. Scott, and Dr. B. W. Wells.

The Association adjourned to 8 P. M.

HANOVER, N. H., Tuesday, July 8, 1884.

EVENING SESSION.

The first Vice-President, Professor Tracy Peck, of Yale College, New Haven, Conn., called the Association to order in Chandler Hall, where a large audience had gathered, to listen to the address of the President, Professor D'Ooge.

---

[1] Boehtlingk and Roth give the citations: Manu i.17, MBh. xii.8521. The latter = xii.233.11, folio 89 b, ed. Bombay.

4. The Historical Method and Purpose in Philology.[1]

The address opened with a brief review of the most noteworthy contributions to the different departments of Philology that have appeared during the current year. Special mention was made of the following: — In English philology, the first fasciculus of the Historical Dictionary of the English Language; the publication by the Early English Text Society of the facsimile of the Epinal Glosses; Sweet's print of Lord Tollemache's famous MS. of King Alfred's Anglo-Saxon translation of Orosius; the publication of an American series of Anglo-Saxon text-books, including Beowulf and Caedmon. In Teutonic and Romance philology, Kluge's Etymological Dictionary of the German Language; Verdam's Dictionary of the Middle-Dutch; Körting's Encyclopaedia of Romance Philology; the *Opuscula* of Diez. In Oriental philology, the monograph of Friedrich Delitzsch on the Hebrew Language as viewed in the light of recent Assyrian researches; the second and third parts of Brugsch's *Thesaurus Inscriptionum Aegyptarum*; a Siamese Grammar, by Rev. S. C. George, in course of preparation. In Indo-European philology, Whitney's work on Sanskrit Verbs, now in press; the Sanskrit Reader of Lanman, which is the first text-book in Sanskrit bearing the imprint of an American publisher that has ever appeared. In classical philology, the contributions to historical syntax under the direction of Schanz in Germany, and of Gildersleeve in this country; the appearance of the first *Heft*, entitled *Archiv für Lateinische Lexicographie und Grammatik*, of the *Thesaurus Linguae Latinae*, which is to be edited under the direction of Wölfflin, and with the aid of the Munich Academy; Vols. IX. and X. of the *Corpus Inscriptionum Latinarum*; the *Inscriptiones Graecae antiquissimae praeter Atticas in Attica repertas*, by Roehl; another instalment of the new *Corpus Inscriptionum Atticarum*; Part II. of the collection of ancient Greek Inscriptions in the British Museum, by Newton; Westphal's treatises on the Rhythmic of Aristoxenus and on ancient Greek Music; Monro's Homeric Grammar.

Attention was called also to the first publication of the Catalogue of the Greek and Latin MSS. of the Vatican library, of which two volumes have recently appeared, and to the projected publication of the catalogue of the famous Orsini library in Rome, which is said to contain many classical MSS. and several early printed texts marginally annotated by scholars of the fifteenth and sixteenth centuries. The speaker also referred to the archaeological surveys and explorations of the year, more particularly those made by Dr. Ramsay, assisted by Dr. Sterrett of the American school at Athens; and congratulated American scholars upon the successful opening of the American school and the work at Assos by the Archaeological Institute, both of which institutions give promise of doing much for the honor of American scholarship, and of promoting the study of classical philology in this country. From this rapid sketch the speaker inferred two facts: (1.) the rapid accumulation of the material of philological study, and (2.) the growth of the historical method and spirit in its pursuit. These facts suggest the theme of the address: *The historical method and purpose in Philology.*

Philology may be defined as the scientific research into the history of man, revealed in language, literature, and art (using "art" in its widest sense). This idea of philology can best be gained from tracing its history and development. The epochs of this history are marked by the names of Scaliger, Bentley, Heyne, Wolf, Bopp, Hermann, Boeckh, and Ritschl. The speaker then characterized

[1] The address is printed in full in the *New Englander*, Vol. XLIII. No. 186 (November, 1884).

the work of each of these scholars. Scaliger was the polyhistor "of infinite reading"; Bentley gave the first example of objective literary and historical criticism; Heyne and Wolf were the first to separate philology from the study of theology, and to make it a separate and more or less complete science in itself. Under Heyne and Wolf philology received its greatest impulse on the archaeological and historical side. Hermann emphasized the grammatical and critical side. Then came Boeckh, whose weight was thrown on the opposite side, that of *realien* and antiquities.

The conflict between the schools of Hermann and Boeckh was described, and it was shown that these two diverse tendencies were after all harmonious in that they worked for a common aim, — the prevalence of an objective and sound method in philology, the historical method. Hermann's historical sense in the treatment of mythology and of metre, and Boeckh's influence in co-ordinating the various departments of philological study, and in relating philology with history, were more fully detailed. Special mention was also made of Boeckh's contributions to our knowledge of antiquities, and to his services as the founder of epigraphy by his *Corpus Inscriptionum Graecarum.*

Attention was next directed to the great influence of the comparative method upon all philological research. This method is essentially the historical and inductive, and is the fruit of comparative philology, whose founder is Franz Bopp. Its earliest and best results thus far have been reaped in the study of linguistics; but the same method is being applied to the study of mythology, of metre, and of antiquities. In the study of mythology, especially, the comparative-historical method has wrought great changes. Compare, for example, such a work as Creuzer's *Symbolik* with the writings of Preuner, Weber, and Roscher.

The address next went on to show how philology in the time of Boeckh was still somewhat vague and indefinite in its aim and scope, and was in danger of becoming simply an auxiliary discipline of history. The scholar to whom belongs the credit of defining the true bounds of this science, and of organizing its parts into one living unit, was Ritschl. He insisted with Boeckh that philology aims to be "the reproduction of the life of classical antiquity through the recognition and contemplation of all its essential representatives and utterances," but he maintains that this reproduction is especially directed to the preservation and restoration of *literary* monuments. Thus he separates philology from general history, while at the same time he makes all philological studies in a certain sense historical. Ritschl affords the best illustration hitherto known of the historical method in philology. He defines this method as inductive and progressive. "No event in the history of civilization springs from the ground all complete, but is conditioned by previous processes, and grows in connection with a steady movement onward." Ritschl applied this principle to the treatment of every question. His method was not alone objective, but also comprehensive. It was his constant effort to place his pupils in the possession of a vivid acquaintance with the whole life of classical antiquity in all its features. Recognizing the fact that the productive study of classical philology must always take its departure from the critical knowledge of the literature, he also insisted that we must know all the conditions of the culture and life of a people before we can properly know and interpret their literature.

After this sketch of the development of philology, the speaker inquired what this historical method may accomplish for philology to-day. As characteristic of the condition of this science to-day he mentioned and illustrated four facts: — (1.) The present unsettled state of many questions in philology. (2.) The vast increase in the material of study, and the new light which is falling upon many points that were supposed to be clearly understood and had been dismissed from discussion. The restatement of many questions is due also to the tendency to treat philology as an exact science. (3.) The absence of systematic co-operation and of co-ordinate advance. This is due to the specializing tendency of our day. This tendency must be counteracted in the interest of true science. (4.) Growing out of this is the failure properly to relate our science with the sciences of the day, and with modern life as a whole. The present discussion as to the place of Greek in a liberal education is at bottom the strife between the ancient and the modern, that comes to issue most sharply here.

The solution of these difficulties and the furtherance of philology is to be found in the recognition and pursuit of philology as a historical science in its widest sense. All special and narrow studies must be pursued and inspired with the aim to interpret some literary or historical monument. We must distinguish between the mere chronicler, the mere linguist, and the philologist. The chronicler is content with recording the simple fact as a fact, and in that sense the mere linguist is a chronicler and not a philologist. To the true philologist every fact, whether of language or of art, of custom or of belief, stands not barely for itself, but is clothed, so to say, with the flesh and infused with the blood of that organic life, of which it is at once an expression and a producing cause. The historical purpose in philology can alone give our science its place in the interest of men of to-day. The speaker thinks that especially in America a broader view of philology needs to be cultivated, and its historical side made more prominent. No one can dispute that our American scholarship in philology has been one-sided. Archaeology and interpretation have had little place in the discussions of the American Philological Association. This fact has been commented on by the *Revue Critique.* Linguistics predominates. Our peculiar situation has something to do with this ; we have no original documents, no inscriptions, no ruins, to collate, to interpret, and to explore. But the work of the Archaeological Institute of America, and of the American School of Classical Studies at Athens, and the enterprise of the London Society for the promotion of Hellenic learning, promise to put into our hands facsimiles of MSS. and original sources of information.

But to popularize the study of philology among us, we need to make evident the truth that this science is vitally connected with the culture of our own times, and can produce the noblest character. And to do this, the study of philology must be infused by the historical spirit which makes the present the child of the past, and the parent of the future.

The Association adjourned to 9 A. M.

HANOVER, N. H., Wednesday, July 9, 1884.

MORNING SESSION.

The President called the Association to order at 9.30 A. M.

The Secretary read the minutes of Tuesday's sessions, and they were approved.

Professor R. B. Richardson, of Dartmouth College, announced that Mr. and Mrs. Hiram Hitchcock would be happy to receive socially at their residence the members of the Association, with their friends, on Wednesday evening, at 8 o'clock.

On behalf of the managers of the Passumpsic Railroad, Professor Richardson extended an invitation to the members of the Association and their friends to join in a pleasure excursion on Friday to Lake Memphramagog.

Both of these invitations were accepted, with thanks.

The President introduced Professor R. C. Jebb, of the University of Glasgow.

Professor Jebb spoke with pleasure of the kindness with which he had been received in our country. He alluded to the oft-made criticism that the work of American scholars concerned itself too much with grammatical and linguistic subjects, and was too often in statistical form. While admitting that such studies might be carried too far and so displace the study of antiquity in its more directly humanizing aspects, he yet enforced the dignity and worth of these severer pursuits as a necessary preliminary for the fruitful study of ancient life and thought.

He added, that the occasions for this criticism were being taken away by the activity of the American archaeologists, who had already achieved such important results at Assos. He spoke of the bright possibilities (as, for instance, at Assos and Babylonia) for American scholars in the future. He concluded by referring to the series of photographic reproductions of the most famous classic manuscripts, such as the Laurentian Sophocles and the Ravenna Aristophanes. These phototypes are fully as good as the originals, and suggest the possibility of studies in palaeography and text-criticism in America under circumstances no less favorable than those of the young German or English student.

The reading of communications was then resumed, at 9.55 A. M.

5. On the Use of the Genitive in Sophokles, by Thomas D. Goodell, Ph. D., of the Hartford High School, Hartford, Conn.; presented by Professor T. D. Seymour, of Yale College.

The aim of the paper was to give, with accompanying statistics, a view of the use of the genitive in the extant plays of Sophocles. From the fragments only such examples were taken as seemed especially noteworthy or significant, and these were not included in the statistics. Incidentally an attempt was made to work out a somewhat better classification than the grammars employ.

As the Greek genitive is a compound case, resulting from the fusion of a part of the ablative with the original genitive, the case should, as far as possible, be treated as two. Accordingly the usage of Sophokles was considered under the following heads : (1.) true genitives, (2.) ablatival genitives, (3.) genitives whose origin and nature are doubtful. For convenience, genitives with prepositions, belonging in all three classes, were treated last.

Under the genitive proper are to be classed 53.6+ per cent of all the genitives in Sophokles, 46 3+ per cent of all being adnominal. The usual varieties of adnominal genitive appear, but no statistics can be given for the genitive subjective, objective, partitive, genitive of possession, material, etc., because no complete subdivision on this basis is possible. The genitives with superlatives were separately enumerated, as were also genitives of the whole dependent on adverbs. The adnominal genitive in the predicate was shown to occur with fourteen or fifteen verbs, the most common being εἰμί. The peculiar usage illustrated in nine passages (Ai. 1236 f., O. T. 102, O. K. 355, 662, El. 317, Tr. 339, 928, 1122, Phil. 439 ff) was explained as a development of the predicate genitive. With these also were classed the genitives translated by "about," with ἀκούω, κλύω, and πυνθάνομαι (O. K. 307, 485, 514, Ant. 1182, El. 35, 481, Tr. 65). Of all the true genitives, 23.3+ per cent occur in lyric lines.

The ablatival genitives, including those of separation, of source, of agent, of cause, of comparison, but not including those with prepositions, are 11.2— per cent of all. The genitive of separation is especially frequent. It occurs with not far from one hundred and fifty words and phrases denoting motion away from or out of, failure, deprivation, distinction, and the like, among which are many simple verbs, such as ἄγω, βαίνω, μολεῖν, ἔρχομαι, κηκίω, πίπτω, στείχω, φέρω. Of ablatival genitives 17.1+ per cent are lyric.

Genitives whose origin and development cannot be traced with certainty are found with a large variety of verbs and adjectives. They belong chiefly to proethnic types, and are not easily classified; but the total number of examples is comparatively small, 9 4 per cent of all, distributed between verbs and adjectives in the proportion of 7.3— to 2.1+. Of those with verbs, 16.1— per cent are lyric; of those with adjectives, 23 0 per cent are lyric.

Among prepositions, ἀπό, ἐξ, παρά, πρό, πρός, and κατά in the single phrase κατ' ἄκρας occurring thrice, were regarded as governing the ablatival genitive. With these are found 15.0 per cent of Sophoklean genitives. With the quasi-prepositions ἄνευ, ἄπωθεν, ἄτερ, ἄτερθε, δίχα, ἐκτός, ἔξω, ἔξωθεν, λάθρα, πάρος, πάροιθεν, πέρα(ν), πλήν, πρόσθεν, χωρίς, occur 2.4— per cent, which are to be added to the ablatival class. In the former subdivision 14.0— per cent are lyric; in the latter, 18.5+ per cent. ἀμφί, ἀντί, διά, ἐπί, κατά, μετά, μερί, ὑπέρ, and ὑπό (ὑπαί) govern only 2.4— per cent, of which 18.0+ per cent are lyric; ἀγχί (ἆσσον), ἀντίον, διαμπερές, ἐγγυτέρω (ἐγγυτάτω), εἵνεκα, ἔνδον, ἔνδοθεν, εἴσω (ἔσω), ἔκατι, ἐναντίον, ἔνερθεν, καθύπερθεν, κάτω, μεταξύ, [μέχρις,] ὄπισθεν, πέλας, πλησίον, govern 1.6+ per cent, of which 9.0+ per cent are lyric.

The most striking fact brought out by these figures is that no less than 28.6 per cent of the genitives in Sophokles are ablatival, while only 17.8— are to be classed as of doubtful character. Several questions suggested by the detailed statistics cannot be answered without similar statistics for other authors, which have not yet been collected.

Remarks upon this paper were made by Professor Jebb. He deemed it a most valuable one, and hoped that it would be printed.

6. On Hanging among the Greeks, by Professor Seymour.

Soph. O. T. 1371 ff. : —

> ἐγὼ γὰρ οὐκ οἶδ' ὄμμασιν ποίοις βλέπων
> πατέρα ποτ' ἂν προσεῖδον εἰς Ἅιδου μολών,
> οὐδ' αὖ τάλαιναν μητέρ', οἷν ἐμοὶ δυοῖν
> ἔργ' ἐστὶ κρείσσον' ἀγχόνης εἰργασμένα.

Eur. Alc. 226 ff. : —

> αἰαῖ αἰαῖ, ἄξια καὶ σφαγᾶς τάδε,
> καὶ πλέον ἢ βρόχῳ δέρην
> οὐρανίῳ πελάσσαι.

Eur. Bacch. 246 f. : —

> ταῦτ' οὐχὶ δεινῆς ἀγχόνης ἔστ' ἄξια,
> ὕβρεις ὑβρίζειν ὅστις ἔστιν ὁ ξένος ;

Eur. Heraclid. 243 ff. : —

> εἰ γὰρ παρήσω τόνδε συλᾶσθαι βίᾳ
> ξένου πρὸς ἀνδρὸς βωμόν, οὐκ ἐλευθέραν
> οἰκεῖν δοκήσω γαῖαν, 'Αργείοις δ' ὄκνῳ
> ἱκέτας προδοῦναι · καὶ τόδ' ἀγχόνης πέλας.

Commentators use these passages to explain each other; but while some understand ἀγχόνης ἄξια as "so bad as to deserve the penalty of hanging," others understand it as "worse than death," i. e. "which I would rather have died by strangling than do." We are assisted to a choice between these interpretations by a consideration of the history of hanging among the Greeks. It is a familiar fact that hanging was the favorite method of suicide by Greek women in the early ages. So died the mother of Odysseus, Anticleia, and Iocasta; so Leda in her shame for Helen (Eur. Hel. 136), so Phaedra, so Antigone, so the daughters of Lycambes. Peleus's wife, Antigone, hangs herself (Apollod. iv. 13. 3). Hanging is proposed for themselves by the suppliants in Aeschylus, and to Helen by Hecuba (Eur. Troad. 1012). Hermione attempts it (Eur. Andr. 811). Clytaemnestra tells her husband on his return (Aesch. Ag. 842) that the noose has often been taken from her neck which she placed there in her desperation. Erigone (Dictys, vi. 4), daughter of Aegisthus and Clytaemnestra, hung herself when she heard of the acquittal of Orestes by the high court at Athens. Other modes of suicide by women were uncommon. The only mythical instance of suicide by poison which has fallen in my way is where the sorceress Medea considers whether she shall take poison (which was quite in her line of business) or the halter (Ap. Rhod. iii. 789). Some few women hurled themselves from rocks.

Doubtless men also hung themselves. This is indicated by Simonides of Amorgos, i. 18: Old age seizes some, diseases wear out others, Ares sends others beneath the ground, others perish in storms on the sea, —

> οἱ δ' ἀγχόνην ἅψαντο δυστήνῳ μόρῳ
> καὐτάγρετοι λείπουσιν ἡλίου φάος.

Here hanging is used for all kinds of suicide, just as in the Alexandrian period, when suicide by starvation was so popular, ἀπέχεσθαι, " to refrain," and ἀποκαρτερῆσαι, came to be used for all suicides. Cf. Suidas, ἀποκαρτερήσαντα· ἑαυτὸν ἢ λιμῷ ἢ ἀγχόνῃ τοῦ βίου ἐξαγαγόντα. But even in the Alexandrian period, hanging seems to have been the favorite mode of suicide for lovers, as Theoc. iii. 9. Suicide by hanging was known at an early time in Rome. Servius on Verg. Aen. xii. 603, (Purpureos moritura manu discindit amictus ‖ et nodum informis leti trabe nectit ab alta,) says that the Pontifical Books directed the corpses of those who hung themselves to be cast out unburied. Bardes, quoted by Eusebius, Praep. Ev. i 320, says of the Germans, Γερμανῶν οἱ πλεῖστοι ἀγχονιμαίῳ μόρῳ ἀποθνήσκουσιν. In Eur. Or. 1036, Orestes mentions the halter or the sword as the last resort of his sister Electra and himself, but he assumes that he will choose the sword. The earliest instance that I find in Greek literature of a man's hanging himself is that of Pantites, one of the three hundred who was sent away from Thermopylae as a messenger, and hung himself from shame at having no part in the battle. Neophron, in his *Medea*, made his heroine prophesy that Jason would hang himself: —

φθερεῖ τέλος γὰρ αὐτὸς αἰσχίστῳ μόρῳ
βροχωτὸν ἀγχόνην ἐπισπάσας δέρῃ.

Another instance is the man who kicked Socrates, according to the story of Plutarch, and hung himself to escape his nickname ὄνος. So the Corcyraean nobles hung themselves (Thuc. iv. 48) when surrounded by the democracy. Strepsiades contemplates the act in order to avoid a suit at law. Heracles suggests it to Dionysus as a way of reaching Hades. Iocasta says of Oedipus (Eur. Phoen. 327 ff.), ὁ πρέσβυς ὀμματοστερής | ἀνῆξε μὲν ξίφους | ἐπ' αὐτόχειρά τε σφαγάν | ὑπὲρ τέραμνά τ' ἀγχόνας. Cf. Apost. xvi. 72, τί οὐκ ἀπήγξω ἵνα Θήβῃσιν ἥρως γένῃ; In general, however, men seem to have been more ready to fall on their swords, or to stab themselves, or to poison themselves with what was said to be bull's blood.

But common as hanging was as a method of suicide, I can find no trace of it as a punishment in the early ages. The act of Telemachus (Hom. χ 462) can hardly be considered normal, when he refuses a pure death to the unfaithful maids, and, making many nooses in a ship's cable, strings the women up in a row. When the Greeks wanted to put a man to a speedy death, corresponding to hanging to a lamp-post or to a tree in our times, they used to stone him. This act of violence, indicated in Hom. Γ 57, is frequently mentioned in the tragedies, and occurred at least as late as the Persian wars at Athens. When hanging is threatened, as by Creon (Soph. Antig. 309), evidently it is not designed that the man should be hung by the neck until he is dead; the hanging is to *precede* death, as a torture; as among the Jews hanging *followed* death, as a disgrace. One apparent arrangement for penal hanging is mentioned by Dem. cont. Timoc. 744 : among the Locrians, the man who proposed a new law did so with his head ἐν βρόχῳ, and, if the law failed to pass, τέθνηκεν ἐπισπασθέντος τοῦ βρόχου. But this is hardly judicial hanging; and the same can be said of Alexander's act when he hung some Brahmins in India, Plut. Alex. 59 *fin.* Agis IV. and his mother were hung or strangled (Plut. Agis, 20); but this was late, about 240 B.C. Where Plutarch (Themist. 22) speaks of the ropes τῶν ἀπαγχομένων, it is uncertain whether the participle is middle or passive, — the ropes with which men were hung or those with which they hung themselves. This word also is used of the bowstring as well as of the halter.

Instances of hanging as a punishment are late or uncertain. A proverb (Paroem. i. 454) says that, under the Thirty Tyrants, the man condemned to death died by sword, *halter*, or hemlock. But this is unsupported by other testimony, although opportunities are offered for the mention of the halter, if it were then used, in Xenophon and the orators; and this *triad* of punishments does not embrace death by *clubbing*, which probably was then practised.

A strong presumption is thus raised against what seems to be the common interpretation of Soph. O. T. 1374, which passage can hardly be separated from the other three quoted at the head of this article. The expressions, ἄξια σφαγᾶς and ἀγχόνης ἄξια, must refer to suicide, and are then excellent illustrations of the original use of ἄξιος, as μνᾶς ἄξιος, properly equivalent to μνᾶν ἄγων. So in Homer ἄξιος is regularly used like ἀντάξιος. Failure to recognize this has led to much unprofitable discussion of Hom. α 318: σοὶ δ᾽ ἄξιον ἔσται ἀμοιβῆς. The original use is preserved very naturally in the proverbial expressions which are treated in this paper.

The later figurative uses of ἀγχόνη were briefly discussed.

Remarks upon the paper were made by Professors Lanman, D'Ooge, and Jebb.

7. On Primary and Secondary Suffixes of Derivation and their Exchanges, by Professor W. D. Whitney, of Yale College, New Haven, Conn.

All structure in language is the joint product of combination and adaptation. The beginnings of speech are roots, or speech-signs having no formal character; then nothing different is possible save by the putting together of these; and observation shows abundantly how the process issues in form-making.

But combination does not necessarily make forms. It is doubtful whether all dissyllabic roots, and even all monosyllabic roots of composite form, are not products of combination. To make a form, there must be a class of words in which a common part adds a preceptible like modification of meaning to the various elements to which it is appended. So *like* is formative in *godly* and *truly*, etc., but not in *such* and *which* (from *so-like* and *who-like*); these are not less radical elements in English speech than are *this* and *mine*; and so with the *pre* contained in *preach* (*predicare*) and the *con* in *cost* (*con-stare*), and in other like cases. It is a great error to assume that roots demonstrably reduced from a fuller form are necessarily relics of grammatical forms. While thus there is combination without forms, but no form-making without combination, adaptation may be active in all stages of language-growth without exception. No forms are possible without an adaptive alteration of the original value of the formative element, such as is seen in the reduction of *like* to the adverbial ending *ly*, of the Latin noun *mente* to an adverbial suffix in Romanic, of *habeo*, 'I have,' to a Romanic future ending, and so on. The same adaptability is seen in all auxiliaries and form-words, in phrases, in moral and intellectual terms, and everywhere else in language; it is a universal characteristic of all speech-material, and dependent on the nature of that material as conventionally significant, and therefore applicable to all the new uses that convenience suggests. It is in greater or less measure shared by languages that have no formal structure ; it is seen, for example, in the Chinese distinction of "full words" and "empty words" : that is, some words are by the mere assignment of usage made to play a subordinate part as indicators of relations, etc. ; or are (like our own *be* and *have*) now principal and now subordinate. The earliest important (probable) case of this kind in Indo-European language-history is the distinction of pronominal from other roots ; this seems to have been the result of a gradual dissimilation and attenuation of meaning, prior to all formal development. Other instances are the gradual distinction of adjective from substantive, of adverb from case-form, of preposition from adverb, of relative from demonstrative or interrogative pronoun, and so on. Allowing for these, the positive growth of our languages is reduced to verb-inflection, noun-inflection, and stem-making by derivative suffixes. Here also original sameness and gradual distinction by use is to be confidently assumed : the difference of verb-form and noun-form even is doubtless the result of differentiation ; so also endings of derivation and of inflection must have been originally of one class. These are conclusions not now demonstrable, but fairly deducible by analogical reasoning. As to the distinction of derivative suffixes into primary and secondary, or those added directly to roots and those added to derivative stems, though in present language a well-marked and important one, it is clearly of later establishment, a part of the general process of inorganic differentiation, or by usage alone. It was the main object of the paper to set this forth, by showing, through the means of examples taken from the Sanskrit, the free convertibility of suffixes of the one class into suffixes of the other class. Prominent examples are the suffixes making gerundives, or future passive participles. The gerundive *karanīˊya* '*faciendus,*' for example, is clearly demonstrable to be a secondary formation, from *karana* ('*fictio*') + *īya*, and not from √*kar* + *anīya*. The equivalent *kartavyà* is likewise from *kartu* + *ya*, not √*kar* + *tavya*. In the light of these analogies, it appears altogether probable that *kāˊrya* and all its kindred, claimed to be made with suffix *ya* added to the root, are really from noun-stems : thus, *kāˊra* + *ya*, and so on. Certainly, the great majority of them are of this character. All these derivatives, now, have assumed in later Sanskrit a primary character (and those in *ya*, even in the earliest known form of the language).

Various other cases of the same kind were noticed and explained : as, the derivatives in *in*, in *aka*, in *uka*. The opposite case, of transfer from primary to secondary office, though it would seem the easier of the two, is much less fully illustrable from Sanskrit. The best examples are the suffixes of comparison *īyas* and *istha* (the latter, at least, probably compound), which have only in small measure won a secondary character ; *man* or *iman*, forming abstract nouns, but only of limited currency ; and the quasi-participial *ta*, which through its use as making participles of denominative verbs has come to be a secondary suffix of possession or affection, precisely like the English *-ed* in such words as *blear-eyed, four-sided.*

These instances are at any rate enough to illustrate the movable nature, dependent on changes of usage, of this particular division-line in grammar. Though itself of minor importance, it instances and exemplifies a truth of wide and deep significance in the history of language.

8. On Latin Glossaries, with especial reference to the Codex Sangallensis, No. 912, by Professor Minton Warren, of the Johns Hopkins University, Baltimore, Md.

The renewed interest of late years in the subject of Latin Glossaries is largely due to the efforts of the late lamented Dr. Gustav Loewe, who published in 1876 his *Prodromus Corporis Glossariorum Latinorum,* and up to the time of his death was diligently engaged in collecting materials for a grand *Corpus.* These collections have now passed into the hands of Loewe's colleague, Professor Georg Goetz of Jena and the Königliche Sáchsische Gesellschaft der Wissenschaften is to furnish the means for the further prosecution of the undertaking. A copy of the Codex Sangallensis, 912, was made by the writer of the paper, at the suggestion of Dr. Loewe, in the summer of 1881. It is one of the oldest glossaries, belonging to the eighth, or perhaps to the latter half of the seventh century. In form duodecimo, it contains 320 pages, with an average of about 16 glosses to the page, and altogether has 5153 glosses, of which the largest number (626) fall under the letter C, while P has 525, and S 456. Of this codex Loewe (*Prodromus,* p. 139) says: "Cum codicibus Vaticano (3320) Vindobonensique (2404) consentit etiam codicis Sangallensis 912 praecipua glossarium materia. Sangallensis praeter Vaticanum 3321 omnium codicum quotquot hac usque noti sunt vetustissimus." Most of the words are Latin, and all are explained in Latin. There are many Greek words in Latin transliteration, and there are a few Hebrew words, mostly proper names drawn from the sacred writings, and, singularly enough, one Gothic word, *baltha: audax,* p. 32. On the margin *Gothice* is written.

The glossary begins on p. 4 with " *abba: pater,*" and closes with " *Zipherus: ventus.* EXPL. ERMENEUMATA DŌ GRATIAS AMEN."

Some of the interpretations furnish rather amusing etymologies. E. g.: — P. 27, *asparagus: quia virgas habet asperas;* which, however, goes back to Varro. P. 18, *allucinatio, lucis alienatio.* P. 20, *alluvium: quotiens flumen alium sivi meatum facit.* P. 127, *idolum: ex dolo nomen accepit, id est dolo diaboli inventum.* P. 135, *indolis: etas iuvenalis qui dolore nescit.*

A number of instances were given in which the superior reading of the Sangallensis furnishes a clue to the emendation of corrupt glosses found elsewhere. E. g.: —

Cod. Leidensis 67 F', *Depalata: manifestata, devolata.* Cod. 912 has, p. 77, *divulgata.*

Cod. Amplonianus has *Tesserarius: praepositus currorum qui bella nutriunt.* Cod. Sangal. 912 has, p. 293, *Tessarius: qui bellum nuntiat.* Cf. Vegetius de Re Mil. ii. 7.

Cod. Parisinus has *Inspicare: diffidere vel modum spicare.* Cod. Sangal., *Inspicare: defendere et in modo spicarum concidere.* · From the two we get the correct reading, *diffindere et in modum spicarum,* etc. Cf. Servius on Verg. Georg. i. 292, and Philargyrius.

Mai (Class. Auct. vi. 550) gives *Veretrum: petosirium.* Cod. Sangal. has, p. 308, *Veretrum: pertusorium.*

Cod. Leidensis 67 F' 1, *Diaria: acibo sed unius diei.* Cod. Sangal., *Diaria: actio sed unius diei.* Cf. Isidorus, Or. i. 63.

In some cases the glosses are very corrupt. E. g.: — P. 31, *bassas: oves.* Cf. Leiden. 67 F', *bassus: pinguis obesus.* P. 116, *gerusa: notrix, conpotrix,* is a corruption of *gerula: nutrix, conportatrix.*

It was sought to establish the following propositions, and to illustrate them from this Codex: —

1. The bad orthography of these glossaries deserves close scrutiny, as it sheds light upon the pronunciation and phonetic changes of a late period, and is therefore of value to the student of late Latin and of the Romance languages.

2. These glossaries contain valuable remains of the words of early grammarians and commentators, often abbreviated and sometimes mutilated beyond recognition, but when properly collated they may be of service to the editors of authors like Varro, Festus, Nonius Marcellus, etc.

3. These glossaries contain many words which, though they cannot be found in any Latin author, may justly be claimed as the property of the Latin language, and, having passed the tests of criticism, even be assigned to definite periods.

4. In the interpretations themselves much material will be found of service to the student of late and vulgar Latin, and in the second instance to workers in Romance. One may see what common classical words went out of use, and what words replaced them.

On motion, the Chair appointed a committee, consisting of Professors Whitney, Owen, and Perrin, to recommend a suitable time and place for the next meeting.

On motion, the Chair appointed Professors T. D. Seymour, Minton Warren, and J. W. White a committee to nominate officers for the ensuing year.

An invitation was extended to the members, through Professor Louis Pollens, to visit the Library of Dartmouth College in Reed Hall.

After several announcements by the Secretary, the Association adjourned till 2.30 P. M.

HANOVER, N. H., Wednesday, July 9, 1884.

AFTERNOON SESSION.

The Association was called to order at 2.30 P. M.

9. On the Relation of the Anglo-Norman Vowel-System to the Norman Words in English, by Professor Hans C. G. von Jagemann, of Earlham College, Richmond, Ind.

The introduction of Latin elements into the English language is due to four principal causes: the occupation of Britain by the Romans, the conversion of the Britons to the Christian Church, the conquest of England by the Normans, and the revival of learning. We are therefore accustomed to speak of these elements respectively as Latin of the first, second, third, and fourth period.

This division is unsatisfactory. It accounts, for instance, for *leal* and *loyal* on the one hand, and *legal* on the other, the first two being Latin of the third period, and the third, Latin of the fourth period; but it fails to explain the doublet *leal* and *loyal*. A similar group is *peer, pair,* and *par,* and others might be mentioned. Again, there is a class of words, a fair specimen of which is *require*, which is decidedly classical Latin in form, and which we should therefore suppose to belong to the Latin of the fourth period; yet it is found in Chaucer. Subdivisions of the above classes are therefore needed, if we wish to account for the various forms in which Latin words appear in English.

The words belonging to the first two classes are few in number, and well known; the third class is the most important one, the words belonging to it being very numerous, and next to the Anglo-Saxon the most important element in the English language.

At the time of the Norman conquest there was no French language in the modern sense of the word, but instead of it we have a number of dialects, the principal ones being the Norman, the Picard, the Burgundian, and the dialect of Île-de-France. These four dialects must be regarded as independent developments of the Low Latin, and not as grown out of a common French type.

The French words which were introduced into English during the first centuries following the Norman conquest came of course directly from the Norman dialect, or rather from that particular species of it known as the Anglo-Norman. Now in consideration of the great differences which existed between the phonetic system of the Anglo-Norman dialect and that of the Old French proper (or dialect of Île-de-France), we must look in the Anglo-Norman for the original types of these words. This has been generally overlooked by English etymologists. Mr. Skeat, in his Dictionary, usually derives English words from their Île-de-France cognates, without accounting for the strange changes which their pronunciation and spelling must have undergone, were they to be derived in that way. A knowledge of the peculiar forms which these words had in Anglo-Norman will show at once that the original Anglo-Norman forms have as a rule been remarkably well preserved, making allowance of course for the changes which the English phonetic system in general has undergone since the Norman conquest, particularly by the mutation of vowel sounds.

The object of this paper was to show in detail how far the influence of the Anglo-Norman vowel-system extends, and it was found that in a general way the present spelling and pronunciation of Norman words in English can be traced back to the Anglo-Norman dialect, irregularities being mostly due to the influence exercised by the analogy of Romance words introduced at other times and belonging to other stages of linguistic development.

10. On Alliteration in Latin, by Professor Tracy Peck, of Yale College, New Haven, Conn.

Alliteration was used throughout the paper in its strictest sense, i. e., as the recurrence of the same initial letter, or its phonetic equivalent, in contiguous words. From a brief historical sketch it appeared that alliteration, though the word is no older than the fifteenth century, was recognized by the Romans themselves as a peculiarity in their diction; that it did not come into the language from an original use by the poets, but that it is found in proverbial and legal and religious phraseology before the rise of formal literature; that though it is prominently found in several prose writers, its frequency is much greater in the poets, especially of the republican period; that it occurs with consonants far oftener than with vowels, and that in poetry its favorite position is at the end of the verse; that, quite exceptionally, related and contrasted ideas naturally fall into alliterative words, so that caution is needed to distinguish unconscious from studied alliteration.

Many examples of evidently conscious alliteration were given to confirm the argument for the guttural pronunciation of *c* before all vowels ; to secure for *o* in all situations its distinctive, unadulterated sound ; to distinguish *ae* from *e*, except in the rustic or in very late speech. Instances of the apparently studied juxtaposition of consonantal and vocalic *u* were adduced against the common view that vowels and semi-vowels were not used for alliterative effect.

Numerous citations, mainly from prose writers, seemed conclusively to show that, of two alliterative words, the one containing *a* regularly follows that containing any other vowel, and that, if the words are of unequal length, the shorter tends to precede.

Finally, attention was called to the legitimate use which may be made of alliteration for purposes of textual criticism.

Remarks were made on this paper by Professors Warren and Perrin.

11. On the Monasteries of Mt. Athos, by Dr. Robert P. Keep, of Williston Seminary, Easthampton, Mass. ; read by Professor J. H. Wright.

[This paper was prepared by the writer in compliance with a request that he would contribute something which, less strictly technical than most of the papers which are read before the Association, should touch upon some aspects of life to-day in Modern Greece.]

Homer mentions the promontory of Athos only once. Apollonius Rhodius preserves the interesting statement, that at certain times in the year the shadow of the mountain extended at sunset to the island of Lemnos, some sixty miles away. Herodotus gives the names of six cities upon the promontory, and describes how Xerxes cut his canal through the isthmus. Thucydides speaks of the mixed population. The sum of this is that the peninsula has no ancient history of importance. Its history really begins with the organization of monastic life there in the tenth century by one Athanasios, a monk of Constantinople.

The peninsula is some forty miles long, by about four miles broad at its point of greatest width. Distinct traces of the canal of Xerxes are thought still to exist at the isthmus. The peninsula rises toward the south until the rocky ridge which forms its backbone reaches an altitude of two thousand to three thousand feet, and at the extreme southern point towers aloft the peak of Mt. Athos, 6,400 feet high, and conspicuous from all points within a radius of fifty to seventy-five miles. It is visible, it is said, from the island of Euboea and from the plain of Troy. This mountain is not only a cause of thunder-storms and hence a terror to sailors, but it also brings down into the peninsula, of which it is the extremity, the temperate climate, and makes it one of the most beautiful spots upon the face of the earth. The Athos peninsula is abundantly watered, and is full of forest trees of almost every variety. Here are found, at different altitudes and exposures, the chestnut, apple, and orange trees, the grape, and the small fruits of New England.

It is impossible to know how numerous the monastic population may, at certain times, have been. Ten thousand may not be an extravagant estimate. The present number of monks is about two thousand, distributed in twenty monasteries. These monasteries are massive stone structures, the plainness of which is sometimes relieved by several rows of light balconies running across their front. They occupy the most picturesque sites, and appear brilliantly white

from the whitewash with which their exterior walls are covered. Certain features of monastic life are common to all the monasteries. These are as follows:—
1. No female is ever admitted to the peninsula, the so-called Holy Mountain.
2. Meat and eggs are never eaten; wine, however, is allowed, in consideration of the severity of the winter. 3. Attendance at the daily services in the monastery church consumes eight to fifteen hours. 4. The remainder of the time is spent in manual labor. 5. No records of individuals are kept, and no tombstones are placed over the dead.

The twenty convents fall into two classes : the *cenobite* and the *idiorrhythmic*. In the cenobite (κοινός, βίος) monasteries, all the monks assemble once a day around a common table, and during their meal a monk reads aloud from a high pulpit from the homilies of the Greek Fathers. In the idiorrhythmic (ἴδιος, ῥυθμός) monasteries, the monks do not come together for a common meal, and, except as far as concerns the church services, regulate their lives more according to their own will. The monasteries have, at all times, suffered much from fire, and the age of most of the present buildings does not exceed one to three centuries. These buildings owe their erection chiefly to the pious gifts of wealthy Greek ruling families of the Danubian Principalities (now called Roumania), where they have until recently possessed great estates, from which most of their revenue has been derived. At present, the monks are poor. They own some farms in the Greek islands, and in various parts of Turkey. Occasionally, they make pilgrimages with their relics through Bulgaria, and thus collect money. Large companies of Eastern Christians at times, too, visit the monasteries and leave gifts behind them. The level of intelligence among the monks is low. Many seek the monasteries as a retreat for indolence ; a few, as a refuge on account of crimes committed; fewer still, as an act of religious consecration.

Aside from the natural beauty of the spot, what most attracts the traveller is the certainty that here he beholds a place where language, occupations, surroundings, have scarcely changed in five hundred years. Perhaps there may not be another place in the world where the present is so like the past. There is much, also, to interest the lover of mediaeval antiquity. There are paintings of the Byzantine school which antedate the fall of the Eastern Empire, and there are sacred vessels and boxes in which relics are kept, the gifts of Greek Emperors of Constantinople.

It is an interesting question what will become of these monastic communities in the near future, when the Turks shall be forced out of Europe. The best use would certainly be to make educational establishments out of some of the larger monasteries. Three of the monasteries possess libraries of great value. In each of these are stored more than two thousand manuscripts. Experts have pronounced upon them, and have declared that the classical philologist has nothing to hope from a further examination. But the recent discovery by Bishop Bryennios, in a monastic library in Constantinople, of the "Teaching of the Apostles," leads us to hope that some valuable discoveries in patristic Greek literature may reward a thorough examination of these convent libraries by modern Greek Hellenists. Possibly the English Hellenic Society and the Archaeological Institute of America may do something to encourage such investigations.

12. **The Ablaut in High German**, by Dr. B. W. Wells, of the Friends' School, Providence, R. I.

One cause for the non-existence of the substantive in many of the illiterate languages is the comparative scarcity of abstract terms and of pure grammatical or relational forms in general. Of all abstractions only those are expressed in words or by grammatic forms, by the ruder populations, which are to them of some deictic import. In languages which have reached the agglutinative stage and are highly synthetic, many ideas are expressed by grammatic forms which we render by separate words, as the definite and indefinite article, potentiality, iteration, beginning, continuation, termination, causation; and one of these forms, either prefixed or suffixed to the radix, is the equivalent of the verb *to be*.

That the idea of existence can be understood in various ways is proved by the fact, that Greek has several substitutes for εἶναι, as ὑπάρχειν, πέλεσθαι, etc.; and that the Aryan languages employ different radices in conjugating *to be*, as in *asmi*, *wësan*, which originally had a more concrete signification. These substitutes plainly show, that *to be* can be taken in at least two acceptations, that of the real, essential existence, and that of the accidental, chancéful, non-essential existence; a distinction which is clearly expressed by the two verbs *to be* and *to exist*, and in Spanish by *ser* and *estar*.

Now the different ways of indicating either one of these two acceptations, or both, can be summed up as follows :

1. A personal pronoun connected with a noun (substantive, adjective) may be used in a predicative sense as a substitute for *to be;* "he enemy," for "he is an enemy."

2. An affix, which is generally a suffix of demonstrative import and origin, and invariable in its form, is connected with a noun and used predicatively for the same purpose. This is done in Cha'hta, for instance. Some languages will use one affix when the object spoken of is near or visible, and another when it is remote, invisible, or simply imaginary; still others, when it stands, sits, lies, or travels.

3. A demonstrative particle of the above description becomes *verbified*, and is then connected in a predicative sense with nouns, to serve as a substantive verb. This we find to be the case in the Klamath language of Southwestern Oregon; it shows an analytic tendency in the language.

4. Nouns become verbified by the appending of inflectional affixes, generally suffixes, and are inflected like verbs. When stems of a qualitative or adnominal signification are inflected in this manner, we call them attributive verbs, and the adjective itself is then usually the participle or a verbal adjective of them. When substantives become thus inflected, we may call them verbified substantives, as in Hitchiti : míki, "chief"; mikólis, "I am chief"; immikólis, "I am their chief."

It will be seen by the instances adduced below, that this fourth method is probably the most frequently used to express the substantive verb *to be* in the languages of North America. But it expresses the idea of the true substantive verb as well as it does that of accidental existence, and I doubt whether there is any language in America which makes any distinction between the two by means of separate grammatic forms.

5. A fifth mode of substitution lies in expressing the idea of existence simply by the position of the attribute or predicate *before* the noun to be qualified, or *after* it, and by distinguishing it through the rhetorical *accent.* Thus, when we say in Latin, *bonus vir*, "that's a good man," we can dispense with the copula *est*, because we have placed the strongly accentuated attribute before the noun to be qualified.

EXAMPLES FROM VARIOUS LANGUAGES.

Káyowē.

kíamat, "lazy"; tsî' kíamat, "a lazy horse."
nû a kíamat, "I am lazy"; ba, ĕmba kíamat, "we, ye are lazy.
dén, "tongue"; ám dén, "your tongue."
ám dén tsé-omki, "your tongue is short."
ám dén kíyumki, "your tongue is long."

Witchita.

hushtákari, "a new house."
tirakā'sha hūshtákari, "this house is new."
hidí akáta kári-i, "an old house."
tirakā'sha hídi akáta kari-i, "this house is old."
tirakā'sha hídi akari-i, "this house was old."
tirakā'sha ga-aká ntsäríwa, "this house will be old."

ni-ikawa na-áshkits, "a blue shirt."
ni-ikawa na-ashkits tî', "the shirt is blue."

Páni.

rákis, "wood"; rakáshish, "hard wood."
tirahātse tihákasish, "this wood is hard."
tikī'skasish, "hard bone."
tirahā'tse tikī'shkasish, "this bone is hard."

Pima.

kĕ'ri, "old"; kĕ'ri tchiō'tch, "old man."
ániut kĕ'ri, "I am old"; ápĕput, áput kĕ'ri, "thou art old."
hĕ'kut kĕ'ri, "he, she is old."
ápi-amut kĕ'keri, "ye are old."
teni kĕ'ri kĕhém, "I was old."
vánto kĕ'rit, "I shall be old."

Yávipai.

gígye, "strong"; pá gigä'ya, "a strong man."
ya'ki pá gigä'gmi, "this man is strong."
pámĕ gigä'gmi, "he is a strong man."
nä'di, mi gigä'gmi, "I am, thou art strong."
áha dúye, "hot water."
(a)háde duígium, "the water is hot."
há χuánia, "clean water."
háve χuánigium, "the water is clean."
wí nimĕsáva, "white stone."
wí nimĕsávigum, "the stone is white."
wí nimĕsáva hamúgium? "is the stone white?"

Isleta Pueblo.

nũ'eg, "night"; nũ'eg nami-í, "a dark night."
nũ'eg nanómim, "the night is dark."

na bā′d'hüi nátufu, "white paper."
nátufu bad'hū′m, "the paper is white."
nátufu funi-í, "black paper."
pám bad'hū′m, "the snow is white" (pám, "snow ").

Uta.[1]

árik úmwi u ? "which (is) your arrow ? "
úngok úmwiung pí-eu ? "who (is) your wife ? "
árik núni pato ? "where (are) my moccasins ? "
ungai-erra ing púnk ? "whose horse (is) this ? "
ing núni púnk, "this (is) my horse."
agávunti nú-intsu érramun ? "what people are you from ? "
úng ure ? "who is it ? " ungámure ? "who are they ? "
ágarr pató-i ? "which (is) the longest ? "
intch pató-i, "this (is) the longest."
intch wēts kóagu, "this (is) the sharpest knife."

The Wítchita and Páni dialects belong to a linguistic family which has an overwhelming tendency to incorporate two or more terms into one by apocope, syncope, aphaeresis, and other means; this also appears from the examples quoted. The verb *to be* is expressed, except in the past and future tenses, by the demonstrative pronoun tirakā′sha, tirahā′tse, used *predicatively.*

No visible sign of *to be* appears in the examples of Káyowē and Pima, while in Yávipai, a dialect of the Yuma stock, the suffix -gium or -igium, in Isleta -m, -ū′m, supplies the copula *is*, and the word standing at the head of the sentence is thereby marked as the subject. In the Uta examples no distinct sign of a predicative suffix, or of affix, appears in any of the terms, nor any other distinct term for *is, are.*

More indications are furnished by the dialects of Kalapúya, which in their verbal inflection seem to approach pretty closely some of the Algónkin languages of the East. The synthetic tendencies of this Oregonian language preponderate over its powers of analysis.

The Kalapúya language of the Willámet Valley, in Western Oregon, presents an undeveloped form of speech, which is extremely archaic in many respects, and deserves to be closely studied by scientists desirous of listening to the rudest attempts of linguistic evolution. I have had the advantage of becoming acquainted with one of its northern dialects once spoken on Wápatu Lake, near Gaston; it is called the Atfálati dialect, a name which was corrupted into Tuálati by the white population.

No substantive verb exists in this dialect, nor in the whole Kalapúya family. The idea of the copula is expressed either by prefixes, or by the position of the rhetoric accent or of the words in the sentence; but when the verb *to be* appears in the past or future tense, the tense is expressed by a separate term or prefix.

Substantive nouns have, when not connected with a possessive prefix, *my, his,* etc., usually the prefix a-, while adjectives, used attributively and predicatively, have wa-, him-, plur. wan-, ni-, prefixed to them (in the third persons). Adjectives can all be inflected as attributive verbs, and the majority of the substantives can also become verbified by means of personal prefixes:

[1] The Uta examples are taken from a linguistic collection made by Major J. W. Powell. All the other languages are illustrated by examples gathered by the author himself.

Ayankē′ld, "a person of the Ayankē′ld tribe."
tchumyankē′ld, "I am of the Ayankē′ld tribe."
máha hintchĕmyankē′ld, "thou art of the A. t."
kōk, kétok miyankē′ld, "he, she is of the A. t."
tchi mē′n gumyankē′ld, "I was of the A. t." (mē′n, "once").
máha mē′n hingumyankē′ld, "thou wert of the A. t."
tchi tibúntcha Ayankē′ld, "I shall be an Ayankē′ld."
máha tabúntcha Ayankē′ld, "thou shalt be an A."

The adjective piéyim, "fat," is verbified into an attributive verb, as follows:

tchi tchpiéyim, "I am fat."
máha hintchpiéyim, "thou art fat."
kōk himpiéyim, "he is fat."
sóto tchidĕpiéyishtu, "we are fat."
miti hintchipiéyishtu, "ye are fat."
kínnuk nipié-ishtu, "they are fat."

One of the past tenses runs as follows:

tchi kupiéyim mē′n, "I was fat once."
máha hinkupiéyim mē′n, "thou wast fat once."
sóto kudĕpieyishtui mē′n, "we were fat once," etc.

The verb *to be* is indicated by the position of the accent, or of the words, or by prefixes, in sentences like the following:

kúmtuk mámpka, "the water is cold" (mámpka, "water").
háshka mámpka kúmtuk, "this water is cold."
awíffie tchéχtem, "the night is dark" (awíffie, "night").
awíffie máwin, "the night is clear, bright."
awē′ himkáski, "the child is bad."
káski *or* kimkáski awé, "the bad child."
méfan káski awé, "a very bad child."
wamóyim akíutan, "the horse is black," and "the black horse."
tchúli-im mámpku, "the water is lukewarm."
yó-iu asháblil, "the wheat is dry."
pé-iu asháblil, "the wheat is ripe."
gúsha ántmat kúmmo, "this chicken is white."
wámmo ántmat, "the white chicken."
nímmo ántmat, "white chickens."
gä′m nímmo, "two are white."
púkĕlfan nímmo, "every one is white."
tchí tánu tch' Atfálatin, "my country is at Atfálati."
Kĕná-i tchi tánkuit, "my name is Kĕnai."
atállim tcha yü′lbiu, "the deer is, *or* deer are, in the woods."

atómp mapítchu apólio tcha túmmai, "there are eggs in the hawk's nest." This example shows that the language substitutes such verbs as *to lie, to be within, to be underneath,* for the verb *to be,* wherever the sense permits it; for mapítchu means "they lie within," mapī′d, "he, it lies in, on, upon, *or* within."

Of all the languages treated in this article, the one most thoroughly studied by me is that of the Klamath Indians. It presents features differing largely from all the others, and I have reason to suppose that the Sahaptin tongues of the Columbia River will exhibit a similar linguistic plan when they shall have been studied more thoroughly.

KLAMATH OF OREGON.

The Klamath language, spoken by the Klamath Lake and Modoc Indians in Southwestern Oregon, furnishes very instructive evidence concerning the Indian equivalents to our verb *to be.*

The substantive verb is rendered here by the verb gî, kî. This is the verbified radix gē, kē, which appears as a pronoun, " this one," " these ones," and as a modal and local adverb, " thus, so," and " here." But this verb gî is used in many other verbal significations besides that of *to be ;* in fact, it unites the functions of an intransitive and substantive verb to those of a transitive verb, and is employed besides as an auxiliary verb, being the only verb of this kind in the Klamath language. Gî originally points, as its origin suggests, to some object close by, in close contiguity, and hence visible or tangible ; from this was developed a reference to *casual* existence, *accidental* being, to a " *happening to be.*" This verbified particle gî is inflected all through, like any other verb, though I have not met with any instance of a distributive form, of which the natives claim the existence : gitko, distr. giggátko, participle of the past. This ubiquitous term, the applications of which form an interesting study in themselves, is also subservient in forming some of the limited number of attributive verbs which the language possesses.

The different functions of gî I present in the order of their logical evolution, which is as follows :

1. *To be here, to be at this* or *that place, to be at such a time.* This is the gî corresponding to the Spanish *estar,* from the Latin *.stare,* " to be standing," and points to accidental existence, or occurrence by chance, generally implying close proximity to the grammatic or logical subject of the sentence. We may render it by *to exist,* though it often corresponds to our *to stay, to remain.* Examples :

kaní gî, " he, she is outside, outdoors."
tídsh gî, " to feel well," ḳú-i gî, " to be unwell."
lápi gî, " there were two (of them)."
kúmmĕtat gíank, " staying in the rocks."

From this definition has been evolved the gî composing the attributive verbs :

lushlúshli, " warm, hot " ; lushlúshgi, " to be warm, to feel hot."
p'laí, " up, above, on high " ; p'laíki, " to be in the culmination point."
ḳá-i, " not, no " ; ḳä'gi, " to disappear, to be absent."

2. *To become, to begin to be.* kú-i gî, " to become, grow worse " ; ḳíllitk tsulä'ks gí-uapk, " the body will become vigorous."

3. *To be really, essentially, intrinsically ; to exist by its own nature.* In this definition gî represents our substantive verb *to be* and the Spanish *ser,* and forms a contrast with definition No. 1. We find it in the following examples :

káni hût gî ? " who is he ? who is she ? "
î a tála gî, " you are right " ; î a ḳú-i gî, " you are wrong."

tchélash pálpali gî, "the stalk (of that plant) is white."
nútakam lúk ḳálḳali gî, "the seed of the nútak plant is round.

As an auxiliary verb, gî forms periphrastic conjugational forms with every verb's verbals and participles :

nánuktua nû papísh gî, "I am a devourer of all (kinds of food)."
p'laíkishtka gî shápash, "the sun was about to culminate."

4. *To be possessed by, to be the property of, to be endowed with.* When used in this sense, gî takes the owner or proprietor in its possessive case (*to be somebody's*), the pronoun possessive in its subjective case, and the object possessed in its subjective case also. The use of the participle gítko is especially frequent : *possessed of*, with objective case :

kánam kēk í-amnash gî ? "whose are these beads ?"
kánam gē látchash gî ? "who owns this lodge ?"
tunépni gé-u wélwash gî, "I have five water-springs."
kailálapsh gítko, "provided with, dressed in leggings."

5. *To do, to act, to perform.* Here and in No. 6 the verbified particle gî assumes the functions of a transitive verb :

tídsh gî, "to do right, to act well."
ḳú-i gî, "to act wickedly, to do evil, to be obnoxious."
wák î gén gîtk ? "what are you doing here ?"
húmasht gíulank, "after having acted thus."

In this signification gî appears also in a few *verba denominativa :*

nkák, "top of the head "; nkā'kgî, "to give birth."
nkásh, "belly, abdomen "; nkáshgi, "to have diarrhœa."

6. *To say, to speak.* Gî is used in this sense only when the words spoken are quoted either *verbatim* or in part; this definition has been evolved from No. 5, *to do,* and the French also sometimes say *il fit,* instead of *il dit.*

nû ná-asht gî, nā'sht ki, "so I said, so he said *or* says."
tsí sha hûn ki, "so they said."
nû gítki gî, "I say they must become."

MASKOKI FAMILY.

The languages of Maskoki affinity, formerly spoken in the Gulf States from the Mississippi to the Atlantic, have the power of expressing accidental and real existence by a verbification of the noun. In *Creek* all adjectives can be verbified in the simple, as well as in the iterative or reduplicated form; but Hitchiti and Cha'hta can verbify substantives also. Thus we have in Creek :

lásti, "black," redupl. lasláti, "black here and black there "; verbified, lánis, "he, she, it is black " ; laslánis, "he, etc. is black in spots."
haúki, redupl. hauháki, "hollow"; haúkäs, "I am hollow "; haúkîs, redupl. hauhákîs, "it is hollow," and "they are hollow."

Hitchiti verbifies in the same manner, and an instance of a verbified substantive, míki, "chief," was presented above.

Cha'hta is able to verbify all nouns and pronouns, even particles, which end in a vowel, by appending 'h, a sound which never varies, to express tense, number, or other grammatic categories. When words end in consonants, they are verbified by advancing the accentuation upon the last syllable. Examples: ála, "child"; ála'h, "it is a child"; hátak, "man"; haták, "he, it is a man"; kállo, "strong"; kállo'h, "he is strong"; fe'hna, "very"; fe'hna'h, "it is very"; taktchi, "to tie"; taktchi'h, "he is tying"; tchúkash, "heart"; tchukásh, "it is the heart."

Another way exists in the Maskoki languages to express existence. It is done by verbs conjugated as regularly as gî is in Klamath, and extensively used as auxiliary verbs. But they do not signify *to be,* but *to be so, to be thus,* or sometimes *to be there.* Thus we have in Creek, ō'mis, mómis, "it is so, it is thus," and the same in Hitchiti; in all dialects, ō'mis can be contracted into ōs, ōsh, and appended to the sentence, even in Cha'hta and Koassáti.

The Association adjourned to 8.30 A. M.

At about eight o'clock, the members of the Association gathered at the residence of Mr. and Mrs. Hiram Hitchcock, meeting there the gentlemen of the Faculty of Dartmouth, with their ladies and friends, and spent the evening in agreeable social intercourse.

HANOVER, N. H., Thursday, July 10, 1884.

The Association was called to order at 9 A. M.

The minutes of Wednesday's sessions were read and approved.

15. Some Peculiarities of a Hebrew Manuscript of the Fourteenth Century of the Christian Era, by Cyrus Adler, of the Johns Hopkins University, Baltimore, Md.

Manuscript copies of the Hebrew Bible are comparatively rare, and, considering the antiquity of the books which compose it, extremely modern. The oldest MS. in the Erfurt library, and according to Lagarde the oldest extant copy of the Massora, has been assigned the date of 1100. The oldest Hebrew MS. Bible in the Bibliothèque Impériale is dated 1286. Moreover, many of the early MSS. and some of the early prints are without vowel points. The most complete copy of the Pentateuch and commentaries in the Bibliothèque Impériale is in this condition. No. 107 of the " Collectio Davidis," now a part of the Bodleian Library, is the oldest punctuated text in the collection. It is a copy of the Psalms, no older than the fourteenth, and possibly as late as the sixteenth century. This unfortunate state of affairs leaves us no facts on which to base a study of the history of the vowel points, and makes textual criticism a hazardous undertaking.

The MS. under discussion is at present the property of Mayer Sulzberger, Esq., of Philadelphia, and was purchased by him from the late Dr. Wickersham, who had himself bought it from Prof. Vincenzo Gustale (now living at Florence, Italy). It was sold as a MS. of the year 1300, and was pronounced from an examination of the handwriting (by Rabbi Iesi of Ferrara) to be of that date.

The MS. contains סליחות, or rather תחנונם, i. e. supplicatory prayers recited, by Jews between New Year's and the day of Atonement. Its first part agrees exactly with Luzzatto's collection, except that where his edition reads, "Here the reader says any prayer which he pleases," our MS. has always inserted one, a confirmation of both the correctness of the editor and of the antiquity of the MS. The MS. 630 of Derenbourg's Catalogue contains six such poetical invocations. Our MS. possesses three such poems which can be recognized (two from their acrostics and the third from its having lived to our own time), and which may furnish some evidence in regard to its date. The first — the acrostic of which is דניאל — is a poem of no merit. It was probably written by an Italian of the twelfth century. The next is the famous ברכי נפשי of Bahya ibn Bakoda, who flourished about the year 1100. The third, and for us most important, connects itself in three ways with the name of Menahem Reqanati, viz. the acrostic, the subscription, and the superscription.

The MS. consists of 34 leaves of mingled parchment and vellum, and was written by a professional scribe. The leaf is 8⅜ inches long and 12⅜ inches broad, and from the aging of the edges, this would appear to have been the original size. The formation of the letters *aliph*, *pe*, *he*, and *gimel* is peculiar.

On the top of the first page there are two lines and a half written in a style of Hebrew known as cursive Italian. They are much blurred and obscured, and were not written by the person who wrote the MS. The inscription warrants us in believing that Isaac Reqanati (there named) either wrote the MS. himself or hired a scribe to do it for him. That Isaac Reqanati was a contemporary and immediate successor of Menahem we may infer from his having preserved the poem, for nothing short of filial affection could have induced him to that step. Menahem Reqanati died in 1290, and is known to the modern world as a great Kabalist. From these facts as well as from the inscription, from the poem of Bakoda and that of Daniel, joined with the tradition and the opinion of the expert referred to, it is safe to assume that the MS. before us is one of the latter part of the thirteenth, or the earlier part of the fourteenth century.

A special interest attaches to the MS. because it contains the text of thirteen Psalms, a comparison of which with the *textus receptus* shows some striking variations. An examination of the vowel points proved even more interesting. In the thirteen Psalms there were over five hundred variations; three hundred are taken up in a confusion of *qameç*, *pathah*, and *hatef-pathah* (all *â*-sounds). The pre-tonic *qameç* is unknown; the article frequently does not take *qameç* before a guttural.

It may be suggested that all this results from pure ignorance, but the fact that the פ כ ד ג ב and ת without *dagesh* have the *raphe* mark is itself sufficient evidence that the MS. has been carefully written. Of course it would be ludicrous to suppose that one MS. could overthrow a well-established system, yet we seem to have an absolutely phonetic system of representation without a knowledge of some of the rules of Hebrew grammar, which at best seem arbitrary.

From a study of the consonantal characters and a comparison with a MS. of the twelfth century, it appears that the MS. style, at least, is made up of initials, medials, and terminals. The present square character corresponds to the initial, which, being the more beautiful, was adopted by printers.

The peculiarities of punctuation seem to show that Qamhi's grammatical system was not without opponents. One MS. is not enough to warrant any positive inferences, yet these facts are important enough to deserve the attention of editors of future critical editions.

16. Greek Ideas as to the Effect of Burial on the Future of the Soul, by Professor F. B. Tarbell, of Yale College, New Haven, Conn.

It was the object of this paper to consider with what degree of clearness and positiveness the ancient Greeks believed in the exclusion from Hades of the souls of the unburied dead. The usual modern authorities on classical antiquities speak of this belief as if it were an unqualified dogma, but a review of the original evidence bearing on the point showed that the doctrine was only fitfully, and for the most part dimly apprehended, while notions inconsistent with it had an equal, if not a stronger, hold on the Greek mind.

True, the idea that the soul continues in the neighborhood of an unburied corpse appears from time to time among the Greeks, as among many other peoples. And once at least in Greek literature (Hom. Ψ 71 ff.) we meet with the less natural fancy that such a soul wanders forlorn on the confines of the underworld, on the hither side of Acheron. But, on the other hand, the soul was habitually spoken of as descending to Hades at the moment of death; and this tendency to think of Hades as the natural habitat of the disembodied spirit was so strong that a Greek might actually picture a shade as fully admitted to Hades, but complaining that his body was still unburied. Of this the most striking instance is in Hom. ω 186 ff. The complete lack of clear, consistent opinions on the subject is well illustrated by the prologue of the *Hecuba* of Euripides, when, at the outset, the ghost of Polydoros announces himself as coming from Hades, and then, thirty lines later. as having just deserted his unburied body.

The belief in the exclusion of the unburied from Hades was too hazy and wavering to account for the extreme importance attached by the Greeks to funeral rites. Such an explanation finds no countenance in the copious passages of Greek literature bearing on the whole matter of burial. The truth probably is, that burial, originating, like lustration, as a sanitary measure, owed its subsequent importance chiefly to immemorial usage and the religious sanction, though it is not denied that the exclusion idea, in so far as it prevailed, would contribute something in the same direction.

Remarks were made on this paper by Professors D'Ooge, Tarbell, and Perrin.

17. The Influence of Written English and of the Linguistic Authorities upon Spoken English, by Professor F. A. March, of Lafayette College, Easton, Pa.

Students of language ar apt to feel powerless amid the changes of language. They know, indeed, that scientific terms ar freely formd by scientific men. They can hardly fail to notice that proper names ar changed by the schoolmaster and by their spelling. But the popular speech is generally thought to be following the laws without regard to grammar men, or lexicografers. An examination of Walker's Pronouncing Dictionary wil surprize many by the extent of the changes which it wil show that ar contrary to the law of least effort, and seem to hav been produced by the spelling and by the authority of the dictionary.

The following classes of sounds wer mentiond as having changed in England, and more in America : —

1. *a* preceded by guttural *g* or *c* softend by the intervention of *e*. "When the *a* is pronounced short, as in the first syllables of *candle, gander*, etc., the interpo-sition of the *e* is very perceptible, and indeed unavoidable; for though we can pronounce *guard* and *cart* without interposing the *e*, it is impossible to pronounce *garrison* and *carriage* in the same manner."

2. *e* before *r* pronounced *a* in *clerk, sergeant, servant, merchant*, etc.

3. *e* pronounced *i* in *yes, pretty, engine*, etc.

4. *i* in the initial syllabl unaccented before a syllabl beginning with a conso-nant has the sound of *e* short; *didactic, digamma, dilate, fidelity*, etc.

5. Words ending in silent *e* after a short vowel: *crocodile, columbine, eglantine, metalline*, etc.

6. The unaccented vowels pronounced in England with the obscure sound ar now in large numbers distinguisht in America.

7. *s* pronounced as *z* between two sonants by Walker, now has its name sound; *disable, disdain, absolve, resignation, nasal*, etc.

8. *d + i* and *d + y*, sounded *j* by Walker, and *t + i, t + y*, sounded *ch*, ar now often *dy* and *ty*: *soldier, educate, nature*, etc.

A large number of anomalous words which Walker notes as having a deplor-abl pronunciation hav become regular: *acceptable, alienate, annihilate, apostle, apothecary, apron, asparagus, authority, been, bellows, chorister, confessor, construe, cucumber, catch, caviare, chap, chart, china, dictionary, oat-meal, ostrich, schedule*, etc., etc.

This kind of change, in which the speling and a desire to improve in speaking hav proved stronger than the law of least effort, is more prevalent in our day than ever before, and in America more than in England. The reason is that traditional pronunciation has givn way to the dictionaries. Very few Ameri-cans now decide how to pronounce a word by recolecting how their grand-mother pronounced it; they refer to Webster or Worcester.

The stronghold of fonetic coruption is among those who cannot spel; but here everybody reads and spels. The influence of authority has become very great. Opinions of experts are easily colected and concentrated and promul-gated. The views of our linguistic scholars would exert an immense influence in favor of improvements in language if they only would take courage and express them, and act on them.

Remarks were made upon this paper by Professor Whitney and others.

18. On the "Teaching of the Twelve Apostles" (Διδαχὴ τῶν δώδεκα Ἀποστόλων), by Rev. Dr. C. K. Nelson, of Brookeville Acad-emy, Maryland.

The proofs required for the authentication of any document must be both historical and internal. No amount of external evidence can establish a claim which is inconsistent with the age and concomitant circumstances of the document in question. On the other hand, no amount of internal evidence can establish a claim which has no historical standing-ground. But when a document is en-tirely wanting in both of these respects, it can only be relegated to the sphere of the apocryphal and spurious; and if itself claim to belong to an historically different period, then it must be pronounced a forgery. The claim for the genuineness and authenticity of the document recently discovered and published by Philotheos Bryennios, Metropolitan of Nicomedia, must be submitted to both of these tests, and sentence must be pronounced upon it in accordance with its fulfilment of the required conditions. The claim is, that the document in question " belongs undoubtedly to the second century ; probably as far back as 120 A. D., hardly later than 160 A. D."

I. As to the historical proofs. The first authority cited is Clement of Alexandria. This authority is much better known for piety than for critical acumen. His proneness to ingenious speculation is proverbial. But even Clement does not use the word Διδαχή, but Γραφή, — a fatal defect in historical proof. The second authority is Athanasius. He is unquestionably more reliable than Clement of Alexandria. But unfortunately this witness is removed some two centuries from the earliest time claimed for the origin of the document. Athanasius does speak of some (so-called, as Eusebius says) apostolical writing as Διδαχή. But there were so many documents in the fourth century claiming to be of apostolic origin, that we cannot attach much importance to this evidence. The third authority cited is Eusebius of Caesarea, also a fourth-century authority. If the document in question is the document referred to by Eusebius, then the authority, to say the least of it, is very questionable ; for Eusebius speaks of it as "the so-called Teachings of the Apostles." To test the value of such historical evidence, what judicious Christian critic would accept the Gospel of St. John, for instance, on such weak historic proof?

II. Internal evidence. In a genuine apostolical document we should expect to find some similarity of thought and language to the writings which are generally accepted as apostolical. But the document in question differs so essentially in linguistic construction and vocabulary from the writings of the New Testament that it is impossible to assign it to the same origin. It is impossible to get a complete idea of the syntactic construction from extracts. I therefore refer to the document *passim* for proof. The vocabulary is marked by many peculiarities. There are twelve words not in general Greek use, and fourteen not found in the New Testament. There are three words which are found only in the Septuagint, and two found only in the Epistle of Barnabas and in Gregory Nazianzen respectively. But lateness of origin is much more fully attested by the character of the teaching. Whatever is not an imitation of the Sermon on the Mount, or of some doctrine of the New Testament already more clearly and strongly expressed, bears marks of lateness. We note a few particulars : — 1st. The distinction between different degrees of Christian perfection. 2d. Making the questioning of the authority of the prophetic teacher the unpardonable sin. 3d. Distinctions in kinds of water to be used in baptism. 4th. The introduction of the doxology in the Lord's Prayer. 5th. Calling the Holy Communion the Eucharist, instead of participation of the Lord's body. Of the three hundred lines of which the document consists I have noted rather more than ten per cent as bearing the most decided marks of lateness of origin. As a conclusion of the whole matter, I am perfectly satisfied that the document neither on linguistic nor on theological grounds can claim for itself an origin anywhere within the first four centuries of the Christian era. On linguistic grounds alone I should assign it a place much later in Christian history, but the document is so comparatively free from later doctrinal errors that its place probably rightfully belongs to the fifth or sixth century. All that has been said is entirely apart from the *a priori* improbability that any important document of the first two centuries of the Christian era should have escaped notice in antiquarian researches. As a general rule, it is the worthless documents that are not brought to the light. If by this very imperfect paper I shall have called attention to a document which by the very pretentiousness of its appellation challenges critical attention, I shall have accomplished all that I could possibly have hoped for or desired.

Professor D'Ooge made some remarks upon this paper.

19. Observations on Vowel-Utterance, by A. Schnyder; reported by Professor W. D. Whitney.

Professor Whitney began by pointing out the great difficulty of defining and classifying the vowel-sounds, and the obstinate differences of view still prevailing among phonetists with regard to even very fundamental points. The system now most in vogue is that of A. M. Bell, somewhat modified in detail by Sweet and others — a pigeon-hole system, finding place for a large variety of differences of sound by distinguishing extreme and medial positions of the back and front of the tongue and of both together ("mixed"), and by adding the modifications of "rounding," and of "wide" utterance as opposed to "primary": the main features of this system may be assumed to be known to all who concern themselves with phonetics. It is sought to be put in place of the older and long-current triangular or linear system, which recognizes *a* (*far*) as medial point, passing to *i* (*pique*) in one direction and to *u* (*rule*) in the other, through the intermediate steps of *e* (*they*) and *o* (*note*) respectively. Even Sievers, who in the first edition of his phonetical manual offers only the latter system, now in the second edition presents both, and gives (a little doubtfully, it is true, and with confession of uncertainty as to sundry points) the preference to the former or "English" system. The speaker said that he had never been able to regard the Bell system as anything at all approaching to a finality, or (however acute it might be in the notation of certain minor differences) as even containing so much and so valuable truth as the other one. It misdefines the *a*, buries the prominence and mutual relations of the five leading historical vowels under a heap of trivialities, and gives to the front of the tongue a primary importance in determining vowel-tone that seems by no means to belong to it. It had been with much satisfaction, then, that he had received from a correspondent in Chicago, Mr. A. Schnyder, some observations upon the subject which seemed to him so interesting and important that he desired (with the consent of their author) to bring them to the attention of the Association. Mr. Schnyder is a native of Switzerland, who, first in his own country and later in this, has been for more than forty years a teacher of articulation to the deaf and dumb, and has come, in connection with that teaching, to the views now held by him. They will be stated here substantially in his own words.

The characteristic distinction of all the simple vowels is conditioned by the position of the back or root of the tongue and of the pharynx, while the palatal cavity and the shape of the mouth add only trifling modifications. It is sufficient proof of this that any one may distinctly pronounce the vowel-series *u, o, a, e, i,* with the anterior organs of speech in very different positions: thus, for example, with the teeth tightly pressed together; with the lips nearly closed in a fixed position; with the tip of the tongue applied to either the lower or the upper lip; with a ring held between the teeth and covered by the lips; with the tip of the tongue bent back upwards against the hard palate [and, it may be added, with the tongue in the position for uttering *l*]. Hence it follows, that Bell's description of the position of the tongue for his "mixed vowels" cannot possibly be correct. But the principal result of my investigations as to the formation of the vowels is the discovery that half the vowel-series is produced by depression of the root of the tongue. All previous descriptions, so far as known to me, make the vowel-sounds originate exclusively by raising the tongue, and hence are only in part correct. Starting from the position of indifference that makes the neutral vowel, the series toward *u* is made by raising the back part of the tongue, that toward *i* by depressing the root of the tongue. The accompanying figure will show the neutral position and those of *u* and *i* respectively; the positions of *e* and *o*, and of any other sounds intermediate between the neutral vowel and the extremes, would be traced between those here given.

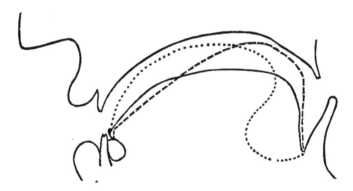

The figure represents a perpendicular section of the mouth cavity, from the lips as far back as the veil of the palate and the epiglottis. The unbroken line shows the neutral position of the tongue; the broken line, the position for uttering *u ;* the dotted line, that for *i.* It is assumed that the point of the tongue is held throughout against the lower teeth.

The depression of the "front" of the tongue in the *u*-position is simply the natural consequence of the humping of the back part of the tongue; and, in like manner, the lifting of the middle and front of the tongue in the *i*-position is only a necessary result of the retraction of the root of the same organ.

In passing from *u* to *i*, or the contrary, only the raising of the middle and front of the tongue is distinctly felt; but one may convince himself of the depression of the root of the tongue by passing the end of a finger in over the back of the tongue between the soft palate and the epiglottis. The resulting disposition to "gag" may be prevented at first by buttering the end of the finger; but after some practice the parts grow accustomed to be meddled with, and make no further resistance.

Professor Whitney said that he and others had fully convinced themselves, in the method last described, of the truth of Mr. Schnyder's account of the *i*-position, and that it seemed to him a capital point in vowel-formation, and calculated to modify seriously the views hitherto entertained by phonetists.

Mr. Schnyder has founded an ingenious and practical system of vowel-notation upon his theory of vowel-formation, and regards it as not less comprehensive and more true to the facts than Bell's. It is to be hoped that he will soon take some opportunity to make a complete report of his observations and views.

20. A Word about the Sonant Fricative Consonants, by Professor Samuel Porter, of the National Deaf-Mute College, Washington, D. C. ; read by Dr. E. D. Perry.

It has been common of late to describe the sonant fricatives, *v*, *th* in *thy*, *z*, etc., as made by means of breath added to tone. They are so described by Melville Bell, Henry Sweet, G. H. von Meyer, and others. Wm. A. Wheeler and Webster's Unabridged (ed. 1863) tell us they are like the corresponding non-sonant forms, only differing in that they have voice for breath. Both of these explanations are either erroneous or inadequate. Even if we soften down an *f* to a whispered *v*, and then add tone, we do not get a sonant *v*. Let two persons give simultaneously, one the breath-sound and the other bare tone from the vocal cords, the impression on the ear will not be that of *v ;* and just so with *z* and the others. There is something more and other than breath-sound added to tone. The contrary explanation derives its deceptive plausibility from an experiment, in which you give first the breath sound, say for *f*, and then add, or seem to yourself to simply add, tone from the larynx. The result will, indeed, be a *v*. But what you do is not what you suppose you do, that is, not the mere adding of tone to breath-sound. Again when you describe the sonant as made by substitution of voice, or tone, for breath-sound, with the mouth organs in the same position, this is not all that you do. Still, this is correct so far as it goes ; only that, in fact, breath-sound is not wholly eliminated. Voice is substituted for the greater part of the breath-sound. But this is not all that is done as respects the voice that is so substituted.

If we attend to our sensations as we utter, for instance, a *v*, we shall be distinctly aware of a vibration in the lip, or between lip and teeth. It is such as we do not feel in the case of an *f*. There is, I think, a tremolo effect, and there certainly is a tone in sympathetic response to the tone from the vocal cords and agreeing with that in pitch. There is also a damping of the tone by the interposed obstruction. And besides this, there is a muffled sound, as in the case of *b*, made by tone injected into a closed or partially closed cavity, with some distention of the elastic walls of the cavity. This kind of action is well understood in the case of the sonant mutes. The sound in that case, we know, comes to the outer air in part through the nasal passage, and a sonant mute, *b*, *d*, or *g*, cannot be perfectly uttered with this passage closed. The same is to be observed, though not in so high a degree, in the case of the sonant fricatives *v*, *th*, *z*, etc. We cannot pronounce them well when the nose is obstructed or closed.

We have thus noted three effects in these articulations as respects the tone ; viz. a tremolo, a tone by responsive vibration, and also a muffling of the tone from the vocal cords.

But there is also, in a greater or less degree, in these consonants a sound of the kind which we call breath-sound, and which has not its origin from the vocal cords, but is made by the action of the breath-current upon some part of the mouth organs. The same current that carries tone from the vocal cords may also act in this other way and give a breath-sound that attends on and blends with the tone. In the case of a *v*, this is very slight, and perhaps hardly perceptible, and is probably limited to the action of the breath between the teeth; — and so it is with the *th*. In a *v* made, in the German way (as the N. German *w*), by the lips alone, it may not exist at all. In the case of *z*, we have the sympathetic or responsive tone vibration made at a place on the tongue somewhat behind the tip, leaving the tip of the tongue nearly free for the hissing sound like that of *s*. The same, or still more, also in *zh*, heard in *azure*, as leaving the front of the tongue free for the *sh* sound.

It is to be added, that in the case of all the sonant fricatives, there may sometimes be a wavering, or unsteady utterance, giving a constantly varying, or oscillating, prominence to the breath-element on the one hand and the tone-element on the other.

21. Remarks on the Shapira Hebrew Roll, deposited in the Rush Library at Philadelphia, by Cyrus Adler.

Dr. Isaac H. Hall has, in a recent report to the American Oriental Society, called attention to a Shapira roll in the Philadelphia Library. It is a leather MS. of the Book of Numbers, and was thought to resemble a Karaite MS. A hasty examination aroused some suspicion, and accordingly a more careful investigation was made. Experts were called in and made some interesting comments. Through the "butcher cuts" on the back it was discovered that the leather had been colored, — rather inexplicable unless to give an appearance of age. The roll is made up of goat and calf hide (no sheep) indiscriminately put together (a combination prohibited by Biblical as well as by Rabbinical law, and therefore not used by Karaites). The appearance of age is given by a number of white stains resembling mildew, but for various reasons it cannot be a vegetable growth. It has attacked only the cuticle and has left the fibre untouched; it has not attacked the ink (naturally inclined to mould); and it has hardened the leather, — a result which could not possibly have been produced by the action of either mildew or water. Dr. Henry Leffmann, an experienced chemist, was inclined to think that corrosive sublimate had been used to give the mildewy appearance. Then again the leather shows in one place what shoemakers call "an invisible patch," quite a modern invention. And finally, the theory having been advanced that the roll was made up of pieces of different ages fitted together, on the oldest-looking piece in the middle of the roll and the newest-looking piece at the end there appears a peculiar formation of the letter *pe* to be found in all probability in no other MS., certainly not to be matched in this one. We are accordingly driven to the unhappy conclusion that this roll was manufactured to meet the wants of a curiosity-seeking age.

Professor March, as Chairman of the Committee on the Reform of English Spelling, presented his report.

The comitte hav taken no oficial action during the last year. Corespondence with the Comitte of the Philological Society of England has been had on the preparation of an alfabetical list of all the words of which the rules adopted last year wil change the spelling, and perhaps a small dictionary following the improved spellings. There has been no very activ movement in regard to the reform. It has been proposed to start a periodical called *Language*, which shal use the spelling recomended by the Philological Associations.

On motion, the Report was aproved, and the comittee apointed in 1875 was continued for another year. It now consists of Messrs. March (chairman), W. F. Allen, Child, Lounsbury, Price, Trumbull, and Whitney.

Dr. E. D. Perry reported on behalf of the Auditing Committee that the account of the Treasurer had been examined and found correct. The report was accepted.

Professor Whitney, as Chairman of the Committee to recommend a suitable place and time for the next meeting, proposed that the Association should meet in New Haven, Conn., on the second Tuesday in July, 1885. The proposal of the Committee was accepted without dissent.

The report of the Committee to nominate officers for the ensuing year was presented by Professor Minton Warren, in the absence of Professors Seymour and White. The Committee made the following nominations : —

For *President,* — Professor William W. Goodwin, Harvard College, Cambridge, Mass.

For *Vice-Presidents,* — Professor Francis A. March, Lafayette College, Easton, Pa.; Professor William D. Whitney, Yale College, New Haven, Conn.

For *Secretary and Curator,* — Professor John Henry Wright, Dartmouth College, Hanover, N. H.

For *Treasurer,* — Professor Edward S. Sheldon, Harvard College, Cambridge, Mass.

For additional members of the *Executive Committee,* —

Professor Basil L. Gildersleeve, John Hopkins University, Baltimore, Md.
Professor Charles R. Lanman, Harvard College, Cambridge, Mass.
Professor Lewis R. Packard, Yale College, New Haven, Conn.
Professor Tracy Peck, Yale College, New Haven, Conn.
Professor Bernadotte Perrin, Adelbert College, Cleveland, Ohio.

The Committee gave notice of a proposition to amend the Constitution, so as to unite the officers of Secretary and Treasurer.

Professors March and Whitney refused to accept nomination as Vice-Presidents. Professor Whitney moved to amend the report of the Committee by inserting the names of Professor Tracy Peck, of

Yale College, and Professor A. C. Merriam, of Columbia College, in place of Professor March's and his own. As a further amendment, it was moved that the names of Professors March and Whitney be put back again on the list of " additional members of the Executive Committee," in place of Professors Peck and Packard.

On behalf of the Treasurer, Professor Sheldon, the Secretary, Professor Lanman, withdrew the name of Mr. Sheldon as candidate for the office of Treasurer. The Secretary explained, at the same time, that a considerable saving of trouble would be made if the duties of the Secretary and those of the Treasurer were performed by the same person. At present the receipts come in part to the Secretary and in part to the Treasurer, and this has sometimes occasioned mistakes and oversights annoying both to officers and to members. Further, according to rule, the disbursements should be made by the Treasurer alone ; but small expenses are constantly incurred by the Secretary, and the responsibility and control of the large expenses falls wholly on the Secretary, who has the sole charge of the printing of the annual publications of the Association. By the election of the same person to both offices, no provision of the Constitution would be violated, and a great deal of correspondence, now necessary, would become unnecessary. The making out of bills and the addressing of envelopes, and similar work, might be done by an experienced man in the employ of the University Press in Cambridge ; so that, on the whole, the labor of the Secretary would not be materially increased by the addition of the duties of Treasurer. The Secretary accordingly moved, as a further amendment, that the place left vacant by Professor Sheldon be taken by Professor Wright.

A vote being taken upon the amendments, the Association assented to them, and the report of the Committee as thus amended was thereupon accepted.

On motion, a resolution to the following effect was adopted : —

The American Philological Association desires to express its hearty thanks to the President and Trustees of Dartmouth College, for the use of their halls for the meetings of the Association; to Mr. and Mrs. Hiram Hitchcock, for their kind reception of the members at their residence; and to the Managers of the Passumpsic Railroad, for their liberality in providing a pleasant excursion to Lake Memphramagog.

The Association adjourned at noon.

On Friday, the 11th, a considerable number of the members of the Association and of the Faculty of Dartmouth College, with their friends, left Hanover, and, after a pleasant morning's ride, in part up the Connecticut Valley, reached Newport, Vermont, at noon. The afternoon was spent most agreeably on the steamer "Lady of the Lake," which took the party to Magog, in Canada, at the farther northern end of Lake Memphramagog. Newport was reached again in the evening, and here the company separated.

OFFICERS OF THE ASSOCIATION.

1884–85.

PRESIDENT.

WILLIAM W. GOODWIN.

VICE-PRESIDENTS.

A. C. MERRIAM.

TRACY PECK.

SECRETARY AND CURATOR.

JOHN H. WRIGHT.

TREASURER.

JOHN H. WRIGHT.

EXECUTIVE COMMITTEE.

The officers above named, and —

BASIL L. GILDERSLEEVE.

CHARLES R. LANMAN.

FRANCIS A. MARCH.

BERNADOTTE PERRIN.

WILLIAM D. WHITNEY.

MEMBERS OF THE AMERICAN PHILOLOGICAL ASSOCIATION.[1]

J. W. Abernethy, Adelphi Academy, Brooklyn, N. Y.
Cyrus Adler, 870 North Eighth St., Philadelphia, Pa.
Eben Alexander, East Tennessee University, Knoxville, Tenn.
Frederic D. Allen, Harvard University, Cambridge, Mass.
William F. Allen, University of Wisconsin, Madison, Wis.
Joseph Anderson, Waterbury, Conn.
Robert Anderson, Episcopal Academy, 1314 Locust St., Philadelphia, Pa.
N. L. Andrews, Madison University, Hamilton, N. Y.
Stephen P. Andrews, 201 East Thirty-fourth St., New York, N. Y.
Robert Arrowsmith, 236 Degraw St., Brooklyn, N. Y.
John Avery, Bowdoin College, Brunswick, Me.
Cecil F. P. Bancroft, Phillips Academy, Andover, Mass.
Grove E. Barber, State University, Lincoln, Nebraska.
E. H. Barlow, Tilden Seminary, West Lebanon, N.H. ·
George A. Bartlett, Harvard University, Cambridge, Mass.
Samuel C. Bartlett, Dartmouth College, Hanover, N. H.
Wm. M. Baskerville, Vanderbilt University, Nashville, Tenn.
Charles C. Bates, Plymouth, Mass.
C. T. Beatty, High School, East Saginaw, Mich.
I. T. Beckwith, Trinity College, Hartford, Conn.
George Bendelari, Yale College, New Haven, Conn.
Charles E. Bennett, 1134 L St., Lincoln, Neb.
T. S. Bettens, "The Kensington," cor. Fifty-seventh St. and Fourth Ave., New York, N. Y.
Louis Bevier, Rutgers College, New Brunswick, N. J.
James S. Blackwell, University of Missouri, Columbia, Mo.
Maurice Bloomfield, Johns Hopkins University, Baltimore, Md.
E. W. Blyden, Monrovia College, Liberia.
James R. Boise, Morgan Park, Chicago, Ill.

[1] This list has been corrected up to November 20, 1884. Names left blank are of members who either are in Europe, or whose addresses are not known to the Secretary.

Hjalmar H. Boyesen, Columbia College, New York, N. Y. (" The Hetherington," cor. Park Ave. and Sixty-third St.).

Charles E. Brandt, Farmington, Conn.

H. C. G. Brandt, Hamilton College, Clinton, N. Y.

Fisk P. Brewer, Iowa College, Grinnell, Iowa.

I. P. Bridgman, Cleveland Academy, Cleveland, Ohio.

Walter Ray Bridgman, Yale College, New Haven, Conn.

LeBaron R. Briggs, Harvard University, Cambridge, Mass.

John A. Broadus, Southern Baptist Theol. Seminary, Louisville, Ky.

Charles J. Buckingham, Poughkeepsie, N. Y.

L. H. Buckingham, English High School, Boston, Mass.

Henry F. Burton, Univ. of Rochester, Rochester, N. Y. (47 North Ave.).

Henry A. Buttz, Drew Theological Seminary, Madison, N. J.

William H. Carpenter, Columbia College, New York, N. Y. (7 East Thirty-first St.).

W. B. Carr, Leesburgh, Loudoun Co., Va.

Franklin Carter, Williams College, Williamstown, Mass.

William C. Cattell, Lafayette College, Easton, Pa.

Miss Eva Channing, Forest Hill St., Jamaica Plain, Mass.

Elie Charlier (Life Member), 108 West Fifty-ninth St., New York, N. Y.

Francis J. Child, Harvard University, Cambridge, Mass.

Bradbury H. Cilley, Phillips Academy, Exeter, N. H.

Herbert M. Clarke, Illinois College, Jacksonville, Ill.

William T. Colville, Kenyon College, Gambier, Ohio.

Albert S. Cook, University of California, Berkeley, Cal.

Joseph Randolph Coolidge, Harvard University, Cambridge, Mass.

Oscar H. Cooper.

Howard Crosby, University of the City of New York, New York, N. Y.

James G. Croswell, Harvard University, Cambridge, Mass.

Edward P. Crowell, Amherst College, Amherst, Mass.

S. E. D. Currier, 2 Cedar St., Roxbury, Mass.

Charles Darwin, Library of the Geological Survey, Washington, D. C.

Edward De Merritte, Berkeley School, Boston, Mass.

Schele De Vere, University of Virginia.

Martin L. D'Ooge, Michigan University, Ann Arbor, Mich.

Louis Dyer, Harvard University, Cambridge, Mass.

T. T. Eaton, Louisville, Ky.

William Wells Eaton, Middlebury College, Middlebury, Vt.

Thomas H. Eckfeldt, Wesleyan University, Middletown, Conn.

August Hjalmar Edgren, University of Lund, Sweden.

Arthur M. Elliott, Johns Hopkins University, Baltimore, Md.

L. H. Elwell, Amherst College, Amherst, Mass.

Alfred Emerson, Johns Hopkins University, Baltimore, Md.

Carl W. Ernst, Boston, Mass.

Ambrose J. Faust, Washington, D. C.

O. M. Fernald, Williams College, Williamstown, Mass.

Mrs. G. W. Field, 204 Columbia Heights, Brooklyn, N. Y.

Gustavus Fischer, Rutgers College, New Brunswick, N. J.

M. M. Fisher, University of Missouri, Columbia, Mo.

Isaac Flagg, Cornell University, Ithaca, N. Y.

A. J. Fleet, University of Missouri, Columbia, Mo.

John Forsyth, Newburgh, N. Y.

W. G. Frost, Oberlin College, Oberlin, Ohio.

Samuel Garner.

James M. Garnett, University of Virginia, Albemarle Co., Va.

Henry Garst, Otterbein University, Westerville, Ohio.

Albert S. Gatschet, United States Bureau of Ethnology, Smithsonian Institution, Washington, D. C.

Charles T. Gayley, University of Michigan, Ann Arbor, Mich.

B. L. Gildersleeve, Johns Hopkins University, Baltimore, Md.

Frank M. Gilley, 27 Marlboro St., Chelsea, Mass.

Farley B. Goddard, Malden, Mass.

Thomas D. Goodell, High School, Hartford, Conn. (176 Sigourney St.).

Ralph L. Goodrich, U. S. Courts, Little Rock, Ark.

William W. Goodwin, Harvard University, Cambridge, Mass.

Richard T. Greener, Howard University, Washington, D. C.

James B. Greenough, Harvard University, Cambridge, Mass.

James M. Gregory, Howard University, Washington, D. C.

F. B. Gummere, Swain Free School, New Bedford, Mass.

Ephraim W. Gurney, Harvard University, Cambridge, Mass.

William Gardner Hale, Cornell University, Ithaca, N. Y.

G. Stanley Hall, Johns Hopkins University, Baltimore, Md.

Isaac H. Hall, 2 East Eighty-sixth St., New York, N. Y.

William G. Hammond, 1417 Lucas Place, St. Louis, Mo.

H. McL. Harding, Brooks Academy, Cleveland, Ohio.

Albert Harkness, Brown University, Providence, R. I.

William R. Harper, Baptist Theological Seminary, Chicago, Ill.

Calvin S. Harrington, Wesleyan University, Middletown, Conn.

J. Rendell Harris, Johns Hopkins University, Baltimore, Md.

Caskie Harrison, Brooklyn Latin School, Brooklyn, N. Y. (185 Montague St.).

James A. Harrison, Washington and Lee Univ., Lexington, Va.

Samuel Hart, Trinity College, Hartford, Conn.

Paul Haupt, Johns Hopkins University, Baltimore, Md.

William H. Hawkes, 1330 New York Ave., Washington, D. C.

B. J. Hawthorne, State Agricultural College, Corvallis, Oregon.

Charles R. Hemphill, Clarksville, Tenn.

Theophilus Heness, 142 Crown St., New Haven, Conn.

Lucius Heritage, University of Wisconsin, Madison, Wis.

W. T. Hewett, Cornell University, Ithaca, N. Y.

Thomas Wentworth Higginson, Cambridge, Mass.

Newton B. Hobart, Hudson, Ohio.

George O. Holbrooke, Trinity College, Hartford, Conn.

Edward W. Hopkins, Columbia College, New York, N. Y.

Selah Howell, Ayer Academy, Ayer, Mass.

E. R. Humphreys, 129 West Chester Park, Boston, Mass.

Milton W. Humphreys, University of Texas, Austin, Texas.

Ashley D. Hurt, State Agricultural College, Lake City, Fla.

Edmund Morris Hyde, Pennsylvania Military Academy, Chester, Pa.

A. V. W. Jackson, Highland Ave., Yonkers, N. Y.

Hans C. G. von Jagemann, Earlham College, Richmond, Indiana.

Frank E. Jennison, Phillips Academy, Exeter, N. H.

Henry Johnson, Bowdoin College, Brunswick, Me.

John L. Johnson, University of Mississippi, Oxford, Miss.

John Norton Johnson, 129 Pike St., Cincinnati, Ohio.

Elisha Jones, Michigan University, Ann Arbor, Mich.

Robert P. Keep, Williston Seminary, Easthampton, Mass.

Martin Kellogg, University of California, Berkeley, California.

Asahel C. Kendrick, University of Rochester, Rochester, N. Y.

T. D. Kenneson.

W. S. Kerruish, 222 Superior St., Cleveland, Ohio.

John B. Kieffer, Mercersburg College, Mercersburg, Pa.

D. B. King, Lafayette College, Easton, Pa.

Louis Kistler, Northwestern University, Evanston, Ill.

George Lyman Kittredge, Phillips Academy, Exeter, N. H.

William I. Knapp, Yale College, New Haven, Conn. (75 Whitney Ave.).

Miss Mary H. Ladd, Chauncy Hall School, Boston, Mass.

Charles R. Lanman, Harvard University, Cambridge, Mass.

Lewis H. Lapham, 68 Gold St., New York, N. Y.

C. W. Larned, U. S. Military Academy, West Point, N. Y.

Albert G. Lawrence, Newport, R. I.

R. F. Leighton, 109 Lefferts Place, Brooklyn, N. Y.

John M. Leonard, University of Cincinnati, Cincinnati, Ohio.

John R. Leslie, Newport, R. I.

Thomas B. Lindsay, Boston University, Boston, Mass.

William S. Liscomb, Providence, R. I.

Thomas R. Lounsbury, Yale College, New Haven, Conn. (22 Lincoln St.).

Rebecca S. Lowrey, 162 West Forty-seventh St., New York, N. Y.

Jules Luquiens, Institute of Technology, Boston, Mass.

Frederick Lutz, Harvard University, Cambridge, Mass.

Merrick Lyon, University Grammar School, Providence, R. I.

James C. Mackenzie, Lawrenceville, N. J.

Irving J. Manatt, State University, Lincoln, Nebraska.

Francis A. March, Lafayette College, Easton, Pa.

Francis A. March, Jr., Lafayette College, Easton, Pa.

Philippe B. Marcou, Johns Hopkins University, Baltimore, Md.
D. S. Martin, Rutgers Female College, New York, N. Y.
Winfred R. Martin, High School, Hartford, Conn.
R. H. Mather, Amherst College, Amherst, Mass.
W. Gordon McCabe, University School, Petersburg, Va.
Irwin P. McCurdy, 723 South Twentieth St., Philadelphia, Pa.
Joseph H. McDaniels, Hobart College, Geneva, N. Y.
Miss Harriet E. McKinstry, Lake Erie Female Seminary, Painesville, O.
H. Z. McLain, Wabash College, Crawfordsville, Ind.
George McMillan, State University, Lincoln, Nebraska.
Charles M. Mead, Leipzig, Saxony.
John Meigs, Hill School, Pottstown, Pa.
Augustus C. Merriam, Columbia College, New York, N. Y. (124 East Fifty-fifth St.).
Elmer T. Merrill, Wesleyan University, Middletown, Conn.
Henry A. Metcalf, Auburndale, Mass.
Hinckley G. Mitchell, Wesleyan University, Middletown, Conn.
Charles D. Morris, Johns Hopkins University, Baltimore, Md.
Wilfred H. Munro, De Veaux College, Suspension Bridge, N. Y.
C. K. Nelson, Brookeville Academy, Brookeville, Md.
Edward North, Hamilton College, Clinton, N. Y.
J. O. Notestein, University of Wooster, Ohio.
Bernard F. O'Connor, Columbia College, New York, N. Y. (136 East Twenty-ninth St.).
Howard Osgood, Rochester Theological Seminary, Rochester, N. Y.
Charles P. Otis, Massachusetts Institute of Technology, Boston, Mass.
W. B. Owen, Lafayette College, Easton, Pa.
*Lewis R. Packard, Yale College, New Haven, Conn. (226 Church St.).
William A. Packard, College of New Jersey, Princeton, N. J.
Charles P. Parker, Harvard University, Cambridge, Mass.
Henry E. Parker, Dartmouth College, Hanover, N. H.
E. G. Parsons, Derry, N. H.
Theodore C. Pease, Malden, Mass.
Ezra J. Peck, Cornell University, Ithaca, N. Y.
Tracy Peck, Yale College, New Haven, Conn. (87 Wall St.).
William T. Peck, High School, Providence, R. I. (350 Pine St.).
William R. Perkins, Cornell University, Ithaca, N. Y.
Bernadotte Perrin, Adelbert College, Cleveland, Ohio (837 Case Ave.).
Edward D. Perry, Columbia College, New York, N. Y. (913 Seventh Ave.).
William C. Poland, Brown University, Providence, R. I. (12 Barnes St.).
Louis Pollens, Dartmouth College, Hanover, N. H.
Samuel Porter, National Deaf-Mute College, Washington, D. C.
L. S. Potwin, Adelbert College, Cleveland, Ohio.
John W. Powell, Washington, D. C.

* Died Oct. 26, 1884.

Henry Preble, Harvard University, Cambridge, Mass.
George Prentice, Wesleyan University, Middletown, Conn.
Thomas R. Price, Columbia College, New York, N. Y.
Sylvester Primer, Charleston, S. C.
Charles W. Reid, Allegheny College, Meadville, Pa.
DeWitt T. Reiley, Rutgers College, New Brunswick, N. J.
Horatio M. Reynolds, Yale College, New Haven, Conn.
William A. Reynolds, Wilmington, Del.
Leonard W. Richardson, Trinity College, Hartford, Conn.
Rufus B. Richardson, Dartmouth College, Hanover, N. H.
W. G. Richardson, Princeton, N. J.
Alfred L. Ripley, Yale College, New Haven, Conn.
Arthur W. Roberts, Hughes High School, Mt. Auburn, Cincinnati, Ohio.
Lawrence Rust, Kenyon College, Gambier, Ohio.
Julius Sachs, Classical School, 38 West Fifty-ninth St., New York, N. Y.
Wesley C. Sawyer, Lawrence University, Appleton, Wis.
W. S. Scarborough, Wilberforce University, Wilberforce, Ohio.
Henry Schliemann, Athens, Greece.
C. P. G. Scott, Columbia College, New York, N. Y.
Walter Q. Scott, Phillips Academy, Exeter, N. H
Jotham B. Sewall, Thayer Academy, South Braintree, Mass.
Thomas D. Seymour, Yale College, New Haven, Conn. (112 College St.).
Joseph Alden Shaw, Trinity School, Tivoli-on-Hudson, N. Y.
Edward S. Sheldon, Harvard University, Cambridge, Mass.
L. A. Sherman, State University, Lincoln, Nebraska.
Charles Short, Columbia College, New York, N. Y.
E. G. Sihler, Classical School, 38 West Fifty-ninth St., New York, N. Y.
Benjamin E. Smith, care of Century Co., Union Sq., New York, N. Y.
Charles Forster Smith, Vanderbilt University, Nashville, Tenn.
Clement Lawrence Smith, Harvard University, Cambridge, Mass.
Frank Webster Smith, Lincoln, Mass.
Edward Snyder, Illinois Industrial University, Champaign, Ill.
Edward H. Spieker, Johns Hopkins University, Baltimore, Md.
George C. S. Southworth, Kenyon College, Gambier, Ohio.
Wm. G. Spencer, Rector of Christ Church, New Haven, Conn.
A. B. Stark, Logan Female College, Russellville, Ky.
Frederick Stengel, School of Mines, Columbia College, New York, N. Y.
William A. Stevens, Rochester Theological Seminary, Rochester, N. Y.
Edward F. Stewart, Easton, Pa.
Austin Stickney, 35 West Seventeenth St., New York, N. Y.
Morris H. Stratton, State Board of Education, Salem, New Jersey.
Charles W. Super, Ohio University, Athens, Ohio.
Miss A. L. Sweetser, Mount Holyoke Seminary, South Hadley, Mass.
Frank B. Tarbell, Yale College, New Haven, Conn.

Franklin Taylor, High School, Philadelphia, Pa. (629 North Twelfth St.).
Zachary P. Taylor, Central High School, Cleveland, Ohio.
John Tetlow, Girls' Latin School, Boston, Mass.
J. Henry Thayer, Harvard University, Cambridge, Mass. (67 Sparks St.).
Calvin Thomas, Michigan University, Ann Arbor, Mich.
William E. Thompson, Genesee Wesleyan Seminary, Lima, N. Y.
Ambrose Tighe, Yale College, New Haven, Conn.
Edward M. Tomlinson, Alfred University, Alfred Centre, N. Y.
Crawford H. Toy, Harvard University, Cambridge, Mass.
James A. Towle, Ripon College, Ripon, Wisconsin.
William H. Treadwell, Yale College, New Haven, Conn.
J. Hammond Trumbull, Hartford, Conn.
Francis W. Tustin, University at Lewisburgh, Pa.
James C. Van Benschoten, American School, ('Οδὸς 'Αμαλίας,) Athens, Greece.
Addison Van Name, Yale College, New Haven, Conn.
Miss Julia E. Ward, Mount Holyoke Seminary, South Hadley, Mass.
Henry C. Warren, 67 Mount Vernon St., Boston, Mass.
Minton Warren, Johns Hopkins University, Baltimore, Md.
W. B. Webster, Military Institute, Norfolk, Va.
R. F. Weidner, Rock Island, Illinois.
James C. Welling, Columbian University, Washington, D. C.
Benjamin W. Wells, Friends' School, Providence, R. I.
J. B. Weston, Christian Biblical Institute, Standfordville, N. Y.
Mrs. A. E. Weston, Christian Biblical Institute, Standfordville, N. Y.
A. S. Wheeler, Sheffield Scientific School, New Haven, Conn.
Benjamin I. Wheeler.
John H. Wheeler, University of Virginia.
Horatio Stevens White, Cornell University, Ithaca, N. Y.
John Williams White, Harvard University, Cambridge, Mass.
William Dwight Whitney, Yale College, New Haven, Conn.
W. H. Whitsitt, Southern Baptist Theological Seminary, Louisville, Ky.
Alexander M. Wilcox, Wesleyan University, Middletown, Conn.
Alonzo Williams, Brown University, Providence, R. I.
R. H. Willis, Norwood, Nelson County, Va.
Edwin H. Wilson, Middletown, Conn.
William Epiphanius Wilson, King's College, Windsor, Nova Scotia.
Henry Wood, Johns Hopkins University, Baltimore, Md.
Henry P. Wright, Yale College, New Haven, Conn. (128 York St.).
John Henry Wright, Dartmouth College, Hanover, N. H.

[Number of Members, 284.]

Albany, N. Y. : N. Y. State Library.
Andover, Mass. : Phillips Academy.
Andover, Mass. : Theological Seminary.
Ann Arbor, Mich. : Michigan University.
Athens, Greece : American School of Classical Studies.
Baltimore, Md. : Johns Hopkins University.
Baltimore, Md. : Peabody Institute.
Berea, Madison Co., Ky. : Berea College.
Berkeley, Cal. : University of California.
Bloomington, Monroe Co., Ind. : Indiana University.
Boston, Mass. : Boston Athenæum.
Boston, Mass. : Boston Public Library.
Brooklyn, N. Y. : The Brooklyn Library.
Brunswick, Maine : Bowdoin College Library.
Buffalo, N. Y. : Young Men's Library.
Burlington, Vt. : University of Vermont.
Cambridge, Mass. : Harvard College Library.
Champaign, Ill. : Illinois Industrial University.
Chicago, Ill. : Public Library.
Cleveland, O. : Adelbert College of Western Reserve University.
Crawfordsville, Ind. : Wabash College Library.
Davidson, N. C. : Davidson College Library.
Easton, Pa. : Lafayette College Library.
Evanston, Ill. : Northwestern University.
Geneva, N. Y. : Hobart College Library.
Greencastle, Ind. : Indiana Asbury University.
Hanover, N. H. : Dartmouth College Library.
Iowa City, Iowa : State University of Iowa.
Ithaca, N. Y. : Cornell University.
Lincoln, Neb. : State University of Nebraska.
Marietta, O. : Marietta College Library.
Middletown, Conn. : Wesleyan University.
Milwaukee, Wis. : Public Library.
Nashville, Tenn. : Vanderbilt University.
Newton Centre, Mass. : Newton Theological Institution.
New York, N. Y. : Astor Library.
New York, N. Y. : The College of the City of New York. (Lexington Ave. and 23d St.)
New York, N. Y. : Union Theological Seminary. (1200 Park Ave.)
Olivet, Eaton Co., Mich. : Olivet College Library.
Philadelphia, Pa : American Philosophical Society.
Philadelphia, Pa. : The Library Company of Philadelphia.

Philadelphia, Pa. : The Mercantile Library.
Providence, R. I. : Brown University.
Providence, R. I. : Providence Athenæum.
Sewanee, Tenn. : University of the South.
Springfield, Mass.: City Library.
Tuscaloosa, Ala. : University of Alabama.
University of Virginia, Albemarle Co., Va. : University Library.
Washington, D. C. : Library of Congress.
Washington, D. C. : United States Bureau of Education.
Waterville, Maine : Colby University.
Wellesley, Mass. : Wellesley College Library.
Windsor, Nova Scotia : King's College Library.
Worcester, Mass. : Free Public Library.

[Number of subscribing Institutions, 54.]

TO THE FOLLOWING LIBRARIES AND INSTITUTIONS HAVE BEEN SENT COM-
PLETE SETS (VOLUMES I. — XIV.) OF THE TRANSACTIONS, GRATIS.

British Museum, London, England.
Royal Asiatic Society, London.
Philological Society, London.
Society of Biblical Archæology, London.
India Office Library, London.
Bodleian Library, Oxford.
Advocates' Library, Edinburgh, Scotland.
Trinity College Library, Dublin, Ireland.
Asiatic Society of Bengal, Calcutta.
Bombay Branch of the Royal Asiatic Society.
North-China Branch of the Royal Asiatic Society, Shanghai.
Japan Asiatic Society, Yokohama.
Public Library of Victoria, Melbourne, Australia.
Sir George Grey's Library, Cape Town, Africa.
Reykjavik College Library, Iceland.
University of Christiania, Norway.
University of Upsala, Sweden.
Russian Imperial Academy, St. Petersburg.
Austrian Imperial Academy, Vienna.
Anthropologische Gesellschaft, Vienna.
Biblioteca Nazionale. Florence, Italy.
Reale Accademia delle Scienze, Turin.
Société Asiatique, Paris, France.
Athénée Oriental, Paris.

Curatorium of the University, Leyden, Holland.
Bataviaasch Genootschap van Kunsten en Wetenschappen, Batavia, Java.
Royal Prussian Academy of Sciences, Berlin, Germany.
Royal Saxon Society of Sciences, Leipsic.
Royal Bavarian Academy of Sciences, Munich.
Deutsche Morgenländische Gesellschaft, Halle.
Library of the University of Bonn.
Library of the University of Jena.
Library of the University of Königsberg.
Library of the University of Leipsic.
Library of the University of Tübingen.

[Number of foreign Institutions, 35.]

[Total, (284 + 54 + 35 =) 373.]

CONSTITUTION

OF THE

AMERICAN PHILOLOGICAL ASSOCIATION.

ARTICLE I. — NAME AND OBJECT.

1. This Society shall be known as "The American Philological Association."

2. Its object shall be the advancement and diffusion of philological knowledge.

ARTICLE II. — OFFICERS.

1. The officers shall be a President, two Vice-Presidents, a Secretary and Curator, and a Treasurer.

2. There shall be an Executive Committee of ten, composed of the above officers and five other members of the Association.

3. All the above officers shall be elected at the last session of each annual meeting.

ARTICLE III. — MEETINGS.

1. There shall be an annual meeting of the Association in the city of New York, or at such other place as at a preceding annual meeting shall be determined upon.

2. At the annual meeting, the Executive Committee shall present an annual report of the progress of the Association.

3. The general arrangements of the proceedings of the annual meeting shall be directed by the Executive Committee.

4. Special meetings may be held at the call of the Executive Committee, when and where they may decide.

ARTICLE IV. — MEMBERS.

1. Any lover of philological studies may become a member of the Association by a vote of the Executive Committee and the payment of five dollars as initiation fee, which initiation fee shall be considered the first regular annual fee.

2. There shall be an annual fee of three dollars from each member, failure in payment of which for two years shall *ipso facto* cause the membership to cease.

3. Any person may become a life member of the Association by the payment of fifty dollars to its treasury, and by vote of the Executive Committee.

ARTICLE V. — SUNDRIES.

1. All papers intended to be read before the Association must be submitted to the Executive Committee before reading, and their decision regarding such papers shall be final.

2. Publications of the Association, of whatever kind, shall be made only under the authorization of the Executive Committee.

ARTICLE VI. — AMENDMENTS.

Amendments to this Constitution may be made by a vote of two thirds of those present at any regular meeting subsequent to that in which they have been proposed.

PUBLICATIONS OF THE ASSOCIATION.

THE annually published "Proceedings" of the American Philological Association contain an account of the doings at the annual meeting, brief abstracts of the papers read, reports upon the progress of the Association, and lists of its officers and members.

The annually published "Transactions" give the full text of such articles as the Executive Committee decide to publish. The Proceedings are bound with them as an Appendix.

The following tables show the authors and contents of the first fifteen. volumes of Transactions:

1869-1870. — Volume I.

Hadley, J.: On the nature and theory of the Greek accent.
Whitney, W. D.: On the nature and designation of the accent in Sanskrit.
Goodwin, W. W.: On the aorist subjunctive and future indicative with ὅπως and οὐ μή.
Trumbull, J. Hammond: On the best method of studying the North American languages.
Haldeman, S. S.: On the German vernacular of Pennsylvania.
Whitney, W. D.: On the present condition of the question as to the origin of language.
Lounsbury, T. R.: On certain forms of the English verb which were used in the sixteenth and seventeenth centuries.
Trumbull, J. Hammond: On some mistaken notions of Algonkin grammar, and on mistranslations of words from Eliot's Bible, etc.
VanName, A.: Contributions to Creole grammar.
Proceedings of the preliminary meeting (New York, 1868), of the first annual session (Poughkeepsie, 1869). and of the second annual session (Rochester, 1870).

1871. — Volume II.

Evans, E. W.: Studies in Cymric philology.
Allen, F. D.: On the so-called Attic second declension.
Whitney, W. D.: Strictures on the views of August Schleicher respecting the nature of language and kindred subjects.
Hadley, J.: On English vowel quantity in the thirteenth century and in the nineteenth.
March, F. A.: Anglo-Saxon and Early English pronunciation.
Bristed, C. A.: Some notes on Ellis's Early English Pronunciation.

Trumbull, J. Hammond : On Algonkin names for man.

Greenough, J. B. : On some forms of conditional sentences in Latin, Greek, and Sanskrit.

Proceedings of the third annual session, New Haven, 1871.

1872. — Volume III.

Evans, E. W. : Studies in Cymric philology.

Trumbull, J. Hammond : Words derived from Indian languages of North America.

Hadley, J. : On the Byzantine Greek pronunciation of the tenth century, as illustrated by a manuscript in the Bodleian Library.

Stevens, W. A. : On the substantive use of the Greek participle.

Bristed, C. A. : Erroneous and doubtful uses of the word *such.*

Hartt, C. F.: Notes on the Lingoa Geral, or Modern Tupí of the Amazonas.

Whitney, W. D. : On material and form in language.

March, F. A. : Is there an Anglo-Saxon language ?

March, F. A. : On some irregular verbs in Anglo-Saxon.

Trumbull, J. Hammond : Notes on forty versions of the Lord's Prayer in Algonkin languages.

Proceedings of the fourth annual session, Providence, 1872.

1873. — Volume IV.

Allen, F. D. : The Epic forms of verbs in $\acute{a}\omega$.

Evans, E. W. : Studies in Cymric philology.

Hadley, J. : On Koch's treatment of the Celtic element in English.

Haldeman, S. S. : On the pronunciation of Latin, as presented in several recent grammars.

Packard, L. R.: On some points in the life of Thucydides.

Goodwin, W. W.: On the classification of conditional sentences in Greek syntax.

March, F. A. : Recent discussions of Grimm's law.

Lull, E. P. : Vocabulary of the language of the Indians of San Blas and Caledonia Bay, Darien.

Proceedings of the fifth annual session, Easton, 1873.

1874. — Volume V.

Tyler, W. S. : On the prepositions in the Homeric poems.

Harkness, A. : On the formation of the tenses for completed action in the Latin finite verb.

Haldeman, S. S.: On an English vowel-mutation, present in *cag, keg.*

Packard, L. R.: On a passage in Homer's Odyssey (x. 81–86).

Trumbull, J. Hammond : On numerals in American Indian languages, and the Indian mode of counting.

Sewall, J. B. : On the distinction between the subjunctive and optative modes in Greek conditional sentences.

Morris, C. D.: On the age of Xenophon at the time of the Anabasis.
Whitney, W. D.: Φύσει or θέσει — natural or conventional?

Proceedings of the sixth annual session, Hartford, 1874.

1875. — Volume VI.

Harkness, A.: On the formation of the tenses for completed action in the Latin
finite verb.
Haldeman, S. S.: On an English consonant-mutation, present in *proof, prove.*
Carter, F.: On Begemann's views as to the weak preterit of the Germanic verbs.
Morris, C. D.: On some forms of Greek conditional sentences.
Williams, A.: On verb-reduplication as a means of expressing completed action.
Sherman, L. A.: A grammatical analysis of the Old English poem "The Owl
and the Nightingale."

Proceedings of the seventh annual session, Newport, 1875.

1876. — Volume VII.

Gildersleeve, B. L.: On εἰ with the future indicative and ἐάν with the subjunctive
in the tragic poets.
Packard, L. R.: On Grote's theory of the structure of the Iliad.
Humphreys, M. W.: On negative commands in Greek.
Toy, C. H.: On Hebrew verb-etymology.
Whitney, W. D.: A botanico-philological problem.
Goodwin, W. W.: On *shall* and *should* in protasis, and their Greek equivalents.
Humphreys, M. W.: On certain influences of accent in Latin iambic trimeters.
Trumbull, J. Hammond: On the Algonkin verb.
Haldeman, S. S.: On a supposed mutation between *l* and *u.*

Proceedings of the eighth annual session, New York, 1876.

1877. — Volume VIII.

Packard, L. R.: Notes on certain passages in the Phaedo and the Gorgias of
Plato.
Toy, C. H.: On the nominal basis of the Hebrew verb.
Allen, F. D.: On a certain apparently pleonastic use of ὡς.
Whitney, W. D.: On the relation of surd and sonant.
Holden, E. S.: On the vocabularies of children under two years of age.
Goodwin, W. W.: On the text and interpretation of certain passages in the
Agamemnon of Aeschylus.
Stickney, A.: On the single case-form in Italian.
Carter, F.: On Willmann's theory of the authorship of the Nibelungenlied.
Sihler, E. G.: On Herodotus's and Aeschylus's accounts of the battle of Salamis.
Whitney, W. D.: On the principle of economy as a phonetic force.
Carter, F.: On the Kürenberg hypothesis.
March, F. A.: On dissimilated gemination.

Proceedings of the ninth annual session, Baltimore, 1877.

1878. — Volume IX.

Gildersleeve, B. L.: Contributions to the history of the articular infinitive.
Toy, C. H.: The Yoruban language.
Humphreys, M. W.: Influence of accent in Latin dactylic hexameters.
Sachs, J.: Observations on Plato's Cratylus.
Seymour, T. D.: On the composition of the Cynegeticus of Xenophon.
Humphreys, M. W.: Elision, especially in Greek.

Proceedings of the tenth annual session, Saratoga, 1878.

1879. — Volume X.

Toy, C. H.: Modal development of the Semitic verb.
Humphreys, M. W.: On the nature of cæsura.
Humphreys, M. W.: On certain effects of elision.
Cook, A S.: Studies in the Heliand.
Harkness, A.: On the development of the Latin subjunctive in principal clauses.
D'Ooge, M. L.: The original recension of the De Corona.
Peck, T.: The authorship of the Dialogus de Oratoribus.
Seymour, T. D.: On the date of the Prometheus of Aeschylus.

Proceedings of the eleventh annual session, Newport, 1879.

1880. — Volume XI.

Humphreys, M. W.: A contribution to infantile linguistic.
Toy, C. H.: The Hebrew verb-termination *un*.
Packard, L. R.: The beginning of a written literature in Greece.
Hall, I. H.: The declension of the definite article in the Cypriote inscriptions.
Sachs, J.: Observations on Lucian.
Sihler, E. G.: Virgil and Plato.
Allen, W. F.: The battle of Mons Graupius.
Whitney, W. D.: On inconsistency in views of language.
Edgren, A. H.: The kindred Germanic words of German and English, exhibited
    with reference to their consonant relations.

Proceedings of the twelfth annual session, Philadelphia, 1880.

1881. — Volume XII.

Whitney, W. D.: On Mixture in Language.
Toy, C. H.: The home of the primitive Semitic race.
March, F. A.: Report of the committee on the reform of English spelling.
Wells, B. W.: History of the *a*-vowel, from Old Germanic to Modern English.
Seymour, T. D.: The use of the aorist participle in Greek.
Sihler, E. G.: The use of abstract verbal nouns in -σις in Thucydides.

Proceedings of the thirteenth annual session, Cleveland, 1881.

1882. — Volume XIII.

Hall, I. H. : The Greek New Testament as published in America.
Merriam, A. C. : Alien intrusion between article and noun in Greek.
Peck, T. : Notes on Latin quantity.
Owen, W. B. : Influence of the Latin syntax in the Anglo-Saxon Gospels.
Wells, B. W. : The Ablaut in English.
Whitney, W. D. : General considerations on the Indo-European case-system.

Proceedings of the fourteenth annual session, Cambridge, 1882.

1883. — Volume XIV.

Merriam, A. C. : The Caesareum and the worship of Augustus at Alexandria.
Whitney, W. D. : The varieties of predication.
Smith, C. F. : On Southernisms.
Wells, B. W. : The development of the Ablaut in Germanic.

Proceedings of the fifteenth annual session, Middletown, 1883.

1884. — Volume XV.

(*In Press.*)

Goodell, T. D. : On the use of the Genitive in Sophokles.
Tarbell, F. B. : Greek Ideas as to the effect of burial on the future life of the
  soul.
Warren, M. : On Latin Glossaries.   Codex Sangallensis, No. 912.
Peck, T. : Alliteration in Latin.
Perrin, B. : The Crastinus episode at Palaepharsalus.
Von Jagemann, H. C. G. : Norman words in English.
Wells, B. W. : The Ablaut in High German.
Whitney, W. D. : Primary and Secondary Suffixes of Derivation and their
  exchanges.

Proceedings of the sixteenth annual session, Hanover, 1884.

The Proceedings of the American Philological Association are distributed gratis upon application until they are out of print.

Separate copies of articles printed in the Transactions are given to the authors for distribution.

The " Transactions *for* " any given year are not always published in that year. To avoid mistakes in ordering back volumes, please .state — not the year of publication, but rather — the year *for* which the Transactions are desired, adding also the volume-number, according to the following table :

The Transactions for 1869 *and* 1870 form Volume I.
"   "   "   1871 form Volume II.
            "   1872   "   "   III.
            "   1873   "   "   IV.
            "   1874   "   "   V.
            "   1875   "   "   VI.
            "   1876   "   "   VII.
            "   1877   "   "   VIII.
            "   1878   "   "   IX.
            "   1879   "   "   X.
            "   1880   "   "   XI.
            "   1881   "   "   XII.
            "   1882   "   "   XIII.
            "   1883   "   "   XIV.
    "   "   1884   "   "   XV.

The price of these volumes is $1.50 apiece. No reduction is made on orders for less than nine volumes. The first two volumes will not be sold separately.

TEMPORARY REDUCTION IN THE PRICE OF COMPLETE SETS.

Single COMPLETE SETS of the Transactions (Volumes I.– XIV.) will be sold, until further notice, at *fourteen* dollars a set.

It is especially appropriate that *American* Libraries should exert themselves to procure this series while it may be had. It is the work of *American* scholars, and contains many valuable articles not elsewhere accessible ; and, aside from these facts, as the first collection of essays in general philology made in this country, it is sure to be permanently valuable for the history of American scholarship.